Rewley House Studies in the Historic Environment
4

PLACES OF WORSHIP IN BRITAIN AND IRELAND
300–950

edited by

P. S. Barnwell

REWLEY HOUSE STUDIES
IN THE HISTORIC ENVIRONMENT

Rewley House Studies in the Historic Environment publishes the proceedings of weekend conferences concerning the historic environment and architectural history held at Oxford University Department for Continuing Education. Volumes in the series, like the weekends themselves, are intended to bring to a wide audience both the results of recent scholarship and overviews of the subjects they address.

Series Editor
P. S. Barnwell

Editorial Board
Malcolm Airs
Geoffrey Tyack
William Whyte

REWLEY HOUSE STUDIES IN
THE HISTORIC ENVIRONMENT, 4

PLACES OF WORSHIP
IN BRITAIN AND IRELAND
300–950

Edited by
P. S. Barnwell

SHAUN TYAS
DONINGTON
2015

© The Contributors, 2015

Typeset from the discs of the authors and designed by the publisher

Published by

SHAUN TYAS
1 High Street
Donington
Lincolnshire
PE11 4TA

ISBN
978-1-907730-48-1

Printed and bound in Great Britain by
Henry Ling Ltd., the Dorset Press, Dorchester, DT1 1HD

Contents

	Foreword	vi
	Colour Plates	vii–xvi
1.	Introduction: Churches and the Christianisation of Early Medieval Britain Barbara Yorke (University of Winchester)	1
2	The Origins of Christian Britain: From Mystery Cult to Christian Mystery Martin Henig (University of Oxford)	15
3.	Christianising the Landscape: The Archaeology of the Early Medieval Church in Wales Nancy Edwards (Bangor University)	33
4.	*More Scottorum*: Buildings of Worship in Ireland, *c*. 400–950 Tomás Ó Carragáin (University College Cork)	56
5.	Physical Evidence for the Early Church in Scotland Sally M. Foster (University of Stirling)	68
6.	The Anglo-Saxon Church in Kent Meg Boulton and Jane Hawkes (University of York)	92
7.	Landscapes of Conversion Among the Deirans: Lastingham and its Neighbours in the Seventh and Eighth Centuries Richard Morris (University of Huddersfield)	119
8.	Northumbrian Churches Rosemary Cramp (Durham University)	153
9.	The Early Medieval Church at Brixworth, Northamptonshire David Parsons (University of Leicester)	170
10.	The Church of St Mary, Deerhurst, Gloucestershire, in the Ninth Century Michael Hare and Maggie Kneen (Independent scholars)	186
11.	Conclusion: Churches, Sites, Landscapes P. S. Barnwell (University of Oxford)	209
	Index	227

Foreword

The essays in this volume represent the substance of a weekend school held at Rewley House, Oxford, in January 2010, the first in a chronological series looking at places of worship in Britain and Ireland from the end of Roman Britain to the present day. Both the weekend itself and the path to publication have been eventful: snow at the last minute prevented three speakers from the north being able to make the journey beyond Derby, and unforeseen events in the editor's life have severely delayed publication. The result is that some of the contributions to the weekend do not appear here, and that one has been added; several authors have updated their original submissions, and where that has not proved possible a note of explanation is included with the paper itself. Editors are always beholden to their authors in various ways, but on this occasion I am more than usually grateful to all who have borne with the difficulties. The weekend, like the others in the series, was conceived in conjunction with Sarah Brown of the University of York: she, also, was prevented from reaching Oxford for the weekend itself, and, while circumstances have meant she has not performed an active editorial role, she has played a significant part in ensuring that the volume has been completed.

The focus of the contributions to this volume is on Christian places of worship from the late Roman period to a point in the tenth century which varies according to the history of the area under discussion in individual chapters: the dates in the title are no more than indicative. Later volumes in the series will include the major non-Christian religions represented in the built environment of the periods they concern. Thematically there is considerable variation, reflecting the diversity of the subject, of the evidence, and of approaches to it, though contributors have been asked that, wherever possible, attention should be paid to the ways in which the sites and buildings they discuss were used for worship. There is no attempt to be comprehensive: rather, the purpose has been to bring together in one place a series of papers which give an insight into the current state of the subject and to enable comparisons to be made between different parts of Britain and Ireland.

P. S. Barnwell

Colour Plate 3.8 Cilgwyn, Nevern: cross-carved stone. (© Crown copyright: Royal Commission on the Ancient and Historical Monuments of Wales / Hawlfraint y Goron: Comisiwn Brenhinol Henebion Cymru.)

Colour Plate 4.4 The Romanesque church at Kilmalkedar, Co. Kerry, shows that Irish carpentry churches must have had antae. In addition to antae, it originally had a pointed barrel vault and skeuomorphs of wooden end rafters running up the gables. Where these intersected was a 'butterfly' finial: a skeuomorph of decorated rafter terminals. (© Copyright Gill Boazman.)

Colour Plate 6.4 St Mary *in Castro*, Dover (Kent), from the north, showing Roman lighthouse to the west. (© Copyright M. Boulton.)

Colour Plate 7.4 Lastingham in its setting. The church of St Mary is lower centre, towards the edge of the village, Spaunton Moor and Rosedale beyond, a trackway rising over Holiday Hill. The age of the oval enclosure to the right of the point where the trackway leaves the village is not yet known. (© Copyright R. Morris.)

Colour Plate 7.6 Crayke (North Riding of Yorkshire), showing monastic site (beside church, centre) and radial field pattern. (© Copyright R. Morris.)

Colour Plate 7.8 Middleton-by-Pickering (North Riding of Yorkshire), looking south. The church stands next to Middleton Hall; its original enclosure appears to have formed part of the planned settlement. (© Copyright R. Morris.)

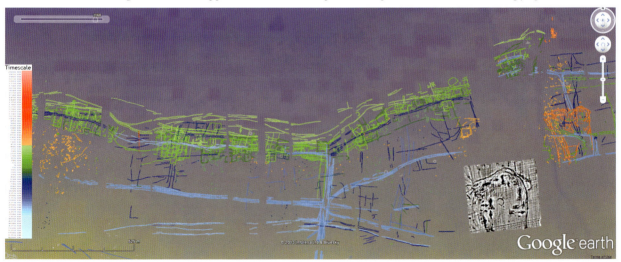

Colour Plate 7.10 Large scale geophysical survey of Sherburn (North Riding of Yorkshire). (© Copyright Landscape Research Centre.)

Colour Plate 8.2 (opposite, above) Escomb (County Durham): church viewed from the south. (Photograph Ian Riddler; © Copyright R. Cramp.)

Colour Plate 8.4 (a) (opposite, below) St Peter's church, Wearmouth (County Durham): west façade (Photograph Jeff Veitch; © Copyright R. Cramp.)

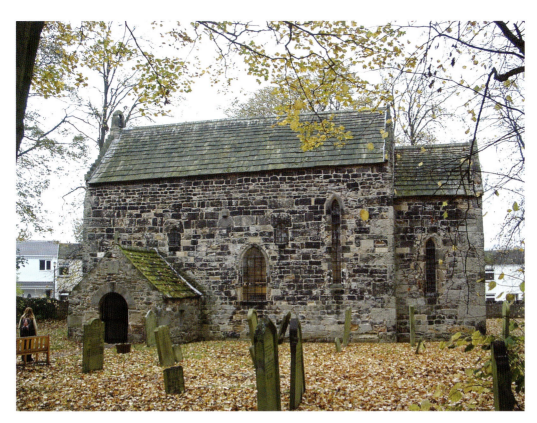

Colour Plate 8.4 (b) St Peter's church, Wearmouth (County Durham): the interior of the west wall of the nave. (Photograph Jeff Veitch; © Copyright R. Cramp.)

Colour Plate 8.6 St Andrew's church, Bywell (Northumberland), viewed from the south. (Photograph E. Rainey; © Copyright R. Cramp.)

Colour Plate 9.1 Brixworth All Saints' (Northamptonshire): general view of church from south east
(© Copyright G. Hammerschmitt.)

Colour Plate 9.4
(a) Brixworth All Saints', fabric survey: west tower, south elevation, colour-coded elevation drawing (C. Unwin, © Copyright D. Parsons.)

and (b), below, key to the colour codes.

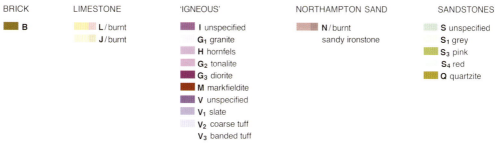

Fig. 1.1 Illaunloughan (Co. Kerry): island monastery, showing its proximity to the mainland. See also Fig. 4.2. (© Copyright B. Yorke.)

(1)
Introduction: Churches and the Christianisation of Early Medieval Britain

BARBARA YORKE

Christianisation and Conversion

The surviving and excavated churches of early medieval Britain and Ireland need to be viewed in the wider context of the adoption and absorption of Christianity in these islands.[1] The Christian religion came first to those parts of Britain under Roman imperial rule in the fourth century. Its progress was complicated by the collapse of centralised Roman control in the following century and the settlement of Germanic peoples in eastern and southern England. The timescale of conversion and Christianisation therefore varied among the different peoples of Britain and Ireland, and arguably between different sectors of society within these groupings. Thus, on analogy with other parts of the western Roman empire, we would expect Christianity to have been more rapidly adopted among the elites of Roman Britain than the rural peasant populations, the *pagani*. Relatively shallow roots in rural societies in eastern Britain may help to explain why the Germanic settlers of eastern England did not adopt Christianity soon after they arrived, unlike, for example, the Franks of northern Gaul who were converted early in the sixth century. However, in the British areas free of an Anglo-Saxon presence Christianity consolidated its hold in the fifth century and, through a variety of contacts, was spread to British areas beyond the old imperial boundaries and to Ireland. By the end of the sixth century the closest neighbours of the Anglo-Saxons—British, Irish and Frankish—were committed to Christianity and conversion of the Anglo-Saxons must have been only a matter of time, even without the prestige of the mission, despatched by Pope Gregory I and led by Augustine, that arrived in 597. Finally, we must not forget the settlement of further northern Germanic pagans, the Vikings from Scandinavia, in many areas of Britain and Ireland in the ninth century and their adoption of Christianity as part of their assimilation with native populations.

Different stages can be recognised in the progress of Christianity among the pagan peoples of early medieval Europe.[2] Conversion itself, in the sense of the

---

[1] R. Fletcher, *The Conversion of Europe: From Paganism to Christianity, 371–1386 AD* (London, 1997); B. A. E. Yorke, *The Conversion of Britain: Religion, Politics and Society in Britain c. 600–800* (Harlow, 2006); H. Pryce, 'Conversions to Christianity', in *A Companion to the Early Middle Ages: Britain and Ireland c. 500–1100*, ed. P. Stafford (Chichester and Malden, MA, 2009), pp. 143–59.

[2] L. Milis, 'La Conversion en profondeur: un procès sans fin', *Revue du Nord* 68 (1986), pp. 187–98.

replacement of the public worship of pagan deities by that of the Christian God, could be a long drawn-out process in which for a period worship of Christian and pre-Christian deities might co-exist, as would have been the case in late Roman Britain.[3] In Anglo-Saxon England where the progress of conversion is particularly well-recorded thanks to Bede's *Ecclesiastical History*, it was some forty or fifty years after the introduction of Christianity into any one kingdom before public worship of the pagan deities was outlawed.[4] From that point a more thorough Christianisation might begin in which the Christian practices introduced from areas that were already Christian were assimilated into native society, a process that would be aided by the training of natives as clergy. The influential portrait of conversion as constructed by Bede is a top-down one, and has been criticised as a simplification that reflects his own authoritarian values. When non-Christian settlers moved into territories where they were in the minority and Christianity in the form of an organised church was thoroughly established, it has been argued that adoption of the natives' religion would be part of the assimilation process. Cases for this type of conversion have been made for Anglo-Saxons moving into the West Midlands in the late sixth and seventh centuries,[5] and for the Scandinavian settlements in the ninth and tenth centuries.[6] However, Christianity needed an organised structure provided by bishops who trained the priests who provided the pastoral care and, if this had to be set up anew, it was dependent on existing secular powers to provide the wherewithal and the legal status to allow it to happen. That is the process Bede describes in the Anglo-Saxon areas of eastern Britain. There are hints of a somewhat similar pattern among the Picts. The integration of bishoprics into the Irish kingdoms suggests something comparable is likely to have occurred there, and, indeed, Patrick's own account of his work shows him working within existing structures of royal power.[7]

Christianisation can be defined as a much more thorough absorption of Christianity into public and private life, individual belief and practice. It must be seen as a two-way process in which many social practices might be modified by the expectations of Christianity, but at the same time the practice of Christianity would

---

[3] D. Petts, *Christianity in Roman Britain* (Stroud, 2003); Henig this volume.

[4] H. Mayr-Harting, *The Coming of Christianity to Anglo-Saxon England*, 3rd edn (London, 1991); B. A. E. Yorke, 'The Reception of Christianity at the Anglo-Saxon Royal Courts', in *St Augustine and the Conversion of England*, ed. R. Gameson (Stroud, 1999), pp. 152–73.

[5] P. Sims-Williams, *Religion and Literature in Western England, 600–800*, Cambridge Studies in Anglo-Saxon England 3 (Cambridge, 1990); S. Bassett, 'How the West was Won: The Anglo-Saxon Take-over of the West Midlands', *Anglo-Saxon Studies in Archaeology and History* 11 (2000), pp. 107–18.

[6] L. Abrams, 'Conversion and Assimilation', in *Cultures in Contact: Scandinavian Settlement in England in the Ninth and Tenth Centuries*, ed. D. Hadley and J. Richards, Studies in the Early Middle Ages 2 (Turnhout, 2000), pp. 135–53.

[7] T. Charles-Edwards, *Early Christian Ireland* (Cambridge, 2000), pp. 182–240.

1. INTRODUCTION

itself be affected by the process of integration into native societies and particularly its integration into their power structures. The balance between these two processes was a precarious one. In the early eighth century Adomnán on Iona and Bede in Northumbria were expressing concerns that the true practice of Christianity was being distorted within their societies.[8] Concerns were to grow amongst leading western European clergy during the century and would climax in the Carolingian Renaissance. A reflex of these reforms can be identified in the actions of Anglo-Saxon bishops in the late eighth and early ninth centuries, but these were compromised by political upheaval and Scandinavian conquests and settlements.[9] Much fuller reform of all levels of church provision was achieved in the newly united Anglo-Saxon England of the later tenth century. It included a return to universal monastic ideals, something which was also a feature of the ascetic *céle Dé* (culdee) reform in Ireland a century before.

Churches in Timber and Stone

Churches might be built in any period, but there were obvious pressure points when they were particularly likely to have been constructed. Thus, there was a particular need for churches when the Anglo-Saxons were first converted to Christianity, and in Kent there are some early church sites identified in written sources which have churches built in a late antique tradition with which Italian and other early missionaries would have been familiar.[10] However, it would also seem, as Richard Gem has argued, that expectations have led to too many churches being assigned to what is known as the 'A' period in the classic scheme provided by Harold and Joan Taylor for the phasing of Anglo-Saxon stone architecture.[11] The dominance of the *topos* of Viking destruction of churches had led also to an assumption that there had been little new church building in the late eighth and ninth centuries whereas this is now seen as a major period of construction of Anglo-Saxon stone churches, especially in Mercia, the dominant kingdom for much of the eighth and early ninth centuries.[12]

---

[8] *Adomnán at Birr, AD 697: Essays in Commemoration of the Law of the Innocents*, ed. T. O'Loughlin (Dublin, 2001); Bede, *Epistola ad Ecgbertum*, in *Venerabilis Baedae Opera Historica*, ed. C. Plummer, 2 vols (Oxford, 1896), pp. 405–23.

[9] N. Brooks, *The Early History of the Church of Canterbury: Christ Church from 597 to 1066* (Leicester, 1984), pp. 111–206; C. Cubitt, *Anglo-Saxon Church Councils c. 650–c. 850* (London, 1995).

[10] E. Cambridge, 'The Architecture of the Augustinian Mission', in *St Augustine*, pp. 202–36; Boulton and Hawkes, this volume.

[11] H. M. and J. Taylor, *Anglo-Saxon Church Architecture*, 3 vols. (Cambridge, 1965–78); R. Gem, 'ABC: How Should We Periodize Anglo-Saxon Architecture?', in *The Anglo-Saxon Church: Papers on History, Architecture, and Archaeology in Honour of Dr H. M. Taylor*, ed. L. A. S. Butler and R. K. Morris, Council for British Archaeology Research Report 60 (London, 1986), pp. 146–55.

[12] R. Gem, 'Architecture of the Anglo-Saxon Church, 735–870', *Journal of the British*

Although surviving mortared stone churches have naturally dominated the study of early medieval church architecture in Britain, we must recognise that such buildings were the exception rather than the norm. The majority of early churches in Ireland and Britain, including in the Anglo-Saxon regions, were built of wood. We can interpret such churches as an example of Christianisation, that is adaptation to vernacular building traditions. In places where timber was not readily available, such as parts of Ireland, other native building traditions might be utilised. In the west of Ireland, for example, there are early examples of sod churches which were replaced by the drystone oratories that are such a feature of the Kerry and Dingle peninsulas.[13] A major distinction can be made between the humbler timber churches, that might be predominantly of wattle construction, and major plank- or stave-built churches with an extravagant use of timber that reflected the great timber halls of secular elites. The surviving Romanesque stave churches of Norway (although somewhat later in date) are a reminder of just how impressive such major timber churches could be.[14] The great church of Kildare described by Cogitosus was surely a building on this sort of scale, and his description implies a division of the interior by wooden screens that replicated stone fittings in other areas of Europe.[15] The excavated timber church of the Northumbrian bishopric at Whithorn also seems to have been architecturally ambitious.[16]

There are a number of reasons why the Anglo-Saxons favoured stone churches, but a significant factor was that they occupied much of a former Romanised province. Major stone structures like forts, or the bridge at Corbridge which seems to have provided much of the stonework of Bishop Wilfrid's crypt at Hexham, appear to have been under the control of kings and the provision of these potential quarries of re-usable stone was part of their patronage for the early church.[17] The early missionaries from Italy would have had an expectation that major ecclesiastical foundations would include stone churches, and it has been suggested that the churches

---

Archaeological Association 146 (1993), pp. 29–66; Parsons, and Hare and Kneen, this volume.

[13] G. D. Rourke and J. W. Marshall, 'The Drystone Oratories of Western Kerry', in J. W. Marshall and C. Walsh, *Illaunloughan Island: An Early Medieval Monastery in County Kerry* (Bray, 2005), 103–24; T. Ó Carragáin, *Churches in Early Medieval Ireland: Architecture, Ritual and Memory* (New Haven and London, 2010), pp. 49–56, and this volume.

[14] G. Bugge, *Stave Churches in Norway: Introduction and Survey* (Oslo, 1983).

[15] C. Neuman de Vegvar, 'Romanitas and Realpolitik in Cogitosius's Description of the Church of St Brigit in Kildare', in *The Cross Goes North: Processes of Conversion in Northern Europe, AD 300–1300*, ed. M. Carver (Woodbridge, 2003), pp. 153–70.

[16] P. Hill, *Whithorn and St Niniian: The Excavation of a Monastic Town, 1984–91* (Stroud, 1997), especially pp. 148–58; T. Ó Carragáin, 'The Architectural Setting of the Mass in Early-Medieval Ireland', *Medieval Archaeology* 53 (2009), pp. 119–54.

[17] T. Eaton, *Plundering the Past: Roman Stonework in Medieval Britain* (Stroud, 2000). P. Bidwell, 'A Survey of the Anglo-Saxon Crypt at Hexham and its Reused Roman Stonework', *Archaeologica Aeliana*, 5th ser. 39 (2010), pp. 53–145.

1. INTRODUCTION

of Canterbury were deliberately laid out to represent the spiritual geography of Rome.[18] Those special links with Rome because of the intervention of Pope Gregory, encouraged kings and churchmen (and women) to visit Rome and then to emulate, however modestly, the type of churches they had seen there or in areas of Francia and Lombard Italy through which they would have travelled.

Bede equated stone churches not just with the architecture of Rome, but also with recognition of the authority and practices of the Roman see and the universal church.[19] Contrariwise, to him the timber building traditions of British and Irish areas symbolised the separatist tendencies and adherence to out-moded traditions to be found in their territories. This, of course, was a highly schematised, polemical view as Anglo-Saxons also built timber churches, and many Irish churchmen were just as concerned with orthodoxy and recognition of Rome. Armagh, which hoped to emulate the status of Canterbury, had a stone church in the eighth century, relics of the Roman saints and an arrangement of extra-mural churches that may also have been intended to recall the topography of Rome.[20] The concentric enclosures of many Irish ecclesiastical sites may have been intended to evoke Jerusalem itself, arguably an even more potent place than Rome in Irish spiritual geography.[21] Nevertheless concern with orthodoxy and of the potency of Rome as a Christian centre were important motivators in the period during which the Anglo-Saxon elites absorbed Christianity. When King Oswiu made the decision at Whitby in 664 that the Northumbrian church should practice Easter in conformity with Rome he was, according to Bede, particularly influenced by the idea that St Peter of Rome was also the gate-keeper who would let him into heaven.[22] The Latin *Petrus*, of course, meant 'stone' and so further reinforced the idea of a link between stone building and Roman orthodoxy.

Oswiu's example in turn seems to have influenced King Nechtan of the Picts. When Nechtan decided in 717 that his churches would also adhere to the Roman Easter, he not only contacted Wearmouth and Jarrow (County Durham) for advice, but also for masons who could erect stone churches in the Roman fashion.[23] Although

---

[18] N. Brooks, 'Canterbury, Rome and the Construction of English Identity', in *Early Medieval Rome and the Christian West: Essays in Honour of Donald A. Bullough*, ed. J. M. H. Smith (Leiden, 2000), pp. 221–47; J. Blair, *The Church in Anglo-Saxon Society* (Oxford, 2005), pp. 66–9.

[19] Bede, *Historia ecclesiastica gentis Anglorum*, ed. and trans. B. Colgrave and R. A. B. Mynors (Oxford, 1969), bk ii c. 14; bk iii c. 25; bk v c. 21.

[20] T. Ó Carragáin, 'The Architectural Setting of the Cult of Relics in Early Medieval Ireland', *Journal of the Royal Society of the Antiquaries of Ireland*, 133 (2003), pp. 130–76, at p. 140 and p. 152.

[21] Ó Carragáin, *Churches*, pp. 57–85.

[22] Bede, *Historia ecclesiastica*, bk iii c. 25.

[23] Bede, *Historia ecclesiastica*, bk v c. 21.

unfortunately none of these churches have yet been identified, his realignment of the Pictish church may have inaugurated new traditions in the use of stone in Pictish ecclesiastical architecture. Concentrations of sculpture at places like the Portmahomack on the Tarbat peninsula (Ross and Cromarty) or St Vigean's in Angus help to identify major church sites that are not otherwise recorded in early medieval sources.[24] These too may have been major centres of Pictish royal patronage and sometimes linked with royal power centres. The surviving arch from Forteviot (Perthshire; see Fig. 5.4) must surely have come from a stone church, and its figures may commemorate royal involvement in founding an ecclesiastical establishment at this major royal centre.[25] In Ireland and Wales mortared stone churches remained rare until the Romanesque period.[26]

The Cult of Saints and Significant Burials

One of the most significant observable differences between ecclesiastical sites in Wales and Ireland and those of the Anglo-Saxons concerns the use of churches for burial and the cult of saints. In Wales and Ireland the major churches were not used for burial or the housing of relics; instead, in the vicinity of the church there might be subsidiary shrine chapels, or other forms of shrine that might be built around the tombs of founders and saints.[27] On the island of Illaunloughan in County Kerry, the reliquary shrine survived as two large slate stones, placed together in the tent-like form of early metal reliquaries, on a grassy mound (see Figs 1.1 and 4.2).[28] Excavation showed that it had been built over two stone cists containing the exhumed bones of two men, perhaps the first two abbots of the small community that inhabited the island, whose reliquary site became a centre of local pilgrimage. The small stone building outside the abbey church of Iona (Argyll) appears be the last stage in the liturgical development of the burial site of St Columba.[29] In Wales such churchyard shrines over significant graves are known as *capeli-y-bedd*, 'chapels of the grave'.

[24] G. Henderson and I. Henderson, *The Art of the Picts: Sculpture and Metalwork in Early Medieval Scotland* (London, 2004); see also Foster, this volume.
[25] N. Aitchison, *Forteviot: A Pictish and Scottish Royal Centre* (Stroud, 2006).
[26] A. Pritchard, 'The Origins of Ecclesiastical Stone Architecture in Wales', in *The Archaeology of the Early Medieval Celtic Churches: Proceedings of a Conference on the Archaeology of the Early Medieval Celtic Churches, September 2004*, ed. N. Edwards, Society for Medieval Archaeology Monograph 29, Society for Church Archaeology Monograph 1 (Leeds, 2009), pp. 245–64; C. Manning, 'A Suggested Typology for Pre-Romanesque Stone Churches in Ireland', ibid., pp. 265–80; Ó Carragáin, *Churches*.
[27] N. Edwards, 'Celtic Saints and Early Medieval Archaeology', in *Local Saints and Local Churches in the Early Medieval West*, ed. A. Thacker and R. Sharpe (Oxford, 2002), pp. 225–66; Ó Carragáin, 'Architectural Setting of the Cult of Relics'.
[28] Marshall and Walsh, *Illaunloughan*, pp. 55–86.
[29] Royal Commission on the Ancient and Historical Monuments of Scotland, *Argyll: An Inventory of Monuments*, 7 vols (Edinburgh, 1971–92), vol. 4, p. 41.

1. INTRODUCTION

From an early date in Anglo-Saxon England practices were rather different and closer to those of continental Europe. Although places of churchyard burial could be significant, an important feature of the development of Anglo-Saxon saints' cults was the translation of the body of the saint from its original place of burial to a shrine inside the church, either adjacent to the main altar or beneath it in a crypt.[30] Major churches might also include special side chapels (porticus) for the burial of significant founders and patrons. One of the best attested examples is St Augustine's, Canterbury where Bede's description of the use of the north porticus for the burial of the archbishops of Canterbury and that in the south for members of the royal house of Kent has been confirmed in excavation.[31] Prominent accommodation for royal burial was a feature of a number of the major surviving Anglo-Saxon churches that were under royal patronage, and may in part be linked with expectations of monumental burial than can be seen in pre-Christian elite practices such as burial under prominent mounds. At Repton in Derbyshire it has been argued that the primary phase of what became the church's crypt was originally a free-standing baptistery converted by the addition of a pillared vault into a mausoleum for King Wiglaf of Mercia (d. 840).[32] The conversion of Wiglaf's burial chamber into the crypt of the church that was extended east over it seems to have been connected with the development of the cult of his murdered grandson Wigstan. The development of a significant number of royal cults, both those of murdered princes and, more conventionally, of queens and princesses who founded nunneries are distinctive features of the way in which Christian practices were absorbed by the Anglo-Saxon elites. Rulers who did not qualify for saintly status could be commemorated in other significant ways. The Repton cross that depicts an Anglo-Saxon warrior in the form of a victorious Roman emperor has been interpreted as a memorial to King Æthelbald of Mercia who was buried there after his murder in 757.[33] It invites comparison with the celebrated St Andrew's sarcophagus whose extensive decorative programme on the theme of King David is surely evidence that it too was a major site of royal burial.[34]

Religious Communities

Consideration of the cult of saints is a reminder that major early medieval churches rarely stood alone, but were part of wider ecclesiastical landscapes that tended to

---

30   A. Thacker, 'The Making of a Local Saint', in *Local Saints*, pp. 45–74; J. Blair, 'A Local Saint for Every Minster? Local Cults in Anglo-Saxon England', ibid., pp. 455–94.
31   Bede, *Historia ecclesiastica*, bk i c. 33; Cambridge, 'Architecture of the Gregorian Mission'.
32   M. Biddle and B. Kjølbye-Biddle, 'Repton', in *The Blackwell Encyclopaedia of Anglo-Saxon England*, ed. M. Lapidge (Oxford, 1999), pp. 390–2.
33   M. Biddle and B. Kjølbye-Biddle, 'The Repton Stone', *Anglo-Saxon England*, 14 (1985), pp. 233–92.
34   *The St Andrews Sarcophagus: A Pictish Masterpiece and Its International Connections*, ed. S. M. Foster (Dublin, 1998).

become more complex as the period progressed with additional cult sites marked by crosses, wells, subsidiary chapels or reliquary shrines. Major ecclesiastical sites had two or more churches and were likely to be but part of complex religious communities containing a variety of buildings. These communities had their origins in eastern monasticism that probably first reached Britain in the sixth century, but underwent some fundamental changes as the concept of monasticism was absorbed into the societies of early medieval Britain and Ireland.[35] From an early stage there were differences in emphasis within monastic communities. Gildas, himself no slouch on matters of ecclesiastical discipline, appears to have been critical of what he considered the ostentatious asceticism of some other communities, including apparently that associated with St David.[36] Major changes occurred when monasticism moved from being outside society to becoming very much part of its kin-based power structures. The process is particularly well-attested and studied for Ireland. By 800 the major religious communities were the property of hereditary clerical families who in many cases were discarded segments of royal families or, like the hereditary abbots of Trim (Meath), the remnants of a royal house ousted from power.[37] The *clasau* of Wales may have had similar origins; certainly when written evidence becomes more readily available for them in the twelfth century the tendency for them to be hereditary in certain families becomes apparent.[38] Irish ecclesiastics who went to Francia in the late sixth and early seventh centuries, most notably Columbanus, seem to have introduced the Frankish nobility to the concept of a religious community effectively owned and run by a family so that it could meet that family's religious needs and provide spiritual endorsement of its temporal authority.[39] Such kin-based communities were therefore an established feature of western Christianity when they were introduced into Anglo-Saxon England through missionaries and other contacts from both Francia and Ireland. Later, Scandinavian settlers in Britain may have sought to underpin their power in similar ways. It has been suggested that what were once identified as the remains of eremitic Celtic communities in Orkney were in fact the family foundations of the leading Norse settlers who were endorsing their status as the new landed powers in what had become an established insular tradition.[40]

[35] M. Dunn, *The Emergence of Monasticism: From the Desert Fathers to the Early Middle Ages* (Oxford, 2000).
[36] D. N. Dumville, *Saint David of Wales*, Kathleen Hughes Memorial Lectures on Mediaeval Welsh History 1 (Cambridge, 2001).
[37] D. Ó Corráin, 'Ireland *c*. 800: Aspects of Society', in *Prehistoric and Early Ireland*, ed. D. Ó Cróinín, New History of Ireland 1 (Oxford, 2005), pp. 549–608, at pp. 582–608.
[38] R. J. Silvester and J. W. Evans, 'Identifying the Mother Churches of North-East Wales', in *Celtic Churches*, pp. 21–41, at pp. 22–4.
[39] P. J. Geary, *Before France and Germany: The Creation and Transformation of the Early Medieval World* (Oxford, 1988), pp. 171–6.
[40] C. Morris, *Church and Monastery in the Far North: An Archaeological Evaluation*, Jarrow Lecture 1989 (Jarrow, 1989)

1. INTRODUCTION

The religious communities of early medieval Britain were encompassed by the Latin term *monasteria*. How far they might be what is generally understood by the term 'monastic' has been the topic of recent debate.[41] Some Anglo-Saxon historians have suggested that the range of religious communities was so varied that it would be more appropriate to refer to them by the more neutral term 'minster', but this has not been taken up in other areas of Britain. 'Ecclesiastical settlement' is now the preferred term in Ireland and has much to recommend it. At a basic level we can say that all early medieval religious communities shared two dominant characteristics: communal living and the performance of regular church services—it was belief in the need for and efficacy of prayer to channel God's support that contributed to the vast investment in religious houses by secular authorities. Surprisingly little is known archaeologically about the buildings in which the ecclesiastical personnel lived or worked (that is, in addition to the churches themselves). Small islands off the Irish and Scottish coasts that allowed recreation of the desert in the ocean, often have traces of the buildings of the hermitages or small communities that lived on them. Excavation of an oratory, two huts and a cemetery on Illaunloughan suggested a small community of five to six men probably established in the late seventh century and abandoned, after gradual reduction in size, by the early ninth century.[42] Rosemary Cramp's excavations at Wearmouth and Jarrow have produced some of the fullest records of the living arrangements of a larger community, with the additional advantage of support from contemporary accounts of the two foundations.[43] Influences from Frankish and Italian monasticism can be seen in features such as painted wall-plaster and the covered walkway at Wearmouth. The large stone communal buildings at Jarrow (see Fig. 8.5) also seem to reflect continental arrangements, but may in addition recall the great timber halls at earlier Northumbrian royal sites such as Yeavering. Excavations at Hartlepool (Durham), a Northumbrian double house of nuns and monks under an abbess, have revealed a different type of arrangement with northern Frankish parallels of small individual dwelling-places or cells.[44]

It has become increasingly apparent that these liturgical centres were but one part of much larger estates, none of which has been investigated in their entirety. Even the eremitic sites of Illaunloughan or Skellig Michael (Kerry) may have been part of larger mainland communities which supplied them with the food they consumed that could not have been raised on the islands.[45] Excavations at a number of religious

---

[41] For overviews see Blair, *Church in Anglo-Saxon Society*, pp. 79–107; S. Foot, *Monastic Life in Anglo-Saxon England c. 600–900* (Cambridge, 2006).
[42] Marshall and Walsh, *Illaunloughan*, especially pp. 125–34.
[43] R. Cramp, *Wearmouth and Jarrow Monastic Sites*, 2 vols (Swindon, 2005–6).
[44] R. Daniels, *Anglo-Saxon Hartlepool and the Foundations of English Christianity: An Archaeology of the Anglo-Saxon Monastery*, Tees Archaeology Monograph Series 3 (Hartlepool, 2007).
[45] E. Murray and F. McCormick, 'Environmental Analysis and the Food Supply', in Marshall and

communities have produced evidence of specialised agricultural and craft activities sited away from the main ecclesiastical foci, including corn-drying kilns at Hoddom (Dumfries),[46] tidal mills at Nendrum (Down),[47] metalworking at Hartlepool,[48] and parchment production at Portmahomack.[49] In Ireland, in particular, concentric enclosures might separate the most sacred, inner areas from the outer, and be in accord with contemporary visualisations of biblical holy sites that in turn reflected those of heaven itself,[50] (though they can also be seen as resembling the enclosures of the raths and cashels of the Irish secular elites).[51]

Although the monastic ideal stressed the separation of lay and religious life, religious communities were prevalent in the early middle ages precisely because they fitted so well into contemporary kin-based power structures. Placing religious communities in the wider landscape has to recognise that this landscape would also contain the dwelling-places of the families which sponsored them. Bede even suggested that some 'false' monasteries were the main dwelling places of secular families.[52] The issue of which features might distinguish a religious and secular community have been examined by Chris Loveluck in a carefully nuanced discussion of Flixborough (Lincolnshire).[53] This is a Middle Saxon site where some of the buildings have been excavated together with the rubbish heaps from a greater part of the settlement. His interpretation is that Flixborough began as a secular settlement that passed in the ninth century into ecclesiastical ownership, a phase that was distinguished by the presence of styli and an inscribed plaque, but also by significant changes in diet, including the disappearance of wild species. Behind such debates are issues over whether religious communities were merely a specialist form of

---

Walsh, *Illaunloughan*, pp. 67–80.

[46] C. Lowe, *Excavations at Hoddom, Dumfriesshire: An Early Ecclesiastical Site in South-West Scotland* (Edinburgh, 2006).

[47] T. McErlean and N. Crothers, *Harnessing the Tides: The Early Medieval Tide Mills at Nendrum Monastery, Strangford Loch*, Northern Ireland Archaeological Monographs 7 (Norwich, 2007).

[48] Daniels, *Hartlepool*, pp. 97–42.

[49] M. O. H. Carver and C. A. Spall, 'Excavating a *Parchmenerie*: Archaeological Correlates of Making Parchment at the Pictish Monastery of Portmahomack, Easter Ross', *Proceedings of the Society of Antiquaries of Scotland* 134 (2004), pp. 1–30.

[50] A. MacDonald, 'Aspects of the Monastic Landscape in Adomnán's *Life of Columba*', in *Studies in Irish Hagiography: Saints and Scholars*, ed. J. Cary, M. Herbert and P. Ó Riain (Dublin, 2001), pp. 15–30.

[51] R. Stalley, 'Ecclesiastical Architecture Before 1169', in *Prehistoric and Early Ireland*, pp. 714–43, at pp. 717–18.

[52] Bede, *Epistola ad Ecgbertum*, pp. 451–6.

[53] C. Loveluck, *Rural Settlement, Lifestyles and Social Change in the Later First Millennium AD: Anglo-Saxon Flixborough in its Wider Context*, Excavations at Flixborough 4 (Oxford, 2007), especially pp. 144–62, and, for a differing interpretation, J. Blair, 'Flixborough Revisited', *Anglo-Saxon Studies in Archaeology and History*, 17 (2011), pp. 101–7.

1. INTRODUCTION

nobleman's estate which can be generally characterised as exploiting land and its inhabitants to fuel the economic boom of the 'long eighth century',[54] or a new form of centralised management of resources which initiated such developments only to be eventually taken over and absorbed into secular society.[55] Should we perhaps expect to see a minster as a regular component of a magnate estate?

A Pastoral Care

So far discussion has centred on churches and communities as manifestations of elite power. In what ways did such foundations impinge on the lives of ordinary people, and to what extent did the pastoral care of the whole community involve use of church buildings? It was the responsibility of bishops to ordain priests and to oversee arrangements for the pastoral care of all the people in their dioceses. In the sixth and seventh centuries the principal of each kingdom having its own bishop seems to have been generally accepted. There was therefore a major contrast between Ireland with its many small kingdoms and correspondingly large number of bishops, and Anglo-Saxon England whose larger kingdoms meant fewer bishoprics, even allowing for subdivision in some of them. The early episcopal arrangements in Wales and Pictland are less well-recorded, and the number of bishoprics and their location is uncertain though some British kingdoms seem to have supported more than one bishop.[56] To begin with, pastoral care, as far as we are able to trace it, was not provided through local churches in individual settlements, but through mother churches (often called 'minsters' in Anglo-Saxon contexts) whose clergy were responsible for the religious needs of subsidiary territories. The foundation of monasteries undoubtedly complicated matters, though not to the extent that episcopal authority was all but extinguished, as was once believed to have occurred in Ireland.[57] Religious communities were often landlords of extensive estates and presumably expected to provide for the religious needs of their tenants. Irish law codes set out in some detail the mutual obligations of ecclesiastical landlords and the tenants who lived on their land (*manaig*).[58] In the Lives of St Cuthbert we get a glimpse of the abbess of Whitby supervising the religious needs of dependent agricultural estates by calling in Bishop Cuthbert to consecrate a church.[59] However, relations were no

---

[54] *The Long Eighth Century: Production, Distribution and Demand*, ed. I. L. Hansen and C. Wickham, Transformation of the Roman World 11 (Leiden, 2000).
[55] Blair, *Church in Anglo-Saxon Society*, pp. 204–12, 246–90.
[56] T. Charles-Edwards, *Wales and the Britons, 350–1064* (Oxford, 2013), pp. 584–98.
[57] R. Sharpe, 'Some Problems concerning the Organization of the Church in Early Medieval Ireland', *Peritia*, 3 (1964), pp. 230–70; C. Etchingham, *Church Organisation in Ireland AD 650 to 1000* (Maynooth, 1999).
[58] Etchingham, *Church Organisation*, pp. 363–454.
[59] Anonymous, *Vita sancti Cuthberti*, in *Two Lives of St Cuthbert*, ed. and trans. B. Colgrave (Cambridge, 1940), c. 10; Bede, *Vita sancti Cuthberti*, ibid., c. 34.

always so harmonious, and Anglo-Saxon founders of monasteries (including some bishops) might seek to exempt their houses from episcopal visitation.[60]

How far all religious communities in the Anglo-Saxon territories were harmonised into a coherent territorial system of pastoral care at a relatively early date forms part of the 'minster controversy'.[61] The earliest arrangements may be obscured by reorganisations in the ninth and tenth centuries when the disintegration of religious communities alongside the political and elite regimes with which they had been associated gave bishops opportunities to regularise provision.[62] Wide scale provision of local churches for worship and burial seems to have been more a feature of the late tenth and eleventh centuries in England, but may have occurred in some other parts of Britain and Ireland somewhat earlier. Ireland seems to have had an extensive network of local churches by 800, and the many ruined, small unmortared stone churches visible in areas such as Kerry may date from this time.[63] There is evidence from Cornwall that its network of parish churches associated with obscure, individual saints who may have been their first priests or patrons, was also likely to have been in place by about 800,[64] and many areas of Wales may have been similarly well provided.[65] One would expect the provision of churches for the population in general to have occurred in Celtic areas before it did in Anglo-Saxon because these areas had been converted earlier. Access to local churches for worship can be seen as part of the trickle-down of deeper Christianisation from elites to the population at large.

That is not to say that a church building was essential for the provision of pastoral care. Mass baptisms of Anglo-Saxons in rivers are described in the conversion period for which there were, of course, impeccable biblical precedents.[66] The use of springs, holy wells and even mill-races for baptism is attested in Ireland.[67] Relatively

---

60 P. Wormald, *Bede and the Conversion of England: The Charter Evidence*, Jarrow Lecture 1984 (Jarrow, 1984).

61 For summary of the debate, see Blair, *Church in Anglo-Saxon-Society*, pp. 153–76.

62 E. Cambridge and D. Rollason, 'The Pastoral Organization of the Anglo-Saxon Church: A Review of the "Minster Hypothesis"', *Early Medieval Europe* 4 (1995), pp. 87–104; F. Tinti, *Sustaining Belief: The Church of Worcester from c. 870 to c. 1100* (Farnham, 2010), pp. 225–314.

63 Ó Corrain, 'Ireland *c.* 800', pp. 594–8; T. Ó Carragáin, 'Cemetery Settlements and Local Churches in Pre-Viking Ireland in Light of Comparisons with England and Wales', in *Anglo-Saxon/Irish Relations Before the Vikings*, ed. J. Graham-Campbell and M. Ryan, = *Proceedings of the British Academy*, 157 (2009), pp. 239–61.

64 O. J. Padel, 'Local Saints and Place-Names in Cornwall', in *Local Saints*, pp. 303–60.

65 H. Pryce, 'Pastoral Care in Early Medieval Wales', in *Pastoral Care Before the Parish*, ed. J. Blair and R. Sharpe (Leicester, 1992), pp. 41–62.

66 S. Foot, '"By Water in the Spirit": The Administration of Baptism in Early Anglo-Saxon England', in *Pastoral Care Before the Parish*, pp.171–92.

67 N. Whitfield, 'A Suggested Function for the Holy Well', in *Text, Image, Interpretation: Studies Anglo-Saxon Literature and its Insular Context in Honour of Éamonn Ó Carragáin*, ed. A. Minnis and J. Roberts, Studies in the Early Middle Ages 18 (Turnhout, 2007), pp. 495–514; T.

1. INTRODUCTION

few free-standing baptisteries for processing adult catechumens have been recognised in Anglo-Saxon England or Ireland, though they seem to have been more a feature of late Roman Britain. Priests could hold services and say mass in the open with the aid or portable altars like the one which was buried with St Cuthbert who was portrayed, particularly by Bede, as touring outlying parts of Northumbria to minister to his congregation.[68] The nun Hugeburg, who had been raised in late seventh-century Wessex, recalled that noblemen might erect crosses (perhaps of wood) on their estates to act as local Christian foci.[69] Worship in the open air at local sacred sites, or within halls that were also lay dwelling places, would presumably have been what people would have been used to,[70] and so an aspect of the gradual introduction of Christianity through the medium of established religious practices as recommended by Pope Gregory I. Even where there were established churches, processions and other liturgical displays might continue to provide a significant open-air aspect to worship.[71]

Burial is one of the best sources of evidence for the gradual intensification of Christianisation and association with churches among the population as a whole, as well as a way of identifying regional differences in the timescale over which it was achieved. In Ireland new forms of burial rite, including supine burial and use of cists, seem to have been part of the influences coming from Britain in the fifth and sixth centuries that included Christianity and so the forms of burial followed by British Christians. However, burial continued in ancestral cemeteries, and it was not until the late seventh and eighth centuries that Irish church leaders made a concerted attempt to move burial to specifically Christian graveyards, associated with churches, where the dead could lie *ad sanctos*, amidst the saints, and receive the attention of the rites for the dead that were being elaborated in Ireland during the same period.[72] Specifically Christian cemeteries began earlier in Wales and might continue for longer, some eventually acquiring their own churches, though this was not an inevitable pattern and a greater number were gradually abandoned between the eighth and twelfth centuries.[73]

Ó Carragáin, 'Archaeology of Early Medieval Baptism at St Mullins, Co. Carlow', *Peritia*, 21 (2010), pp. 285–302.

[68] E. Coatsworth, 'The Pectoral Cross and Portable Altar from the Tomb of St Cuthbert', in *St Cuthbert, His Cult and His Community to AD 1200*, ed. G. Bonner, D. Rollason and C. Stancliffe (Woodbridge, 1989), pp. 267–301; Bede, *Vita sancti Cuthberti*, c. 26.

[69] *The Anglo-Saxon Missionaries in Germany: Being the Lives of SS. Willibrord, Boniface, Sturm, Leuba and Lebuin, together with the Hodoeporicon of St Willibald and a Selection of the Correspondence of St Boniface*, ed. and trans. C. H. Talbot (London, 1954), pp. 154–5.

[70] S. Semple, *Perceptions of the Prehistoric in Anglo-Saxon England: Ritual, Religion, and Rulership in the Landscape* (Oxford, 2013).

[71] H. Gittos, *Liturgy, Architecture, and Sacred Places in Anglo-Saxon England* (Oxford, 2013).

[72] Ó Carragáin, 'The Cult of Relics'; E. O'Brien, 'Pagan or Christian? Burial in Ireland During the 5th to 8th Centuries AD', in *Celtic Churches*, pp. 135–54.

[73] D. Longley, 'Early Medieval Burial in Wales', in *Celtic Churches*, pp. 105–32.

Among the Anglo-Saxons, the earliest Christian burials were likely to be in established family cemeteries. New cemeteries might be created in the succeeding centuries though it is not clear whether this was the result of ecclesiastical intervention, as in Ireland, or of the settlement migration that was a feature of the Middle Saxon period. Burial in association with churches took longer to be established except on the estates of religious communities such as Hartlepool. The local church with its burial ground only became a regular feature of the English landscape from the end of the tenth century when the tenth-century reformation within the church combined with the impact of growing manoralisation.[74] However, many of the earliest surviving stone 'parish' churches from this time seem to have originated as lordly chapels rather than specifically parochial structures. Excavations at Furnells Manor, Raunds (Northamptonshire) suggested the community graveyard was a secondary addition to what had been originally a small manorial chapel.[75] Many of the distinctive features of tenth and eleventh century Anglo-Saxon churches such as their prominent towers seem to have been designed to meet a variety of needs that demonstrated the lordly status of their owners,[76] just as founding religious communities had done for a more narrowly focused group of the elite in the late seventh and early eighth centuries. We can conclude that churches are an essential part of the narrative of the spread of Christianity in these islands, and that, like many other aspects of Christianity, they only gradually became part of the lives of all members of its communities.

---

[74] Blair, *Church in Anglo-Saxon Society*, pp. 228–45; 368–425.
[75] A. Boddington, *Raunds Furnells: The Anglo-Saxon Church and Churchyard*, English Heritage Archaeological Report 7 (London, 1996).
[76] M. Shapland, 'St Mary's, Broughton, Lincolnshire: A Thegnly Tower-Nave in the Late Anglo-Saxon Landscape', *Archaeological Journal* 165 (2008), pp. 471–519.

(2)
The Origins of Christian Britain: From Mystery Cult to Christian Mystery

MARTIN HENIG

This paper inevitably builds on the research of others, many of whom have been good friends who have encouraged my own studies and whose work on the subject remains vibrant and fresh. Foremost amongst them are the late Professor Jocelyn Toynbee's pioneering papers, then Professor Charles Thomas' magisterial study of the church in Roman Britain and amongst younger scholars the elegant survey by David Petts.[1] However, our story starts earlier than Christian times for the history of religion in Britain is a continuum, and it is doubtful whether there was ever a time at which people living here did not attempt to venerate the powers which controlled earth and heaven. The degree of sophistication varied but the fact of worship taking place did not. My own starting point has always been one of empathy with seekers after God, very much in line with the view of the great late Roman statesman, pagan philosopher and man of letters, Quintus Aurelius Symmachus, who, in a famous speech addressed to the emperor Gratian requesting the return of the altar of Victory to the Roman Senate, famously proclaimed: 'Not by a single path can mankind comprehend so great a mystery'.[2]

In the fourth century, the first century of Christian hegemony in the Roman Empire, Britain, like Italy, was a land where many cults flourished. Churches and other places of Christian worship cannot and should not be viewed in isolation but rather as part of a rich tapestry of religious life in which there may frequently been some lack of precision in the minds of worshippers (who were not theologians) in distinguishing between pagan and Christian practice. Thus the mosaic floors of a villa or more probably a building associated with a sanctuary at Frampton in Dorset were embellished with scenes from pagan myth and representations of Bacchus and Neptune but also with a prominently placed chi-rho.[3] Then again a curse tablet from

---

[1] J. Toynbee, 'Christianity in Roman Britain', *Journal of the British Archaeological Association*, 3rd ser. 16 (1953), pp. 1–24, and J. Toynbee, 'Pagan Motifs and Practices in Christian Art and Ritual in Roman Britain', *Christianity in Britain 300–700: Papers Presented at a Conference on Christianity in Roman and Sub-Roman Britain held at the University of Nottingham 17–20 April 1967*, ed. M. W. Barley and R. P. C. Hanson (Leicester, 1968), pp. 177–92; C. Thomas, *Christianity in Roman Britain to AD 500* (London, 1981); D. Petts, *Christianity in Roman Britain* (Stroud, 2003).

[2] Symmachus, *Relatio* iii, 9. in *Prefect and Emperor: The Relationes of Symmachus AD 384*, ed. R. H. Barrow (Oxford, 1973), p. 41.

[3] S. R. Cosh and D. S. Neal, *Roman Mosaics of Britain*, 3 vols in 4 (London, 2002–10), vol. 2, pp. 130–40 especially pp. 134–7 mosaic 168.2.

the sacred spring of Sulis Minerva at Bath is addressed to the thief ('whether he be Pagan or Christian') with the implication that someone who identified himself or herself as a Christian might have been present in the sanctuary.[4] Even more strikingly, amongst the church plate from a church at Water Newton in Cambridgeshire discussed below, votive leaves or feathers embellished with the chi-rho attest a continuing pagan rite, albeit in what is now surely a Christian context.[5]

There are not likely to have been many Christians in Britain c. 300, the time of the Great Persecution unleashed by Diocletian and his colleagues in the Tetrarchy against Christianity. Despite attempts to push the history of the church in Britain further back there is no reliable evidence before about the beginning of the fourth century, when in all probability Alban was martyred at Verulamium and Julius [or Julian] and Aaron most probably at Caerleon (Monmouthshire). I have argued that St Alban, the best attested British martyr, and the others are most likely to have suffered then at the hands of Constantine's father Constantius, who would, presumably, have had little choice other than to execute the orders of his senior colleague Maximian.[6] Alban was most probably a local, convicted of sheltering a fugitive, and was not a member of any established Christian community. The name Aaron is of course Hebraic, and in any case both he and Julius were associated with a legionary base so could well have been foreigners.

The position was to change after Constantine was proclaimed emperor at York on the death of his father in 306, so that a bare decade later at the 314 Council of Arles bishops are attested at York, Lincoln and London, respectively capitals of the late Roman provinces of *Flavia Caesariensis*, *Britannia Secunda* and *Maxima Caesariensis*. The apparent absence of a bishop of what was probably the largest and richest province, *Britannia Prima*, may simply be chance, a vacancy at the time, but it may attest the minority position of Christianity amongst other competing cults, mainly native but also exotic (such as Mithraism and the Isiac cult), which continued to flourish.[7] No archaeological evidence has yet emerged either from London or Lincoln attesting a Christian presence in the early decades of the fourth century, while

---

[4] R. Tomlin in *The Temple of Sulis Minerva at Bath*, ed. B. Cunliffe, P Davenport, V. Care and R. Tomlin, University of Oxford Committee for Archaeology Monographs 7 and 16, 2 vols in 3 (Oxford, 1985–8), vol. 2, pp. 232–4 no. 98.

[5] K. S. Painter, 'The Water Newton Silver: Votive or Liturgical?', *Journal of the British Archaeological Association*, 152 (1999), pp. 1–23, especially pp.1–2, Fig. 1, and pl. I B–D.

[6] M. Henig, 'Religion and Art in St Alban's City', *Alban and St Albans Roman and Medieval Architecture, Art and Archaeology*, ed. M. Henig and P. Lindley, British Archaeological Association Conference Transactions 24 (Leeds, 2001), pp. 13–29 at pp. 24–5.

[7] For Constantine see E. Hartley, J. Hawkes, M. Henig and F. Mee, *Constantine the Great: York's Roman Emperor* (York and Aldershot, 2006); for the relevant extract from the *Acta Concilii Arelatensis* see A. L. F. Rivet and C. Smith, *The Place-Names of Roman Britain* (London, 1979), pp. 49–50.

2. THE ORIGINS OF CHRISTIAN BRITAIN

at York, apart from the marble head of Constantine from near the *principia* of the Fortress (rather indicating veneration of the Emperor than the religion he was to adopt), there is only a cornelian intaglio found in excavations at Wellington Row in the Colonia, depicting the well-known Christian motif of an anchor and two fish, almost certainly to be dated to the time of Constantine or even earlier.[8] Jeffrey Spier, who has published many similar gems, believes it is the product of a Syrian workshop, and if so it is more than likely that like the wearer of the sardonyx intaglio from Corbridge, Northumberland, depicting the chief god of Baalbek, Zeus [Jupiter] Heliopolitanus, the owner hailed from the Levant.[9] Even under Constantine Christians may have been a small community, with a strong foreign element within it, including its hierarchy such as it was. For religious architecture we have to turn to the temples of the myriad pagan cults.

Pagan Temples

Temples varied widely in type and style. Large official temples, notably the Temple of the Imperial Cult at Colchester, Essex, evidently dedicated to *Divus Claudius* after his death in 54, together with the chief temples in the larger towns, notably London and the *coloniae*, proclaimed the hegemony of Rome. They would have housed statues of the major gods of the Roman state especially the Capitoline Triad of Jupiter, Juno and Minerva, and upon their altars set up in their sacred precinct libations and sacrifice were regularly offered for the well-being of the state.[10]

The temple of *Sulis Minerva* at Bath, perhaps originally built in the first century by the client king Tiberius Claudius Togidubnus, may have partaken of this rather formal aspect of cult, though it had as much in common with the myriad temples of local deities which were often square or octagonal in plan with central towers pierced by windows for clerestory lighting, and surrounding ambulatories.[11] Such temples,

---

[8] Hartley, Hawkes, Henig and Mee, *Constantine the Great*, pp. 120–1, cat. no. 9; M. Henig, 'Sealed in Stone: Roman Gem Stones Excavated in York by YAT', *Yorkshire Archaeology Today*, 20 (Spring 2011), pp. 7–9 at p. 9.

[9] Jeffrey Spier (pers. comm.). For many other gems depicting the anchor and fishes, see J. Spier, *Late Antique and Early Christian Gems*, Spätantike, frühes Christentum, Byzanz, Reihe B: Studien und Perspektiven 20 (Wiesbaden, 2007), pp. 42–8. It is worth mentioning that a second cornelian with the same subject, set in a silver ring, was excavated in a fourth-century layer in the baths at Binchester, County Durham, in the summer of 2014 (inf. David Petts), presumably implying the presence of a Christian, if not a church. For Zeus Heliopolitanus on a gem from Corbridge, see M. Henig, *A Corpus of Roman Engraved Gemstones from British Sites*, British Archaeological Reports British Series 8, 3rd edn (Oxford, 2007), p. 134 and pl. xii, no.351 (Zeus Heliopolitanus).

[10] M. J. T. Lewis, *Temples in Roman Britain* (Cambridge, 1966), chapter 2; P. J. Drury, 'The Temple of Claudius at Colchester Reconsidered', *Britannia*, 15 (1984), pp. 7–50.

[11] *Temple of Sulis Minerva at Bath*, vol. 1, and cf. M. Henig, 'A New Star Shining over Bath', *Oxford Journal of Archaeology*, 18 (1999), pp. 419–25.

Fig 2.1 The Roman temple next to the forum at Caerwent, Monmouthshire
(a): General view. (b): Entrance hall to temple with apsidal east end.
(© Copyright M. Henig.)

especially when located in the countryside as at Springhead in Kent, Nettleton in Wiltshire and Uley and Lydney Park in Gloucestershire, might be considerable magnets for pilgrimage, and their sanctuaries often contained ancillary buildings like baths and accommodation for priests and pilgrims. The main cult activities comprise sacrifice, prayer (including petitions scratched on lead tablets for the restoration of stolen property) and the presentation of offerings (sometimes explicitly directed to the recovery of the health of the votary); such activities point to direct personal, and sometimes even emotional, relationships with the gods.[12] Although these activities at first sight might seem rather foreign to Christians, it should be recalled that the Jewish Temple where Jesus and his disciples worshipped was distinguished by the self same activities of sacrificial and votive prayer. Moreover, intercession and offertory remained central to Christian cult throughout its history. Sometimes temples of Romano-Celtic form served as civic temples, an interesting fourth-century example of which can be seen at Caerwent (Monmouthshire) (Fig. 2.1a) with an apse attached to the north side of the *cella*.[13] What sort of cult was practiced here?

A third temple type, generally of basilican form, allowed for activity within the building. Most familiar, at least in Britain, from the well-known examples from beside the Walbrook, London, and Hadrian's Wall, especially Carrawburgh (Fig. 2.2) were *mithraea*, temples dedicated to the god Mithras who was believed to have slain the primeval bull from whose blood all life flowed at the beginning of time.[14] Votaries of Mithras congregated for sacred feasts and rituals within the temple and passed through a series of grades. Some descriptions of Mithraic liturgy and a few lines of sacred text are preserved, as they are of other mystery cults from the east, such as those

---

[12] Lewis, *Temples*, chapter 1; M. Henig, *Religion in Roman Britain* (London, 1984) especially chapters 2 and 6.

[13] R. J. Brewer, *Caerwent Roman Town*, 3rd edn (Cardiff, 2006), pp. 44–7.

[14] Henig, *Religion in Roman Britain*, pp. 98–109, ills 41 and 42; J. Shepherd, *The Temple of Mithras, London: Excavations by W. F. Grimes and A. Williams at the Walbrook*, English Heritage Archaeological Report 12 (London, 1998).

Fig. 2.2 Mithraeum at Carrawburgh, Northumberland (© Copyright Institute of Archaeology, Oxford.)

of the Egyptian Isis from Egypt and of the Magna Mater (Cybele) from Phrygia. These suggest a generic relationship between them, which in some ways links them to Christianity too. They not only offered to initiates closer personal union with the deity than traditional religions, often through cult acts including a sacred meal, but also held out the promise of personal salvation. In Isaea and temples of the Magna Mater cult activity seems to have been centred in the courtyard rather than the temple itself, but Mithraea were either caves or small basilicas which conform to the type of building we associate with churches save that they were windowless. The London *mithraeum* has yielded a small hoard of silver plate consisting of a now fragmentary silver bowl and an infuser in a canister. I have elsewhere assigned these to the late fourth-century Bacchic phase at the site.[15] Although dedicated to the native healing god Mars Nodens, and set within what was effectively a local healing sanctuary the fourth-century temple in Lydney Park approximated to this type. Small chambers constructed within an ambulatory are thought to be for *incubation* where the god could visit and cure votaries suffering from health complaints in their sleep. A separate long building of multiple chambers (an *abaton*, a 'place apart') served the same purpose.[16]

[15] Shepherd, *Temple of Mithras*, pp. 179–81, Figs 208–11, and Henig, 'The Temple as a *Bacchium* or *Sacrarium* in the Fourth Century', in the same volume, pp. 230–2.
[16] R. E. M. Wheeler and T. V. Wheeler, *Report on the Excavation of the Prehistoric, Roman and*

Finally there were private shrines in villas, including a tri-conch building with Orphic mosaics from Littlecote, Wiltshire, and what appears to be Bacchic chamber, again with mosaics, established by the villa-owner Quintus Natalius Natalinus at Thruxton, Hampshire.[17] In addition there were mausolea, sometimes quite grand and even in the form of temples, though perceived dangers of pollution meant that they were visited only on particular occasions in the year and not for regular worship. A good example of such a temple-mausoleum was excavated at Lullingstone, Kent.[18]

The fourth-century world in which Christianity emerged as a potent force in Britain was one where all these varieties of Pagan shrine flourished and indeed co-existed with the nascent churches, which again can be divided into types, some of which approximate (albeit with differences) to pagan temples.

Christian Churches

As far as Britain is concerned the rarest type of church is the grand intra-mural basilica. Such may well have existed as the sees of bishops, but even London and the other capitals of the late Roman provinces ranked far below Trier, where there are still notable remains of a great double basilica redolent of Imperial power.[19] The only possible example of such a grand church yet discovered in Britain, late Roman in date, is the robbed out foundations of an aisled building in south-east London dated to the second half of the fourth century.[20] The excavator sees similarities with the plan of St Tecla, Milan, and the presence of fragments of marble casing albeit in a secondary context hint at a luxuriously appointed building, but there can be no certainty.

The function and date of the 'church' at Silchester in Hampshire (Fig. 2.3), albeit a building of basilican type with side chapels, is far from certain. It may indeed not have been a church, but rather have served as a centre of some other unknown cult or even a quasi-secular purpose.[21] If it was a church, its complex plan looks later than

---

Post-Roman Site in Lydney Park, Gloucestershire, Reports of the Research Committee of the Society of Antiquaries of London 9 (London, 1932); Henig, *Religion in Roman Britain*, pp. 51–2 and 56, ill.16.

17 B. Walters, 'The "Orpheus" Mosaic in Littlecote Park, England', *III colloquio internazionale sul mosaico antico: Ravenna, 6–10 settembre 1980*, ed. R. Farioli Campanati, 2 vols (Ravenna, 1984), vol. 2, pp. 433–42; M. Henig and G. Soffe, 'The Thruxton Roman Villa and its Mosaic Pavement', *Journal of the British Archaeological Association*, 146 (1993), pp. 1–28.

18 Henig, *Religion in Roman Britain*, pp. 196–7, ill. 97.

19 E. M. Wightman, *Gallia Belgica* (London, 1985), pp. 288–91, Fig. 43.

20 D. Sankey, 'Cathedrals, Granaries, and Urban Vitality in Late Roman London', *Roman London: Recent Archaeological Work, Including Papers given at a Seminar held at the Museum of London on 16 November 1996*, ed. B. Watson, Journal of Roman Archaeology Supplementary Series 24 (Portsmouth, Rhode Island, 1998), pp. 78–82, and Fig. 17.

21 For a traditional view see S. S. Frere, 'The Silchester Church: The Excavations by Sir Ian Richmond in 1961', *Archaeologia*, 105 (1975), pp. 277–302, and for a more skeptical appraisal, A. King, 'The Silchester Church Reconsidered', *Oxford Journal of Archaeology*, 2

Fig. 2.3 Roman church(?) at Silchester, Hampshire (© Copyright Institute of Archaeology, Oxford.)

the fourth century and it may fit in with what is now perceived as the very late fifth or sixth phase at the site. The plan reminded Dr John Wilkinson of Syrian churches of that period,[22] and, although altogether a much grander building, Phase IV of the basilica at Petra is not dissimilar, with squared-off chambers flanking the apse and a fairly narrow narthex.[23] In front of the building a squarish tile platform might have served as the seating for a font, and it may be noted that Petra had a baptistery in approximately the same position. If Silchester is, indeed, a church it can be no more than a simple urban church for a small Christian community; nobody could call it a grand example of religious patronage. Possibly the temple beside the forum at Caerwent, cited above,[24] came to function as an urban church, at least on occasions. At its entrance is a hall oriented east–west; it has an apse at the east end, and this part of the complex looks church-like (see Fig. 2.1b). Could it have served as a Christian chapel alongside, maybe (pagan) civic cult? Another more certain example of what

---

[22] (1983), pp. 225–37.
Pers. comm.
[23] Z. T. Fiema, C. Kanellopoulos, T. Waliszewski and R. Schick, *The Petra Church* (Amman, 2001), pp. 158–66, Figs 17–23.
[24] See note 13.

Fig. 2.4 Roman font at Richborough, Kent (© Copyright Society of Antiquaries of London.)

may be regarded as an urban intra-mural church, although one whose plan is merely suggested by a line of re-used stone blocks photographed at the time of totally inadequate excavations, is a putative example within the late Roman Saxon Shore fort at the port of Richborough in Kent, first recognised by P. D. C. Brown in 1971.[25] The *enceinte* at Richborough is essentially the same as the reduced town walls of Gaulish cities and, like them, incorporates re-used material. The church may thus be regarded as being as much urban as military. An important feature here was the hexagonal, niched font (Fig. 2.4) which must have been a beautiful and elaborate part of the complex before losing its casing. Very probably it was enclosed in a baptistery building the robber trenches of which were not recognised in the excavation. Late Roman Christianity is represented at Richborough also by a bronze signet-ring inscribed: 'Iustine vivas in Deo', giving a name, no doubt that of a member of the congregation.[26] There must also have been a church in the small town of Water Newton. Although no

[25] P. D. C. Brown, 'The Church at Richborough, Kent', *Britannia*, 2 (1971), pp. 225–31.
[26] S. S. Frere, M. Roxan and R. S. O. Tomlin, *The Roman Inscriptions of Britain, II. Instrumentum Domesticum (Personal Belongings and the Like)*, 9 vols (Stroud, 1990–5), vol. 3, p. 30, no. 2422.70.

2. THE ORIGINS OF CHRISTIAN BRITAIN

church building has yet been recognised, a set of silver plate employed for the celebration of the Mass has been recovered.[27] Dating from the second half of the fourth century, the importance of this small group of Christian objects can hardly be over stated, for it is the earliest group of such plate to have survived anywhere. Amongst the material, too, are the votive plaques, to which reference has been made, one of them dedicated by a woman called Amcilla. Of two deep bowls, perhaps used for the Eucharistic wine, one was given by Innocentia and Viventia and another by Publianus, so clearly both men and women were involved. Publianus' bowl bears the legend, 'Sanctum altare tuum Domine subnixus honoro' ('Prostrating myself, I honour your sacred sanctuary'[28]). The word *altare* has a Christian rather than a Pagan resonance: a Pagan altar was always an *ara*, and the language of the invocation, as Kenneth Painter argues, echoes that of the Old Latin Mass. The association with the bowls of a handled cup, jug, dish and strainer, every item embellished with a chi-rho, is powerful evidence for the practice of the sacrament here.

Although religious rituals were practiced at Pagan mausolea they were limited to specific times of the year and the appeasing of the spirits, the *manes*, of deceased relatives. Christianity was unique in honouring the graves of the deceased, especially those of what Peter Brown has styled 'the very special dead', with special rites.[29] In Rome itself there was a clear distinction between the urban Lateran basilica and the basilicas outside the walls of the city, such as St Peter's, dedicated to martyrs. It is all but certain that such a martyrial church existed at St Albans, outside *Verulamium*, where Alban was buried in a late Roman cemetery partly excavated by the Biddles.[30] The original church may have been quite simple like St Severin at Cologne or the church outside Xanten (*ad sanctos*). An excavated basilican building at Butt Road, Colchester, may have been a church of this type, and it looks as though St Martin's, Canterbury, mentioned by Bede, and St Martin's-in-the-Fields, London, were originally cemetery churches.[31] Both churches are situated approximately a mile beyond the walls of their respective cities.

---

[27] Painter, 'The Water Newton Silver'.
[28] Translation: *Roman Instcrpitions of Britain*, II, vol. 3, p. 31, no. 2414.2.
[29] P. Brown, *The Cult of the Saints* (Chicago, 1981), chapter 4.
[30] M. Biddle and B. Kjølbye-Biddle, 'The Origins of St Albans Abbey: Romano-British Cemetery and Anglo-Saxon Monastery', *Alban and St Albans*, pp. 45–77.
[31] N. Crummy, P. Crummy and C. Crossan, *Excavations of Roman and Later Cemeteries, Churches and Monastic Sites in Colchester, 1971–88*, Colchester Archaeological Reports 9 (Colchester, 1993), pp. 164–202, Figs 3.24–3.27; Thomas, *Christianity in Roman Britain*, pp. 170–4, seems to me to be over skeptical in the face of Bede's statement, the dedication, and now the evidence from another St Martin's church, London. See A. Telfer, 'New Evidence for the Transition from the Late Roman to the Saxon Period at St-Martin-in-the-Fields, London', *Intersections: The Archaeology and History of Christianity in England, 400–1200. Papers in Honour of Martin Biddle and Birthe Kjølbye-Biddle*, ed. M. Henig and N. Ramsay, British Archaeological Reports British Series 505 (Oxford, 2010), pp. 49–58.

Christianity was not a merely urban (or military) phenomenon as, at least in Britain, other exotic, non-native pagan 'mystery' cults, apart from that of Bacchus, tended to be. Indeed, in some ways the evidence from villas is the most interesting and instructive for it provides the sort of evidence which leads us on to consider how British (sometimes regarded—wrongly—as Celtic) Christianity came into existence. Lullingstone was not one of the larger villas but it had a long and intriguing history including, it appears, at one stage being a country hideaway in the late second century for the governor, later emperor, Publius Helvius Pertinax.[32] One of the rooms certainly seems to have contained a contemporary shrine of the nymphs, presumably of the river Darent, and it appears that later offerings were made to the marble busts of Pertinax and his father. A shrine and an early fourth-century mausoleum, apparently pagan, beside the building suggest that there was a powerful religious aspect to the site. In the mid-fourth century a mosaic was laid in an apsed *stibadium* and an adjoining chamber showing Europa and the bull, and Bellerophon slaying the Chimaera. Although a two-line verse inscription between the scenes has been seen merely as a reflection of literary culture, it in fact encodes the name of the owner, Avitus, together with 'Iesus'.[33] In other rooms, above, wall-paintings of *orantes* (praying figures with raised hands), one supporting a yoke on his shoulders, chi-rhos and biblical scenes, attest this was a house church probably some ten or twenty years after the mosaics.[34] The Christian chambers lacked the formal planning of the other churches we have considered but do show the flexibility of Christian witness. At Hinton St Mary in Dorset a two-chambered suite with mosaic floors showing respectively Bellerophon slaying the Chimaera and a bust of Our Lord as central features, with dogs chasing deer around both scenes, allude to Psalm 22 and again suggest a house-church. A third example, at Frampton, in the same county is more problematic: although there is an apse on one side of a chamber, with a chalice as a feature of its mosaic and a chi-rho on the cord of the apse, the other figural scenes are pagan, though one of them depicts Bellerophon. The fourth example of a Bellerophon mosaic, possibly in the light of the others suggestive of a villa house-church was excavated at Rawler Manor, Croughton, Northamptonshire. It may be suggested that the myth of Bellerophon expressed something of the eclectic character of insular Christianity in the fourth century, and it certainly suggests that an active approach to

---

[32] M. Henig, 'The Victory-Gem from Lullingstone Roman Villa', *Journal of the British Archaeological Association*, 160 (2007), pp. 1–7.

[33] M. Henig, 'The Lullingstone Mosaic. Art, Religion and Letters in a Fourth-Century Villa', *Mosaic*, 24 (1997), pp. 4–7.

[34] N. Cronin, '*Sumus novi dei*: Approaches to a Renewed Understanding of the Identity of the Romano-British Church', *Roman Art, Religion and Society: New Studies from the Roman Art Seminar, Oxford 2005*, ed. M. Henig, British Archaeological Reports International Series 1577 (Oxford, 2006), pp. 127–40 at p. 137, Fig. 6.

Fig. 2.5 Late fourth-century mosaic in a villa at Bradford-on-Avon, Wiltshire, partly overlain by a font. The apsed exedra with dolphins and cantharus probably served as a church in the fifth and sixth centuries. (a). General view with seating for a font. (b): Exedra
(© Copyright Bryn Walters.)

fighting evil was a formative element in the upbringing of our one native-born Roman heresiarch, Pelagius.[35]

At the villa of Bradford on Avon, Wiltshire, which flourished in the fourth century, a mosaic-covered chamber was modified in the fifth century to take an octagonal font, though the chamber beyond which retained its cantharus and dolphin mosaic in its apse could well have served as a church (Fig. 2.5a and b). Only the seating for the font remained, but in all probability it was a masonry structure like that at Richborough. The worn threshold stone to the font chamber reveals that many people flocked to this baptistery, very probably over many decades.[36] In this instance there is good reason to posit continuity between the Romano-British church and the later Christian activity at Bradford. The same was probably true of other villa sites and at Croughton, for example, a polychrome bead of 'Anglo-Saxon' sixth-century type lying on top of the mosaic is a hint of a similar trajectory of villa to church. Such modifications of parts of villas for Christian use were probably common; there is another undated instance at Chedworth where an ornamental hexagonal pool (Fig. 2.6), probably originally a nymphaeum, was converted into a baptistery by having

---

[35] Cosh and Neal, *Roman Mosaics of Britain*, vol. 2, p. 1346 mosaic 168.2 (Frampton) and pp. 156–60 mosaic 172.1 (Hinton St Mary); vol. 1, pp. 234–6 mosaic no.86.1. See M. Dawson, 'Excavation of the Roman Villa and Mosaic at Rawler Manor, Croughton, Northamptonshire', *Northamptonshire Archaeology* 35 (2008), pp. 45–93; M. Henig in Hartley, Hawkes, Henig and Mee, *Constantine the Great*, pp. 92–3; M. Henig, 'From Romano-British Hero to Patron Saint of England: The Transformations of Bellerophon and his Chimaera', *Myth, Allegory, Emblem: The Many Lives of the Chimaera of Arezzo. Proceedings of the International Colloquium, Malibu, the J. Getty Museum (4–5 December 2009)*, ed. G. C. Cianferoni, M. Iozzo and E. Setari (Rome, 2012), pp. 137–50.

[36] M. Corney, 'The Roman Villa at Bradford-on-Avon—Investigations at St Laurence School', *ARA*, 16 (2004), cover and pp.10–13; K. Bowes, *Private Worship, Public Values, and Religious Change in Late Antiquity* (Cambridge, 2008), pp. 176–7, Fig. 53.

Fig. 2.6: Nymphaeum at Chedworth villa, Gloucestershire,
converted in a baptistery in the fourth or fifth century (a): General view (© Copyright Martin Henig.);
(b): Chi-Rho monogram scratched on a flagstone at Chedworth
(© Copyright the late Ralph Merrifield.)

chi-rhos incised into its flag-stones, transforming a pagan structure into a Christian one.[37]

There is plentiful evidence for religious activity in rural sanctuaries, and just occasionally there are traces of a Christian presence, co-terminous with pagan worship at the site or even succeeding it. At Ivy Chimneys, Witham, in Essex, an octagonal font was found to the east of a small two-cell structure which may have served as a church and the same arrangement of rectangular building and a tank, this time, rectangular and apsed on the east was recorded at Icklingham, Suffolk.[38] A third, perhaps less certain case, is known at West Hill, Uley, Gloucestershire, where a possible simple church and baptistery have been proposed succeeding a temple dedicated to the god Mercury.[39] Such very basic structures are a far cry from the Roman period churches familiar from Mediterranean lands.

Both Uley and Icklingham have provided material evidence for Christianity. At Uley this takes the form of a piece of sheet bronze, the covering of a small casket, displaying Biblical scenes: the sacrifice of Isaac, Jonah beneath the gourd, Christ and the centurion, and Christ healing the blind man. As the sheeting was folded and apparently an offering to Mercury it arguably does not attest living faith at the site,[40] but two lead tanks found at Icklingham are another matter. Although our present theme is centred on Christian buildings, the lead tanks of late Roman Britain are of crucial importance for understanding the progress of the faith in the province.[41] They

---

[37] R. Goodburn, *The Roman Villa Chedworth* (London, 1972), p. 24 and pl. 11.
[38] Petts, *Christianity in Roman Britain*, pp. 91–3, Fig. 35.
[39] Petts, *Christianity in Roman Britain*, pp. 70–1, Fig. 21; R. White, *Britannia Prima: Britain's Last Roman Province* (Stroud, 2007), p. 95, Fig. 37.
[40] Henig in Hartley, Hawkes, Henig and Mee, *Constantine the Great*, pp. 224–5 no. 227.
[41] Thomas, *Christianity in Roman Britain*, pp. 220–7; Petts, *Christianity in Roman Britain*, pp. 96–9; and now especially B. Crerar, 'Contextualising Romano-British Lead Tanks: A Study in Design, Destruction and Deposition', *Britannia*, 43 (2012), pp. 135–66.

2. THE ORIGINS OF CHRISTIAN BRITAIN

are quite numerous in the east and south east of England extending as far as Bourton on the Water, Gloucestershire, and are found in all sorts of sites, sanctuaries like Icklingham, villas such as Wigginton in Oxfordshire, small towns (including Bourton on the Water) and the open countryside. Many of them are ornamented with the chi-rho, but one discovered not long go at Flawborough, Nottinghamshire, is also embellished with figures of *orantes*, such as we have observed frescoed in the Lullingstone house-church.[42] A fragmentary font from Walesby, Lincolnshire, has been thought to portray an actual scene of baptism with a central nude neophyte with her two sponsors, and on each side three members of the community, being initiated within a columnar building.[43] However, as Crerar points out, the scene is badly damaged by the plough which brought it to the surface and other explanations are possible; she believes that it bears a greater resemblance to Romano-British pagan iconography, including *genii cucullati* and perhaps here an image of Venus holding an apple.[44]

It has generally been agreed that these lead tanks were intended to be fairly portable, perhaps taken to villas, farms and small settlements on an ox-cart by the bishop who would have wanted to make sure that the vessels were only used in the manner intended for them; they could be placed in the open air or in a barn for the baptismal rite and then returned to store. Crerar is not convinced by this explanation, and concludes that 'for the time being, the tanks remain enigmatic and a convincing explanation for their original intended use is elusive';[45] nevertheless I still think that they are most probably portable fonts.

When discovered, they are generally deliberately buried and most are deliberately damaged, sometimes as at Walesby carefully cut and in other instances as at Flawborough simply crushed or pierced. It has sometimes been suggested that they met their fate as the result of an anti-Christian reaction in the late fourth century.[46] There is a perfectly valid reason why, if they were fonts, they were slighted when they became redundant as it was customary through the middle ages, and indeed now, to break redundant fonts to make sure that they cannot be re-used in impious rites,

---

[42] L. Elliott and S. Malone, 'Iron Age/Romano-British Features and a Fourth-Century A.D. Christian Lead Tank from Flawborough, Nottinghamshire', *Transactions of the Thoroton Society*, 109 (2005), pp. 25–43, especially pp. 29–36; P. Booth, E. Cameron and B. Crerar, 'A Roman Lead "Tank" from Wigginton, North Oxfordshire', *Oxoniensia*, 76 (2011), pp. 266–72; R. Wilson in Hartley, Hawkes, Henig and Mee, *Constantine the Great*, 208–9 no. 195.
[43] Henig in Hartley, Hawkes, Henig and Mee, *Constantine the Great*, p. 208 no. 194.
[44] Crerar, 'Romano-British Lead Tanks', pp. 146–50.
[45] Crerar, 'Romano-British Lead Tanks', p.156.
[46] C. J. Guy, 'Roman Circular Lead Tanks in Britain', *Britannia*, 12 (1981), pp. 271–6 at p. 275; D. Watts, *Religion in Late Roman Britain: Forces of Change* (London, 1998), pp. 147–53: Watts suggests that Christians themselves attempted to save the sacred monogram from misuse by Pagan zealots.

though as they are consecrated they have to be disposed of in a reverent manner.[47] This means of disposal was most likely the custom of the church in Roman Britain. Lead had a fairly high monetary value, and the fact that it was not recycled as scrap metal is surely of significance. There is increasing archaeological evidence, from Bradford on Avon, London (for example, St Martin-in-the-Fields), and St Albans, not to mention the literary evidence of St Patrick and Constantius' *Life of St Germanus*, of quite a different trajectory, indeed of a church rapidly gaining both in numbers of its adherents and in confidence. In an island where an increasingly large percentage of the population was Christian, portable fonts such as these may have given way to larger and far more permanent structures such as that recently discovered at Bradford on Avon. We should look for others.

In Northern Britain, too, there are remains of buildings which can probably be identified as churches. They appear to be of late date, *c.* 400 or even later at Vindolanda, Northumberland, over the courtyard of the *principia*, and at Housesteads, also Northumberland, towards the north-west corner of the fort. Both have apses.[48] They were not very different in architectural conception from earlier pagan temples in the region such as the Temple of Antenociticus at Benwell (Northumberland) or the Carrawburgh *mithraeum* (see Fig. 2.2).

Romano-British Christianity began in a pluralist society in which, as far as can be seen, pagan cults operated alongside churches (or in the case of Lullingstone where offerings were buried in pots before the two busts, beneath the church). Sophisticated mosaic-floored cult rooms dedicated to Bacchus or Orpheus at the villas at Thruxton, Hampshire, and Littlecote, Wiltshire, served analogous functions to the probable Christian house chapels at Lullingstone and Hinton St Mary. The pagan jewellery dedicated by well-to-do votaries to the Latian god Faunus at his temple near Thetford, Norfolk, mirrored the fine jewellery worn by contemporary Christian aristocrats, amongst them the owners of the Hoxne Treasure.[49]

Structural changes in society during the fifth century, including the virtual collapse of a regular currency and consequent economic dislocation, meant that the sort of luxury item proclaimed by its ornamentation or inscription became rare. In western Britain continuities are easy enough to assume, even without the recent dramatic evidence from Bradford on Avon. The Roman town of Caerwent became the *Llan*, the ecclesiastical centre, of St Tatheus, though no early church has yet been

---

[47] A. Doig, *Liturgy and Architecture from the Early Church to the Middle Ages* (Aldershot, 2008), p. 50.

[48] R. Birley, *Vindolanda: A Roman Frontier Fort on Hadrian's Wall* (Stroud 2009), pp. 151–2; R. Rushworth, *Housesteads Roman Fort: The Grandest Station. Excavation and Survey at Housesteads, 1954–95, by Charles Daniels, John Gillam, James Crow and others*, 2 vols (Swindon, 2009), vol. 1 pp. 321–5.

[49] C. Johns, *The Jewellery of Roman Britain: Celtic and Classical Traditions* (London, 1996), pp. 215–18 and passim.

2. THE ORIGINS OF CHRISTIAN BRITAIN

excavated here, while at Llandough and Llantwit Major similar monasteries evidently developed from villas. The inscribed stones of Wales, south-west Scotland and the far south-west of England proclaim an active Christian culture from the fifth century onwards. Moreover the career of the British Christian Patricius (St Patrick) attests the continued evangelisation of Ireland where Christianity took deep root. Gildas who probably wrote somewhere in south-west Britain in the mid-sixth century, and achieved a European reputation for his sagacity, was almost too successful in following the prophecies of Jeremiah in revealing a Britain fallen to the barbarian foe as a price of the sins of its princes, in a missionary work of theology which has too often, and for far too long, been conflated with history.

Eastern Britain has thus been assumed (and still is by many) to have been overrun by invading Angles and Saxons. Even if this were so, there is evidence for the survival of towns as central places, and from some of them there are indications of Christian continuity.[50] Moreover a case is now being made for the native languages of the eastern tribes of Britain, including Cantii, Iceni and Corieltauvi, to have been related to the 'Belgic' or Germanic dialects spoken by the Batavii, the Menapii and other tribes, just across the North Sea, though the exact configuration of the ethnic and cultural maps of England in late antiquity and the early middle ages will never be fully elucidated even with the—often contradictory—DNA evidence, and must have been very complex indeed. Cultural and ethnic continuity offers an explanation of how and why the churches of St Martin at London and Canterbury, both evidently Roman cemetery churches, remained as Christian centres, each with a seventh-century conversion period cemetery. Moreover, in the neighbourhood of Dorchester in Oxfordshire, the Queensford Farm cemetery which seems to overlap in date with the contiguous cemetery at Wally Corner, Berinsfield,[51] provides a further indication of a town continuing to be populated until after the Augustinian mission with the advent of St Birinus (as the late Birthe Kjølbye-Biddle pointed out to me, scion of the great Roman family of the Virinii) it eventually became the seat of a bishop. No early church building has yet been located around the site of the later abbey, immediately outside the east gate of the town, though this is a prime position for a *martyrium* or cemetery church.

There was, however, the famous *martyrium* site at St Albans, according to Constantius of Lyon's biography of the saint, evidently visited by St Germanus in 429 during his campaign to collect relics and confront the Pelagians, and still well known to Gildas in the sixth century.[52] Excavation by the Biddles not only located a late

---

[50] M. Henig, 'The Fate of Late Roman Towns', *The Oxford Handbook of Anglo-Saxon Archaeology*, ed. H. Hamerow, D. A. Hinton and S. Crawford (Oxford, 2011), pp. 515–33.

[51] C. M. Hills and T. C. O'Connell, 'New Light on the Anglo-Saxon Succession : Two Cemeteries and Their Dates', *Antiquity*, 83 (2009), pp. 1096–1108.

[52] Constantius, *Vita Germani*, ed. R. Borius, *Vie de Saint Germain d'Auxerre*, Sources chrétiennes

Roman cemetery but a silver-hand pin dated to the fifth or sixth century and a fine decorative escutcheon of the seventh century which perhaps goes some way towards confirming the near presence of a late Roman church, either destroyed by subsequent work in the construction of the Abbey or still awaiting discovery, although it is possible that until Offa built his church, pilgrims would have found facilities exceedingly modest even here.[53] Apart from Alban there seem to have been cults of other more shadowy local saints, perhaps martyrs, in south-eastern Britain such as Augulius in London and a St Sixtus in Kent or perhaps the Middle Thames region.[54] The fact that Augustine and his missionaries were confronted by British bishops concerned, it would seem, by the Levitical purity laws to the extent that he felt obliged to consult Pope Gregory as to the official Roman attitude to them, is eloquent testimony to a thriving Christian presence even in the south east.[55] Even if at this period there is a dearth of Christian artifacts, several fifth- to sixth-century Christian objects, mainly from graves, confirm the continuity of the Church in south-east England. The great series of hanging-bowls is now, since the discovery of the hoard of vessels from Drapers' Gardens, London, confirmed as having begun by the late-fourth or early fifth century; they were most probably employed for hand-washing, and the three escutcheons of Vermand style from a grave at Faversham, Kent, which take the form of crosses supported in each case by two dolphins, are consonant with liturgical use in Church;[56] a bronze-bound vessel from Strood near Rochester, also in Kent, which figures Christ in Majesty between two Apostles, is most likely to have served a liturgical purpose (perhaps foot-washing).[57]

---

112 (Paris, 1965), chapter iii, paras 17–18; Gildas, *De Excidio Britonum*, ed. and trans. M. Winterbottom, *Gildas: The Ruin of Britain and Other Documents*, Arthurian Period Sources 7 (Chichester, 1978), cc. 10–11.

53 Biddle and Kjølbye-Biddle, 'The Origins of St Albans Abbey'.

54 R. Sharpe, 'Martyrs and Local Saints in Late Antique Britain', *Local Saints and Local Churches in the Early Medieval West*, ed. A. T. Thacker and R. Sharpe (Oxford, 2002), pp. 75–154 at pp. 122–4.

55 Bede, *Historia ecclesiastica gentis Anglorum*, ed. and trans. B. Colgrave and R. A. B. Mynors (Oxford, 1969), bk 1 c. 27; cf. R. Meens, 'Ritual Purity and Gregory the Great', *Unity and Diversity in the Church*, ed. R. N. Swanson, Studies in Church History 32 (Oxford, 1996), pp. 31–43 at p. 35.

56 J. Gerrard, 'The Drapers' Gardens Hoard: A Preliminary Account', *Britannia*, 40 (2009), pp. 163–83 at pp. 168–71, no. 1; A. Harris and M. Henig, 'Hand-washing and Foot-Washing, Sacred and Secular in Late Antiquity and the Early Medieval Period', *Intersections*, pp. 25–38; R. Bruce-Mitford, *A Corpus of Late Celtic Hanging-Bowls* (Oxford, 2005), pp. 163–5 no. 37. Cf. M. Henig, *The Heirs of King Verica: Culture and Politics in Roman Britain* (Stroud, 2002), p. 142, Fig. 63 (Faversham).

57 G. Chenet, 'La Tombe 319 du cimetière mérovingien de Lavoye (Meuse)', *Préhistoire*, 4 (1935), pp. 34–118 at pp. 87–91; V. I. Evison, *The Fifth-Century Invasions South of the Thames* (London, 1965), pp. 23 and 34, Fig. 14.1.

2. THE ORIGINS OF CHRISTIAN BRITAIN

Even more interesting is the beaker from a grave at Long Wittenham, near Dorchester, Oxfordshire, which figures three New Testament scenes, the marriage at Cana, Zacchaeus in a tree, and Christ healing the blind man; it is quite close in style to similar work from Belgium, and, although very probably a local product, attests both a continuing church and continuing relations between Britain and the near continent.[58] The owner could well have worshipped with other Christians in nearby Dorchester. The beaker is also a potent reminder that British Christians were 'people of the Book' who did not have to wait for the arrival of St Augustine's Gospels to learn to celebrate their faith in visual form.

Further to the north east there was possible Christian continuity of St Paul in the Bail, Lincoln, where a church of simple form in the area of the forum at once suggests a Christian presence at the site and, because that presence was associated with graves, the breakdown of Roman civic standards.[59] York too, ancient *Eboracum*, is a place where one might have expected continuity from the Roman past into the early middle ages. As the headquarters building of the fortress may have continued to stand it could have served as a church or even a cathedral, but proof is lacking. The Roman layers are, as in London, very deep and often under later buildings of historic importance, so this aspect of York's early history may be hard to elucidate. Again this evidence can be supplemented by items of material culture, including the spectacular (originally) late fourth- or early fifth-century gilt-silver jug with Biblical scenes including Adam and Eve and the Adoration of the Magi from a mid fifth-century *hacksilber* cache found on Traprain Law, East Lothian, and probably originating in Northern Britain.[60]

In conclusion we can view Christianity in Roman Britain as beginning as one amongst many cults. Pagan buildings were generally grander, and churches would not have been especially notable amongst them. Rooms in villas, which might carry frescoed or mosaic embellishment, would not have been at all prominent architecturally. Churches were certainly present in Britain through the fifth and sixth centuries and probably throughout the island, and, although pagan cults surely also survived, the evidence of the literary sources we have over this period tends to suggest that Christianity was gaining the ascendancy over them. Despite this, churches have been hard to recognise, and such large Roman-style churches as did exist probably did not remain in use; it is possible that a few Roman secular buildings known to have

---

[58] Chenet, 'Tombe 319', pp. 87–91; Evison, *Fifth-Century Invasions*, p. 23 and Fig.13c; M. Henig and P. Booth, *Roman Oxfordshire* (Stroud, 2000), pp. 85–6, Fig. 7.4.

[59] B. Gilmour, 'Sub-Roman or Saxon: Pagan or Christian. Who was Buried in the Early Cemetery at St-Paul-in-the-Bail, Lincoln?', *Pagans and Christians: From Antiquity to the Middle Ages. Papers in Honour of Martin Henig, Presented on the Occasion of his 65th birthday*, ed. L. A. Gilmour, British Archaeological Reports International Series 1610 (Oxford, 2007), pp. 229–56.

[60] K. Painter, 'A Roman Silver treasure with Biblical Scenes from the Treasure Found at Traprain Law', *Intersections*, pp. 1–24.

stood into the middle age, and pagan temples, were converted to Christian use, even before the Augustinian mission as I have suggested elsewhere.[61] But for the most part Christian buildings were modest and have left little or no physical evidence. This is just as true in western Britain and in Wales, with its plentiful epigraphic evidence, as it is in the east.

The Roman mission associated with Pope Gregory the Great and his emissary St Augustine in the last years of the sixth century, is famously well reported by Bede. Evidently it brought Christianity to a Britain where there was clearly a local 'British' church, even in Kent, and where theological issues of some complexity between Britons and Romans required resolution. Certainly, then, as previously, there were pagans but perhaps Anglo-Saxon heathendom needs to be viewed much more in association with the continuing rustic cults indigenous to the region rather than as novel Anglo-Saxon imports. The purpose of the Roman mission was frankly propagandist, designed to strengthen the allegiances of Christian communities that, from the viewpoint of Pope Gregory, were very much following a local path rather than central direction. Its programme may have included suppressing some local cults as well as strengthening doctrinal orthodoxy. Most important for us today, it saw a programme of building or rebuilding churches, albeit small, in a thoroughly 'Roman' manner in eastern England and beyond. Buildings such as the Carrawburgh *mithraeum* (see Fig. 2.2), and the Temple of Antenociticus at Benwell whose foundations at least in rebuilt form still confront visitors to Hadrian's Wall, remind us that native architecture may have played a part in the new movement, alongside more metropolitan prototypes, though we should not forget what may have been similar but less well-preserved churches at Vindolanda, Housesteads and no doubt elsewhere, mentioned above.[62] Early Anglo-Saxon churches and monasteries such as those at Bradwell-on-Sea, Essex, St Augustine's, Canterbury and Reculver in Kent, Old Minster, Winchester, Hampshire, and in the north, Monkwearmouth (Durham), Jarrow (also Durham) and Hexham (Northumberland) undoubtedly mark a new stage, both organisationally and architecturally in what should surely be seen as the continuing history of the church in Britain. However just as we would be wrong to ignore the influence of what has been misnamed 'Celtic Christianity' in the west, so too the direct legacy of Roman Britain should no longer be ignored.

61 M. Henig, '"And Did Those Feet in Ancient Times": Christian Churches and Pagan Shrines in South-East Britain', *Ritual Landscapes of Roman South-East Britain*, ed. D. Rudling (Great Dunham and Oxford, 2008), pp. 191–206.
62 M. Henig, '"*Murum civitatis, et fontem in ea a Romanis mire olim constructum*". The Arts of Rome in Carlisle and the Civitas of the Carvetii and their Influence', *Carlisle and Cumbria: Roman and Medieval Architecture, Art and Archaeology*, ed. M. McCarthy and D. Weston, British Archaeological Association Conference Transactions 27 (Leeds 2004), pp. 11–28 at 25, with Figs 6 and 7.

(3)
Christianising the Landscape: The Archaeology of the Early Medieval Church in Wales

NANCY EDWARDS

The last half century has seen a great expansion in our knowledge and considerable progress in our understanding of the archaeology of the early medieval church in Britain and Ireland. Initially this was largely driven by the documentary record. For example, the monasteries at Monkwearmouth and Jarrow (both County Durham)[1] and, to a lesser extent, Whithorn (Wigtownshire)[2] figure in the works of Bede and other writers, while Iona (Argyll) is the setting for Adomnán's Life of Columba,[3] and Armagh for some of the hagiographical tales associated with St Patrick.[4] Furthermore in England it is still possible to recognise a variety of sites from surviving Anglo-Saxon fabric in church buildings, mostly still in use, as well as stone sculpture.[5] A similar picture emerges in Ireland, though comparatively few sites now remain in use.[6] In Scotland, though the survival of early medieval church buildings is rare and written sources are almost non-existent, the presence of early medieval stone sculpture has led to the recognition of a great many sites, including the recently excavated monastery at Portmahomack.[7]

In contrast, until recently the archaeology of the early medieval church in Wales has received less overt attention.[8] Written sources which illuminate the development of the early church are sparse before the late eleventh century and, apart from Gildas,[9]

---

[1] R. Cramp, *Wearmouth and Jarrow Monastic Sites*, 2 vols (Swindon, 2005–6), vol. 1, pp. 31–4.
[2] P. Hill, *Whithorn and St Ninian: The Excavation of a Monastic Town, 1984–91* (Stroud, 1997), pp. 17–19.
[3] Adomnán of Iona, *Life of St Columba*, trans. R. Sharpe (Harmondsworth, 1995).
[4] *The Patrician Texts of the Book of Armagh*, ed. and trans. L. Bieler, Scriptores Latini Hiberniae 10 (Dublin, 1979).
[5] See J. Blair, *The Church in Anglo-Saxon Society* (Oxford, 2005), especially pp. 182–245.
[6] N. Edwards, *The Archaeology of Early Medieval Ireland* (London, 1990), pp. 99–131; T. Ó Carragáin, *Churches in Medieval Ireland: Architecture, Ritual and Memory* (New Haven and London, 2010).
[7] M. Carver, *Portmahomack: Monastery of the Picts* (Edinburgh, 2008).
[8] For recent publications see *The Archaeology of the Early Medieval Celtic Churches*, ed. N. Edwards, Society for Medieval Archaeology Monograph 29, Society for Church Archaeology Monograph 1 (Leeds, 2009), which includes several papers on Wales; also D. Petts, *The Early Medieval Church in Wales* (Stroud, 2009).
[9] Gildas, *De Excidio Britonum*, ed. and trans. M. Winterbottom, *Gildas: The Ruin of Britain and Other Documents*, Arthurian Period Sources 7 (London and Chichester, 1978).

largely confined to terse entries[10] in the annals—the only earlier hagiography relevant to Wales is the probably seventh-century Breton Life of St Samson of Dol.[11] Despite the existence of a late eleventh-century Life of St David by Rhygyfarch of Llanbadarn Fawr (Cardiganshire),[12] there has been no rush to dig up St Davids (Pembrokeshire), a site where later building campaigns have all but obliterated any early medieval remains.[13] There have also been remarkably few excavations on other church sites, whether abandoned or still in use. Furthermore, apart from Presteigne (Radnorshire), where the architectural remains are Anglo-Saxon,[14] there are no securely identifiable stone churches in Wales surviving before the advent of the Romanesque.[15] Nevertheless, all is not doom and gloom: over the last decade or more there have been some significant advances, most notably the identification of a range and hierarchy of sites and an evolving Christian landscape in the period *c*. 400–1100. Regional differences are also beginning to emerge. This contrasts sharply with the rather small number of sites, taken largely from documentary sources, which Wendy Davies was able to identify in 1982, though she greatly expanded the number for the south-east by using the Llandaf charters, which were compiled in their final form in the early twelfth century, but incorporate earlier material.[16]

This paper will explore how this transformation has taken place. It will discuss the different types of site which have been identified in Wales and their relationships to each other—burial and cemeteries, mother churches and the development of Christian landscapes—using examples, taken as far as possible, from different parts of the country; it will also consider the origins and functions of these sites and how they evolved over time.

The Identification and Investigation of Sites
In the introduction to *The Early Church in Wales and the West* published in 1992 Alan Lane and I advocated the critical use of a multi-disciplinary approach to facilitate

---

[10] *Annales Cambriae A.D. 682–954: Texts A–C in Parallel*, ed. and trans. D. N. Dumville, Basic Texts in Brittonic History 1 (Cambridge, 2002).

[11] *The Life of St. Samson of Dol*, trans. T. Taylor (London, 1925, reprinted Felinfach, 1991); T. M. Charles-Edwards, *Wales and the Britons 350–1064* (Oxford, 2013), pp. 66, 637–40.

[12] R. Sharpe, 'Which Text is Rhygyfarch's *Life* of St David?', in *St David of Wales: Cult, Church and Nation*, ed. J. W. Evans and J. M. Wooding, Studies in Celtic History 24 (Woodbridge, 2007), pp. 90–106; 'Rhygyfarch's *Life* of St David', ed. and trans. R. Sharpe and J. R. Davies, ibid., pp. 107–55.

[13] J. W. Evans, *St David's Cathedral* (Andover, 2002); J. W. Evans and R. Turner, *St David's Bishop's Palace*, 3rd edn (Cardiff, 2005).

[14] H. M. Taylor and J. Taylor, *Anglo-Saxon Architecture*, 3 vols (Cambridge, 1965–78), vol. 2, pp. 497–99.

[15] For a recent review of the evidence, see A. Pritchard, 'The Origins of Ecclesiastical Stone Architecture in Wales', in *Archaeology of Celtic Churches*, pp. 245–64.

[16] W. Davies, *Wales in the Early Middle Ages* (Leicester, 1982), Figs 49–50.

3. CHRISTIANISING THE LANDSCAPE

the identification of early medieval sites. This would combine a range of archaeological evidence, such as the presence of early medieval burials, later grave-chapels (*capeli-y-bedd*) thought to be associated with the relics of the founding saint, curvilinear enclosures, stone sculpture and other early medieval Christian artefacts, with that of the documentary sources, contemporary, later medieval and antiquarian, as well as place-names and dedications.[17] In large measure this approach has now borne fruit since it was influential on the criteria adopted by the Cadw-funded *Early Medieval Ecclesiastical Sites* project which was carried out regionally by the four Welsh archaeological trusts and completed in 2004.[18] It set out 'to identify and rank the evidence for potential early medieval ecclesiastical and related sites throughout Wales' with the aim of setting up a strategy for the future protection of the archaeological resource.[19] The results were illuminating and, interestingly, also varied considerably from region to region; those for the south-west proved particularly rich.[20]

The second major breakthrough has been as a result of the methodology adopted to analyse the early medieval inscribed stones and stone sculpture for the new *Corpus of Early Medieval Inscribed Stones and Stone Sculpture in Wales*.[21] It used to be thought that, since many of the monuments had been moved to churches and other sites for safe-keeping, it was virtually impossible to recover their original archaeological contexts.[22] However, with the construction of individual monument 'biographies', drawing on a range of antiquarian and other sources, this view has been proved incorrect.[23] Instead, the number and type(s) of monuments associated with an

---

[17] N. Edwards and A. Lane 'The Archaeology of the Early Church in Wales: An Introduction', in *The Early Church in Wales and the West*, ed. N. Edwards and A. Lane, Oxbow Monograph 13 (Oxford, 1992), pp. 1–11 at pp. 3–8; see also N. Edwards, 'Identifying the Archaeology of the Early Church in Wales and Cornwall', in *Church Archaeology Research Directions for the Future*, ed. J. Blair and C. Pyrah, Council for British Archaeology Research Report 104 (York, 1996), pp. 49–62.

[18] Findings are published in *Archaeology of Celtic Churches*, chapters 2–6.

[19] N. Edwards, 'The Archaeology of the Early Medieval Celtic Churches: an Introduction', in *Archaeology of Celtic Churches*, pp. 1–18, at pp. 6–7.

[20] N. Ludlow, 'Identifying Early Medieval Ecclesiastical Sites in South-West Wales', in *Archaeology of Celtic Churches*, pp. 61–84.

[21] M. Redknap and J. M. Lewis, *A Corpus of Early Medieval Inscribed Stones and Stone Sculpture in Wales, Vol. I, Breconshire, Glamorgan, Monmouthshire, Radnorshire, and geographically contiguous areas of Herefordshire and Shropshire* (Cardiff, 2007); N. Edwards, *A Corpus of Early Medieval Inscribed Stones and Stone Sculpture in Wales, Vol. II, South-West Wales, Vol. III, North Wales* (Cardiff, 2007–13); hereafter *Corpus*.

[22] J. M. Lewis, 'A Survey of the Early Christian Monuments of Dyfed, West of the Taf,' in *Welsh Antiquity: Essays Mainly on Prehistoric Topics Presented to H. M. Savory upon his Retirement as Keeper of Archaeology*, ed. G. C. Boon and J. M. Lewis (Cardiff, 1976), pp. 177–92 at p. 184.

[23] N. Edwards, 'Early Medieval Inscribed Stones and Stone Sculpture in Wales: Context and Function', *Medieval Archaeology*, 45 (2001), pp. 15–39.

individual site can give an indication of its origins, evolution, functions, regional and cultural affiliations, as well as the role of patronage. The value of the sculptural evidence can also be enhanced when other forms of evidence are brought into play. Finally, archaeological excavations, though mainly in the form of rescue digs and other recording prior to destruction or church restoration, rather than larger research projects, have also played an increasing role. Though these have often been comparatively modest compared with work on similar sites elsewhere in Britain and Ireland, the results have been of considerable value. On the one hand, there have now been a small number of informative excavations on individual church sites, notably Capel Maelog (Radnorshire), Pennant Melangell (Montgomeryshire) and Llanelen (Glamorgan),[24] which have cast light on their origins, development and functions up to the present. On the other, a significant number of early medieval cemetery excavations have taken place, many on sites which were subsequently abandoned and never acquired a church.

Burial and Cemeteries
In *The Early Christian Archaeology of North Britain* published in 1971 Charles Thomas argued that what he termed 'undeveloped [inhumation] cemeteries' spanned the period of conversion to Christianity. Some of these sites were later abandoned; others subsequently acquired church buildings and a significant number eventually developed into parish churches.[25] In Wales these models of 'undeveloped' and 'developed' cemeteries continue to be of value though, as a result of recent excavations, especially where a sequence of radiocarbon dating is available, we are now able to reconstruct a more detailed and nuanced picture, which includes a growing recognition of links with both the prehistoric and Roman past.[26] The majority of recent excavations have been concentrated in north-west and south-west Wales, especially Anglesey and Pembrokeshire, where identification has been aided by the frequent though not exclusive use of stone-lined graves, but excavations elsewhere have also been instructive allowing for regional comparisons and contrasts to be made.

On Anglesey, there is a particularly interesting group of 'undeveloped' cemeteries which are focussed on prehistoric monuments. These include Arfryn, Capel Eithin and Tŷ Mawr, though the first has yet to be fully published.[27] The site of Capel Eithin had a complex history of use and re-use beginning in the Neolithic

---

[24] W. J. Britnell, 'Capel Maelog, Llandrindod Wells, Powys: Excavations 1984–87', *Medieval Archaeology*, 34 (1990), pp. 27–96; W. J. Britnell, 'Excavation and Recording at Pennant Melangell Church', *Montgomeryshire Collections*, 82 (1994), pp. 41–102; A. Schlesinger and C. Walls, 'An Early Church and Medieval Farmstead Site: Excavation at Lanelen, Gower', *Archaeological Journal*, 153 (1996), pp. 104–47.
[25] C. Thomas, *The Early Christian Archaeology of North Britain* (Oxford, 1971), pp. 48–90.
[26] D. Longley, 'Early Medieval Burial in Wales', in *Archaeology of Celtic Churches*, pp. 105–32.
[27] Longley, 'Early Medieval Burial', pp. 106, 110–11, 118–19, 122, 125; *Corpus III*, no. AN1,

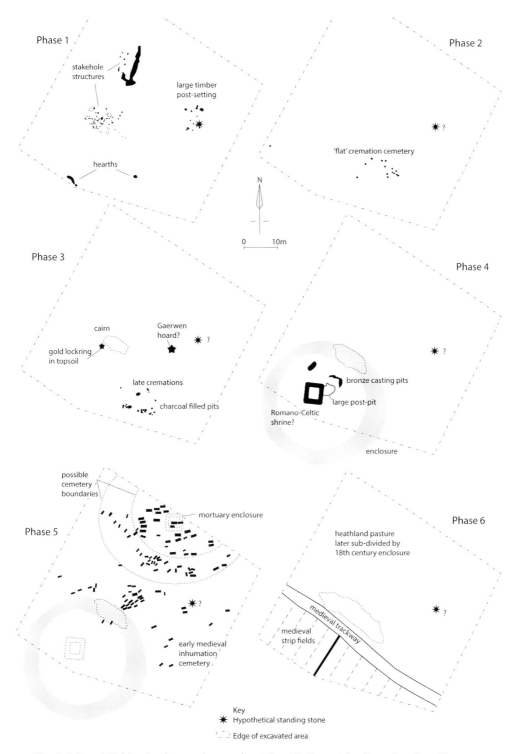

Fig. 3.1 Capel Eithin, Anglesey: phases of activity. (© Copyright. Drawing, Jane Kenney, after White and Smith, 'Funerary and Ceremonial Centre' (as n. 27), Fig. 51. By permission of Gwynedd Archaeological Trust.)

(Fig. 3.1). In the early Bronze Age a small cremation cemetery was established. Later a cairn was constructed to the north west of the cremation cemetery which remained a prominent feature in the landscape up to the time of excavation. The fourth phase of activity spans the late first and early second centuries AD and consisted of a small square stone structure set within a circular enclosure. This building, later dismantled, was originally interpreted as either a Roman military signal station or watch-tower, but a Romano-Celtic shrine, which would have continued the emphasis on ritual functions, now seems more likely.[28] In the early medieval period the site once again became the location of funerary activity with the establishment of an inhumation cemetery partly focussed on the upstanding cairn. Over one hundred findless inhumations were identified, the graves of adults, juveniles and infants. Most were dug graves, but the rest were wholly or partially stone-lined, and almost all were broadly oriented east/west. Near the north-eastern edge of the excavated area was a square-ditched mortuary enclosure with a wooden structure enclosing a partially encisted grave with a plank on the bottom and an infant burial nearby; a third long-cist grave had subsequently been set in the entrance. A group of other burials were focussed on this structure.[29] A sixth-century inscribed memorial stone with the personal name *Devorix*, literally 'divine king', which would have acted as a high status grave-marker, possibly indicating the founder's grave, was recorded *c*.1699, but is now lost. Patrick Sims-Williams has noted that the name should not be regarded as either a title or an indication of paganism, though the form does have pre-Christian origins.[30]

What is certain is that there is nothing specifically Christian about this cemetery or the inscribed stone. Instead, based partly on analogies with Ireland,[31] it may be interpreted as one of an increasing number of community or kin-group cemeteries which have been identified on Anglesey, as well as elsewhere in Wales, which is focussed on an earlier monument, often a Bronze Age barrow or cairn. It may well have contained both pagan and Christian graves and is dated to before the more general establishment of churchyard burial, probably from around the eighth century onwards.[32] To what extent such early cemeteries also acted as the foci for conversion

---

pp. 143–5; R. Cuttler, A. Davidson and G. Hughes, *A Corridor Through Time: The Archaeology of the A55 Road Scheme* (Oxford and Oakville, 2012), pp. 104–21, 258–68; S. I. White and G. Smith, 'A Funerary and Ceremonial Centre at Capel Eithin, Gaerwen, Anglesey', *Transactions of the Anglesey Antiquarian Society and Field Club* (1999), pp. 9–166.

28 White and Smith, 'Capel Eithin', pp. 29–127, 150–3; Longley, 'Early Medieval Burial', p. 120, Fig. 6.5.
29 White and Smith, 'Capel Eithin', pp. 128–45, 155–8.
30 *Corpus III*, no. AN20, pp. 173, 175.
31 E. O'Brien, 'Pagan or Christian? Burial in Ireland during the 5th to 8th Centuries AD', in *Archaeology of Celtic Churches*, pp. 135–54.
32 White and Smith, 'Capel Eithin', p. 158; D. Petts, 'Cemeteries and Boundaries in Western Britain', in *Burial in Early Medieval England and Wales*, ed. S. Lucy and A. Reynolds, Society for Medieval Archaeology Monograph 17 (London, 2002), pp. 24–46 at pp. 42–5.

Fig. 3.2 Tywyn y Capel, Anglesey: mounds over the Phase 1 graves.
(© Copyright. By permission of Gwynedd Archaeological Trust.)

and pastoral care is much more difficult to say but the re-use of sites with prehistoric monuments is indicative of the manipulation of the past to new ends which is at least partially connected with signifying the ownership of land.

Recent excavations at another important site, Tywyn-y-Capel, in coastal sand-dunes in north-west Anglesey, do not show any links with the prehistoric past, but instead indicate the gradual development of a mixed cemetery of men, women and children between the sixth and twelfth centuries.[33] The earliest graves, with radiocarbon dates spanning the mid-sixth to mid-seventh centuries, were in stone-lined cists marked above ground by rare surviving evidence of circular mounds outlined by stones (Fig. 3.2). A second phase with radiocarbon dates spanning c. 650–1220 consisted of over one hundred dug graves and the positions of the skeletons in some of these suggested that they may have been wrapped in shrouds, a clear indication of Christian burial.[34] Unusually for Wales the bone evidence survived and indicated that the earlier group may have been more healthy and lived longer than those in the later phase.[35] The earliest evidence for a building on the site was a stone

[33] A. Davidson, 'Excavations at Tywyn y Capel, Treaddur Bay, Anglesey, 1997 and 2002–3', *Archaeologia Cambrensis*, 128 (2009), pp. 167–223.
[34] O'Brien, 'Pagan or Christian', p. 146.
[35] R. Adlam and M. Wysocki, 'The Human Skeletal Remains', in Davidson, 'Tywyn y Capel', pp. 210–19, at p. 219.

chapel (no longer extant) which probably dated to the twelfth century. It was dedicated to St Ffraid (Brigit) and is indicative of a Hiberno-Scandinavian connection.[36]

Nevertheless, a substantial group of fifth- and sixth-century inscribed memorial stones from north-west Wales with a range of Christian formulae, notably *hic iacit* ('here lies') and expansions of it, and the occasional use of chi-rho and cross symbols, suggest the presence of a Christian elite and an organised church which had links with the Roman past. In several instances the practice of Roman roadside burial persisted and many of those commemorated continued to have Roman names. For example, the Latin inscription on Trawsfynydd 2 (Merioneth), commemorates *Porivs / hic in tvmvlo iacit / homo [x]p(ist)ianvs fvit* ('Porius lies here in the tomb, he was a Christian man') using the Greek letters chi and rho at the beginning of *[x]p(ist)ianvs*.[37] The stone was originally located on open moorland above the line of the Roman road running south from the fort at Tomen-y-Mur.[38] The inscription on Penmachno 4 (Caernarfonshire), found in association with two graves on the line of the Roman road running north from Tomen-y-Mur, has a chi-rho cross (Fig. 3.3) and the wording, *Caravsivs / hic iacit / in hoc con/geries la/pidvm* ('Carausious, here he lies, in this heap of stones') indicates that the grave it marked was covered by a cairn,[39] perhaps similar to those in the earlier phase at Tywyn-y-Capel.

There were also inscribed stones set up to mark burials beside Roman roads in the uplands of south Wales.[40] However, the most important cemetery excavated in this region to date is Llandough in the Vale of Glamorgan. This presents a very different picture from those in the north and is indicative of connections with the more heavily Romanised parts of south-west England and possibly of continuity from the Roman period since there is a Roman villa nearby. The site is presumed to have been a monastery, most likely founded in the late fifth or early sixth century by St Dochdwy, to whom the parish church is dedicated. There are several references to Llandough in the later charters associated with Llandaf and Llancarfan (both in Glamorgan) suggesting its importance from the seventh century onwards, though it was finally eclipsed by the establishment of a bishopric at Llandaf in the early eleventh century.[41] Until recently, the only known archaeological evidence from the site was a

---

36 Davidson, 'Tywyn y Capel', pp. 209–10; N. Edwards, 'Viking-influenced Sculpture in North Wales: Its Ornament and Context', *Church Archaeology*, 3 (1999), pp. 5–16 at p. 14.
37 *Corpus III*, no. MR23.
38 Edwards, 'Early Medieval Inscribed Stones', p. 25.
39 *Corpus III*, no. CN38.
40 A. Fox, 'The Siting of Some Inscribed Stones of the Dark Ages in Glamorgan and Breconshire', *Archaeologia Cambrensis*, 94 (1939), pp. 30–41; C. Fox, 'The Re-erection of Maen Madoc, Ystradfellte, Breconshire', *Archaeologia Cambrensis*, 95 (1940), pp. 210–16; *Corpus I*, *e.g.*, nos B50, G7, G27, pp. 270–2, 251–3, 302–5, 562–4.
41 J. K. Knight, 'From Villa to Monastery: Llandough in Context', *Medieval Archaeology*, 49 (2005), pp. 93–107 at pp. 101–3.

Fig. 3.3 Penmachno, Caernarfonshire: Latin-inscribed memorial stone with a chi-rho cross. (© Crown copyright: Royal Commission on the Ancient and Historical Monuments of Wales / Hawlfraint y Goron: Comisiwn Brenhinol Henebion Cymru.)

cross-shaft of late tenth- or early eleventh-century date.[42]

Whether the monastery was founded *de novo* or had its origins in a Christian chapel and/or cemetery on the villa estate is now impossible to say. However, in 1994 over 1,000 almost exclusively east/west inhumations were excavated north of the church and the surviving skeletal evidence suggested a mixed population of men, women and children. Radiocarbon dating of individual burials proved imprecise and it was impossible to tell whether any were of Roman date; though some had Roman finds in the grave-fills, these could have been residual. Late fifth- and early sixth-century imported amphorae sherds from the eastern Mediterranean and scraps of late sixth- or seventh-century imported glass suggest links with the nearby high status hillfort at Dinas Powys (Glamorgan). The latest burials are likely to be eleventh-century and contemporary with the historical eclipse of the foundation. It has been argued that the burials represent members of the ecclesiastical community and their families as well as the elite of the surrounding area who were their patrons.[43]

Monasteries, Mother Churches and *Clasau*

Like Llandough, most of the churches which were of sufficient status to be mentioned in the early medieval documentary sources, were the most important Christian foundations in their localities and have been variously termed monasteries, mother churches (*mam eglwysi*) or *clasau*, though the last is only relevant to the end of the period. From the sixth century onwards it has been shown that the most important foundations were given the Latin term *monasterium* and were staffed by a community of priests headed by an abbot or occasionally a bishop.[44] In the seventh and eighth centuries these are presumed to have functioned in a similar way to Anglo-Saxon minsters and to have provided pastoral care for lay communities in the surrounding area, perhaps aided by the establishment of daughter houses. There is likewise evidence that some foundations also included a hermitage, perhaps on a nearby offshore island, which acted as a retreat from the world. However, it is also clear that not all of the establishments which are recorded as mother churches in the twelfth- and thirteenth-century documentary sources necessarily had early origins. At least some are likely either to have been founded or to have risen to prominence from the ninth century onwards, while the fortunes of others, such as Llandeilo Fawr, Carmarthenshire,[45] and later Llandough faltered. Indeed, their prospects were linked

[42] *Corpus I*, no. G42, pp. 329–37, 570–2.
[43] N. Holbrook and A. Thomas, 'An Early-Medieval Monastic Cemetery at Llandough, Glamorgan: Excavations in 1994', *Medieval Archaeology*, 49 (2005), pp. 1–92 at p. 91.
[44] H. Pryce, 'Pastoral Care in Early Medieval Wales', in *Pastoral Care Before the Parish*, ed. J. Blair and R. Sharpe (Leicester, 1992), pp. 41–62 at pp. 44–55.
[45] J. R. Davies, 'The Saints of South Wales and the Welsh Church', in *Local Saints and Local Churches in the Early Medieval West*, ed. A. T. Thacker and R. Sharpe (Oxford, 2002), pp. 361–95 at pp. 368–9.

3. CHRISTIANISING THE LANDSCAPE

to the patronage of local elites, including the rulers of the various kingdoms in early medieval Wales.

Therefore, though the evidence is sometimes sparse, it is clear that these major foundations, their layout, structures and functions, evolved over time. By the twelfth century, it has been shown that such regional mother churches were owned, staffed and administered by a hereditary body of canons or *claswyr* led by an abbot who saw themselves as descendants of the founding saint.[46] The best known example of such a church is Llanbadarn Fawr (Cardiganshire), which, in the eleventh and twelfth centuries, was controlled by three successive generations of the learned family of Sulien (d. 1091), who was also the bishop of St Davids.[47]

How can we identify such sites archaeologically? What did they look like in, say, the seventh or eighth centuries as opposed to the eleventh or twelfth? What can the archaeological evidence, when used in conjunction with other sources, tell us about their evolving functions, the role of patronage and their changing fortunes? It has to be said that we are only at the beginning of trying to answer such questions, but some of these issues will now be addressed using three examples: Bangor (Caernarfonshire), Llantwit Major (Glamorgan), and Llandanwg (Merioneth).

Bangor, the place-name of which refers to the horizontal plaited wattles which bound the top of a fence together, and hence to the ecclesiastical enclosure,[48] is located in a narrow, steep-sided valley near the Menai Strait. It was the most important ecclesiastical foundation in the kingdom of Gwynedd. Documentary testimony is thin, but suggests that the foundation had early origins. The obit of the patron saint, Bishop Deiniol, is noted retrospectively in the *Annales Cambriae* as 584[49] and his cult was of sufficient importance to have spread to Ireland by the early ninth century.[50] Elfoddw, who in 768 finally persuaded the Welsh to adopt the

---

[46] R. J. Silvester and J. W. Evans, 'Identifying the Mother Churches of North-East Wales', in *Archaeology of Celtic Churches*, pp. 21–40 at pp. 22–4.

[47] J. E. Lloyd, 'Bishop Sulien and his Family', *National Library of Wales Journal* 2(1) (1941), pp. 1–6; M. Lapidge, 'The Welsh-Latin Poetry of Sulien's Family', *Studia Celtica* 8–9 (1973–4), pp. 69–106; N. Edwards, '11th-century Welsh Illuminated Manuscripts: The Nature of the Irish Connection', in *From the Isles of the North: Early Medieval Art in Britain and Ireland. Proceedings of the Third International Conference on Insular Art, held in the Ulster Museum, Belfast, 7–11 April 1994*, ed. C. Bourke (Belfast, 1995), pp. 147–55; J. W. Evans, 'The Survival of a *Clas* as an Institution in Medieval Wales: Some Observations on Llanbadarn Fawr', in *Early Church*, pp. 33–40.

[48] R. J. Thomas, *Geiriadur Prifysgol Cymru: A Dictionary of the Welsh Language*, 4 vols (Cardiff, 1950–2002), vol. 1, p. 254; J. E. Lloyd, 'Presidential Address', *Archaeologia Cambrensis*, 92 (1937), pp. 193–207 at pp. 201–2.

[49] *Annales Cambriae*, ed. and trans, J. Morris, *Nennius: British History; and the Welsh Annals*, Arthurian Period Sources 8 (London and Chichester, 1980), pp. 45, 86.

[50] *The Martyrology of Tallaght from the Book of Leinster and MS. 5000–4 in the Royal Library, Brussels*, ed. R. I. Best and H. J. Lawlor, Henry Bradshaw Society 68 (1931), p. 71; P. Ó Riain,

Fig. 3.4 Bangor, Caernarfonshire: aerial photograph looking northwards and showing the curved line of the monastic enclosure preserved in the street-plan stretching eastwards from the cathedral on the left of the picture. (© Copyright. By permission of Gwynedd Archaeological Trust.)

Roman method for computing Easter, is later noted as 'archbishop of Gwynedd', in all probability located in Bangor; another bishop, Morglais, is recorded in 943/4.[51] By the tenth century Anglesey and the adjacent mainland had become a sphere of Viking interest and a raid is recorded on Bangor in 1073.[52] In the late eleventh century it was briefly captured by the Normans, but recovered by the ruler of Gwynedd, Gruffudd ap Cynan, who was buried in the cathedral in 1137.[53] The earliest upstanding church fabric is Romanesque and is thought to date to this period.[54]

'The Tallaght Martyrologies, redated', *Cambrian Medieval Celtic Studies*, 20 (1990), pp. 21–38.

[51] *Annales Cambriae*, pp. 6–9, 16–17; *Brenhinoedd y Saeson*, *'The Kings of the English'*, *A.D. 682–954: Texts P, R, S in Parallel*, ed. and trans. D. N. Dumville, Basic Texts for Mediaeval British History 1 (Aberdeen, 2005), pp. 38–9.

[52] W. Davies, *Patterns of Power in Early Wales* (Oxford, 1990), pp. 51–4; *Brut y Tywysogyon, or, The Chronicle of the Princes: Peniarth MS. 20 Version*, ed. T. Jones, History and Law Series 11 (Cardiff, 1952), p. 16.

[53] H. Pryce, 'Esgobaeth Bangor yn Oes y Tywysogion', in *'Ysbryd Dealltwrus ac Enaid Anfarwol', Ysgrifau ar Hanes Crefydd yng Ngwynedd*, ed. W. P. Griffith (Bangor, 1999), pp. 37–57 at pp. 43–4.

[54] Royal Commission on Ancient and Historical Monuments of Wales (hereafter RCAHMW), *An Inventory of the Ancient Monuments in Caernarvonshire*, 3 vols (London, 1956–64), vol. 2, pp. 1–4; M. Thurlby, *Romanesque Architecture and Sculpture in Wales* (Little Logaston, 2006), pp. 193–5.

3. CHRISTIANISING THE LANDSCAPE

The archaeological evidence is equally fragmentary but, in Welsh terms, it is comparatively rich and varied. Topographically, it is evident that the present cathedral and its former precinct shape the layout of the historic town and the line of the enclosure may still be preserved in that of the modern High Street (Fig. 3.4).[55] However, the date at which this was established and the stages by which it evolved are unclear, though there would certainly have been a wooden church at an early date, most likely located under the present cathedral, and possibly more than one fulfilling different functions.[56] There have been several excavations within the former precinct north-east of the cathedral. The earliest feature, probably a fence line, was radio-carbon dated to between the mid-sixth and eighth centuries.[57] Adjacent excavations at Berllan Bach uncovered an early medieval cemetery of seventy-six dug graves, some cut by a boundary ditch, the radiocarbon dates from which centre on the tenth century.[58] By this time the environs of the site may also have functioned as a focus for commercial activity as suggested by the discovery of two Anglo-Saxon coins of Edgar and a Viking silver hoard.[59] The latter, dated to c. 925, contains part of an ingot, a fragment of Hiberno-Scandinavian armband, Sāmānid dirhams, and pennies of Edward the Elder and from Viking York. However, the evidence is insufficient to point to nascent urban origins at this time. The only indications of craft-working which have so far come to light are six small and rather poorly executed fragments of stone sculpture which survived by being broken up for re-use as masonry making their original forms difficult to determine. A couple are most likely parts of freestanding crosses of tenth- or eleventh-century date, which presumably stood in the churchyard, but the rest, which are all two-sided with borders of frets and interlace, are more intriguing. Indeed, they may be fragments of either architectural sculpture or parts of church fixtures and fittings, such as screens. Dating is difficult because the use of insular ornament persists in north Wales well into the twelfth century, but if they are of a similar date to the cross fragments, they belong to an otherwise unknown pre-Romanesque stone church on the site.[60]

---

[55] See John Speed's map 1610: D. Longley, 'Excavations at Bangor, Gwynedd 1981–1989', *Archaeologia Cambrensis*, 114 (1995), pp. 52–70 at pp. 53–4, Fig. 2.
[56] For a possible reconstruction of the plan, see Edwards, 'Identifying the Archaeology', Fig. 3.5.
[57] Calibrated AD 545–771 (2 sigma) (CAR-1221, 1390±60BP): Longley, 'Excavations at Bangor', pp. 65, 69.
[58] Longley, 'Excavations at Bangor', pp. 58–65; two samples from the ditch were radiocarbon dated to calibrated AD 690–983 and 894–1161 (2 sigma) respectively (CAR-950; 951).
[59] G. C. Boon, *Welsh Hoards, 1979–81* (Cardiff, 1986), pp. 92–7; Anon., 'Saxon Coins found at Bangor, Caernarvonshire', *Archaeologia Cambrensis*, 1 (1846), p. 276.
[60] *Corpus III*, nos CN4–9; N. Edwards, 'The Early Medieval Sculpture of Bangor Fawr yn Arfon', in *The Modern Traveller to Our Past. Festschrift in Honour of Ann Hamlin*, ed. M. Meek (Dublin, 2006), pp. 105–11 at pp. 106–9; Pritchard, 'Origins of Stone Architecture', pp. 255–8.

Llantwit Major (*Llanilltud Fawr*) is located in the fertile Vale of Glamorgan. The documentary record for the foundation, described in the ninth century as a *monasterium*, is considerably better than for Bangor, and it is first referred to in the probably seventh century Life of St Samson of Dol.[61] There is also a twelfth-century Life of St Illtud[62] and the foundation is referred to numerous times in the Llandaf and Llancarfan charters. There has been speculation that the establishment could have originated in the vicinity of a Roman villa, where early medieval burials have been found, three-quarters of a mile (just over 1 km.) north-west of the present church, and the relationship between the two has been compared with Llandough.[63] Whether or not there was any link, the presence of a fine collection of stone sculpture datable to the later eighth century onwards, which provides the only archaeological evidence for the foundation, indicates that by that time it was located on the site of the present church. The sculpture mainly consists of now incomplete stone crosses carved with both interlace and fret patterns and lengthy inscriptions demonstrating, not only the importance of the foundation as a centre of literacy and learning, but also its wealth and significance as a focus for artistic endeavour fostered by the patronage of the rulers of Glywysing, who were buried in the cemetery. The inscription on one cross-shaft records that it was prepared by Abbot Samson for his soul and those of King Iuthahel and Artmail and Tecan. It has been argued that these men are the same as those named in Llandaf charters datable to the later eighth century, thereby dating the monument.[64] A century or so later another cross (Fig. 3.5) was prepared by Houelt for the soul of his father Res; Hywel ap Rhys may be identified as the king of Glywysing who died in 886.[65] A third is dated art-historically to the early tenth century and names St Illtud, Samson the king, who set up the cross, and two other men with Old Testament names, Samuel and Ebisar, most likely clerics.[66] There are other pieces which may be architectural fixtures or fittings, notably a cylindrical pillar nearly 8 ft (over 2 m.) high with a vertical groove running the length of the column which has been dated to the tenth or eleventh century. It might be identified as a door-post or a pillar supporting an internal arch or screen,[67] again suggesting the former presence of a pre-Romanesque stone church.

---

[61] *Life of St. Samson*, cc. 7–19, p. 14, n. 1.
[62] *Vitae Sanctorum Britanniae et Genealogiae*, ed. and trans. A. W. Wade-Evans, History and Law Series 9 (Cardiff, 1944), pp. 193–233.
[63] *Corpus I*, p. 575.
[64] *Corpus I*, no. G65.
[65] *Corpus I*, no. G63.
[66] *Corpus I*, no. G66; J. R. Davies, 'Old Testament Personal Names among the Britons: Their Occurrence and Significance before the Twelfth Century', *Viator*, 43 (2012), pp. 175–92 at pp. 177, 183–7.
[67] *Corpus I*, no. G67; Thurlby, *Romanesque Architecture*, pp. 71–2.

Fig. 3.5 Llantwit Major, Glamorgan: Cross of Houellt. (© Crown copyright: Royal Commission on the Ancient and Historical Monuments of Wales / Hawlfraint y Goron: Comisiwn Brenhinol Henebion Cymru.)

Fig. 3.6 Llandanwg Church, Merioneth. (© Copyright N. Edwards.)

Bangor and Llantwit Major are well-attested sites, both historically and archaeologically. However, recent research in north Wales as part of the Early Medieval Ecclesiastical Sites project has demonstrated that by the end of period there was a network of mother churches, many of which were comparatively modest, and it has been argued that these had *parochiae* co-terminous with regional administrative units, either *cantrefi* or later commotes.[68] But at what date were these establishments founded and when did they acquire the status of a mother church?

Llandanwg, Merioneth, provides an interesting example which, it has been argued, was the mother church of the *cantref* of Ardudwy.[69] The present later medieval building (Fig. 3.6) which was formerly contained within a curvilinear churchyard and bears the unique dedication to St Tanwg,[70] is sited in sand-dunes on the coast near the mouth of the Afon Artro close to a sheltered landing-place, and it is this, and the importance of seaborne contacts, which may provide a key to its significance. However, the only contemporary evidence to suggest the early medieval origins of the site is the unusually large cluster of stone monuments spanning the period. Firstly, there are three early inscribed memorial stones indicating that the origins of the site lie in a cemetery established by the beginning of the sixth century. All have Christian formulae, *hic iacit* or *nomine* ('by name'), and commemorate men with Latin names. The third is a recent discovery made while clearing wind-blown sand west of the church. Unusually, it is cut with a knife rather in the manner of graffiti and reads *Geronti hic iacit / fili Spectati* ('Gerontius, here he lies, son of

[68] A. Davidson, 'The Early Medieval Church in North-West Wales', in *Archaeology of Celtic Churches*, pp. 41–60 at pp. 46–50; Silvester and Evans, 'Identifying the Mother Churches', pp. 24–36.
[69] H. Pryce, 'The Medieval Church', in *History of Merioneth, Volume II: The Middle Ages*, ed. J. B. Smith and L. B. Smith (Cardiff, 2001), pp. 254–96 at pp. 266–7.
[70] A. Davidson, 'Parish Churches', *History of Merioneth*, pp. 326–85 at pp. 343–4.

3. CHRISTIANISING THE LANDSCAPE

Spectatus').[71] Secondly, there is a later simple linear cross-carved stone, which probably functioned as an anonymous grave-marker, perhaps datable between the seventh and ninth centuries, suggesting the continuing use of the cemetery.[72] Finally, there is another new discovery, a small and rather crudely shaped free-standing cross with an incised cross in a lozenge, which may date to the ninth century or later.[73] Was this also a grave-marker or did it act as a focus for worship? It is impossible to say when the first church was built on the site and at what point the foundation rose to prominence. However, by the end of the twelfth century it was weakened by the establishment of a new church nearby at Llanfihangel y Traethau (Merioneth)[74] and its *parochia* became fragmented.[75]

Christianising the Landscape

In the case of more minor sites, we have already seen how some 'undeveloped' cemeteries, which had their origins in the conversion period, fell out of use with the foundation of new sites, some of which were centred around churches, from about the eighth century onwards. Others, however, continued in use and at some point acquired church buildings; many of these evolved into parish churches or chapels-of-ease, though some were later abandoned.[76] There has been very little archaeological excavation on sites which have continued in use. A notable exception is Pennant Melangell (Montgomeryshire), the site of a possible hermitage associated with the female saint Melangell. In the limited areas excavated Bronze Age activity was uncovered later superseded by early medieval burials, including the possible special grave of the saint, but the earliest known building is the twelfth-century stone church with its remarkable Romanesque shrine.[77]

Three other sites have been excavated, all churches which were subsequently abandoned, but the evidence is not always easy to interpret. The first is the probable hermitage on Burry Holms, a tidal islet off the Gower peninsula (Glamorgan).[78] Here a rectangular post-hole structure under the twelfth-century stone church has been identified as an earlier wooden church, though the sketchy nature of the evidence[79]

---

[71] *Corpus III*, nos MR10–12.
[72] *Corpus III*, no. MR13.
[73] *Corpus III*, no. MR14.
[74] V. E. Nash-Williams, *The Early Christian Monuments of Wales* (Cardiff, 1950), no. 281 has an inscription recording the new foundation.
[75] Pryce, 'The Medieval Church', pp. 266–7.
[76] Edwards and Lane, *Early Church*, Fig. 1.1.
[77] Britnell, 'Pennant Melangell'.
[78] D. B. Hague, 'Some Welsh Evidence', *Scottish Archaeological Forum*, 5 (1974), pp. 17–35 at pp. 29–32; RCAHMW, *An Inventory of the Ancient Monuments in Glamorgan*, 4 vols in 8 (Cardiff, 1976–2000), vol. 1 part 3, pp. 14–15.
[79] Pritchard, 'Origins of Stone Architecture', p. 251, Fig. 13.1.

has meant that not all accept its existence. The other two most likely functioned as estate churches. At Llanelen, also on Gower, a structure comprising seven post-holes was likewise interpreted as a wooden church, with the adjacent pit possibly functioning as a baptistery, but the evidence is decidedly thin. A small cemetery was excavated nearby, some of the graves overlying earlier structural features. The only dating evidence was a scrap of later sixth- or seventh-century imported glass found in the fill of one of the graves. In the second phase a platform was constructed over the earlier remains and a small stone church was built, presumably of twelfth-century date, with a later chancel. It has been argued that this was abandoned in the early thirteenth century and the building converted to a farm.[80] At Capel Maelog (Radnorshire) a cemetery was excavated and dated to between the ninth and twelfth centuries, but only in the late eleventh or twelfth century was a small stone church built on the site, later altered by the addition of apses at either end. Interestingly, the position of the junction of the nave and chancel was determined by the presence of an earlier special grave.[81]

Even though excavations have been comparatively rare, in recent years there has been considerable progress made in identifying a large number of more minor sites in different parts of Wales and in analysing their development over time and their relationship to the major churches in their localities. Heather James' study of the cult of St David and the ritual landscape of Dewisland published in 1993 was pioneering.[82] She used a multi-disciplinary approach incorporating topographical evidence from Rhygyfarch's late eleventh-century Life of St David with later sources, including antiquarian records, alongside the archaeological evidence, to identify a range of sites: the probable hermitage on Ynys Dewi (Ramsey Island), several chapels, including St Non's, and St Justinian's and St Patrick's which were associated with landing places and the development of pilgrimage routes, as well as several cemeteries and holy wells.

The presence of early medieval sculpture has also proved an important tool. In the case of St Davids, there is a significant collection of early medieval sculpture dating from the ninth century to the early twelfth and includes fragmentary free-standing crosses and cross-slabs as well as grave-markers, some with inscriptions. One cross-carved stone (Fig. 3.7) commemorates the sons of Bishop Abraham who was killed in 1080, the victim of a Viking raid.[83] There are also monuments from Ramsey Island, St Non's Chapel, St Patrick's Chapel and an otherwise unknown site on Pen-Arthur Farm.[84] But it is also possible to identify several other sites in the western half of

---

[80] Schlesinger and Walls, 'Llanelen'.
[81] Britnell, 'Capel Maelog'.
[82] H. James, 'The Cult of St. David in the Middle Ages', in *In Search of Cult: Archaeological Investigations in Honour of Philip Rahtz*, ed. M. Carver (Woodbridge, 1992), pp. 105–12.
[83] *Corpus II*, nos P90–8, the grave-slab is no. P97.
[84] *Corpus II*, nos P99–106.

Fig. 3.7 St Davids, Pembrokeshire: cross-slab commemorating Isaac and Heth, the sons of Bishop Abraham.
(© Crown copyright: Royal Commission on the Ancient and Historical Monuments of Wales / Hawlfraint y Goron: Comisiwn Brenhinol Henebion Cymru.)

Pembrokeshire where the sculpture shows close similarities with that of St Davids and in some instances makes use of a distinctive purplish Caerbwdi sandstone quarried on the coast nearby.[85] This indicates not only that they are products of the same workshop based at St Davids, but also demonstrates the existence of a much wider area of influence for the most important foundation in south-west Wales which, by the ninth century, was also the seat of a bishop.[86] Indeed, comparison with the documentary sources indicates that two of these sites were daughter houses: St Ismaels and Llawhaden are identified in a legal text, possibly datable to the late ninth or tenth century, as two of the seven bishop-houses of Dyfed, each of which was located in a different *cantref*, the former in Rhos, the latter in Daugleddau.[87]

Further east Nevern was the mother church of the *cantref* of Cemais and was the centre of the cult of St Brynach. Two early inscribed stones indicate the origins of the site in the fifth or early sixth centuries and the presence of a large freestanding stone cross and a cross-carved stone testify to its importance in the tenth and eleventh centuries.[88] Nevern is an unusually large parish which stretches southwards from the coast and up into the Preseli Hills. Within this area of Pembrokeshire are four other sites with simple cross-carved stones which presumably functioned as grave-markers and are indicative of local cemeteries. The first is Cilgwyn, one of the chapels-of-ease which belonged to Nevern in the thirteenth century. Two carved stones with linear crosses have been found built into the nineteenth-century church on the site; the second (Colour Plate 3.8) was only discovered in 2009 when the redundant church was converted into a dwelling.[89] However, the other three sites, Pen Parke, Tre-bwlch and Tre-haidd, which all have one or more similar cross-carved stones, have, until recently, functioned as farms.[90]

To the west is the Gwaun Valley where the process of parish formation is very different. The area is made up of several small parishes and most of the churches have cross-carved stones associated with them. At Llanychlwydog, for example, four carved grave-markers came to light during demolition of the medieval church, two incised with linear crosses and two with outline ones.[91] An excavation carried out when the church was converted into a dwelling also uncovered a group of long-cist graves, one of which was radiocarbon dated between the eighth and eleventh centuries.[92]

---

[85] *Corpus II*, nos P7, P126, P129, P132.
[86] *Corpus II*, pp. 84–7.
[87] T. M. Charles-Edwards, 'The Seven Bishop-Houses of Dyfed', *Bulletin of the Board of Celtic Studies*, 24(2) (1971), pp. 247–62.
[88] *Corpus II*, nos P70–3.
[89] *Corpus II*, no. P74; *Corpus III*, no. P140, pp. 478–9.
[90] *Corpus II*, nos P74–9.
[91] *Corpus II*, nos P51–4.
[92] K. Murphy, 'Excavations at Llanychlwydog Church, Dyfed', *Archaeologia Cambrensis*, 136 (1987), pp. 77–93.

3. CHRISTIANISING THE LANDSCAPE

It is interesting that by the end of the period these two adjacent areas have such contrasting patterns of parish formation. The large parish of Nevern surely indicates the extent of the lands, rights and privileges, including sanctuary (*noddfa*), of the *parochia* of St Brynach at that time. Did the minor sites with cross-carved stones, which never developed into parish churches, function as the community cemeteries of the tenants who farmed the lands of St Brynach, an analogy broadly comparable with the monastic *manaig* in Ireland? Was it the descendants of these tenants who later became the portioners of the *clas*? In contrast, the small parishes of the Gwaun Valley, with one exception, have churches dedicated to St David rather than St Brynach, demonstrating the expansion of the cult of Dewi beyond the bounds of Dewisland to the west.[93] Do these sites have similar origins to those in the parish of Nevern, but subsequently developed into parish churches because they changed allegiance? Or, might they have a different pattern of formation, with one or more obscure sites unassociated with churches, such as Cilrhedyn in Llanychaer parish (Pembrokeshire), where an unusual cross-carved pillar with a crucifixion was found,[94] being superseded by the establishment of local cemeteries and perhaps estate churches from the ninth century onwards?

Finally, Penmon in south-east Anglesey, is strategically located at the eastern entrance to the Menai Strait, and was the most important foundation in the *cantref* of Rhosyr. In addition to the site on the mainland, Penmon also had a hermitage on the adjacent island of Ynys Seiriol, which is named after the patron saint. Penmon is first mentioned in the documentary record when it was raided by the Vikings in 971.[95] When it was founded is unclear, but there is now cumulative historical, archaeological and place-name evidence that, from the late ninth century onwards, Hiberno-Scandinavian settlements were established in the south-eastern part of the island and there were attempts, which may well have been temporarily successful, to wrest control of Anglesey, which was strategically situated between Dublin and Chester, from the rulers of Gwynedd.[96] The only early medieval archaeological evidence at Penmon is the Viking Age sculpture, which includes three free-standing stone crosses (one now lost), but in contrast with many monuments in south Wales, they do not have inscriptions. One of these, dated art-historically to the tenth century, is carved with a distinctive Viking Borre ring-chain of the type found on the Isle of Man, and a

---

[93] H. James, 'The Geography of the Cult of St David: A Study of Dedication Patterns in the Medieval Diocese', in *St David of Wales*, pp. 41–83 at pp. 53–5.
[94] *Corpus II*, no. P49.
[95] *Brut y Tywysogyon*, pp. 8, 143.
[96] Davies, *Patterns of Power*, pp. 51–4; N. Edwards, 'Viking-Age Sculpture in North-West Wales: Wealth, Power, Patronage and the Christian Landscape', in *TOME: Studies in Medieval Celtic History and Law in Honour of Thomas Charles-Edwards*, ed. F. Edmonds and P. Russell (Woodbridge, 2011), pp. 73–87 at pp. 82–6.

scene depicting the Temptation of St Anthony, suitable iconography for a monastic site, with parallels in Ireland.[97] However, the secular scenes showing a horseman, a stag and other animals may hint at the aristocratic pastime of the patron, who may himself have been of Hiberno-Scandinavian extraction. There is also a font, probably of a similar date, since it is carved with insular interlace and frets comparable with the crosses and has no Romanesque features; it must have stood in a church constructed on the site before the present Romanesque building.[98]

Like the Gwaun Valley, much of Anglesey is divided into a patchwork of small parishes. A significant number of churches across the southern and eastern part of the island have pieces of early medieval sculpture, mainly cross-carved grave-markers, but also free-standing crosses of various sizes, some undecorated, and two fonts, all broadly datable from the tenth to earlier twelfth centuries. The largest collection is at Llangaffo which is first mentioned *c*.1200 in the life of St Cybi as *Merthyr Caffo*, a place-name denoting the presence of the relics of St Caffo on the site.[99] At Llanfihangel Tre'r Beirdd in eastern Anglesey, for example, there is a recently discovered plain free-standing cross and a fragmentary cross-carved stone with ring-and-dot ornament,[100] while at Cerrig Ceinwen there is a carved stone font[101] indicating the presence of a church building. The sculpture indicates a fairly dense landscape of sites, possibly identifiable as foundations on landed estates, a pattern seen in many other parts of Britain and Ireland in the Viking Age. In contrast, there is very little stone sculpture in the north-western half of the island. Recent research by Jana Horák and Heather Jackson of National Museum Wales has suggested that the stone from which both the Penmon crosses and the other groups of monuments were carved—a coarse-grained, Carboniferous quartz arenite—is derived from local sources in southern and eastern Anglesey, including sandstone strata associated with limestone near Penmon. The same stone was also employed for the making of carved monuments considerably further afield.[102] Both the font decorated with a derivative of Borre-style ring-chain at Pistyll on the north coast of Llŷn and the cross-shaft from the important ecclesiastical foundation on Bardsey Island off the tip of the peninsula (some 60 miles (100 km.) by sea) utilised this stone, and in all likelihood to the east a

---

[97] Edwards, 'Viking-influenced Sculpture'; *Corpus III*, nos AN51–3.
[98] *Corpus III*, no. 54; Pritchard, 'Origins of Stone Architecture', pp. 254–5; R. Gem, 'Gruffudd ap Cynan and the Romanesque Church at Penmon, Anglesey', in *Archaeology of Celtic Churches*, pp. 301–12.
[99] *Corpus III*, nos AN27–37; Wade-Evans, *Vitae Sanctorum Britanniae et Genealogiae*, ch. 17; T. Roberts, 'Welsh Ecclesiastical Place-Names and Archaeology', in *The Early Church*, pp. 41–4 at p. 42.
[100] *Corpus III*, nos AN17–18.
[101] *Corpus III*, no. AN2.
[102] J. Horák and H. Jackson, 'Geological Sources and Selection of Stone', in *Corpus III*, pp. 31–40 at pp. 36–7.

cross and cross-base at Dyserth (Flintshire), arguing for the role of secular patrons with large boats capable of transporting it such a long distance by sea.[103]

Conclusion

Therefore recent research on the early medieval church in Wales using a multi-disciplinary approach has greatly increased our ability to identify a range of different types of site and enabled us to tease out their relationship to each other and to chart their foundation, development and change over the period *c.* 400–1100. However, there is still a very long way to go and it is equally important to recognise what we do *not* know. Though there were undoubtedly wooden churches on the major sites, which from perhaps the tenth century onwards may in some instances have been replaced by stone, we know next to nothing about their appearance. Though the Lichfield Gospels were displayed on the altar of St Teilo at Llandeilo Fawr in the early ninth century,[104] and the shrine of Gwenfrewi[105] was at Gwytherin, Denbighshire, probably from around the same date, it remains impossible to conjure up how the sacred space of the church was used and how this related to the liturgy. Many more minor sites did not necessarily have a church at all before the twelfth century. Where there is some ephemeral evidence of a possible wooden building, as at Llanelen, it was extremely small. In many instances one has to imagine that cemeteries remained the main foci for pastoral care throughout the period and that worship may often have been centred around a carved stone cross or simply the mounds of the graves.

---

[103] *Corpus III*, nos. CN12, CN39, F2–3, p. 112.
[104] D. Jenkins and M. E. Owen, 'The Welsh Marginalia in the Lichfield Gospels: Part I', *Cambrian Medieval Celtic Studies*, 5 (Summer, 1983), pp. 37–66.
[105] L. Butler and J. Graham-Campbell, 'A Lost Reliquary Casket from Gwytherin, North Wales', *Antiquaries Journal*, 70 (1990), pp. 40–8; N. Edwards and T. G. Hulse, 'A Fragment of a Reliquary Casket from Gwytherin, Denbighshire', *Antiquaries Journal*, 72 (1992), pp. 91–101; N. Edwards and T. G. Hulse, 'Gwytherin (Denbs.). A Second Fragment of the Shrine of Gwenfrewi', *Archaeology in Wales*, 37 (1997), pp. 87–8; C. Bourke, 'The Shrine of St Gwenfrewi from Gwytherin, Denbighshire: An Alternative Interpretation', in *Archaeology of Celtic Churches*, pp. 375–88.

(4)
More Scottorum:
Buildings of Worship in Ireland, c.500–950

TOMÁS Ó CARRAGÁIN

In the period covered in this paper the vast majority or churches in Ireland were of timber or other organic materials. No fabric from any of these buildings survives and, with the exception of a few at unrepresentative minor sites, virtually no evidence for them has been recovered through archaeological excavation. A few congregational mortared stone churches were built before the mid tenth century but, as we shall see, they rarely survive either. This, then, is a paper about a group of buildings that have left very few physical traces. And yet we can discuss their form and character with a fair degree of confidence, more confidence perhaps than in the case of many of their non-extant Anglo-Saxon counterparts. In part, this is because of contemporary textual and art historical sources, but the principal reason is the tenacity of tradition in early Irish architecture: as a result of this it can be inferred that the later (tenth to twelfth century) churches of mortared stone which still survive at many sites provide us with a good indication of what their predecessors looked like.

In keeping with the scope of this publication, this paper presents a broad overview of ecclesiastical architecture in Ireland from the fifth century to the mid tenth century. It should be pointed out that the mid tenth century is a somewhat artificial chronological break, for the English monastic reform movement had little impact on Ireland, architectural or otherwise. In Ireland, the most significant reform movement prior to the late eleventh century was the eighth- to ninth-century Céli Dé (Servants of God) movement. There are no indications, either in the archaeological record or in the abundant texts produced at Céli Dé establishments, that the leaders of the movement sought to instigate architectural change, though they did promote some liturgical changes, such as an increase in the frequency of Masses,[1] which may have encouraged the construction of ever more single-altar churches at major sites. Their aim was to revive the ascetic ideals embodied by Ireland's first monastic founders and so they were happy to perpetuate the predominant church form, which was becoming closely associated with these early founding saints. While no contemporary Céli Dé churches survive, this conclusion is supported by the fact that their tenth- and eleventh-century mortared stone replacements at powerhouses of the movement such as Derrynaflan (Tipperary), Terryglass (also Tipperary) and Dysert Aenghusa (Limerick), are in this simple conservative tradition.

---

[1] W. Follett, *Céli Dé in Ireland: Monastic Writing and Identity in the Early Middle Ages*, Studies in Celtic History 23 (Woodbridge, 2006), p. 202.

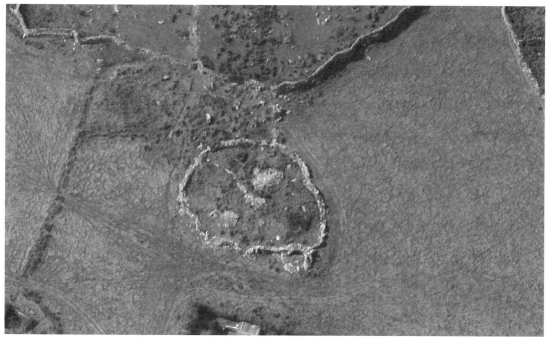

Fig. 4.1 Aerial view of the minor ecclesiastical site of Currauly on the Dingle peninsula, Co. Kerry. The vast majority of Irish ecclesiastical sites are delimited by curvilinear enclosures, usually somewhat larger than this. (© Copyright T. Ó Carragáin.)

In this paper I will consider the small number of excavated churches of organic materials and the advent of stone construction in the eighth and ninth centuries. Of necessity, the treatment here is far from exhaustive and the arguments are set out in greater detail elsewhere.[2] To begin with, let us briefly consider the range of sites at which these churches stood. While some ecclesiastical sites were established in the fifth century, the sixth and seventh centuries saw a great increase in the rate of foundation. Far fewer were founded after 800, and (in contrast to England) very few new ecclesiastical settlements were established between 900 and 1100.[3] This is testimony to the great density of sites that had been established by 900: on average there was a church for about every 10–20 square kilometres (4–8 square miles) according to a preliminary analysis carried out as part of the 'Making Christian Landscapes' Project.[4] These sites varied greatly in character from great episcopal-

[2] T. Ó Carragáin, *Churches in Early Medieval Ireland: Architecture, Ritual and Memory* (New Haven and London, 2010).

[3] T. Ó Carragáin, 'Church Buildings and Pastoral Care in Early Medieval Ireland', *The Parish in Medieval and Early Modern Ireland: Community, Territory and Building*, ed. E. FitzPatrick and R. Gillespie (Dublin, 2006), pp. 91–123 at pp. 92–101; T. Ó Carragáin, 'Cemetery Settlements and Local Churches in Pre-Viking Ireland in Light of Comparisons with England and Wales', *Anglo-Saxon/Irish Relations before the Vikings*, ed. J. Graham-Campbell and M. Ryan, = *Proceedings of the British Academy*, 157 (2009), pp. 239–61 at p. 241.

[4] T. Ó Carragáin, 'Church Sites and Other Settlements in Early Medieval Ireland: Densities, Distributions, Interactions', in *Converting the Isles, vol. 2: Converting Landscapes*, ed. N. Edwards (Turnhout, forthcoming).

monastic *civitates* like Armagh and Clonmacnoise (Offaly) to community churches associated with particular population groups to minor hermitages and proprietary churches established for particular families or kin-groups (Fig. 4.1). While in England church foundation was restricted to kings and the more important nobles, in Ireland the relatively numerous nobles, and probably also some non-noble freemen, were entitled to found a church where they and their kin could be buried. Other families chose to be buried at a range of non-ecclesiastical cemeteries, some of which continued in use until well into the Viking Age.[5] Despite their diversity of function, virtually all Irish ecclesiastical settlements follow the same basic grammar when it comes to layout: most are delimited by one or two curvilinear enclosures. The function of ecclesiastical sites is best expressed in the size and composition of their cemeteries (for example, segregated burial at monastic sites) and, as we shall see, by the size of their churches. Indeed, where both variables are known, there seems to be quite a close positive correlation between them.

Timber Churches

The sparse distribution of early stone churches in most areas, and their virtual absence from large regions (notably Ulster and east Connacht), illustrates the ubiquity of churches built of other materials even in the period *c.* 900–1130 when all but a handful of these stone churches were built. While excavation may yet make a significant contribution to our understanding of early timber churches, two factors are against this. The first is the possibility that many important churches were of sill beam construction which, even in ideal conditions, would leave little archaeological trace. The second is the strong Irish tradition of burial within ruined medieval churches, which means that most of the key sites are not available for excavation, and in any case the evidence is probably badly disturbed if not obliterated. To date, a handful of minor sites with relatively few post-medieval burials, along with one or two subsidiary churches at important sites (Iniscealtra (Clare), Cashel (Tipperary)), have produced substantial evidence for organic churches.

A few of them were of turf construction. Liam de Paor excavated a subsidiary church, about 18 by 13 ft (5.5 by 4 m.) internally, at Iniscealtra.[6] Its 8 ft 3 in. (2.5 m.) thick turf walls were supported by close-set wattles. In contrast, the walls of the seventh-century example on Illaunloughan, Co. Kerry were just over one metre wide and were delimited at the base by upright stones, while posts set at intervals along the wall supported the roof (Fig. 4.2).[7] New radiocarbon dates from Church Island, Co.

[5] *Death and Burial in Early Medieval Ireland in the Light of Recent Excavations*, ed. C. Corlett and M. Potterton, Research Papers in Irish Archaeology 2 (Bray, 2010).

[6] L. de Paor, 'Inis Cealtra: Report on Archaeological and other Investigations of the Monuments on the Island', Report submitted to the National Monuments Service, Department of the Environment Heritage and Local Government (Dublin, 1997), pp. 85–6.

[7] W. Marshall and C Walsh, *Illaunloughan Island: An Early Medieval Monastery in County*

4. MORE SCOTTORUM: BUILDINGS OF WORSHIP IN IRELAND, c.400–950

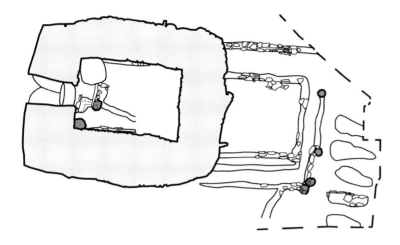

Fig. 4.2 Foundations of a sod-built church were excavated under the drystone church on the tiny island monastery of Illaunloughan, Co. Kerry. (After Marshall and Walsh as n. 5; © T. Ó Carragáin.)

Kerry, suggest that the probable turf-built oratory there was maintained from the seventh/eighth century to the tenth/eleventh century. All that survived of it was a rectangular arrangement of postholes but, as Hayden has pointed out, the metre-wide gap between postholes and burials suggests perhaps a turf-built church.[8] A number of other posthole arrangements may represent churches of upright corner posts with walls of horizontal planks, or else post-and-wattle churches. For example, at Caherlehillan (Kerry) burials occur immediately outside the line of postholes ruling out the possibility that it was of turf construction.[9] There are a few references to wattle churches in Irish hagiography. Thus, according to his Latin Life, before founding his principal establishment St Kevin 'constructed for himself a little oratory from rods [*ex virgiis*] so as to pray to God daily'.[10]

Most of our sources, however, describe or depict high-quality carpentry churches and *dairthech*, literally 'oak house,' was the most common term for 'church'. There is no evidence for churches of palisade construction of the sort sometimes found in Britain (such as Whithorn (Wigtownshire), Greensted (Essex)), but there is evidence for sill-beam construction: both interrupted by earthfast posts and continuous sill-beam construction without earthfast posts. Usually sill-beams are laid

---

Kerry (Bray, 2005).
[8] A. Hayden, 'A Terraced Shrine and Other Structures on Church Island, Valentia, Co. Kerry (Licence No. 03E1518)', Report for the Department of the Environment, Heritage and Local Government (Dublin, 2008), p. 3.
[9] J. Sheehan, 'A Peacock's Tale: Excavations at Caherlehillan, Iveragh, Ireland', in *The Archaeology of the Early Medieval Celtic Churches: Proceedings of a Conference on the Archaeology of the Early Medieval Celtic Churches, September 2004*, ed. N. Edwards, Society for Medieval Archaeology Monograph 29, Society for Church Archaeology Monograph 1 (Leeds, 2009), pp. 191–206 at p. 195.
[10] *Vitae sanctorum Hiberniae*, ed. C. Plummer, 2 vols (Oxford, 1910), vol. 2, p. 243.

directly on the ground, and so they tend to leave little archaeological trace. As a result the only archaeological evidence for churches of interrupted sill-beam construction is often an arrangement of postholes. It is generally agreed that most posthole churches in mainland Europe were constructed in this way.[11] A possible Irish example was found under the chancel of Cormac's Chapel at Cashel. The evidence comprised two parallel rows of four rock-cut posts, representing successive phases of the south wall of a small church (c. 19 ft 6 in. × 13 ft, or 6 × 4 m.), probably a royal chapel like its successor.[12] Buildings of uninterrupted sill-beam construction are much more elusive archaeologically, but most Irish watermills (which survive because of water-logging) are built in this way.[13] A number of documentary sources suggest some churches were also. For example, in the Latin *Life of Samthanne*, it is recorded that a wooden church was moved from part of the monastery to another without dismantling it.[14] Such episodes suggest familiarity with well-jointed churches without earthfast posts.

Virtually all of our art historical and documentary sources suggest that, like their mortared stone successors, the wooden churches were rectangular with short proportions and a single door in the west wall. We should be ever conscious of the possibility that churches of other forms were built. In particular Cogitosus' description suggests that the seventh-century church at Kildare had a door in each of its sidewalls, but this is an unusual case.[15] I have suggested elsewhere that the basic form of Irish churches arrived from Roman Britain in the late fourth/early fifth century: most of the basic tenets of Irish church-design are found there and, especially in western Britain, the majority of new churches in this period were of wood rather than stone.[16] Unicameral churches (*Saalkirchen*) were quite common elsewhere in early medieval Europe. What is different about Ireland is the minimal amount of variation. The unwillingness to experiment suggests that, already, the unicameral form had become a defining characteristic of a church.

---

[11] C. Ahrens, *Die Frühen Holzkirchen Europas*, Schriften des archäologischen Landesmuseums 7, 2 vols (Stuttgart, 2001), vol. 2; G. Descoeudres, 'Die Pfarrkirche von Ursenbach', *Archéologie Suisse*, 16 (1992–3), pp. 97–8.

[12] B. Hodkinson, 'Excavations at Cormac's Chapel, Cashel, 1992 and 1993: A Preliminary Report', *Tipperary Historical Journal*, 7 (1994), pp. 167–74; B. Hodkinson, *Excavations at Cormac's Chapel, Cashel* (Dublin, forthcoming).

[13] C. Rynne, 'Waterpower in Medieval Ireland', in *Working with Water in Medieval Europe: Technology and Resource-Use*, ed. P. Squatriti, Technology and Change in History 3 (Leiden, 2000), pp. 1–50.

[14] Translated from *Vitae sanctorum Hiberniae*, vol. 2, p. 257.

[15] S. Connolly and J.-M. Picard, 'Cogitosus: Life of Saint Brigit', *Journal of the Royal Society of Antiquaries of Ireland*, 117 (1987), pp. 11–27 at pp. 25–6.

[16] T. Ó Carragáin, 'Skeuomorphs and *Spolia*: The Presence of the Past in Irish Pre-Romanesque Architecture', in *Making and Meaning in Insular Art*, ed. R. Moss (Dublin, 2007), pp. 95–109 at p. 98; Ó Carragáin, *Churches*, pp. 36–8.

This may be partly because the form had become associated with Ireland's first and most important evangelisers. For example, in several texts it is specified that the churches built by Patrick, and therefore reputedly the first built in Ireland, were quadrangular. This form may also have become sacrosanct because it was associated with the Jerusalem Temple (the historical Temple), and especially with the idea of the Temple as a metaphor for the institution of the Church made up of the community of believers (the metaphorical Temple).[17] The 'Judaizing tendencies' of the early Irish Church are well documented: Irish clerics identified themselves closely with the Levites and considered the layout of their ecclesiastical sites to be based on that of Jerusalem.[18] It is therefore not surprising that the Temple is the predominant model for churches in Irish documentary sources. In Insular exegesis on the metaphorical Temple it is depicted as a simple quadrilateral. This is because the world was metaphorically conceived as quadrangular. In Jennifer O'Reilly's words,

> space, time and matter were seen as part of a fourfold ordering: the four winds or cardinal directions; the four season of the year; the elements of earth, air, fire and water [...] The underlying unity of this quadripartite world was seen to flow from its divine Creator made known in Christ and revealed in the harmonious testimony of the four gospels.[19]

Within this framework it is not surprising that there is a marked emphasis in exegesis on the four corners of the metaphorical Temple. These are described as being supported on the four cardinal virtues, which represent the four evangelists whose message has been brought to the four corners of the world.[20] Thus the Temple, and by extension any church which alluded to it, was a microcosm and a foreshadowing of the world to come.

The singular design feature of pre-Romanesque mortared churches in Ireland is the monumentalisation of their corners in the form of antae: square-sectioned projections of the side walls beyond the end walls (Fig. 4.3). That these are skeuomorphs of features found in wooden churches is confirmed by St MacDara's, Co. Galway, and the Romanesque church at Kilmalkedar, Co. Kerry: the only two

---

[17] *Die Irische Kanonensammlung*, ed. H. Wasserschleben, 2nd edn (Leipzig, 1885), § 40:14; C. Swift, 'Forts and Fields: A Study of "Monastic Towns" in Seventh- and Eighth-Century Ireland', *The Journal of Irish Archaeology*, 9 (1998), pp. 105–125 at pp. 107, 120.
[18] M. Herren, 'The "Judaizing tendencies" of the Early Irish Church', *Filologia mediolatina*, 3 (1996), pp. 73–80.
[19] J. O'Reilly, 'Patristic and Insular Traditions of the Evangelists: Exegesis and Iconography', *Le Isole Britanniche e Roma in età romanobarbarica*, ed. A. M. Luiselli Fadda and É. Ó Carragáin (Rome, 1998), pp. 49–94 at pp. 54, 79–81.
[20] M. Krasnadębska-D'Aughton, 'The Four-Symbols Page in Cracow Cathedral Library MS. 140: An Image of Unity', *Peritia*, 14 (2000), pp. 323–41 at p. 331; also N. Hiscock, *The Symbol at Your Door: Number and Geometry in Religious Architecture of the Greek and Latin Middle Ages* (Aldershot, 2007), p. 198.

Fig. 4.3 Pre-Romanesque church with antae and plain trabeate doorway at Kilree, Co. Kilkenny. It is probably tenth to early twelfth century. (© Copyright T. Ó Carragáin.)

churches in which antae are combined with a stone roof. In these churches the antae are one element of a skeuomorphic package including stone copies of end-rafters and finials (Colour Plate 4.4).[21] But why were wooden churches given such prominent corner-posts? There is no obvious functional explanation; for example, they were not needed to carry the roof over the gable, for extensions of the wall places facilitate this in churches throughout Europe. One possibility is that that an interest in the cosmological connotations of the quadrangle contributed to the appeal of antae in Ireland and discouraged the addition of extra cells that would compromise this sacred form.[22]

As far as we can tell, there could be no straying from this model. It seems that the particular function of a church was expressed only in its size and probably in its internal layout. Though there is little archaeological evidence for them, we know that churches had chancel screens, usually referred to as *crann-chaingel*, a compound of 'wood' and '*cancellus*'.[23] A number of sources indicate that the altar was near the chancel screen and that the celebrant stood in the small space between them during the mass. Probably in the larger churches there was considerable room behind the

21 P. Harbison, *Pilgrimage in Ireland: The Monuments and the People* (London, 1991), p. 98.
22 Ó Carragáin, *Churches*, pp. 38–46.
23 T. Ó Carragáin, 'The Architectural Setting of the Mass in Early Medieval Ireland', *Medieval Archaeology*, 53 (2009), pp. 119–54 at p. 125.

4. *MORE SCOTTORUM*: BUILDINGS OF WORSHIP IN IRELAND, c.400–950

chancel screen and altar. This was usually the case elsewhere in early medieval Europe, including for example the eighth-century church excavated at Whithorn.[24] In the case of the later Irish stone churches the position of the altar is suggested by that of the solitary south window.[25] The altar in the larger examples seems to have been positioned further west than that in the smaller examples. In part at least this was probably to facilitate more elaborate liturgies in the important episcopal and/or monastic churches. This space may also have had other purposes: some of the clergy may have sat here and, by analogy with churches on the Continent, it is possible that in some cases some of the space was used as a library and/or vestry. In contrast, the altars of smaller churches, which in many cases probably had a pastoral function, were located closer to the east wall so that a greater proportion of the more limited available space was available for the congregation. Depending on the function of the church the nave could also be subdivided. The clearest example of this is Cogitosus' famous description of the church of the double monastery of Kildare, the nave of which was divided longitudinally with the lay women and nuns at the left of the partition and the lay men and monks on the right.[26]

The Advent of Stone Construction

In peninsular Kerry a local tradition of drystone domestic buildings and churches with corbelled stone roofs developed, probably during the eighth century, and as a result this is the only area in Ireland where even very minor sites acquired stone churches.[27] These buildings had little or no influence on architecture elsewhere in Ireland. By contrast, the mortared stone churches built before 950 are usually at very important sites whose other church, or churches, were still of wood. In part at least, mortared stone construction was chosen to express the fact that these particular churches were special.

We know from the *Annals of Ulster* that there was an 'oratorium lapideum' at Armagh by 789.[28] Other written sources hint that this was built in the eighth century and that it was a congregational church.[29] But, if so, what changed during the eighth century to convince Armagh clerics to rebuild their church in mortared stone? One possible explanation is the influence of the writings of Bede. During the seventh century, Armagh instigated a campaign to have the successors of Patrick recognised, at home and abroad, as archbishops of the Irish. Among other strategies, it did so by

[24] P. Hill, *Whithorn and St Ninian: The Excavation of a Monastic Town, 1984–91* (Stroud, 1997), Fig. 4.15.
[25] Ó Carragáin, 'Architectural Setting', pp. 135–43.
[26] Connolly and Picard, 'Cogitosus', pp. 26–7.
[27] Ó Carragáin, 'Church buildings', p. 109.
[28] *The Annals of Ulster (to AD 1131)*, ed. S. Mac Airt and G. MacNiocaill (Dublin, 1983).
[29] *Annals of the Four Masters*, in *Annala Rioghachta Eireann: Annals of the Kingdom of Ireland by the Four Masters*, ed. J. O'Donovan, 7 vols (Dublin, 1851), vol. 2 *s.a.* 1020.

acquiring relics of Peter and Paul and other Roman martyrs.[30] Already in late seventh-century Northumbria the use of mortared stone was itself considered an expression of *romanitas* but this idea is not evident in Ireland before the arrival there of Bede's writings in the eighth century.[31] It is in Bede's *Ecclesiastical History*, completed in 731, that we get by far the clearest expression of the symbolic dichotomy between stone churches built 'in the Roman manner' and wooden churches built 'in the Irish manner' ('more Scottorum');[32] and we know that, on the Continent, the dissemination of this text bedded down the idea that mortared stone construction was an expression of *romanitas*.[33] In a similar way, it may be no coincidence that this relatively early Irish annalistic reference to a stone church concerns a site which was particularly anxious to cultivate links with Rome.[34]

The only other mortared stone churches which seem to have been built before 900 are a small group of diminutive churches at a number of important sites such as Clonmacnoise, Iona (Argyll) and Labbamolaga (Cork) which I have termed shrine-chapels (Fig. 4.5).[35] These seem to have been built over the graves of founder saints in order to house their relics. There was no shrine-chapel at Armagh, as far as we know: Patrick was believed to have been buried at Downpatrick (Co. Down) so Armagh was only major site which did not possess the grave and corporeal relics of its founder. When radiocarbon-dated by Rainer Berger, mortar from three or four shrine-chapels produced date ranges centring on the eighth and ninth centuries suggesting they may be earlier than any extant congregational church.[36] This relatively early date range makes historical sense, for it is in the eighth and ninth centuries that we get evidence for the translation of the corporeal relics of a minority of Irish saints. Translation was not necessary for the development of an Irish saint's

---

[30] R. Sharpe, 'Armagh and Rome in the Seventh Century', in *Ireland and Europe: The Early Church*, ed. P. Ní Chatháin and M. Richter (Stuttgart, 1984), pp. 58–72; Bieler, 'Patrician Texts', pp. 122–3, pp. 186–9.

[31] R. Stalley, *Early Medieval Architecture* (Oxford, 1999), p. 34; T. M. Charles-Edwards, *Early Christian Ireland* (Cambridge, 2000), pp. 329–30; R. Cramp, *Wearmouth and Jarrow Monastic Sites*, 2 vols (Swindon, 2005–6), vol. 1, p. 352.

[32] R. Gem, 'Towards an Iconography of Anglo-Saxon Architecture', *Journal of the Warburg and Courtauld Institutes*, 46 (1983), pp. 1–18 at p. 1.

[33] N. Gauthier, 'Note annexe: les églises en bois du VIe siècle d'après les sources littéraires', *Grégoire de Tours et l'éspace gaulois: actes du congrès international, Tours, 3–5 novembre 1994*, ed. N. Gauthier and H. Galinié, Supplement à la revue archéologique du centre de la France 13 (Tours, 1997), pp. 237–40 at pp. 237, 240.

[34] Further: Ó Carragáin, *Churches*, pp. 61–6.

[35] T. Ó Carragáin, 'The Architectural Setting of the Cult of Relics in Early Medieval Ireland', *Journal of the Royal Society of Antiquaries of Ireland*, 133 (2003), pp. 130–76 at p. 130.

[36] R. Berger, '14C Dating Mortar in Ireland', *Radiocarbon*, 34 (1992), pp. 880–9; R. Berger, 'Radiocarbon Dating of Early Medieval Irish Monuments', *Proceedings of the Royal Irish Academy*, 95C (1995), pp. 159–74.

Fig. 4.5 The shrine-chapel of St Molaga at Labbamolaga, Co. Cork, is believed to mark the saint's grave. Immediately north of it are the foundations of a congregational Romanesque church which probably replaced a wooden pre-Romanesque church. (© Copyright T. Ó Carragáin.)

cult: most remained in their original graves and the shrine chapels, along with other 'outdoor' reliquary foci such as gable shrines, show that even there they were translated their bones were usually kept at the gravesite. An exception is Kildare where, according to Cogitosus, the shrines of Brigit and the first archbishop Conlaed were to either side of the altar in the main congregational church: an arrangement much more common in contemporary Francia and England. In documentary sources shrine-chapels seem to have been equated with the little ædicule built over the tomb of Christ in Jersualem.[37] Stone was therefore an appropriate choice of materials for according to Adomnán this was 'carved out of one and the same rock [… and] covered with choice marble'.[38] Of course, as Harbison has pointed out, the relics they contained were safer in a building of mortared stone than they would have been in one of wood.[39]

Clonmacnoise cathedral appears to be both the largest and the oldest congregational stone church surviving in Ireland (Fig. 4.6). It served as a cathedral in the high medieval period when its south was rebuilt to reduce its size, but Conleth

[37] Ó Carragáin, 'Architectural Setting of the Cult of Relics', pp. 142–6.
[38] *Adamnán's De Locis Sanctis*, ed. D. Meehan, Scriptores latini Hiberniae 3 (Dublin, 1958), pp. 45–7.
[39] Harbison, *Pilgrimage*, p. 151.

Manning has shown that it was originally about 240 square yards (200 square metres) internally.[40] Unfortunately none of its original apertures survive. It was built in 909 by Abbot Colmán and King Flann of the Southern Uí Néill immediately after the latter's victory over the men of Munster at the battle of Belach Mugna, in which he was recognised as high king of Ireland. They also commissioned the famous Cross of the Scriptures and placed it immediately west of the cathedral and repositioned older high crosses at equal distances north and south of it. As a result, though the cathedral was unicameral rather than cruciform its axis represented the shaft of a cross inscribed across the sacred core of the site. This early tenth-century scheme may perpetuate one of *c.* 700, for excavation revealed large postholes under the extant high crosses presumably for wooden ones.[41]

Conclusion

As far as we can tell, this cathedral was the first congregational stone church built in Ireland since Armagh's *damliac mór* almost two centuries before. From then on, however, such buildings became increasingly common at important sites, especially those patronised by the two most important royal powers in the country, the Southern Uí Néill and the Dál Cais. The only other major architectural change around this time is the advent of the round tower, a monument type first referred to in 950. Both of these developments will be considered in the next volume in this series, along with the changes in church form that one finally sees from the end of the eleventh century, mainly as a result of liturgical and theological imperatives. Until then the quadrangular form established during the conversion period predominated. This church type could, with variations in size and internal layout, serve a wide range of purposes. As we have seen, despite its formal simplicity, this was also symbolically sophisticated architecture.

Fig. 4.6 (opposite) Clonmacnoise Cathedral, Co. Offaly, along with the Cross of the Scriptures that stands due west of it, was erected in 909. Its inserted Romanesque doorway (and the pre-Romanesque one that it replaced) was originally at the centre of the west wall, but in the later medieval period the south wall was entirely rebuilt in order to reduce the size of the cathedral. (© Copyright T. Ó Carragáin.)

[40] C. Manning, 'Clonmacnoise Cathedral', in *Clonmacnoise Studies, Volume 1: Seminar Papers 1994*, ed. H. King (Dublin, 1998), pp. 56–86.
[41] H. King, 'Burials and High Crosses at Clonmacnoise', in *Death and Burial in Medieval Europe*, ed. G. de Boe and F. Veraeghe, Papers of the Medieval Europe Brugge Conference 1997, 2 (Zellik, 1997), pp. 127–31.

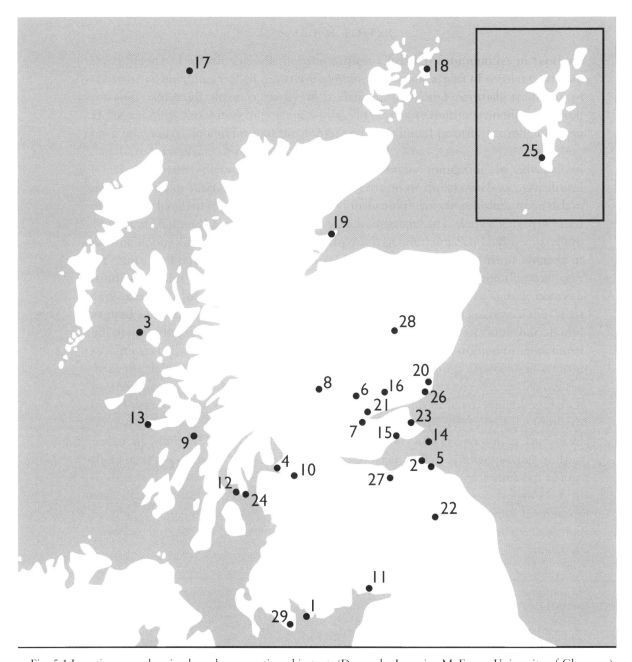

Fig. 5.1 Location map showing key places mentioned in text. (Drawn by Lorraine McEwan, University of Glasgow.)

1. Ardwall Island
2. Auldhame
3. Canna
4. Dumbarton Rock
5. Dunbar
6. Dunkeld
7. Forteviot
8. Fortingall
9. Garvellachs
10. Govan
11. Hoddam
12. Inchmarnock
13. Iona
14. Isle of May
15. Lundin Links
16. Meigle
17. North Rona
18. Papa Stronsay
19. Portmahomack
20. Redcastle
21. Scone
22. Sprouston
23. St Andrews
24. St Ninian's Isle, Bute
25. St Ninian's Isle, Shetland
26. St Vigeans
27. Thornybank
28. Tullich
29. Whithorn

(5)
Physical Evidence for the Early Church in Scotland

SALLY M. FOSTER

> Early monastic complexes [...] consisted of scatterings of crude huts around an equally unambitious oratory, and with a defensive rampart either encircling the site or cutting across the approach to it [...] there are few signs of any striving after architectural effects in Scotland before the eleventh century even though the adjacent areas had already seen the emergence of a more monumental approach to design before then.[1]

> A people may be highly cultured in other respects without possessing a single structure that an architect would care to look at.[2]

Separated by just over a hundred years, these two quotes are both apologies for the nature of the physical evidence for the early church buildings in Scotland. In the thirty years since publication of the second of them, new evidence from archaeological excavations invites us to think far more ambitiously and creatively about the possibilities, as do different ways of looking at existing resources, particularly sculpture and place-names. The aim of this paper is to bring out some of the key characteristics of this material, and in doing so to highlight some of its potential to recover an increasingly detailed and nuanced picture of the early church in northern Britain. As a preliminary to that, some brief scene-setting is necessary: a few words about chronological scope; landmarks in past study; an introduction to the types of evidence we have for the physical form of the church; and what the recent key developments are. Figure 5.1 shows the location of the main places mentioned in the text.

The Fifth to Tenth Centuries in Scotland

For Scottish purposes, the scope of this paper is the fifth to early tenth centuries. During this time there was no such political entity as Scotland: that part of northern Britain was a place of enormous diversity, home to five peoples (Britons, Picts, Gaels, incoming Angles and Norse) with six languages spoken (the church brought or reintroduced Latin).

---

[1] R. Fawcett, *Scottish Medieval Churches: An Introduction to the Ecclesiastical Architecture of the 12th to 16th Centuries in the Care of the Secretary of State for Scotland* (Edinburgh, 1985), p. 28.

[2] J. Anderson, *Scotland in Early Christian Times*, The Rhind Lectures in Archaeology, 1879 (Edinburgh, 1881), p. 128.

This half millennium of considerable change begins with some evidence for sub-Roman Christianity in southern Scotland (the late fifth-century inhabitants of Dumbarton Rock (Dunbartonshire) were Christian). While the best-known missionaries are Saints Ninian (probably St Finnian, d. 579), Columba and Cuthbert, the process of conversion and Christianisation involved many, was by no means linear, and was highly local in its character and manifestations. It was possibly not until the late seventh century that conversion was largely completed, the time from which begins widespread evidence for Christianisation—a *visibly* formal relationship between secular and ecclesiastical powers, coincident, in Pictland at least, with a concerted extension and consolidation of royal authority. Verturians of northern Pictland took over southern Pictland and used the idea of a single church to bind their territories, further drawing on the Columban church. The evidence speaks of a maturing and strengthening relationship over time, in which the line between secular and church politics arguably becomes blurred. At the same time, kings and aristocrats increasingly co-resided with church establishments. At the other extreme, the ultimate strength of the movement clearly lies in local community observance and practices.[3]

Our exercise ends around 900, the time when a consolidated nation of Picts and Gaels was forging a new identity for itself as Alba, with a redefined type of kingship. This is particularly evident in the events of 906 when Scone (Perthshire) emerged as a new ceremonial centre for Alba with explicit associations with the church. Here King Constantine, Bishop Cellach, 'and the Scots likewise, upon the hill of Faith near the royal city of Scone, swore to preserve the laws and disciplines of the Faith and the rights in church and gospels'. This reflects a strong church and strong kingship with a mature and sophisticated mutual dependency.[4]

At the end of Constantine's reign in 943, the kingdom of Scots ran from the Mounth to the Forth; he was overlord of Northumbria; and the neighbouring kingdoms of Cumbria (including Strathclyde) and Moray may have acknowledged his overlordship. Govan, just 2½ miles (4 km.) west of the ecclesiastical heart of later medieval Glasgow, was the principal royal centre of the king of the Strathclyde

---

[3] The best historical overview lies in J. Fraser, *From Caledonia to Pictland: Scotland to 795*, New Edinburgh History of Scotland, 1 (Edinburgh, 2009). A. Maldonado, 'What does Early Christianity look like? Mortuary Archaeology and Conversion in Late Iron Age Scotland', *Scottish Archaeological Journal*, 33 (2011), pp. 39–54 offers a useful theoretical perspective on changing archaeological approaches to what conversion involved in general, in the Scottish context in particular. I. Smith, 'The Origins and Development of Christianity in North Britain and Southern Pictland', in *Church Archaeology: Research Directions for the Future*, ed. J. Blair and C. Pyrah, Council for British Archaeology Research Report, 104 (York, 2006), pp. 19–37, reviews the sub-Roman evidence.

[4] S. Driscoll, *Alba. The Gaelic Kingdom of Scotland 800–1124* (Edinburgh, 2002), p. 8: Constantine, who retired to a monastery in 943, was 'in many respects the real architect of medieval Scotland'.

5. PHYSICAL EVIDENCE FOR THE EARLY CHURCH IN SCOTLAND

Britons. Here a place took shape with a strikingly similar monumentality and topography to Scone: an assembly place/court hill at Doomster Hill adjacent to a major church used for high-status ecclesiastical or secular burials (recumbent slabs, free-standing cross-slabs, hogbacks and a special tomb-shrine), all within sight of the royal estate lying on the other (north) side of the river Clyde.[5] Elsewhere in Scotland, we find the earldom of Orkney with Caithness, and fledgling kingdom of the Isles and the Kingdom of Galloway.

Landmarks in the Study of the Physical Evidence for the Early Medieval Church in Scotland

There is no up-to-date modern review that brings together all the different sources for the early church across Scotland, or even a single detailed treatment of the full range of physical evidence. Ian Fisher and Ian Smith published short overviews of the current state of knowledge and issues in 1996; partial surveys and more recent introductory texts also exist.[6] Charles Thomas is the first and last person so far to attempt anything magisterial, in 1971, with his inspirational *The Early Christian Archaeology of North Britain*.[7] Among other things, he introduced the influential concept of undeveloped and developed cemeteries. Ninety years previously in his Rhind lectures for 1879, *Scotland in Early Christian Times*, Joseph Anderson struggled with the dating of simple architectural structures in much the same way as we do today.[8] Between 1971 and 1992 the Royal Commission on the Ancient and Historical Monuments of Scotland published seven inventories for Argyll, a highly significant regional recording exercise, notable to us here for its surveys of chapel sites and monasteries, including many upstanding but undatable remains, and its detailed

---

[5] Driscoll *Alba*, p. 37; C. Dalglish and S. T. Driscoll, *Historic Govan: Archaeology and Development* (York and Edinburgh, 2009), pp. 28–50.

[6] Smith, 'Origins and Development of Christianity'; I. Fisher, 'The West of Scotland', in ibid., pp. 37–42. Carver, *Portmahomack*, pp. 87–92, and R. Cramp, *The Hirsel Excavations*, Society for Medieval Archaeology Monograph, 36 (Leeds, 2014), pp. 313–18 are useful on the form of early church buildings in Scotland. Professor Thomas Clancy is writing *The Making of Scottish Christianity: A History to 1215*. Examples of introductory archaeological texts are E. Campbell, *Saints and Sea-Kings: The First Kingdom of the Scots* (Edinburgh, 1999), M. Carver, *Surviving in Symbols: A Visit to the Pictish Nation* (Edinburgh, 1999), Driscoll, *Alba*, S. M. Foster, *Picts, Gaels and Scots*, 3rd edn (Edinburgh, 2014), chapter 5, C. Lowe, *Angels, Fools and Tyrants: Britons and Anglo-Saxons in Southern Scotland, AD 450–750* (Edinburgh, 1999), and O. Owen *The Sea Road: A Viking Voyage Through Scotland* (Edinburgh, 1999). A. D. S. Macdonald and L. R. Laing produced two surveys: 'Early Ecclesiastical Sites in Scotland: A Field Survey, Part 1', *Proceedings of the Society of Antiquaries of Scotland* 100 (1968), pp.123–34, and 'Early Ecclesiastical Sites in Scotland: A Field Survey, Part 2', *Proceedings of the Society of Antiquaries of Scotland,* 102 (1970), pp. 129–45.

[7] C. Thomas, *The Early Christian Archaeology of North Britain: The Hunter Marshall Lectures Delivered at the University of Glasgow in January and February 1968* (London, 1971).

[8] Anderson, *Scotland in Early Christian Times*, p. 123.

drawings and excellent photographs of carved stone monuments. The techniques they developed in recording carved stones have extended to their work on *Early Medieval Sculpture in the West Highlands and Islands*,[9] and drawing of Pictish sculpture by John Borland, bolstered by the continuing work of Ian G. Scott in his retirement.

The Nature of Evidence for the Physical Form of the Early Church

In general terms, the surviving evidence takes the form of visible upstanding remains, excavated evidence, cropmarks, carved stones, textual sources and ecclesiastical artefacts. Between them these forms of evidence help to build up a picture of the form of ecclesiastical buildings and settlements, what they might have looked like, the activities that took place at them and where, as well as having implications for the wider environmental footprint of ecclesiastical settlements. Place-names, as characterised by Simon Taylor, reflect different aspects of the early church—places for worship, usually a church or chapel; places where religious communities lived and worked; places set aside for sanctuary; places whose income supported the church; names containing allusions to saints' names or allusions to incidents in their lives; and places to which people attached some religious quality—but do not illuminate their physical form.[10]

Sites vary in scale, of course. Some fulfilled more regional than local functions, and some smaller sites were linked to more important ones, while some others were, towards the end of the first millennium, probably proprietorial (independently established by local lords and their families). Some sites are more remote (in geographical and/or topographical senses) than others and are assumed to be eremitic, including caves with internal structures or carvings on their walls. While we know some places were bishoprics, or bishops were present (for example, Iona, Argyll), we have to allow for a more flexible organisation than 'monastic' and 'episcopal': 'the early medieval church throughout Europe had a strong monastic impulse at every level, and this impulse waxed and waned, and took on different levels of standardisation'.[11]

Visible Upstanding Remains

If Scotland was like Ireland, and in the north and west this seems likely, small, early dry-stone churches will mostly date to the eleventh and twelfth centuries, although a few could date to the tenth, or in exceptional circumstances even as early as the eighth century. With the exception of shrine-chapels, most mortared examples were built

---

[9] I. Fisher, *Early Medieval Sculpture in the West Highlands and Islands* (Edinburgh, 2001).
[10] S. Taylor, 'Place-Names and the Early Church in Scotland', *Records of the Scottish Church History Society*, 28 (1998), pp. 1–22.
[11] T. Clancy, 'Deer and the Early Church in North-Eastern Scotland', in *Studies on the Book of Deer*, ed. K. Forsyth (Dublin, 2008), pp. 363–97 at p. 390.

5. PHYSICAL EVIDENCE FOR THE EARLY CHURCH IN SCOTLAND

after 900, particularly from the eleventh century.[12] In the absence of excavation it is not possible to say how many of the visible foundations in northern and western Scotland may pre-date 900, although attributes such as length/width ratios may help, and the form of churches/chapels and their enclosures sometimes parallels dated Irish examples.[13] 'Classic' structures include the corbelled cells surviving on remote islands. The enclosure with its corbelled buildings on North Rona (Ross and Cromarty), including the so-called oratory—a small stone building measuring 11 by 8 ft (3.4 by 2.4 m) internally and 10 ft 6 in. (3.2 m) high—is the most complete complex of buildings. Carved stones suggest a seventh- to ninth-century phase of activity on the site, but there is no scientific date for the corbelled structures, examples of which in Ireland seem unlikely to date before the tenth century. Scientific dates are equally lacking for the corbelled double beehive cell and a second possible corbelled structure on Eileach na Naoimh in the Garvellachs (Argyll). Its clay-mortared chapel is no longer thought to have been corbelled, and is most likely eleventh or twelfth century in date. The small church of St Flannan's on Eilean Mor in the Flannan Isles (Ross and Cromarty) was also possibly corbelled, on the basis of an antiquarian account.[14] The structural complexities and monumental biographies of such places are certainly masked, but some sophistication is evident even on unexcavated sites.[15] Sgòr nam Bán-Naoimha (cliff of the holy women) on the island of Canna (Inverness-shire) is a likely eremitic site, about 2 miles (3 km.) from a presumed monastery. Here, among a range of buildings, recognisable only from their grassed-over foundations, its builders channelled springs into a sophisticated water system that includes a probable horizontal water mill, and the latrine lies by the outflow.[16]

The earliest surviving upstanding church structures in eastern Scotland are immediately pre-Romanesque buildings at Abernethy (Perthshire), Brechin and Restennth (Angus), Egilsay (Orkney), Edinburgh Castle (Midlothian) and St Andrews (Fife) that Eric Fernie dates to between around 1090 and 1130.[17] Early church

---

[12] T. Ó Carragáin, *Churches in Early Medieval Ireland: Architecture, Ritual and Memory* (New Haven and London, 2010), pp. 15, 52, 57, 61, 64.

[13] M. O. H. Carver, *Portmahomack: Monastery of the Picts* (Edinburgh, 2008), p. 90.

[14] N. Fojut, D. Pringle and B. Walker, *The Ancient Monuments of the Western Isles: A Visitors' Guide to the Principal Historic Sites and Monuments* (Edinburgh, 1994), pp. 22–5; Fisher, *Early Medieval Sculpture*, pp. 114–16; A. O'Sullivan, F. McCormick, T. R. Kerr and L. Harney, *Early Medieval Ireland AD 400–1100: The Evidence from Archaeological Excavations* (Dublin, 2014), pp. 169–70; Ó Carragáin, *Churches*, p. 321, n. 13.

[15] High Island (Galway) is a good example of how an apparently simple church building reveals great complexity: J. W. Marshall and G. D. Rourke, *High Island: An Irish Monastery in the Atlantic* (Dublin, 2000).

[16] Fisher, *Early Medieval Sculpture*, p. 101.

[17] E. C. Fernie, 'Early Church Architecture in Scotland', *Proceedings of the Society of Antiquaries of Scotland*, 116 (1986), pp. 393–411; E. C. Fernie, *Romanesque Architecture: The First Style of the European Age* (New Haven and London, 2014). Traditionally little surviving fabric of

buildings may lie within or close to present church sites, or abandoned in woodland and under cultivated fields. At Tullich (Aberdeenshire) the presence of early sculpture, the sub-circular shape of the graveyard and dedication speak loudly of an early church foundation.[18] What *may* be upstanding early medieval fabric survives at Portmahomack (also known as Tarbat, Ross and Cromarty) where Martin Carver originally suggested a Pictish date for the east wall of the crypt, although he is now more cautious about this.[19] Peter Yeoman argues it is no earlier than the tenth century;[20] as such it raises questions about the physical nature of any church on the site after the Viking raids of around 800 that Carver argues led to the destruction of the monastery and a change in the overall function of the site.

Excavated Evidence

With notable exceptions (see below) work on known early sites—even very important ones such as Iona—has been keyhole in nature, with modern sensitivities and regulations meaning that little significant archaeological excavation occurs at churches or graveyards still in use in some way. Only through excavation can archaeologists hope to recover stone, let alone timber and possibly also turf and earthen, ecclesiastical buildings. The vestigial evidence for these structures may only survive as subtle changes in soils; waterlogged structural timbers surviving from monastic buildings at Iona remind us of the techniques and skilled carpentry we are missing.[21]

Structures found in early medieval field cemeteries are generally interpreted as mortuary structures rather than churches. Excavations in 1996 at Thornybank (Midlothian) revealed over 100 burials in varied grave forms (including log coffins), aligned approximately east to west and carefully laid out with no intercutting.

---

medieval date has been recognised either, but systematic survey of the dioceses of Dunblane and Dunkeld has shown that a considerable amount does survive: R. Fawcett, R. Oram and J. Luxford, 'Scottish Medieval Parish Churches: The Evidence from the Dioceses of Dunblane and Dunkeld', *Antiquaries Journal*, 90 (2010), pp. 261–98.

[18] I. A. G. Shepherd and M. K. Greig, *Grampian's Past: Its Archaeology from the Air* (Aberdeen, 1996), p. 34.

[19] Carver, *Portmahomack*, pp. 82–92; M. Carver, J. Garner-Lahire and C. Spall, *Portmahomack on Tarbat Ness: An Iron Age Estate, Pictish Monastery, Scots Trading Farm and Medieval Township in North-East Scotland* (Edinburgh, forthcoming).

[20] P. Yeoman, 'Investigations on the May Island, and other Early Medieval Churches and Monasteries in Scotland', in *The Archaeology of the Early Medieval Celtic Churches: Proceedings of a Conference on the Archaeology of the Early Medieval Celtic Churches, September, 2004*, ed. N. Edwards, Society for Medieval Archaeology Monograph, 29, Society for Church Archaeology Monograph, 1 (Leeds, 2009), pp. 227–44 at p. 233; H. F. James and P. Yeoman, *Excavations at St Ethernan's Monastery, Isle of May, Fife 1992–7*, Tayside and Fife Archaeological Committee Monograph, 6 (Perth, 2008), p. 171.

[21] J. Barber, 'Excavations on Iona, 1979', *Proceedings of the Society of Antiquaries of Scotland*, 111 (1982), pp. 282–380.

Fig. 5.2 Plan of excavated features at Hallow Hill. (Source: Proudfoot, 'Hallow Hill' (as n. 23), illustration 5. Reproduced with kind permission of the Society of Antiquaries of Scotland and Edwina Proudfoot.)

Radiocarbon dates suggest a *floruit* of burial in the sixth century. The burials include a four-posted dug grave (possibly with a wooden mortuary structure over) and two square-ditched graves.[22] Hallow Hill, St Andrews, is a large long-cist cemetery with a *floruit* in the seventh century (Fig. 5.2). This cemetery developed on either side of a road (to and from where? So far most known early medieval laid roads are *within* monasteries), and the site may be associated with an *eccles* (church) place-name. The organisation of the cemetery is again formal with the suggestion of some foundation graves containing Roman heirlooms. A six-post timber structure in a prominent hilltop location, aligned east to west and measuring 23 by 10 ft (7 by 3 m.), is a possible mortuary chapel, if not in this instance a church.[23] This example illustrates

22 A. R. Rees, 'A First Millennium AD Cemetery, Rectangular Bronze Age Structure and Late Prehistoric Settlement at Thornybank, Midlothian', *Proceedings of the Society of Antiquaries of Scotland*, 132 (2002), pp. 313–55 at pp. 349–50.
23 E. Proudfoot, 'Excavations at the Long Cist Cemetery on the Hallow Hill, St Andrews, Fife', *Proceedings of the Society of Antiquaries of Scotland*, 126 (1996), pp. 387–454.

the difficulty of identifying whether the earliest Christian communities in Scotland constructed buildings at their cemeteries designed for some aspect of regular Christian worship, although there certainly is a British, Irish and Scottish tradition of architecturally elaborating important tombs.[24] Their more routine worship could well have taken place in and around the home, and their initial priority for religious foci may have been places of baptism rather than burial.

Larger-scale interventions driven particularly by mitigation in advance of development, or rescue in advance of coastal erosion or threats such as agricultural ploughing, have led to the discovery of previously unknown church sites. In an urban context at Dunbar (East Lothian), Leslie Alcock suggested an L-shaped length of faced walling dating from the Anglo-Saxon occupation of southern Scotland compares to the Northumbrian church of Escomb (Durham).[25] Nearby in a rural context at Auldhame (East Lothian) ploughing-up of human remains prompted the discovery and excavation of a Northumbrian (Anglian) monastic settlement dating between around 650 and 1000. This was succeeded by a parish church and graveyard that went out of use in the seventeenth century, and its location was forgotten. Some burials and structural evidence pre-date a tenth-century, unicameral, stone-footed timber chapel of probable mid-eighth- to mid-ninth-century date, set within an enclosed coastal promontory. Historic Scotland did not permit the excavators to excavate below the first-floor levels that they encountered but a short length of narrow bedding trench hints at an earlier timber structure that the excavators interpret as part of the southern wall of an oratory.[26] Ploughing also led to the discovery and excavation of The Hirsel (Berwickshire) with its extensive burials and sequence of stone-built churches (judged to start in the tenth century with a unicameral building with a west entrance), but no earlier structures.[27] In Orkney, archaeologists found pre-Norse remains at St Nicholas' chapel on the island of Papa Stronsay: a corbelled cell beneath the church produced a piece of imported green porphyry and a central rectangular stone setting containing the stump of an upright stone. This may be a ritual structure associated with a Pictish monastery.[28]

[24] D. Petts and S. Turner, 'Early Medieval Church Groups in Wales and Western England', in *Early Medieval Celtic Churches*, pp. 281–99 at p. 294. The recent discovery of a *leacht* at Balisclate (Argyll) is undated but there are seventh to ninth-century burials nearby: C. Ellis, 'Data Structure Report: Balisclate Chapel, Isle of Mull. A Research and Community Excavation' (unpublished report).

[25] L. Alcock, *Kings and Warriors, Craftsmen and Priests in Northern Britain AD 550–850* (Edinburgh, 2003), p. 216.

[26] E. Hindmarch and M. Melikian, 'Baldred's Auldhame: An Early Medieval Chapel and Cemetery', *Church Archaeology*, 10 (2006), pp. 97–100; A. Crone, *Living and Dying at Auldhame, East Lothian: The Excavation of an Anglian Monastic Settlement and Medieval Parish Church* (Edinburgh, forthcoming).

[27] Cramp, *Hirsel*.

[28] Royal Commission on the Ancient and Historical Monuments of Scotland, record HY 62 NE 14.

5. PHYSICAL EVIDENCE FOR THE EARLY CHURCH IN SCOTLAND

Overall, on the basis of recent excavations, we have to question the dates that earlier excavators have attributed to their church buildings. At St Ninian's Point (Buteshire), excavated in the 1950s, burials aligned north–south were overlain by east-west ones. A chapel built of undressed rubble set in clay overlay at least two graves, its altar interpreted as having a box-like cavity; Raleigh Radford argued for a pre-Viking date.[29] On Ardwall Island (Kirkcudbrightshire), excavated by Thomas in the 1960s, Phase I extended inhumations related to the focus of a rock-cut slab shrine, a form interpreted as coming from Ireland. Phase II saw the construction of a small timber structure (oratory or chapel) and possibly another shrine of 'corner-post' type. According to the excavator, in around 700, in Phase III, a stone church with composite hollow altar was constructed: bone inside the altar is assumed to have been disturbed during construction of the chapel. There were two rows of inhumations to the west.[30] Neither site produced any direct scientific dating evidence and better dated, recently excavated stone buildings—The Hirsel, St Ronan's on Iona, Isle of May (Fife), Inchmarnock (Buteshire), Brough of Deerness (Orkney)—belong to the ninth or tenth century and later.[31] The use of clay bonding and lime mortar finds its parallels at Ardwall, Whithorn (Wigtownshire) and St Ninian's Point. The dated exceptions to these later dates are limited for now to Northumbrian Scotland: the small, partially excavated stone-footed structure at Auldhame (see above) and the large eighth-century timber church at Whithorn (see below).

Not only do we need to question the date of buildings, but several scholars have successfully challenged the interpretation of the pre-Northumbrian levels at Whithorn as ecclesiastical, seeing them instead as an aristocratic, Christian settlement.[32] The associated finds indicate considerable prosperity, widespread evolving trade contacts, including with the Continent, and innovative technological skills. So, with the

---

[29] Thomas, *Early Christian Archaeology*, pp. 54–6, 71, 179–80. W. G. Aitken, 'Excavation of a Chapel at St. Ninian's Point, Isle of Bute', *Transactions of the Buteshire Natural History Society*, 14 (1955), pp. 62–76.

[30] C. Thomas, 'An Early Christian Cemetery and Chapel on Ardwall Isle, Kirkcudbright', *Medieval Archaeology*, 11 (1967), pp. 127–88.

[31] J. O'Sullivan, 'Excavation of an Early Church and a Women's Cemetery at St Ronan's Medieval Parish Church, Iona', *Proceedings of the Society of Antiquaries of Scotland*, 124 (1994), pp. 327–65. In general, there is little hard evidence for pre-Norse churches in the northern isles, although the timber predecessor of the stone church at Brough of Deerness, Orkney, may be pre-Norse: C. D. Morris, 'The Chapel and Enclosure on the Brough of Deerness, Orkney: Survey and Excavations, 1975–77', *Proceedings of the Society of Antiquaries of Scotland*, 116 (1986), pp. 301–74 at p. 357. See also R. C. Barrowman, *The Chapel and Burial Ground on St Ninian's Isle, Shetland: Excavations Past and Present*, Society for Medieval Archaeology Monograph, 32 (Leeds, 2011), where there was an undated but earlier structure beneath the surviving eleventh- or twelfth-century church.

[32] Summarised in A. R. Maldonado. 'Christianity and Burial in Late Iron Age Scotland, AD 400–650', PhD thesis, University of Glasgow (2011), chapter 6.

exception of the manufacture of ecclesiastical artefacts, the nature of the activities taking place on large church sites may in many respect be little different from what took place at hill-top power centres (see below).

Significant invasive or non-invasive exploration around the periphery of large church settlement sites, likely to extend beyond the present-day churchyard boundaries, is also lamentably rare. Excavations at Portmahomack, Whithorn and Hoddam (Dumfries-shire) vividly demonstrate the potential of these areas to contain significant archaeological evidence that illuminates our understanding of the early church in Scotland (see below).

Cropmarks

There is an unavoidable skew in our potential to recognise early church sites from cropmarks because the conditions for creating them is generally restricted to lowland, mainly eastern, Scotland, and anyway limited because many sites will be built over. Such cropmarks can be particularly helpful in demonstrating how a modern churchyard is one small part of a large, presumed ecclesiastical settlement, such as at Portmahomack, Hoddam and Fortingall (Perthshire). Cropmarks can provide a high level of resolution, a particularly notable example being Whitmuirhaugh near Sprouston (Roxburghshire) where a cemetery of at least 280 graves visible on aerial photographs appear to focus on a rectangular building in the south-west corner of the cemetery. Ian Smith interpreted this as a seventh-century Anglian church belonging to a royal estate.[33]

Carved Stones

Carved stones are the major accessible resource for trying to understand ecclesiastical monuments and buildings in early medieval Scotland to around 1000, after which proprietorial church building became the more significant vehicle for social expression.[34] (Although we should not under-estimate the importance of possible early timber churches.) They provide evidence for different forms of monuments, including burial markers, church furniture, fittings and architecture, and hint at what may also have existed in timber.[35] Examples include a gable finial from the Phase III chapel at Ardwall Island, which the excavators suggested is of Irish type. This implies

---

[33] I. M. Smith, 'Sprouston, Roxburghshire: An Early Anglian Centre of the Eastern Tweed Basin', *Proceedings of the Society of Antiquaries of Scotland*, 121 (1991), pp. 261–94.

[34] S. T. Driscoll, 'Christian Monumental Sculpture and Ethnic Expression in Early Scotland', in *Social Identity in Early Medieval Britain and Ireland*, ed. W. Frazer and A. Tyrell (Leicester, 2000), pp. 233–52 at pp. 251–2.

[35] At the time of writing, prompted by excellent night-time photography of the ninth-century Sueno's Stone by Alan Braby, Katherine Forsyth (pers. comm.) is exploring the possibility that the feature depicted above a series of decapitated bodies might represent a building of the period, conceivably a church.

a complete stone roof.[36] The range of Pictish sculptural monuments continues to expand, with what may be the decorated finial of a stone ecclesiastical chair from Portmahomack, further evidence for the fittings within churches, if not their original settings. In the absence of datable inscriptions, dating of carved stones is stylistic and therefore imprecise and often broad.

Textual Sources

For Scotland, the period is largely devoid of local sources. For present purposes, the most important surviving document is Adomnán's *Life of Columba* in which, in passing, he paints a picture of the church on Iona (see below). Archaeology continues to discover undocumented sites, such as the Pictish monastery at Portmahomack.

Ecclesiastical Artefacts

Surviving artefacts with a demonstrable ecclesiastical function are rare: there are some stone objects, such as portable altars or a cross-marked sandstone vessel from Whithorn, possibly a *mortarium* for preparing the host;[37] some fine metalwork (notably the eighth-century Monymusk (Aberdeenshire) reliquary); manuscripts (the Book of Kells was probably made on Iona); crosiers; bronze and iron bells. Much is simply lost and/or destroyed, or was made of organic materials and is unlikely to survive. The exceptionally rare leather book satchel recovered from a crannog at Loch Glashan (Argyll) is the earliest surviving Insular example and reminds us that possible ecclesiastical artefacts can be recovered from non-church sites.[38] As well as helping to furnish church interiors, some of these objects may provide evidence for the appearance of churches: possibly the principal church on Iona was the model for the Temple of Jerusalem in the Book of Kells, and the form of the Monymusk reliquary is likely to reflect the architecture of churches.[39]

---

[36] Thomas, 'Early Christian Cemetery', pp. 127–88 at p. 175.

[37] P. Hill, *Whithorn and St Ninian: The Excavation of a Monastic Town 1984–91* (Stroud, 1997), pp. 46, 437.

[38] A. Crone and E. Campbell, *A Crannog of the First Millennium AD: Excavations by Jack Scott at Loch Glashan, Argyll, 1960* (Edinburgh, 2005), pp. 81–92. See also E. Campbell, 'The Archaeology of Writing at the Time of Adomnán', in *Adomnán of Iona: Theologian, Lawmaker, Peacemaker*, ed. J. M. Wooding (Dublin, 2010), pp. 139–44 on the material evidence for literacy on secular sites.

[39] Ó Carragáin, *Churches*, pp. 15, 79; D. V. Clarke, A. Blackwell and M. Goldberg, *Early Medieval Scotland: Individuals, Communities and Ideas* (Edinburgh, 2012), p. 35. The aisled basilican-style church incised on a slate at Inchmarnock (Argyll) is thought to be tenth- or eleventh-century in date and unlikely to represent a building on Inchmarnock: C. Lowe, *Inchmarnock: An Early Historic Island Monastery and its Archaeological Landscape* (Edinburgh, 2008), pp. 160–1.

New Knowledge, New Ways of Seeing

There are a several main reasons why our understanding of early church sites, and recognition of their existing and future potential, has leapt enormously in the last decade or so. A series of excavations at key sites have produced a mass of new evidence, most of it now in print: Iona (excavated 1979 and 1992), The Hirsel (1979–82, 1984); Whithorn (1984–91), Hoddam (1991), Isle of May (1992–7); Portmahomack (1994–2007), Govan (1994–6), Inchmarnock (1999–2004), and Auldhame (2005).[40] While most of these are on a relatively large scale, they are still only partial excavations of very large sites; the location of the excavations in relation to what we understand to be the original church site varies and obviously influences what they can tell us.

This period has also seen detailed new studies of Pictish art and new approaches to extracting meaning from sculpture.[41] Beyond Columba, Ninian and Cuthbert, place-name and textual studies are playing a particularly important role in identifying the territories in which more local saints and their followers worked, and the possible relationship of these to secular territories.[42] The historians have also furnished us with refreshingly new models against which to contextualise and consider the archaeological evidence.[43] Adrián Maldonado has also successfully questioned and revised our understanding of the relationship between burial types and practices, conversion and Christianisation. This includes demolishing earlier ideas about what constituted a Christian burial type (and hence our ability to recognise the presence of the first Christians) and the theory that 'undeveloped cemeteries' (usually unenclosed and

---

[40] Barber, 'Iona'; Cramp, *Hirsel*; Hill, *Whithorn*; C. Lowe, *Excavations at Hoddam, Dumfriesshire. An Early Ecclesiastical Site in South-West Scotland* (Edinburgh, 2006); James and Yeoman, *St Ethernan's*; M. O. H. Carver, 'An Iona of the East: The Early Medieval Monastery at Portmahomack, Easter Ross', *Medieval Archaeology*, 48 (2004), pp. 1–30; Carver, *Portmahomack*; M. Carver et al., *Portmahomack*; S. T. Driscoll, 'Govan: An Early Medieval Royal Centre on the Clyde', in *The Stone of Destiny: Artefact and Icon*, eds R. Welander, D. Breeze and T. O. Clancy (Edinburgh, 2003), pp. 77–83; Lowe, *Inchmarnock*; Crone, *Auldhame*.

[41] E.g., *The St Andrews Sarcophagus: A Pictish Masterpiece and its International Connections*, ed. S. M. Foster (Dublin, 2006); *Able Minds and Practised Hands: Scotland's Early Medieval Sculpture in the 21st Century*, ed. S. M. Foster and M. Cross, Society for Medieval Archaeology Monograph 23 (Leeds, 2005); G. Henderson and I. Henderson, *Art of the Picts: Sculpture and Metalwork in Early Medieval Scotland* (London, 2004); and Clarke et al., *Early Medieval Scotland*.

[42] T. Clancy, 'Deer', pp. 386, 392, demonstrates that there is negative evidence for the development of the church in north-east Scotland having non-'Columban' roots and having been open to other influences, including internal ones and ones from elsewhere in Ireland. The sculpture supports an early establishment of local churches in this area. He suggests that the key period for formation of these churches is 670–720 during the *floruits* of Nechtan, Drostan and Fergus; this is the same period as new centres emerged in Fife, Fothrif, Atholl and Easter Ross.

[43] Fraser, *Caledonia to Pictland*.

5. PHYSICAL EVIDENCE FOR THE EARLY CHURCH IN SCOTLAND

without a church) progressed to 'developed cemeteries' (with a church, usually enclosed).[44] By the end of our period, burial in churchyards was the norm, but this did not generally occur until the eighth century. Clusters of burials might precede the establishment of a church, but not necessarily.

The remainder of this paper will ring some of the changes: changing perceptions of church architecture; the physical manifestations of saints' cults; the structured use of space at church settlements; and the associated crafts, industries and technologies.

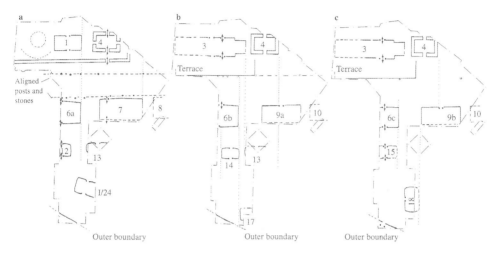

Fig. 5.3 Summary of phasing for the Period II minster church at Whithorn. (Source: Hill, *Whithorn* (as n. 37), Fig. 4.1. Reproduced with kind permission of The Whithorn Trust.)

Changing Perceptions of Church Architecture

The Anglian, eighth-century, minster church excavated at Whithorn is a complete revelation, illustrating how complex and sophisticated timber churches might be, and that for the Anglo-Saxons it *was* perfectly acceptable to build important, large 'Roman' churches in timber (Fig. 5.3); we now know that European architecture elsewhere was commonly timber too.[45] The Whithorn minster's internal divisions have much in common with Cogitosus' description of the large seventh-century church at Kildare in Ireland, which Neuman de Vegvar argues exhibits *romanitas* in

---

44   Maldonado, 'Christianity and Burial'; A. Maldonado, 'Burial in Early Medieval Scotland: New Questions', *Medieval Archaeology*, 57 (2013), pp. 1–34; A. Maldonado, 'What Does Early Christianity Look Like?' See also S. Winlow, 'A Review of Pictish Burial Practices in Tayside and Fife', in *Pictish Progress: New Studies on Northern Britain in the Early Middle Ages*, eds. S. T. Driscoll, J. Geddes and M. A. Hall, Northern World 50 (Leiden, 2010), pp. 335–69; and D. E. Cowley, 'Early Christian Cemeteries in South-West Scotland', in *St Ninian and the Earliest Christianity in Scotland*, ed. J. Murray, British Archaeological Reports, British Series 483 (Oxford, 2009), pp. 43–56.

45   O'Carragáin, *Churches*, pp. 15–17.

its form.[46] Importantly, the Whithorn minster shows the potential for the survival of fragile and slight evidence about the division of church interiors, where the altars and doorways were, where people walked and where water used in rituals might be disposed of. Such evidence may provide insights into liturgy.[47] Churches also had a need for places safely to store and display reliquaries, as well as the exotic ecclesiastical treasures that were clearly circulating (as analysis of Pictish art suggests).

However, we know that after the Synod of Whitby (North Riding of Yorkshire) in 664, an important way in Northumbria of signalling allegiance to the Roman church (*romanitas*) was to build in mortared *stone* rather than timber, and that timber church architecture was, according to Bede, associated with the Irish. There is a reasonable case for some large Anglo-Saxon churches in Scotland being stone, at Hoddam and Dunbar. We know from places such as St Andrews that major churches could have more than one church, and that the Anglian tradition, as at Whithorn and possibly Hoddam, could include aligned churches, part of a wider linear trend.[48] Whithorn was also home to the church that Bede describes in 731 as St Ninian's *Candida Casa*, interpreted as a white-washed stone church. While there is evidence for lime preparation in its Phase I deposits, pointing to the construction of a sophisticated, mortared and perhaps lime washed building in the vicinity of the Glebe Field excavated area, there is no proof that such a building is the one Bede describes, or indeed a church at all.

The monastery at Iona is the obvious starting point for the form of Irish churches in Scotland, but sadly we have no archaeological evidence for the nature and form of any of its early churches. The principal church is likely to have been under the Abbey church.[49] Adomnán describes it in either its sixth- or seventh-century form (or how he imagined it to have been). He gives no indication that the church is stone—it was probably timber—but he reveals that the floor space was large enough to accommodate the entire monastic community or those present at a given time. Singing took place in a choir, and there may have been a window above the altar and possible extra windows along the south wall to help illuminate the altar further. Adomnán only mentions one main door, probably in the gable and possibly protected by a porch. Apart from the altar, there is no mention of any furniture. He describes an *exedra*,

46 C. Neuman de Vegvar, 'Romanitas and the Realpolitik in Cogitosus' Description of the Church of St Brigit, Kildare', in *The Cross Goes North: Processes of Conversion in Northern Europe AD 300–1300*, ed. M. Carver (Woodbridge, 2003), 153–70.
47 See for instance, T. Ó Carragáin, 'The Architectural Setting of the Mass in Early-Medieval Ireland', *Medieval Archaeology*, 53 (2009), pp. 119–54.
48 See useful summary in Petts and Turner, 'Early Medieval Church Groups', pp. 292–3.
49 Early twentieth-century excavations under the Abbey located some earlier structures: Royal Commission on the Ancient and Historical Monuments and Constructions of Scotland, *Argyll: An Inventory of the Ancient Monuments*, 7 vols (Edinburgh, 1971–92), vol. 4 (Iona), p. 152, n. 275.

thought (unusually in the context of Irish church architecture) to be an annex adjoining the church wall on its north or south side and entered from the church, possibly serving as a sacristy or side chapel. On top of this we must consider the possibility of ornately carved and painted walls, wall tapestries, and gleaming and colourful metalwork adorning the altar.[50] According to Adomnán, the monks on Iona had to import timber for building projects. Whether the early Irish church would have required all its early churches in western and northern Scotland to be timber is unknown and seems inherently unlikely given the sophisticated prehistoric building tradition of north and west Scotland and wide availability of stone rather than timber.

In Pictland, in around 716, the Pictish King Nechtan sent messengers to Abbot Ceolfrith of Wearmouth (Durham) seeking advice on changing the Pictish Church from Columban to Roman observance, and for architects to build a church in the Roman style. The location of the stone church that Nechtan dedicated to St Peter is uncertain. Traditionally it has been associated with *Egglespethir* somewhere near Restenneth but Rosemarkie on the Black Isle (Ross and Cromarty), the seat of the bishop for northern Pictland, now seems likely.[51] This begs the question of the extent to which there was stone churches in Pictland, and whether they all belong to after the 710s. Elsewhere in the Isles, beyond areas of Anglo-Saxon (that is, continental) architectural influence, the sense is that we should not expect much by way of stone buildings before the tenth century.[52]

Nechtan's reforms appear to have been extensive. It seems that a strategy for implementing his agenda, and a measure of its success, was a programme of erecting symbol-bearing cross-slabs, found throughout much of Pictland. Their content seems in various ways to reflect the way in which the local aristocracy gave support to the king and the church. Their form and the adoption of interlace decorative elements is an imaginative and distinctive response by Pictish masons to the artistic and technical inspiration of their Northumbrian counterparts. Stone monuments such as these conceivably symbolised the persuasion of the church and identity of the local patrons, even if any church besides them was still of timber.[53]

---

50 A. MacDonald, 'Adomnán's Monastery of Iona', in *Studies in the Cult of St Columba*, ed. C. Bourke (Dublin, 1997), pp. 24–44 at pp. 29–31; Ó Carragáin, *Churches*, p. 34.
51 Pers comm. T. Clancy; Fraser, *Caledonia to Pictland*.
52 A. Pritchard, 'The Origins of Ecclesiastical Stone Architecture in Wales', in *Medieval Celtic Churches*, pp. 245–64; C. Manning, 'A Suggested Typology for Pre-Romanesque Stone Churches in Ireland', in ibid., pp. 265–80.
53 In a recent study, James Fraser suggests that many Picts in the early eighth century 'had convinced themselves that a mutual lack of interest in "the Romans", however they defined them, was central to their ethnic identity', and that non-engagement with the continent was part of that Pictishness (J. Fraser, 'From ancient Scythia to *The Problem of the Picts*: Thoughts on the Quest for Pictish Origins', in *Pictish Progress*, pp. 15–43 at p. 38). The implication of this for Nechtan's Roman church 'drive' needs further work.

Aside from the possible proxy of the symbol-bearing cross-slabs, there is no evidence of an extensive programme of stone *church* building in the early eighth century, although this is probably the context in which we should now consider the establishment of the major Pictish monastery at Portmahomack under Ionan influence (noting that Romanising tendencies existed in the Columban church). The number and range of the surviving carved stones point to the existence of an impressive stone church, if not a series of early medieval churches here, but they were not definitively located in the excavation of the church.

Later in the ninth century a growing corpus of carved stones throws a light on what we may be missing in terms of stone architecture. Carved panels may be cladding for the interior and exterior of buildings. At Rosemarkie panels appear to be part of the same architectural scheme as a decorated stone altar. Distinctive panels and corner-post shrines clearly belonged to an interior setting, although one that was possibly modest in scale and could have been timber.[54] However, Clarke *et al.* suggest that these fittings long interpreted as shrines (including the St Andrews Sarcophagus) were in fact precinct barriers within a church, in much the same way as the continental post-and-panel technique they are ultimately believed to derive from, via the Northumbrian masons.[55] In general, there are strong indications that quite a lot of the sculpture was designed for internal spaces, as Geddes' re-analysis of the St Vigeans (Angus) collection shows.[56] Isabel and George Henderson speculate that the monumental cross-slab known as Meigle 2 (Perthshire) could have acted as the focus of a funerary chapel containing graves over which were placed Meigle's cross-bearing recumbent monuments. They also suggest that at least one of the series of major cross-slabs erected on the Tarbat peninsula at the end of eighth century was designed for use in an internal space.[57] The placing of sculpture within buildings raises interesting questions about how these internal spaces were illuminated, as well as how such spaces acted on the emotions and sense of visitors.

The so-called arch from Forteviot (Perthshire) is certainly the only surviving vestige of a very grand, ninth-century church, part of the royal palace complex (Fig. 5.4).[58] Aitchison argues that it stood above the chancel. He reinterprets its iconography as not biblical but showing a king, a prominent cross, the Agnus Dei and clerics, the rods in their hands depicting the iconography of ecclesiastical foundation (on the basis of Irish parallels). He makes the case that the king is Unuist (820–34), and that the

---

54 Henderson and Henderson, *Art of the Picts*, p. 208; C. Thomas, 'Form and Function', in *The St Andrews Sarcophagus*, pp. 84–96.
55 de Vegvar, 'Romanitas', p. 161; Clarke *et al.*, *Early Medieval Scotland*, pp. 95–7.
56 J. Geddes, *Early Medieval Sculpture at St Vigeans, Angus* (Edinburgh, forthcoming).
57 Henderson and Henderson, *Art of the Picts*, pp. 180–1, 201.
58 N. Aitchison, *Forteviot: A Pictish and Scottish Royal Centre* (Stroud, 2006), p. 146 describes it more accurately as a 'round-arched monolithic lintel'.

Fig. 5.4 Forteviot arch. (Reproduced with permission of the Trustees of the National Museums Scotland.)

Agnus Dei is evidence of promotion of the Roman liturgical rite. He suggests the church was on the same scale as Escomb (which held an estimated 84 adults), and that the iconography of the arch may have formed part of a coherent programme that encompassed the whole church in a 'graphic and potent testament to royal patronage of the Pictish church'.[59] Mark Hall widens possibilities for the arch in suggesting that it might be a pillared canopy over an altar or formed part of the superstructure of a baptistery, as well as querying Aitchison's interpretation of the 'rods'.[60]

So, we can feel more confident that the later Picts could, with high-status secular and ecclesiastical patronage, build quite splendid stone buildings at key church sites, such as major monasteries or royal chapels, but we are probably missing what could have been large-scale and impressive timber churches.

The Manifestation of Saints' Cults

As Stephen Driscoll observes, with exception of St Andrew, the great Scottish saints are all firmly linked to particular regions of Scotland, and their distribution is a manifestation of ethnic differences apparent in languages and cultural practices: the distribution of cults may in fact represent 'eroded footprints' of ancient polities.[61]

[59] Aitchison, *Forteviot*, p. 208. The chancel arch at Escomb is different in scale (5 ft 3 in. (1.6 m.) wide in comparison to about 4 ft (1.2 m.) inner diameter at Forteviot) and form (at Escomb the arch is created from well-cut voussoirs and is probably re-used Roman masonry): H. M. and J. Taylor, *Anglo-Saxon Architecture*, 3 vols (Cambridge, 1965–78), vol. 1, pp. 234–8.

[60] M. Hall, 'Tales From Beyond the Pict: Sculpture and Its Uses in and around Forteviot, Perthshire from the Ninth Century Onwards', in *Pictish Progress*, pp. 135–68 at pp. 141–3.

[61] Driscoll, 'Christian Monumental Sculpture', pp. 233–52.

Driscoll argues that the vigorous growth of such cults in Scotland is 'perhaps the best documented of the innovative social and political developments that provided the framework for the Scottish kingdom', and their growth provides the clearest indication of the increasing power of leading churches.[62] Using place-names, the slight documentary evidence and the surviving sculpture we can infer how the aristocracy and royalty patronised such cults for political as well as devotional reasons. Examples include sixth-century Serf in the Forth Valley and Strathearn area and Ethernan (d. 669) in the Fife area, native saints who had direct associations with local royalty.

Glasgow University's Leverhulme-funded 'Commemoration of Saints in Scottish Place-Names' project has the exciting potential to offer us insights into dedications to early saints, and the tools better to analyse them.[63] Aside from inscriptions on stone monuments that very occasionally refer to a named individual who could be a particular saint, it is nigh on impossible to identify from the *physical* evidence which saints prevailed where.[64] Yet sometimes cumulative sources of evidence can hint at programmes of ecclesiastical activity. Place-names, cropmarks indicating a monastery at Fortingall similar in its enclosure to Iona, a newly discovered eighth-century cross-slab with Ionan parallels from Dull (Perthshire),[65] and a high concentration of handbells and cross-incised stones from Atholl appear to indicate the activities of Gaelic Columban churchmen in southern Pictish affairs in the early eighth century, where they were promoting Roman practices.[66]

The development of cults is linked to architectural innovation, as Tomás Ó Carragáin shows in his study of shrine-chapels found in Ireland and Iona in the eighth and ninth centuries. He makes the case for the chapel on Iona known as 'St Columba's Shrine' (Fig. 5.5) being built to house a reliquary shrine, clearly before 843 when the saint's relics were split between Dunkeld (Perthshire) and Kells (Ireland). Such shrines were free-standing structures that stood in the burial grounds. The Iona example is probably the earliest example, possibly relating to a mid-eighth-century translation of Columba's remains.[67]

[62] Driscoll, *Alba*, pp. 9–11.
[63] Due to be launched as an online resource in November 2014.
[64] It is questionable the extent to which, for example, schools of sculpture can be used in this way. They are, anyway, difficult to establish for the Picts: Henderson and Henderson, *Art of the Picts*, p. 212.
[65] Sculpture found close to a north–south clay-bonded wall that is likely to be an earlier undated church.
[66] See, for example, S. Taylor, 'Seventh-Century Iona Abbots in Scottish Place-Names', *Innes Review*, 48 (1997), pp. 45–72; N. M. Robertson, 'The Early Medieval Carved Stones of Fortingall', in *The Worm, the Germ and the Thorn: Pictish and Related Studies Presented to Isabel Henderson*, ed. D. Henry (Balgavies, 1997), pp. 133–48; and R. S. Will, K. Forsyth, T. O. Clancy and G. Charles-Edwards, 'An Eighth-Century Inscribed Cross-Slab in Dull, Perthshire', *Scottish Archaeological Journal*, 25 (2003), pp. 57–72.
[67] O'Carragáin, *Churches*, p. 69–70.

Fig. 5.5 (opposite) St Columba's Shrine, Iona.
(Reproduced with kind permission of David Breeze.)

In comparison to Ireland, few saints' reliquaries—such as metal shrines, crosiers, bells—survive in Scotland, although sculptural detail and monument form regularly betray inspiration from sacred treasuries. Various forms of monuments are possibly shrines and/or had a reliquary function. Examples include the eighth-century so-called St Andrews Sarcophagus and related composite monuments (but see alternative possibilities above), and the ninth-century Govan tomb-shrine carved from a single block of stone. The latter probably stood on the south side of the east end of the church at Govan, while the St Andrews Sarcophagus, if a shrine, would have worked to best advantage on the north side.[68] A characteristic form of recumbent burial marker that develops in the eighth to ninth centuries sometimes had a secondary reliquary role by means of recesses designed to hold things. Concentrations of such monuments suggest aristocratic or royal patronage at key places like St Andrews, Meigle and St Vigeans. Programmes of monument creation may relate in some way to the translation of saints' relics.

The Structured Use of Space

A structured use of space is visible in the cemeteries, often with multiple foci, and also in the overall layout of sites. But as Maldonado's reinterpretation of Whithorn shows, the boundaries between places of burial and industrial activities can fluctuate.[69] An overall structured use of space is also obvious at the larger church sites where significant excavations have taken place: evidence for inner and outer enclosures (Inchmarnock; Portmahomack by implication) and roads (Iona; Portmahomack; Isle of May). We have to bear in mind that these places were designed not just for the monks and clerics who used them but also for visiting pilgrims, the dead and their mourners. Enclosures may date from the mid-sixth century at Whithorn, and the fifth- or sixth-century date from the earliest burials at Govan could imply that its enclosure also dates from this period. However, there is increasing evidence that enclosures around churches, as in Ireland, do not need to be primary or may be later than anticipated.[70]

Within the enclosures, landscaping can be a feature. On the Isle of May in the Firth of Forth there was four centuries of burial before the earliest dated building appears (probably in the late tenth century, a simple rectangle with a west door, overlying some earlier burials). At an early date the raised beach was transformed into something resembling a platform cairn measuring at least 200 ft (60 m.) from north to south by 72 ft (22 m.) transversely. Within this area, the Group 2/3 burials were

---

68   J. R. Davies, *The Cult of St Constantine* (Glasgow, 2010), p. 4; I. Henderson, '*Primus inter pares*: The St Andrews Sarcophagus and Pictish Sculpture', in *The St Andrews Sarcophagus*, pp. 97–167 at p. 155.
69   Maldonado, 'Christianity and Burial', chapter 6.
70   O'Sullivan *et al.*, *Early Medieval Ireland*, p. 148.

aligned differently suggesting some segregation of burials in the eighth to ninth centuries. Another example of landscaping is the construction of revetments at Whithorn in the eighth century that transformed the excavated part of this site.

Whithorn also provides detailed evidence of considerable experimentation with access for people passing between the site's outer and inner precincts. In this area, the clay-bonded building to the east of the eighth-century minister church at Whithorn appears to have been a mortuary chapel that doubled as a gateway to the inner precinct. With its rare evidence for coloured window glass, this implies that a particular value attached to the burial of high status individuals (some were buried in chests) at the entrance to an important church.

Patterns are also visible in where other activities took place. Inchmarnock produced over a hundred pieces of incised slate that imply a monastic school or equivalent to the north or west of the church. This mirrors the location of the Nendrum schoolhouse (Down), and Inishmurray (Sligo) in Ireland. The excavators believe it was a place where young children were fostered, possibly functioning as a primary or elemental school.[71]

There is good evidence for a wide range of activities taking place in association with church sites, frequently beyond the bounds of the historical or modern graveyard (agricultural activities at the perimeter; more specialised craft activities often closer to the site core (Fig. 5.6)): 'the evidence from Hoddam [and Portmahomack] should also lead us to reconsider the physical size of these early settlements and reassess the complexity of their associated parts'.[72] Sometimes there is also evidence for the presence of domestic architecture, including possible guesthouses, as at Whithorn, or timber buildings at Iona.

Associated Industries and Technologies
This final example introduces the expanded evidence for a wider range of crafts, industries and technologies present in association with the churches: fine metalworking and glass working (for example, Portmahomack, where the 'pieces' are in place for manufacture of reliquaries); unique evidence for a vellum-manufacturing workshop at Portmahomack, which supports the evidence for not only the presence but also the manufacture of decorated manuscripts here;[73] a workshop specialising in oil-shale artefact production to the north of the church at Inchmarnock, and a metalworking area (both dating to the last quarter of the first millennium);

---

[71] Lowe, *Inchmarnock*, pp. 257–63.
[72] Lowe, *Hoddam*, p. 198.
[73] M. Carver and C. Spall, 'Excavating a *Parchmenerie*: Archaeological Correlates of Making Parchment at the Pictish Monastery at Portmahomack, Easter Ross', *Proceedings of the Society of Antiquaries of Scotland*, 134 (2004), pp. 183–200.

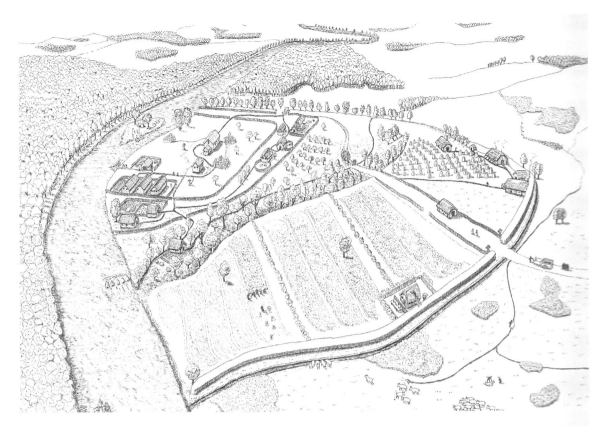

Fig. 5.6 A reconstruction of the Northumbrian monastery at Hoddam in the eighth century. Note the church buildings close to the river and the agricultural area around the site's perimeter. (Source Lowe, *Excavations at Hoddam* (as n. 40), Fig. 9.1, drawn by Sheena Williamson. Reproduced with kind permission of the Society of Antiquaries of Scotland and Headland Archaeology (UK) Ltd.)

metalworking from Govan;[74] smithing at Portmahomack; leather tanning at Hoddam; possible milling (water management was certainly a feature at Portmahomack); and good evidence for agricultural activities in the form of an arc of corn-drying kilns around the inner perimeter of the vallum at Hoddam, which has implication for access to resources (cereal and fuel).

Concluding Remarks

Building churches in stone features in Scotland from the eighth century, although that is not to preclude the discovery in future of dated chapels in northern and western Scotland where stone was the most ready building material. While the 'architectural effect' so sought by architectural historians was not on a par with the developments in Anglo-Saxon England and the Continent at this time, such as western towers, crossing-like bays and crypts, there were instances when under the patronage of royal or high status churchmen, impressive stone and timber churches were being built at

[74] Dalglish and Driscoll, *Historic Govan*, p. 39.

important monasteries.[75] These could have complex, divided interiors as well as decoration, and be a small element of well-laid out, resource-intensive, agricultural, economic and technological enterprises. Contemporary buildings elsewhere on church sites such as Iona, the mortuary chapel at Whithorn with its coloured glass windows, and the geometrically laid-out building known as S1 ('the smith's hall') at Portmahomack highlight the available technological skills.[76]

In focussing on the physical evidence this short paper has skipped over the expected complexities and diversity of early Christian religious establishments across what is now Scotland, including key questions such as who founded and supported the churches (communities, lay persons, lords, kings), and how this changed across time and space. Our period saw the transformation of how and where critical rites of passage took place (individual baptism and burial; inauguration of kings, etc.), so that by the tenth century the church had acquired control of these. For places that lie at the heart of understanding the development of early medieval settlement as a whole, we know lamentably little about church sites in general, particularly about the church buildings themselves. The archaeological revelations have primarily come from excavations taking place *around* surviving churchyards, in the outer perimeters of what were mostly some of the largest religious establishments of this period. With opportunities for significant exploration of the heart of early church sites generally slight unless we discover more Auldhames and Hirsels, the greatest future potential for understanding the physical nature of the church in Scotland largely lies in understanding what happened around the perimeter of larger sites, and in understanding how these sites fitted into the wider social and economic landscape, as well as continuing to explore the possibilities of the carved stones, new discoveries and old.

Acknowledgements

I am pleased to have the opportunity to thank the people and organisations who kindly lent me slides to use in the original lecture this paper derives from, and subsequently: Martin Carver (University of York), Erlend Hindmarch (AOC Archaeology Ltd), Chris Lowe (Headland Archaeology Ltd) and Peter Yeoman (Historic Scotland). This paper was written in 2010 with adjustments in 2014.

---

[75] Fernie, *Romanesque Architecture*, chapter 6.
[76] M. Carver, 'Early Scottish Monasteries and Prehistory: A Preliminary Dialogue', *Scottish Historical Review*, 88 (2009), pp. 332–51 at pp. 342–3.

(6)
The Anglo-Saxon Church in Kent

MEG BOULTON AND JANE HAWKES

There has been considerable scholarly interest in the early medieval architecture of Kent which has seen the publication of several studies devoted to cataloguing, classifying and describing the extant architecture succeeding Rickman's foundational *Attempt to Discriminate the Styles of English Architecture* in 1817,[1] as well as more recent work that seeks to address the importance and significance of the architecture in a more synthetic manner following Gem's examination of the ecclesiastical architecture at Canterbury.[2] Together, these have made considerable contributions to our understanding of the (fragmentary) Anglo-Saxon architectural forms extant in the region today.

[1] T. Rickman, *An Attempt to Discriminate the Styles of English Architecture from the Conquest to the Reformation* (London, 1817); see *e.g.*, J. T. Micklethwaite, 'Description and History of the Church of St Pancras', *Archaeological Journal*, 55 (1896), pp. 343–4; G. Baldwin Brown, *The Arts in Early England, vol. 2: Anglo-Saxon Architecture*, 2nd edn (London, 1925); A. W. Clapham, *English Romanesque Architecture Before the Conquest* (Oxford, 1930); E. A. Fisher, *An Introduction to Anglo-Saxon Architecture and Sculpture* (London, 1962); E. Fernie, *The Architecture of the Anglo-Saxons* (London, 1983); H. M. Taylor and J. Taylor, *Anglo-Saxon Architecture*, 3 vols (Cambridge, 1965–78); R. Morris, *The Church in British Archaeology*, Council for British Archaeology Research Report, 47 (London, 1983); C. B. McClendon, *The Origins of Medieval Architecture: Building in Europe A.D. 600–900* (London and New Haven, 2005).

[2] R. Gem, 'Towards an Iconography of Anglo-Saxon Architecture', *Journal of the Warburg and Courtauld Institutes*, 46 (1983), pp. 1–18; R. Gem, 'The English Parish Church in the Eleventh and Early Twelfth Centuries: A Great Rebuilding?', in *Minsters and Parish Churches: The Local Church in Transition 950–1200*, ed. J. Blair, University of Oxford Committee for Archaeology Monographs, 17 (Oxford, 1988), pp. 21–30; R. Gem, 'Reconstructions of St Augustine's Abbey, Canterbury, in the Anglo-Saxon Period', in *St Dunstan: His Life, Times and Cult*, ed. N. Ramsay, M. Sparks and T. Tatton-Brown (Woodbridge, 1992), 57–73; R. Gem, 'Architecture of the Anglo-Saxon Church, 735 to 870: From Archbishop Ecgberht to Archbishop Ceolnoth', *Journal of the British Archaeological Association* 146 (1993), pp. 29–66; R. Gem, 'The Anglo-Saxon and Norman Churches', in *St Augustine's Abbey, Canterbury*, by R. Gem (London, 1997), pp. 90–122; see also, *e.g.*, H. Gittos, 'Architecture and Liturgy in England c. 1000: Problems and Possibilities', in *The White Mantle of Churches: Architecture, Liturgy and Art Around the Millennium*, ed. N. Hiscock, International Medieval Research, 10 (Turnhout, 2003), pp. 91–106; H. Gittos, *Liturgy, Architecture, and Sacred Places in Anglo-Saxon England* (Oxford, 2013); M. G. Shapland, 'Buildings of Secular and Religious Lordship: Anglo-Saxon Tower-nave Churches', Ph.D. thesis, University College London (2012); M. G. Shapland, 'Meanings of Timber and Stone in Anglo–Saxon Building Practice', in *Trees and Timber in the Anglo-Saxon World*, ed. M. D. J. Bintley and M. G. Shapland (Oxford,

6. THE ANGLO-SAXON CHURCH IN KENT

According to Taylor and Taylor's seminal three-volume study, thirty churches in Kent can be considered to contain visible evidence of Anglo-Saxon fabric, with a further four presenting archaeological evidence.[3] These range in date from the Roman (reputed) chapel of St Martin just outside the city walls of Canterbury, which was re-used by the Frankish princess, Bertha and her retinue, upon her marriage to Æthelberht of Kent in the late sixth century,[4] to a number of churches constructed after the conquest of England by William I in the eleventh century.[5] Even in their current incomplete state these churches, incorporating stone and brick in their fabric, are remarkable structures that, in their contemporary context, would have been striking features of the built Anglo-Saxon world, existing in a now 'vanished landscape of locally distinctive structures and techniques',[6] and forming an active element in the built topography of Anglo-Saxon England.

This discussion does not seek to rehearse the considerable body of scholarship on the Anglo-Saxon ecclesiastical architecture of Kent, nor to enumerate the totality of extant buildings which remain in the region,[7] beyond providing a brief historiography of the scholarship and discussion of the manner in which it has been constructed. Rather, in addition to the more usual concerns of dating, style and the transmission of sources, it seeks to explore the ways in which the Church was brought to Kent; the manner in which it was constructed by Augustine and his successors; the

---

2013), pp. 21–44; M. G. Shapland, 'The Cuckoo and the Magpie: The Building Culture of the Anglo-Saxon Church' (forthcoming).

[3] Those churches containing Anglo-Saxon fabric have been identified as St Martin's, SS Peter and Paul, St Pancras and St Mary's, St Mildred's and St Dunstan's (in and around Canterbury), and those at Cheriton, Coldred, Darenth, Dover (St Mary *in Castro*), East Langdon, Leeds, Lower Halstow, Lydd, Kingsdown, Kingston, Milton Regis, Minster in Sheppey, Northfleet, Orpington, Paddlesworth, Reculver, St Margaret's at Cliffe, Shorne, Stone by Faversham, Swanscombe, West Peckham, West Stourmouth, Whitfield, Willesborough, Wilmington and Wouldham; churches for which archaeological evidence of the Anglo-Saxon buildings underlying the later medieval churches has been confirmed are Christ Saviour (under the current Cathedral of St Peter in Canterbury), and those at Lyminge, Minster-in-Thanet and Rochester; no material evidence of the Anglo-Saxon churches of St Mary, Holy Cross and *Quatro Coronati* in Canterbury, and that at Lullingstone, all mentioned in the textual sources, has been identified. See Appendix.

[4] Gem, 'Anglo-Saxon and Norman Churches', pp. 90–122.

[5] Gem, 'English Parish Church'; Fernie, *Architecture*; T. Tatton-Brown, 'Survey of Kent Churches', Kent Archaeological Society (www.kentarchaeology.org.uk/01/03/00.htm; accessed 25 June 2013).

[6] M. Bintley and M. G. Shapland, 'Introduction', in *Trees and Timber*, pp. 1–14, esp. p. 4, and n. 20.

[7] For full accounts see *e.g.*, Taylor and Taylor, *Anglo-Saxon Architecture*; Fernie, *Architecture*; W. Rodwell, *The Archaeology of the English Church: The Study of Historic Churches and Graveyards* (London, 1981); J. Blair, *The Church in Anglo-Saxon Society* (Oxford, 2005); S. Foot, *Monastic Life in Anglo-Saxon England, c. 600–900* (Cambridge, 2006); Gittos, *Liturgy*.

way the 'imported' ecclesiastical architecture was subsequently translated across Kent; and the symbolic significance of the spaces and structures of this early Church.

In terms of the scholarship on Anglo-Saxon architecture in England the ecclesiastical structures of Kent hold a unique position, as the extant spaces and forms built or restored by the Augustinian mission after its arrival in 597 tend to be employed as the 'bedrock' upon which to construct the narrative of conversion of Anglo-Saxon England.[8] The significance of this date in such accounts was recognised by Gem who, in the introduction to his discussion of the Saxon church complex constructed at Canterbury by the mission, explained how:

> 597 is one of those key dates in English history that are known to many people, even if they have a less sure understanding of its precise significance other than that it was the year in which Augustine arrived in Kent to bring Christianity to the English. With all such key dates there is something symbolic about them; that is, they are only a shorthand for historical events that were more drawn out in reality. Yet, for all the symbolism of this particular date, it corresponds to a very real historical process that saw the establishment of the Christian religion as one of the principle bases for the development of English political, social and cultural life up to modern times.[9]

In the conversion narrative common to the scholarship, however, it is not simply this date which is redolent with significance. Within Kent Canterbury occupies an equally notable position, being the 'point of origin' of the papal mission's presentation of a Romanised Christian topography. Against the backdrop of such significant dates and places in the construction of an early ecclesiastical 'identity' in England the architecture of the period is, all too frequently, *assumed*, used as a stable (if featureless) background against which to examine the material evidence of the early ecclesiastical culture of Anglo-Saxon England and, more recently, its liturgical practices—in so far is these may be determined.[10] Alternatively, the architecture is examined in detail through its salient features, such as round-headed, single- or double-splayed windows, through-stones and masonry types, becoming a discursive

---

[8] Bede, *Historia ecclesiastica gentis Anglorum*, ed. B. Colgrave and R. A. B. Mynors, *Bede: Ecclesiastical History of the English People* (Oxford, 1969), bk i, cc. 22–7; see also D. Farmer, 'St Augustine's Life and Legacy', in Gem, *St Augustine's Abbey*, pp. 15–32; R. C. Jenkins, 'On the Connection Between the Monasteries of Kent in the Saxon Period in Illustration of the Ruined Church of Dover Castle', *Archaeologia Cantiana* [hereafter *Arch. Cant.*], 3 (1860), pp. 19–34; C. F. Routledge, 'Roman Foundations at St Pancras, Canterbury', *Arch. Cant.*, 14 (1882), pp. 103–7; W. St John Hope, 'Recent Discoveries in the Abbey Church of St Austin at Canterbury', *Arch. Cant.*, 32 (1917), pp. 1–25; R. U. Potts, 'The Plan of St Austin's Abbey, Canterbury', *Arch. Cant.*, 46 (1934), pp. 179–94; H. F. Ding, 'St Augustine of Canterbury and the Saxon Church in Kent', *Arch. Cant.*, 62 (1949), pp. 108–39; F. Spiegel, 'The Tabernacula of Gregory the Great and the Conversion of Anglo-Saxon England', *Anglo-Saxon England*, 36 (2007), pp. 1–15.

[9] Gem, 'Anglo-Saxon and Norman Churches', p. 9.

[10] Gittos, *Liturgy*.

genre reliant on stylistic taxonomies, classifications and dating. Only recently has there been a shift toward engaging with the symbolic significance of the materials and forms of the architecture itself.[11]

Both approaches have much to recommend them: the first engages with the buildings in relation to the other cultural artefacts of Anglo-Saxon England, noting that the institution of the Church (often seen as synonymous with its architectural structures),[12] was a major force of production in the creation of visual objects in this culture, as well as the place that housed and displayed them. At the same time, this approach rather curiously neglects detailed examination of these architectural 'containers' with a rigour analogous to that applied to the objects housed within. Conversely, the second has produced a highly detailed identification of the various building phases and specific features, examining them in terms of sources of influence, chronology, and stylistic groupings.[13] Yet, this methodology does not fully consider the architecture in the light of the wider visual culture of the Christian Anglo-Saxon *milieu*, limiting it to a linear and chronological progression of increasingly large-scale, sophisticated buildings, without considering the architecture as part of a symbolic nexus intended to construct ecclesiastical identity in England.

It is noteworthy, however, that despite these discrete approaches much of the discussion of the architecture of Anglo-Saxon England (from Clapham onwards) systematically embeds the narrative of conversion into the accounts of the extant material exemplars; in this respect, it could be said to follow the example set by the

[11] For discussions see J. O'Reilly, 'Introduction', in *Bede: On the Temple*, trans. S. Connolly, Translated Texts for Historians, 21 (Liverpool, 1995), pp. xvii–lv; C. Farr, *The Book of Kells: Its Function and Audience* (London, 1997); H. Pulliam, 'Guarded Thresholds: Sight as Sentinel', *Manuscripta*, 57 (Forthcoming, 2013); É. Ó Carragáin, 'The Term *Porticus* and *Imitatio Romae* in Early Anglo-Saxon England', in *Text and Gloss: Studies in Insular Learning and Literature Presented to Joseph Donovan Pheifer*, ed. H. C. O'Briain, A. M. D'Arcy and J. Scattergood (Dublin, 1999), pp. 13–34; T. Ó Carragáin, *Churches in Early Medieval Ireland: Architecture, Ritual and Memory* (London and New Haven, 2010); McClendon, *Origins*; J. Hawkes, '*Iuxta Morem Romanorum*: Stone and Sculpture in Anglo-Saxon England', in *Anglo-Saxon Styles*, ed. C. Karkov and G. Hardin Brown (Albany, 2003), pp. 66–99; M. Boulton, 'The Conceptualisation of Sacred Space in Anglo-Saxon Northumbria in the Sixth to Ninth Centuries', Ph.D. thesis, University of York, 2 vols (2011); Shapland, 'Meanings of Timber and Stone'.

[12] J. Hawkes, 'The Church Triumphant: The Masham Column and the Art of the Church in Ninth-Century Anglo-Saxon England', *Hortus Artium Medievalium*, 8 (2002), pp. 337–48; J. Hawkes, '*Iuxta Morem Romanorum*'; J. Hawkes, 'The Legacy of Constantine in Anglo-Saxon England', in *Constantine the Great: York's Roman Emperor*, ed. E. Hartley, J. Hawkes and M. Henig (London, 2006), pp. 104–14; J.Hawkes, 'The Church Triumphant: The Figural Columns of Early Ninth-Century Anglo-Saxon England', in *Shaping Understanding: Form and Order in the Anglo-Saxon World, 400–1100*, ed. H. Hamerow and L. Webster (Oxford, 2009), pp. 29–42; Boulton, 'Conceptualisation of Sacred Space'; Gittos, *Liturgy*.

[13] For notable exceptions to this mode of scholarship see Gem, 'Towards an Iconography'; Gittos, *Liturgy*; Shapland, 'Meanings of Timber and Stone'; Shapland, 'Cuckoo and Magpie'.

earliest (medieval) 'scholarship' on the foundation of the early churches in the country:[14] Bede (672/3–735), who provides retrospective accounts of the first buildings (re-)used and constructed by the papal mission in Kent and accounts of the 'Roman' churches he knew in Northumbria; Eddius Stephanus, whose *Vita Wilfridi*, composed before 720, recounts the refurbishing and construction of elaborate stone churches as part of Wilfrid's mission to establish the Roman Church in the North; Alcuin (c. 735–804), who eulogised the Church in York with its origins in the activities of the papal mission under Paulinus and Edwin; Goscelin's accounts of the early saints and Church in Kent, centred on Canterbury; and those of his near contemporaries: Eadmer, whose account of the church in Canterbury was written to support its primacy over that of York (1060–1126),[15] and William of Malmesbury (c. 1120), who wove accounts of the 'old' churches and saints into his discussions of the spiritual nature of England, its Church and its rulers.[16]

The early associations of history and architecture thus constructed were subsequently taken up by Clapham and further re-evaluated by Fisher,[17] with the Taylors recounting the medieval references to the churches in some detail.[18] Their approach was comprehensively utilised by Fernie,[19] and more recently by Tatton-Brown (although his dating is frequently at a variance with that supplied by the Taylors),[20] and has been re-addressed by Gem, Gittos and Shapland.[21]

[14] The connection is absent from Rickman's work as its relevance seems to have been realised only as Bede and other medieval authors came to be more widely available during the nineteenth century (see Colgrave and Mynors, *Bede*, p. lxx).

[15] Bede, *Historia ecclesiastica* (c. 731); Eddius Stephanus, *Vita sancti Wilfrithi* (c. 709–20), ed. B. Colgrave, *Eddius Stephanus: The Life of Bishop Wilfrid* (Cambridge, 1927); Alcuin, *The Bishops Kings and Saints of York* (c. 780–1), ed. P. Godman (Oxford,1982); Goscelin of Saint-Bertin, *Vita maior s. Augustini*, ed. J-P. Migne, *Patrologiae cursus completus, series latina*, 221 vols (Paris, 1844–65), vol. 80, cols 41–94; *Vita minor s. Augustini, Patrologiae cursus completus, series latina*, vol. 150, cols 743–64; H. Taylor, 'The Anglo-Saxon Cathedral Church at Canterbury', *Archaeological Journal*, 126 (1969), pp. 101–130; see also R. Willis, *The Architectural History of Canterbury Cathedral* (London, 1845); *Eadmer of Canterbury: Lives and Miracles of Saints Oda, Dunstan, and Oswald*, ed. B. J. Muir and A. J. Turner (Oxford, 2006).

[16] William of Malmesbury, *Gesta Regnum Anglorum*, ed. R. A. B. Mynors, R. M. Thomson and M. Winterbottom, 2 vols (Oxford, 1998–9), bk i, c. 280; Fernie, *Architecture*, p. 8; J. Hawkes, 'Creating a View: Anglo-Saxon Sculpture in the Sixteenth Century', in *Making Histories: Proceedings of the Sixth International Conference on Insular Art, York 2011*, ed. J. Hawkes (Donnington, 2013), pp. 372–84, at pp. 373–7.

[17] Clapham, *English Romanesque Architecture*; Fisher, *Introduction*.

[18] Taylor and Taylor, *Anglo-Saxon Architecture*.

[19] For overviews of the scholarship see Fernie, *Architecture*; McClendon, *Origins*.

[20] Tatton-Brown, 'Survey'; see also R. Gem, 'ABC: How Should We Periodize Anglo-Saxon Architecture?', in *The Anglo-Saxon Church: Papers on History, Architecture and Archaeology in Honour of Dr H.M. Taylor*, ed. L. A. S. Butler and R. K. Morris, Council for British Archaeology Research Report, 60 (London, 1986), pp. 146–55.

6. THE ANGLO-SAXON CHURCH IN KENT

In part, the tendency to embed the narrative of conversion into the architectural fabric of extant churches has arisen because of the largely fragmentary nature of the material evidence and the dichotomy that exists between those structures that remain extant and those that are discussed in the medieval accounts. The site of the church of *Quatro Coronati* in Canterbury, for example, cited by Bede, has yet to be identified;[22] conversely, the church at Lydd, which preserves an impressive amount of the original Anglo-Saxon building (Fig. 6.1), is ignored in the early sources, and so the question of its dating has revolved around its stylistic details, comparisons made with churches such as Reculver (which are included in the sources), and evidence from later charters and Domesday Book.[23]

The enumeration and identification of such Anglo-Saxon architectural details of the Kentish churches, like those elsewhere in England, has been a subject of considerable concern in the scholarship since the early identification of 'Saxon' architectural features by Rickman, who first provided the means for separating the 'Saxon' from those styles which preceded it and those which followed. In his chapter on 'English Architecture',[24] when addressing 'Anglo-Saxon Architecture or such buildings as may be presumed to have been erected in England before the Norman Conquest',[25] he proceeded on the premise that 'it is most likely that in some obscure country churches some *real* Saxon work […] may exist', despite the fact that 'hitherto, […] none has been ascertained to be of so great an age'.[26] For Rickman, the task was to identify that which was pre-Norman in the extant fabric of the churches, and he went about this by systematically discussing and *identifying* the various features he deemed to be 'Saxon',[27] moving from towers, through masonry, to openings, before

---

[21] Gem, 'Towards an Iconography'; Gittos, *Liturgy*; Shapland, 'Meanings of Timber and Stone'; see also Foot, *Monastic Life*.

[22] Bede, *Historia ecclesiastica*, bk ii, c.7; Hawkes, '*Iuxta Morem Romanorum*', p. 75; E. Cambridge, 'The Architecture of the Augustinian Mission', in *St Augustine and the Conversion of England*, ed. R. Gameson (Stroud, 1999), pp. 202–37.

[23] F. C. Elliston Erwood, 'Notes on the Churches of Romney Marsh in the County of Kent, 1923', *Arch. Cant.*, 37 (1925), pp. 177–208; G. M. Livett, 'Lydd Church', *Arch. Cant.*, 42 (1930), pp. 61–92; Taylor and Taylor, *Anglo-Saxon Architecture*, vol. 1, pp. 405–8.

[24] Rickman, *Attempt to Discriminate*, pp. 35–45.

[25] Rickman, *Attempt to Discriminate*, p. i.

[26] 'These questions were more fully treated in an article "On Saxon Architecture", which first appeared in the *Archaeologia*, but was subsequently incorporated in the fourth edition of Rickman's "Architecture".' This note, still included in Rickman's publication (*Attempt to Discriminate*, p. 45), speaks to a changing scholarly awareness of Anglo-Saxon architecture in the early nineteenth century, from being undervalued and marginalised, separated from the history of medieval English architecture, to being incorporated into the architectural canon, demonstrated here by its changing placement over the course of four editions of the text, from exclusion to inclusion, albeit as an appendix.

[27] Rickman, *Attempt to Discriminate*, pp. i, iv.

Fig. 6.1 Lydd, north aisle, showing west end and north arcade of the Anglo-Saxon church. (© Copyright M. Boulton.)

Fig. 6.2 Site of SS. Peter and Paul, Canterbury, looking towards the remains of St Pancras, with north porticus on the left. (© Copyright J. Hawkes.)

ending with notes on architectural decoration.[28] This methodology has become entrenched in studies of Anglo-Saxon (and subsequent medieval) ecclesiastical architecture, being clearly evident in the approaches adopted by Taylor and Taylor and Tatton-Brown.[29]

Although this method, which frequently combines examination of extant architectural evidence alongside contemporary textual sources and archaeological excavation, provides the means by which to identify an Anglo-Saxon church, it tends not, in itself, to reveal information about who built the structures, why they were built, or how they were used. It does, however, go some way to demonstrating the scale and scope of Anglo-Saxon architecture, its complexity, grandeur and sophistication. The archaeological investigations of the monastic church of SS. Peter and Paul ('*fuori le mura*') in Canterbury, for example (Fig. 6.2), demonstrate that it extended almost the full length of the later medieval building, incorporating three aisles and funerary porticus in imitation of Old St Peter's in Rome, and in its final (Anglo-Saxon) phase incorporated transepts, a west-work, and east and west apses.[30] While no concrete information is produced about the lived specifics of such a building through the remaining archaeological details, or the extant architectural details of the (possibly earlier) monastic church of St Pancras lying to the east, much of what remains does give rise to further discussion: such as possible sources of influence lying behind the Anglo-Saxon structures, be those of the sub-Roman world of early Christian Europe or more Germanic traditions;[31] and of the relationships between architectural articulations across the Christianised kingdoms of Anglo-Saxon England, and within the wider context of the early Christian West.

The question of architectural influence is important as, until recently, scholarship on Anglo-Saxon architecture has focused almost exclusively on those buildings constructed of stone. While being highly significant in terms of the ecclesiastical architectural profile of the period, this was atypical of the wider architectural traditions in Anglo-Saxon England, or indeed in the Irish Christian tradition in the region, where building in wood remained the norm.[32] This distinction, in addition to

---

[28] Rickman, *Attempt to Discriminate*, p. iv.

[29] Taylor and Taylor, *Anglo-Saxon Architecture*, vol. 1, pp. 1–16; Tatton-Brown, 'Survey'; Gem, 'ABC'.

[30] W. St John Hope, 'Excavations at St Austin's Abbey, Canterbury', *Arch. Cant.*, 25 (1902), pp. 222–43; St John Hope, 'Recent Discoveries'; R. U. Potts, 'The Tombs of the Kings and Archbishops in St Austin's Abbey', *Arch. Cant.*, 38 (1926), pp. 97–112; R. U. Potts, 'A Note on the Plan of St Augustine's Abbey Church', *Arch. Cant.*, 40 (1928), pp. 65–6; R. U. Potts, 'The Plan of St Austin's Abbey, Canterbury', *Arch. Cant.*, 46 (1934), pp. 179–91; A. W. Clapham, 'A Note on the Layout of the Cloister at St Austin's Abbey, Canterbury', *Arch. Cant.*, 46 (1934), pp. 191–4; Taylor and Taylor, *Anglo-Saxon Architecture*, vol. 1, pp. 134–43.

[31] Fernie, *Architecture*, pp. 32–46; McClendon, *Origins*, pp. 59–66; Gittos, *Liturgy*, pp. 55–64; Shapland, 'Meanings of Timber and Stone', pp. 28–31.

[32] P. Addyman, 'The Anglo-Saxon House: A New Review', *Anglo-Saxon England*, 1 (1972), pp.

the frequent use of the 'foreign' materials of stone, glass, brick and tile within these structures, has allowed scholars to identify certain features (such as high set round-headed single-splayed windows, or the proportional dimensions of buildings) in terms of their 'Roman' or 'continental' prototypes, and discuss the potential symbolic significances of the structures and their materiality invoked by those who were responsible for their construction. This is, of course, particularly significant in Kent where the initial impetus for building and restoring ecclesiastical architecture potentially came directly from Rome.

Alongside the question of influence, the relationship between the documentary and material evidence is also important as, although it provides a more nuanced understanding of the structures than the architectural details alone, it also poses a potential problem—particularly for the later period of church building in the region for which near contemporary references survive in Domesday Book and *Domesday Monachorum*.[33] While some have assumed that mention of a church in Domesday Book indicates a late Anglo-Saxon/pre-Conquest date, others assume a post-Conquest/pre-1080s construction is denoted. Thus, Taylor and Taylor identify Coldred as including late Anglo-Saxon fabric in the form of its roughly worked flint quoins (later patched with Norman Caen stone), and the small round-headed single-splayed windows in the north and west walls (Fig. 6.3),[34] while Tatton-Brown considers the same features as indicative of a date not much before the church is cited in Domesday.[35]

This raises another issue relating to the documentary evidence surrounding Anglo-Saxon church building in the region. As noted, much of it is retrospective and its use by scholars can be selective, while many churches which are considered to display Anglo-Saxon architectural features receive no mention in the textual sources leading to dating by association of stylistic features—a reasonable solution to the

---

273–307; essays in *The Archaeological Study of Churches*, P. Addyman and R. Morris, Council for British Archaeology Research Report, 13 (London, 1976); P. Rahtz, 'Buildings and Rural Settlements', in *The Archaeology of Anglo-Saxon England*, ed. D. M. Wilson (Cambridge, 1976), pp. 49–98; Fernie, *Architecture*, pp. 8–31; M. Kerr and N. Kerr, *Anglo-Saxon Architecture* (Aylesbury, 1983), pp. 57–63; P. Dixon, 'Secular Architecture', in *The Making of England: Anglo-Saxon Art and Culture AD 600–900*, ed. L. Webster and J. Backhouse (London, 1991), pp. 67–70; McClendon, *Origins*, pp. 59–84; Shapland, 'Meanings of Timber and Stone', pp. 21–38.

[33] G. Ward, 'The Lists of Saxon Churches in the Domesday Monachorum, and White Book of St Augustine', *Arch. Cant.*, 45 (1933), pp. 60–89; *The Domesday Monachorum of Christ Church, Canterbury*, ed. D. C. Douglas (London, 1944). For *Domesday*, see The Domesday Book Online (http://www.domesdaybook.co.uk/kent1.html; accessed: 24 June 2013).

[34] Taylor and Taylor, *Anglo-Saxon Architecture*, vol. 1, pp. 164–5; see also E. P. L. Brock, 'The Saxon Church at Whitfield, near Dover, Kent', *Arch. Cant.*, 21 (1895), pp. 301–7, at p. 302.

[35] Tatton-Brown, 'Survey'.

Fig. 6.3 Coldred, from the south-west, showing possible Anglo-Saxon work in the west wall. (© Copyright J. Hawkes.)

dearth of information. However, almost no record survives of any ecclesiastical activity in the course of the ninth century, and this has resulted in a certain reluctance among architectural historians to date any church fabric to that period. An odd 'gap' in the presumed chronology of church buildings in the region is thus manifest.[36]

With such caveats in mind, it is possible to turn to look more closely at the earlier architectural structures which are seen as synonymous with the coming of (Roman) Christianity to Kent/Anglo-Saxon England. The association of 'English' Christianity with a Roman style of building is so intertwined that Bede, for whom description of architecture other than that of the exegetical or symbolic, seems not to have been of particular importance,[37] devoted considerable attention to Canterbury in his *Historia ecclesiastica*, describing both how the papal mission entered the city, and how they chose to articulate and actualise their presence on the landscape through the renovation and construction of churches.

[36] See Appendix
[37] See *e.g.*, Bede, *De Templo* and *De Tabernaculo*, in *Bedae Venerabilis Opera, Pars II: Opera Exegetica*, ed. D. Hurst, Corpus christianorum series latina, 118–21, 4 vols in 6 (Turnhout, 1960–83), vol. 2a (119a), trans. Connolly, *On the Temple*, and A. G. Holder, *Bede: On the Tabernacle*, Translated Texts for Historians, 18 (Liverpool, 1994).

Their acts of building (or restoration) are, in Bede's narrative, highly charged, with the initial conversion of the Anglo-Saxon people to the 'new' religion of Christianity being accompanied by the apparently self-conscious adoption of stone as a building material by the early Church to house and instruct the converted pagan people; it was an act of material selection which changed the architectural vocabulary of the Anglo-Saxon world. The advent of these new 'stone spaces' located the Church within an architectural environment, literally grounding the theology of the Roman Church solidly to the Anglo-Saxon earth through Roman building traditions, tying the metaphysical to the actual, and monumentalising the presence of the Church in the Anglo-Saxon landscape through the material choices of its construction.

In addition to this physical manifestation of ecclesiastical presence on the Anglo-Saxon landscape, however, and the inherent ideal of Rome suggested by the (re-)use of *spolia*,[38] such as the Roman brick-and-tile work common to the Kentish churches, or the deliberate employment of *romanitas*, such as that displayed by St Mary *in Castro* at Dover constructed in close proximity to the standing Roman lighthouse, and echoing many of its features (see Colour Plate 6.4),[39] these acts of symbolic (re-)building and the deliberate choice of material also evoked a further layer of significance. The conversion of Anglo-Saxon England was a deliberate papal act.[40] Gregory I had sent Augustine across the post-Imperial space of sub-Roman Europe to convert a barbarian (or potentially heretical) people, in a land that, if not entirely unknown in Rome, was certainly one that did not have the most favourable of reputations.[41] The sending out of the mission is of interest here for, with it, not only

---

[38] The topic of *spolia* and its myriad significances is too large to cover here in full but for a general discussion see D. Kinney, '"*Spolia Damnatio*" and "*Renovatio Memoriae*"', *Memoirs of the American Academy in Rome*, 42 (1997), pp. 117–48; D. Kinney, 'Roman Architectural Spolia', *Proceedings of the American Philosophical Society*, 145 (2001), pp. 138–61; D. Kinney, 'Spolia', in *St Peter's in the Vatican*, ed. W. Tronzo (Cambridge, 2005), pp. 16–47; D. Kinney, 'The Concept of Spolia', in *A Companion to Medieval Art: Romanesque and Gothic in Northern Europe*, ed. C. Rudolph (Oxford, 2006), pp. 233–52; for a selected discussion of the deliberate employment of *spolia* in Anglo-Saxon England, see J. Higgitt, 'The Roman Background to Medieval England', *Journal of the British Archaeological Association*, 36 (1973), pp. 1–15; R. Cramp, 'The Anglo-Saxons and Rome', *Transactions of the Architectural and Archaeological Society of Durham and Northumberland*, n.s. 3 (1974), pp. 27–38; Hawkes, '*Iuxta Morem Romanorum*'.

[39] G. G. Scott, 'The Church on the Castle Hill, Dover', *Arch. Cant.*, 5 (1862–3), pp. 1–18; Jenkins, 'Connections'; Taylor and Taylor, *Anglo-Saxon Architecture*, vol. 1, pp. 214–17

[40] Bede, *Historia ecclesiastica*, bk. i, c. 23; see also H. Mayr-Harting, *The Coming of Christianity to Anglo-Saxon England* (London, 1972), p. 51–68; C. Neuman de Vegvar, 'The Value of Recycling: Conversion and the Early Anglo-Saxon Use of Roman Materials', *The Haskins Society Journal*, 9 (1997), pp. 123–35; M. Lambert, *Christians and Pagans: The Conversion of Britain from Alban to Bede* (New Haven and London, 2010), pp. 164–200.

[41] Tacitus, *Agricola*, trans. A. Church and W. Broadribb (Cambridge, 1869), bk i, c. 11; see also R. A. Markus, 'Gregory the Great's Pagans', in *Belief and Culture in the Middle Ages: Studies*

would the conversion of a land at the 'edge of the world' render the Universal Church complete, Anglo-Saxon England would be tied to the papacy in Rome, a potent act in a time of relative instability for the Church.

As far as the introduction of the C/church in the region is concerned, Bede tells us that Gregory, 'prompted by divine inspiration' ('diuino admonitis instinctu'),[42] was adamant that his mission be completed, despite Augustine's repeated wishes to call a halt to the 'dangerous, wearisome and uncertain task'.[43] Notwithstanding such reluctance, once the mission arrived in England it did so with the full pomp of the ecclesiastical institution behind it.[44] Upon arrival, Bede records that the monks were initially restricted by order of Æthelberht to the Isle of Thanet, home to 600 families but segregated from the wider population they had come to convert.[45] Yet even his brief account of the initial meeting between the Roman Christian ecclesiastics and pagan Anglo-Saxon king makes it clear that space and architecture played a pivotal role from the very outset of the conversion process. Basing his account on records acquired for him from Rome and Canterbury,[46] Bede recounts that the first meeting occurred in the open air because Æthelberht 'held the traditional superstition that if he entered a building and they were practicing any magic art it would work against him as soon as he entered.'[47] This perception of buildings as spaces that could shelter, or indeed amplify a malevolent force is familiar from the vernacular oral poetry which, written down at a later date, refers to ancient stone buildings as 'the work of giants' ('enta geweorc');[48] architecture, in the Anglo-Saxon imagination could clearly be alien and other. It was a superstition that was certainly at odds with Christian beliefs surrounding architecture current in the early Church: namely, that they were spaces which functioned to house the Divine, to make present the space of heaven for

---

Presented to Henry Mayr-Harting, ed. R. Gameson and H. Leyser (New York, 2001), pp. 24–34.

[42] Bede, *Historia ecclesiastica*, bk i, cc. 22–3.
[43] Bede, *Historia ecclesiastica*, bk i, cc. 22–3: 'Nec mora, Augustinum [...] disposuerat , domum remittunt qui a beato Gregorio humili supplicatu obtineret, ne tam periculosam, tam laboriosam, tam incertam peregrinationem adire deberent'.
[44] Bede, *Historia ecclesiastica*, bk i, cc. 24–26.
[45] Bede, *Historia ecclesiastica*, bk i, cc. 24–5.
[46] Bede, *Historia ecclesiastica*, Preface.
[47] Bede, *Historia ecclesiastica*, bk i, c. 25: 'Post dies ergo uenit ad insulam rex, et residens sub diuo iussit Augustinum cum sociis ad suum ibidem aduenire colloquium. Cauerat enim ne in aliquam domum ad se introirent, uetere usus augurio, ne superuentu suo, siquid maleficae artis habuissent, eum superando deciperent.'
[48] *The Wanderer*, in *The Exeter Book*, ed. G. P. Krapp and E. van K. Dobbie (London and New York, 1936), ll. 76–87; see also *Beowulf*, in *Beowulf and The Fight at Finnsburg*, ed. F. Klaeber (Boston and New York, 1922), l. 2774; *The Ruin*, in *Exeter Book*, pp. 227–9; J. P. Frankis, 'The Thematic Significance of *enta geweorc* and Related Imagery in *The Wanderer*', *Anglo-Saxon England*, 2 (1973), pp. 253–69.

the earth-bound faithful, and to signify the glory of the heavenly Jerusalem to come for those encountering and entering them.

At the initial meeting between Church and king, which apparently avoided the loaded encounters of vernacular tradition that would have resulted from situating the gathering in a building, the monks, around forty in number,[49] nevertheless made full visual display of their beliefs, 'bearing as their standard a silver cross and the image of our Lord and Saviour painted on a panel'.[50] While displays of highly decorated and precious metalwork objects, albeit in forms dissimilar to that of the cross, would have been familiar to and appreciated by Anglo-Saxon viewers, especially in the context of social elites and personal adornment,[51] the figural painted panel would have arguably appeared somewhat foreign in an Anglo-Saxon setting.[52] The use of the wooden board as a standard, its painted medium, and its display of the human figure were all phenomena alien to the visual culture of the region.[53] They were, however, integral to the visual tradition of the Church, and Bede's invocation of them makes it clear that, in the absence of built space, these specific signs of the Church were being deliberately employed in such a way as to indicate that they were considered a significant part of the meeting between the two parties. Indeed, they could perhaps be understood as signifying the symbolic space and institutional identity of the Church *in lieu* of an architectural articulation as yet not widely familiar in the Anglo-Saxon landscape of the late sixth century. Certainly, Bede records that, on receiving promise of Æthelberht's support and the use of land in and around Canterbury,[54] the monks' *adventus* into the old Roman cantonal capital was also preceded by the cross and painted figure of Christ, and accompanied by the sound of the sung liturgy of the Roman mass.[55] Thus, from its first entry the Church announced and negotiated its

---

[49] Bede, *Historia ecclesiastica*, bk i, c. 25.

[50] Bede, *Historia ecclesiastica*, bk i, c. 25: 'crucem pro uexillo ferentes argenteam, et imaginem Domini saluatoris in tabula depictam.'

[51] See *e.g*, J. D. Richards, 'Anglo-Saxon Symbolism', in *The Age of Sutton Hoo: The Seventh Century in North-Western Europe*, ed. M. O. H. Carver (Woodbridge, 1992), pp. 131–48, at pp. 145–6.

[52] While such objects may have been familiar to Æthelberht as being part of the visual vocabulary of Bertha and Liudhard's religion, reflected in religious and liturgical objects brought from Francia, the artefacts brought by Augustine as part of the Papal mission are nonetheless indelibly tied to the institutional identity of the Roman Church as it marked its arrival into the Anglo-Saxon landscape in 597.

[53] C. R. Dodwell, *Anglo-Saxon Art: A New Perspective* (Manchester, 1982), p. 84.

[54] Bede, *Historia ecclesiastica*, bk i, c. 25.

[55] Bede, *Historia ecclesiastica*, bk i, c. 25: 'Fertur autem, quia adpropinquantes ciuitati more suo cum cruce sancta et imagine magni regis Domini nostri Iesu Christi'. The liturgical chant cited in bk i, c. 26 has been demonstrated by I. N. Wood ('The Mission of Augustine of Canterbury to the English', *Speculum*, 69 (1994), pp. 1–17) to be that current in his day rather than Augustine and Gregory's, but this does not affect his account of the visual aspect of the entry procession into Canterbury.

visual presence through a dramatic display of its symbolic forms and significant rituals, forcibly imprinting itself as a visual force on the English landscape,[56] as it would continue to do through the medium of architecture.

Through such accounts, it can be seen that public ritual and display were integral to the Church in Anglo-Saxon England from its inception,[57] and such associations were only heightened once the papal mission began to construct architectural spaces, for, in a potent act of architectural symbolism they set out to rebuild Rome in Canterbury.[58] Bede again recounts how, 'as soon as they had entered the dwelling place allotted to them, they began to imitate the way of life of the apostles and of the primitive church',[59] going on to relate that, while initially meeting 'to chant the psalms, to pray, to say mass, to preach, and to baptise' in the church of St Martin,[60] built 'while the Romans were still in Britain', once Æthelbert had been converted 'they received greater liberty to preach everywhere and to build or restore churches'.[61] Of these acts of building and restoration he tells us that, having:

> received his episcopal see in the royal city, [Augustine] with the help of the king restored a church in it, which, as he was informed, had been built in ancient times by the hands of Roman believers. He dedicated it in the name of the holy Saviour, our Lord and God, Jesus Christ; and there he established a dwelling for himself and his successors. He also founded a monastery not far from the city, to the east, in which Æthelbert, encouraged by him, built from its foundations the church of the Apostles St Peter and St Paul and endowed it with various gifts, so that the bodies of Augustine himself and all the bishops of Canterbury and the kings of Kent might be placed in it.[62]

---

[56] See N. J. Higham, *The Convert Kings: Power and Religious Affiliation in Early Anglo-Saxon England* (Manchester, 1997).

[57] See full discussion in L. Izzi, 'Representing Rome: The Influence of 'Rome' on Aspects of the Public Arts of Early Anglo-Saxon England (c. 600–800)', Ph.D. thesis, 2 vols, University of York (2010); L. Izzi, 'The Visual Impact of Rome in Anglo-Saxon Eyes: The Evidence of Architecture', in Hawkes, *Making Histories*, pp. 105–20.

[58] Gem, 'Towards an Iconography'.

[59] Bede, *Historia ecclesiastica*, bk i, c. 26: 'At ubi datam sibi mansionem intrauerant, coeperunt apostolican primitiuae ecclesiae uitam imitari.'

[60] Co-incidentally, this church shares its dedication with a chapel lying to the west of Old St Peter's in Rome; see É. Ó Carragáin, *Ritual and the Rood: Liturgical Images and Old English Poems of the Dream of the Rood Tradition* (London and Toronto, 2005), pp. 263–6.

[61] Bede, *Historia ecclesiastica*, bk. i, c. 26: 'Erat autem prope ipsam ciuitatem ad orientem ecclesia in honorem sancti Martini antiquitus facta, dum adhuc Romani Brittaniam incolerent, in qua regina, quam Christianam fuisse praediximus, orare consuerat. In hac ergo et ipsi primo conuenire psallere orare missas facaere praedicare et baptizare coeperunt, donec rege ad fidem conuerso maiorem praedicandi per Omnia et ecclesias fabricandi uel restaurandi licentiam acciperent.'

[62] Bede, *Historia ecclesiastica*, bk i, cc. 32–3: 'At Augustinus, ubi in regia ciuitate sedem episcopalem, ut praediximus, accepit, recuperauit in ea, region fultus adminiculo, ecclesiam auam inibi antique Romanorum fidelium opera factam fuisse didicerat, et eam in nomine sancti Saluatoris Dei et Domini nostri Iesu Christi sacrauit, atque ibidem sibi habitationem statuit et

These accounts are well known, and have been much discussed in the scholarship, but what has been less widely recognised is that the complex string of ecclesiastical structures which served to actualise Rome in Canterbury existed within a wider network of significant places associated with the mission.[63]

The earliest of the Kentish churches (with the possible exception of the space initially used by Bertha),[64] were thus those of the Cathedral, just within the city walls, and those of the monastery founded outside.[65] This arrangement and the associated dedications can be considered echoic of early Constantinian building practices in Rome, with the Emperor's Cathedral dedicated to Christ Saviour inside the city walls on the Lateran, and the martyrium basilicas (including those built over the remains of Peter and Paul) constructed *fuori le mura*.[66] The main church of the monastic complex, dedicated to Peter and Paul (*c.* 602) included funerary porticus for both the archbishops of Canterbury and the Christian members of the royal family—a practice replicating that found at St Peter's in Rome where, from the time of Leo the Great (440–61), the bodies of high ranking ecclesiastics were housed in the eastern 'porticus'.[67] This was followed by a small chapel dedicated to Mary to the east (*c.* 620),[68] which Gem has suggested may reference the chapel of St Mary that stood over the entrance into Old St Peter's.[69] Further east lay a third, small, single-aisled church with transeptual porticus and a triple arch framing the chancel articulated by reused Roman columns, dedicated to St Pancras in the later middle ages (see Fig. 6.8a, b). Unrecorded in the early accounts of the site, it has been suggested on archaeological evidence that this may have been set up while the main basilica was being constructed at the turn of the seventh century.[70]

---

cunctis successoribus suis. Fecit autem at monasterium non longe ab ipsa ciuitate ad orientem, in quo eius hortatu Aedilberct ecclesiam beatorum apostolorum Petri et Pauli a fundamentis construxit ac diuresis donis ditauit, in qua at ipsius Augustini et omnium episcoporum Doruuernensium, simul et regnum Cantiae poni corpora possent.'

[63] Gittos, *Liturgy*, p. 2, notes that the reasons underpinning the use of multiple churches remain unexplained.
[64] Although A. J. Beresford Hope recorded a tradition that Bertha's Chapel originally stood on the site which became the location for St Pancras, see 'Architectural Notes on St Augustine's College, Canterbury', *Archaeologia Caniana*, 4 (1861), pp. 57–66.
[65] Bede, *Historia ecclesiastica*, bk i, c. 33; bk. ii, c. 3.
[66] Gem, 'Anglo-Saxon and Norman Churches'; Hawkes, '*Iuxta Morem Romanorum*'; Gittos, *Liturgy*, p. 64; Izzi, 'Visual Impact of Rome'.
[67] See Ó Carragáin, 'The Term *Porticus*'; Hawkes, '*Iuxta Morem Romanorum*'; see also St John Hope, 'Recent Discoveries'.
[68] Bede, *Historia ecclesiastica*, bk ii, c. 5; see also Taylor and Taylor, *Anglo-Saxon Architecture*, vol. 1, p. 145.
[69] R. Gem, pers. comm.
[70] St John Hope, 'Excavations', pp. 222–43; for recent discussion on the development and context of these axial churches see Gittos, *Liturgy*, pp. 55–102.

Fig. 6.5 St Martin's, Canterbury
(a): west wall; (b): south wall of chancel showing Roman brick work and inserted Anglo-Saxon doorways.
(© Copyright J. Hawkes.)

The tendency for arranging churches 'in procession' in this way has, of course, been noted,[71] but John Blair has suggested that its origins may lie in late antiquity, in Merovingian Gaul,[72] and Gittos, drawing on earlier recognitions that such church groups can also include other features of the local landscape (such as wells, cemeteries and older ritual sites),[73] has usefully introduced St Martin's church into the debate. Standing at the eastern end of the east-west axis of churches stretching from Christ Saviour and incorporating those of the monastery, it stands adjacent to an ancient spring. While acknowledging the longevity of popular association with the main body of churches in the monastic complex, and the spatial relations of these churches, she notes that in the eleventh century St Martin's was tied to the cathedral rather than the monastery,[74] suggesting that the monastery is perhaps 'best considered as having been situated in order to make reference to St Martin's with its putative links to Queen Bertha'.[75]

Here, however, it is also necessary to recognise the long-standing association of St Martin's with fabric of Roman origin, which may well have served as a symbolic lode-stone for the subsequent placement of the run of churches founded as part of the monastic complex set up between it and the Roman city of Canterbury (Fig. 6.5a, b). The west wall of the nave of St Martin's clearly incorporates red Roman brick

---

[71] E.g., Rodwell, *Church Archaeology*, pp. 15–21.
[72] J. Blair, 'Anglo-Saxon Minsters', in *Pastoral Care before the Parish*, ed J. Blair and R. Sharpe (Leicester, 1992), pp. 246–58; J. Blair, *Church in Anglo-Saxon Society*, pp. 199–202; see also McClendon, *Origins*, pp. 60–4.
[73] Gittos, *Liturgy*, pp. 55–102; esp. p. 59.
[74] N. Brooks, *The Early History of the Church of Canterbury: Christ Church from 597 to 1066* (Leicester, 1984), pp. 34, 251, 295–6, 300.
[75] Gittos, *Liturgy*, p. 60.

Fig. 6.6 Stone-by-Faversham, showing Roman brick work of the 'chancel' and the original sill stone between the Anglo-Saxon chancel and nave. (© Copyright J. Hawkes.)

tile-work in single, double and even triple courses, picking out the blocked central arch over the present door, and forming the turnings of the two flanking windows, while pounded Roman tile has been mixed with lime and sand to form the mortar used for the windows and the north and south walls of the nave, indicating subsequent Anglo-Saxon rebuilding *more Romano*. The south wall of the chancel, however, retains much of the original Roman build of tiled bricks into which two doorways were inserted. The overall result is an Anglo-Saxon building constructed in two distinct phases: one Roman and the other early (seventh-century) Anglo-Saxon, which incorporated Roman fabric and *reproduced* Roman building techniques.[76]

Similar practises were also employed at Stone-by-Faversham (Fig. 6.6) where a small square Roman mausoleum of squared tufa stone blocks and ragstone, with regular courses of red brick tiles and *opus signinum* flooring, was extended west to form the nave of an early (probably seventh-century) Anglo-Saxon church, the shrine incorporated to form the chancel.[77] More notably, at St Mary's *in Castro*, not only were the distinctive red Roman brick tiles incorporated into the flint work of the church fabric, forming the turnings of the apertures, but they were clearly arranged in keeping with the Roman lighthouse, still standing next to the church, making the

[76] C. F. Routledge, 'St Martin's Church Canterbury', *Arch. Cant.*, 22 (1897), pp. 1–28; Taylor and Taylor, *Anglo-Saxon Architecture*, vol. 1, pp. 143–5.
[77] E. Fletcher and G. W. Meates, 'The Ruined Church of Stone-by-Faversham: Second Report', *Antiquaries Journal*, 57 (1977), pp. 67–72.

Fig. 6.7 Richborough, site of 'St Augustine's Chapel' looking west to the remains of the Roman tetrapylon. (© Copyright M. Boulton.)

one appear to be integral to the other (see Colour Plate 6.4). Here, the Roman building was incorporated into the subsequent (tenth-century) Anglo-Saxon church as a western tower, linked to the nave by means of a doorway in an upper gallery.[78] While at Rochester, Richborough (Fig. 6.7) and Reculver (see Fig. 6.9a), the Anglo-Saxon churches set up in the seventh century were sited in the *principium* area of the earlier Roman forts, that at Richborough stood close to the remains of the tetrapylon that was erected as the 'gateway' to Roman Britannia under Domitian (81–96).[79]

Such Roman associations are, of course, redolent with symbolic significance, providing visible articulation of the place of the Anglo-Saxon Church in Kent alongside the papal and Universal Churches centred in Rome. But there is another

---

[78] Scott, 'Church on the Castle Hill'; Taylor and Taylor, *Anglo-Saxon Architecture*, vol. 1, p. 146.
[79] For Rochester, see G. M. Livett, 'Foundations of the Saxon Cathedral Church at Rochester', *Arch. Cant.*, 18 (1889), pp. 261–78; G. M. Livett, 'Medieval Rochester', *Arch. Cant.*, 21 (1895), pp. 17–72; G. Payne, 'Roman Rochester', *Arch. Cant.*, 21 (1895), pp. 1–16; W. St John Hope, 'The Architectural History of the Cathedral Church and Monastery of St Andrew at Rochester', *Arch. Cant.*, 23 (1898), pp. 194–328; W. St John Hope, 'The Architectural History of the Cathedral Church and Monastery of St Andrew at Rochester, II: The Monastery', *Arch. Cant.*, 24 (1900), pp. 1–85; Taylor and Taylor, *Anglo-Saxon Architecture*, vol. 2, pp. 518–19; for Reculver, see G. Dowker, 'Reculver Church', *Arch. Cant.*, 12 (1879), pp. 248–68; Taylor and Taylor, *Anglo-Saxon Architecture*, vol. 2, pp. 503–9; for Richborough, see *e.g.*, S. Harris, *Richborough and Reculver* (London, 2001); see also Cambridge, 'Architecture of the Augustinian Mission'.

potential set of Christological significances being referenced in the material structures of these early churches. As noted, Augustine and his mission, with their unknown practices and alien visual traditions, were initially confined to Thanet, off the coast of Kent, enforcing a physical separation between the space of the (mostly) pagan land of the kingdom and the liminal space of the island. Once allowed to leave the island there is again evidence of a significant place being created on the landscape, recorded at the former Roman fort of Richborough (Fig. 6.7). Here, a rock understood to preserve the footprint of Augustine made at the point of his first stepping onto English soil was enshrined in the church.[80] Such acts of leaving sacred imprints upon the earth of Anglo-Saxon England were memorialised in the popular consciousness in a later event related by Goscelin, who recorded how Mildrith (694–716/33), daughter of the founder of the nunnery at Minster-in-Thanet, left a footprint in the rock at the point of her return from Chelles. Like Augustine's arrival, this event was considered to have left a trace on the landscape which became a site of popular devotion, inspiring a chapel (*oratorium*) to be built in her honour with the rock later preserved in a porticus. As Gittos has pointed out, the story of Mildrith's footprint is, 'in part, a story about how a holy place came into being'.[81] These footprints, and the subsequent architecture that housed them, monumentalised the sites in a pattern whereby, for Gittos, sacred places are revealed by God, made through human action, transformed by the Church through meditation on their significance, and consecrated through ritual. What Augustine's initial imprinting of the Church on to Anglo-Saxon stone (and Mildrith's subsequent footstep) would also reference, however, is a rich matrix of associations based on Peter, as the rock of the Christ's Church (Matthew, xvi, 17–19), and Christ himself.[82] It is a subject discussed by Jennifer O'Reilly in her seminal introduction to Bede's *De Templo*,[83] where Christ is presented as corner stone, the apostles and prophets as foundation, and Solomon's Temple, 'the house of God […] built in Jerusalem […] as a figure of the holy universal Church', is presented as constructed of white, dressed stone.[84] While Gittos has postulated that Mildreth

[80] For a full account of this legend following the 1849 excavation of the church when the stone was reportedly discovered, see C. R. Smith, *The Antiquities of Richborough, Reculver and Lymne, in Kent* (London, 1850), pp. 160–1; J. R. Planché, *A Corner of Kent; or, Some Account of the Parish of Ash-next-Sandwich, its Historical Sites and Existing Antiquities* (London, 1864), pp. 28–31; see further, R. Mackintosh, *Augustine of Canterbury: Leadership, Mission and Legacy* (Norwich, 2013), pp. 150–1.

[81] Gittos, *Liturgy*, p. 21.

[82] See, *e.g.*, Gregory I, *Moralia in Iob*, ed. M. Adriaen, *Gregorius Magnus: Moralia in Iob*, Corpus christianorum series latina, 143, 3 vols (Turnhout, 1985), bk. xxx, c. 48.1: 'In sacro elopuio cum singulari numero petra nominator quis alius quam christus accipitur?'

[83] O'Reilly, 'Introduction'; Farr, *Book of Kells*; H. Pulliam, *Word and Image in the Book of Kells* (Dublin, 2006).

[84] Bede, *De Templo*, bk i, c. 1.1: 'Domus dei quam aedificauit rex salomon in hierusalem in figuram facta est sanctae uniuersalis ecclesiae' (trans. Connolly, *On the Temple*, p. 5).

may have alighted onto a 'block of white Carrera marble from the triumphal arch at nearby Richborough',[85] the setting of Augustine's foot-imprinted rock within a church at the base of the remains of that structure would have unequivocally established the Church in Anglo-Saxon Kent as established in Christ through Rome. Indeed, the leaving of footprints is itself an act of *imitatio Christi* with Christ being understood to have left his own final footprint on the rock of the Mount of Olives at the point of his Ascension—that stone being initially enshrined in the Church of the Ascension built over the site. Described by Adomnán, and later, Bede in their various accounts of *De Locis Sanctis*,[86] the rock marked the last moments of Christ's footsteps on earth before he was taken into heaven. This was a potent relic, as are all secondary Christological relics,[87] and the fact that the moment of the mission's arrival into England was apparently monumentalised and memorialised through a similar imprint is not insignificant; while the footprint in the Holy Land serves to link the earth to the heavens through the triumphant salvation offered by Christ's sacrifice, in Kent it would have served to herald the arrival of the institution through which the same salvation would be made possible in Anglo-Saxon England.

Furthermore, there is a powerful association not just with the Christological prototype, but also between the Anglo-Saxon saints themselves, as Mildreth was 'produced' and memorialised as a saint by the very monastery which Augustine had founded; her relics were translated from Minster-in-Thanet into the abbey church at Canterbury at the same time as the remains of the 'founding fathers' of Canterbury were re-sited during Wulfric's re-building project carried out between 1047 and 1059.[88] This serves to produce a historiography of sanctity in Anglo-Saxon Kent on a lived and local level—a powerful statement tied to the actions of Christ and the places in which he was memorialised.[89] The imprints become performative relics that both commemorate and monumentalise the moment of the *adventus* of the Church of Rome into Anglo-Saxon England,[90] and create an Anglo-Saxon lineage of sanctity in Kent, while also powerfully recalling the analogous imprint left by Christ at the moment of his ascension, perhaps foreshadowing the ultimate entry into the heavenly

---

[85] Gittos, *Liturgy*, p. 23.
[86] Adomnán, *De Locis Sanctis*, ed. D. Meehan (Dublin, 1958), p. 64–9; Bede, *De Locis Sanctis*, ed. J. Fraipont, in *Itineraria et alia geographica*, Corpus christianorum series latina, 175–6, 2 vols (Turnhout, 1965), vol. 1, pp. 262 4.
[87] R. P. Harrison, *The Dominion of the Dead* (Chicago, 2003), p. 106–23.
[88] St John Hope, 'Recent Discoveries', p. 4–6, 9–11, 13–21; Potts, 'Tombs of the Kings and Archbishops', pp. 100–1; Farmer, 'Augustine's Life and Legacy', pp. 26–31; S. Kelly, The Anglo-Saxon Abbey', in Gem, *St Augustine's Abbey*, pp. 33–49, at p. 48; Gittos, *Liturgy*, p. 25.
[89] For ideas of local sanctity and cult practice see essays in *Local Saints and Local Churches in the Early Medieval West*, ed. A. Thacker and R. Sharpe (Oxford, 2002), and in *Oswald: Northumbrian King to European Saint*, ed. C. Stancliffe and E. Cambridge (Stamford, 1995).
[90] The triumphal connotations are of particular interest here, given the proximity of the monumental tetrapylon which once stood in the centre of the fort of Richborough.

kingdom which would now also be possible for the Anglo-Saxon people through their inclusion in the Universal Church.

Whether this is indeed the case, this mark upon the landscape, which forcibly inscribes the institution of the Church into the landscape, embedding it irrevocably into the rock of England, can be seen as a type of pre-cursor to the sophisticated and highly political use of space implemented in Canterbury once the mission started to restore and rebuild structures. There, Augustine and his monks, with royal support, (re-)constructed a series of churches which are recognised as a conscious act of building deliberately meant to create a 'new' Rome on Kentish soil, 'a focus second to none in importance for the unfolding of the historical process begun by Augustine's mission',[91] and recognised as such by the Anglo-Saxons. As Gem has put it:

> To Bede conversion to Christianity was essentially conversion to the religion of the Roman Church, with its customs and language. This was not the Rome of the remote past that he had in mind, but the continuing Rome centred on the papacy, in continuity with the apostolic past. Against this background, Augustine's [monastery] in the first century may be seen as an essential link in the cultural chain that reattached Anglo-Saxon England to a continental culture.[92]

This link is clearly actualised and perpetuated in the architectural programme implemented in Canterbury—along with the personnel, books, images, furnishings and liturgical objects that were sent to support the mission, the dedications of the early churches, and the symbolic identity systematically created through the shared use of *spolia*, stone, brick, glass and tile as a building material. All combined to form a powerful visual language that served to reproduce 'Rome' in the region.

Of these, the practices and processes of architecture employed by the mission and its successors are perhaps the most visible evidence of the process of building and embedding the history and tradition of the Church into the sacred spaces, sites and structures reclaimed, restored and constructed by the early church founders in Kent. It was certainly distinct from that built elsewhere in Anglo-Saxon England, as is evident, for example, in the early Northumbrian architecture, where expressions of Roman identity are articulated in very different ways.[93] While the Kentish churches, for instance, reuse red Roman brick, setting it in the building fabric of flint rubble or re-used stone from earlier Roman structures to echo the designs picked out by brick in Roman buildings, in Northumbria, where blocks of stone marked Roman structures, it is this material, and not brick, that is used to invoke *romanitas*. Likewise, the churches in Kent share a distinctive Roman architectural vocabulary with the employment of apsed structures, and arches dividing the nave from the chancel. The

---

[91] Gem, 'Towards an Iconography', p. 9.
[92] Gem, 'Towards an Iconography', p. 11.
[93] For an overview of the Northumbrian architecture, see Boulton, 'Conceptualising Sacred Space'; Cramp, this volume.

6. THE ANGLO-SAXON CHURCH IN KENT

use of the eastern apse was widespread, found in Canterbury at St Pancras, Christ Saviour, and possibly St Martin's, and further afield at, Rochester (*c.* 604), Reculver (*c.* 669), Lydd and Lyminge (*c.* 633).[94] It is a spatial layout ubiquitous to the basilicas of early Christian Rome, being seen not just in the Constantinian foundations of Christ Saviour, St Peter's and St Paul's or San Lorenzo *fuori le mura*, but also in subsequent papal foundations, such as Santa Pudenziana (*c.* 400), Santa Sabina (*c.* 420), Santa Maria Maggiore (*c.* 435), SS Cosmas and Damian (526–30), Sant'Agnese *fuori le mura* (625–38), San Marco (792–833), and those of the ninth-century 'revival' in Rome, at Santa Cecelia in Trastevere and Santa Prassede (817–24). This apsidal plan is notably distinct from the two-celled, squared-chancel design favoured in the earliest large-scale stone foundations of Northumbria (at Hexham, Wearmouth and Jarrow),[95] suggesting some significance was intended for the deliberate use of this style across Kent.

With Canterbury replacing London, intended by Gregory as the southern metropolitan of Anglo-Saxon England,[96] the two spaces of Rome and Canterbury become intimately and irrevocably associated with each other, one being actively re-built to overlie and symbolically map the other. The 'ruinous and sparsely populated place' that was Canterbury, made a *romano*-centric rebuilding both possible and probable,[97] as the ex-cantonal capital provided a plethora of Roman fabric with which to construct the new version of Roman *ecclesia*, while the symbolic

---

[94] St Martin's: Routledge, 'St Martin's Church'; Taylor and Taylor, *Anglo-Saxon Architecture*, vol. 1, pp. 143–5. St Pancras: St John Hope, 'Excavations'; Taylor and Taylor, *Anglo-Saxon Architecture*, vol. 1, pp. 146–8. Christ Saviour: see D. Parsons, 'The Pre-Conquest Cathedral at Canterbury', *Arch. Cant.*, 84 (1969), pp. 175–84; K. Blockley, M. Sparks and T. Tatton-Brown, *Canterbury Cathedral Nave: Archaeology, History and Architecture*, Archaeology of Canterbury, n.s., 1 (Canterbury, 1997). Rochester and Reculver: see references in n. 77. Lydd: Livett, 'Lydd Church'; Elliston Erwood, 'Churches of Romney Marsh', 177–90; Taylor and Taylor, *Anglo-Saxon Architecture*, vol. 2, pp. 405–8. Lyminge: R. C. Jenkins, 'The Basilica of Lyminge: Roman, Saxon and Medieval', *Arch. Cant.*, 9 (1874), pp. 205–23; R. C. Jenkins, 'Remarks on the Early Christian Basilicas, in Connection with the Recent Discoveries at Lyminge', *Arch. Cant.*, 10 (1876), pp. ci–ciii; R. C. Jenkins, 'Observations on the Remains of the Basilica of Lyminge', *Arch. Cant.*, 18 (1889), pp. 46–54.

[95] The form of the original east end of Ripon is unknown; for Hexham see E. Gilbert, 'Saint Wilfrid's Church at Hexham', in *Saint Wilfrid at Hexham*, ed. D. Kirby (Newcastle upon Tyne, 1974), pp. 81–113; R. N. Bailey, 'The Abbey church of St Andrew, Hexham', *Archaeological Journal*, 133 (1976), pp. 197–202; E. Cambridge, 'C. C. Hodges and the Nave of Hexham Abbey', *Archaeologia Aeliana*, 5th ser., 7 (1979), pp. 159–68; Izzi, 'Visual Impact of Rome', pp. 105–20, esp. pp. 111–12; for Wearmouth and Jarrow, see R. Cramp, *Wearmouth and Jarrow Monastic Sites*, 2 vols (Swindon, 2005–6); an exception to this can be seen in the small single-cell apsed structure that lay to the east of St Andrew's at Hexham.

[96] Bede, *Historia ecclesiastica*, bk. i, c. 29, ed. Colgrave and Mynors, pp. 104–5, and esp. n. 3.

[97] Editorial, 'The Columns of Reculver Church', *Arch. Cant.*, 3 (1860), pp. 135–6; Dowker, 'Reculver Church'; Taylor and Taylor, *Anglo-Saxon Architecture*, vol. 2, pp. 506–7; Kelly, 'Augustine's Life and Legacy', p. 34.

re-building at Canterbury was a deliberate act carried out at the 'the uttermost part of the earth' (Acts, i, 8), 'completing' the Church in the face of a coming eschatology.[98]

While the inherent *romanitas* of Anglo-Saxon architecture is evident from the design and extant fabric of the surviving buildings, if one knows where, or perhaps more importantly, *how* to look,[99] and becomes quickly apparent when reading the contemporary literature,[100] it is perhaps pertinent here to consider more closely what it means to consciously (re-)build a place in this manner. Place and space are complex constructs and, this being so, despite the striking lack of liturgical evidence for the early Christian milieu of Anglo-Saxon Kent which would provide a more relational understanding of the use of ecclesiastical space, it is nonetheless relevant to ask how the spaces of the Anglo-Saxon church were articulated architecturally. In general (although there are notable exceptions), the churches were two-celled structures which were often apsed, and sometimes had side porticus. These latter features had a consistent architectural identity characterised as squared adjuncts to the main body of the church, accessed both from each other and the church, and although differing widely from the architectural arcading marking the Roman porticus, are widely acknowledged to reference these porticus in their funerary functions: in Anglo-Saxon England the term becomes a functional frame of reference rather than an architectural descriptor. These porticus spaces, which in some instances directly precede the church, as at St Pancras or Lydd, taken together with the evidence for a processional use of these spaces argued for by Ó Carragáin, into and through the long narrow naves lit by deeply set single-splayed windows, the remains of which survive at Reculver,[101] toward the spoliated archways which herald the chancel (as at St Pancras and Reculver—see Figs 6.8b, 6.9a, b), all serve to give a sense of movement through the architectural space of the church, demarcated by architectural features and various forms of threshold, toward the apse and altar. Considered together with the carefully constructed associations with the lineage and authority of the papal city of Rome (which itself drew on a tradition of association with its apostolic foundations produced by the reuse of *spolia*), the pre-existing structures and the choice of dedications which had direct Roman relevance, the churches of Kent may well have been created to embody further symbolic associations: namely, the triumph of the Church, both on earth and in heaven.

The church at Reculver (Fig. 6.9a, b) provides a particularly noteworthy example of this phenomenon, despite its ruined state, as it preserves evidence of the form and

---

98 For summary, see J. Hawkes, 'The Road to Hell: The Art of Damnation in Anglo-Saxon Sculpture', in *Listen, O Isles, unto me: Studies in Medieval Word and Image in honour of Jennifer O'Reilly*, ed. E. Mullins and D. Scully (Cork, 2011), pp. 230–42.

99 See Brook, 'The Saxon Church', particularly p. 302: 'How can such work as this be actually proved to be of Saxon date?'.

100 See also Gem, 'Towards and Iconography'; Hawkes, '*Iuxta Morem Romanorum*', pp. 69–70.

101 Taylor and Taylor, *Anglo-Saxon Architecture*, vol. 2, p. 508.

Fig. 6.8 St Pancras, Canterbury
(a): looking east from the western narthex. (b): view of chancel and base of re-used Roman column.
(© Copyright a: M. Boulton; b: J. Hawkes.)

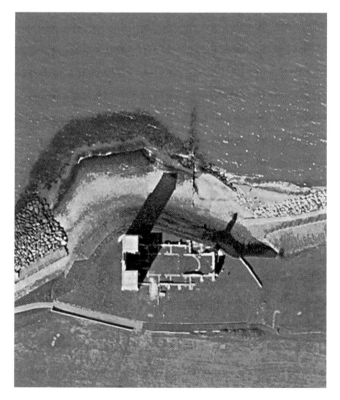 

Fig. 6.9 Reculver

(a): aerial view of the remains of the Anglo-Saxon church.

(b): columns from chancel arch.

(© Copyright
a: Google Earth: 2014 Google;
b: J. Hawkes.)

scale of the triple 'triumphal' arch which separated the nave from the apse, held a clerical bench running around the inner arc of the apse, with the altar set before the arch and flanked by a free-standing 'triumphal column'.[102] Today housed in the crypt of Canterbury cathedral, the columns of the arch are monumental in scale and size, their bases preserving details of their (original Roman) decoration, thus providing a clear insight to the architectural ambition of this church, originally set up in the *principium* area of the Roman shore fort. This complex ecclesiastical space was clearly demarcated internally with an emphasis placed, unsurprisingly, on the east end of the building and although, like most Anglo-Saxon architecture, it is articulated in a manner distinct from the architectural examples of Rome, it nevertheless serves to recall not only the ubiquitous traces of *romanitas*, but also the idea of moving toward a space which is perhaps representative of the wider Universal Church, the institutional identity of other churches across the Christian world, and the metaphysical spaces of the heavenly Jerusalem beyond.

In this respect, the triple opening formed by the columns at Reculver (apparently exceptional in the Anglo-Saxon architectural record in both size and scale) echoes that marking the entry to the courtyard of Old St Peters,[103] itself recalling the triumphal forms of Imperial Rome.[104] This being so, the arch forms a powerful statement about the triumphal 'entry' offered by the Church into salvation, heralding the coming of the New Jerusalem.[105] This possible Jerusalemic reference is noteworthy as the twin earthly centres of Christian authority and history represented by Rome and Jerusalem are both presented on the ecclesiastical landscape of Anglo-Saxon England through the active use of symbolic materials and iconographically resonant architectural forms.

These symbolic significances have begun to be considered as a part of the architectural milieu of the Anglo-Saxon Church. Boulton, for example, has argued for the comprehensive material significance of both Rome and Jerusalem being presented in the early Anglo-Saxon churches in Northumbria,[106] which commonly evoke the Heavenly Jerusalem through symbolic materials and forms and the conceptualisation of place. Likewise, Gittos has noted the potential Jerusalemic symbolism of ecclesiastical structures from the dedication ceremonies of churches.[107] Shapland, too

---

[102] Taylor and Taylor, *Anglo-Saxon Architecture*, pp. 508–9; R. Kozodoy, 'The Reculver Cross', *Archaeologia*, 108 (1986), pp. 67–94; D. Tweddle, M. Biddle and B. Kjølbye-Biddle, *Corpus of Anglo-Saxon Stone Sculpture, 4: South-East England* (Oxford, 1995), pp. 46–61, 138, 151–61, Figs 108–20; Hawkes, 'Anglo-Saxon Legacy', pp. 109–10; Hawkes, 'Church Triumphant: The Figural Columns', pp. 36–41; Hawkes, 'Creating a View', pp. 373–6.

[103] Later replicated by the gateway to the ecclesiastical complex of Lorsch (*c*. 800).

[104] Izzi, 'Visual Impact of Rome', pp. 116–19.

[105] Boulton, 'Conceptualisation of Sacred Space', pp. 233–65.

[106] Boulton, 'Conceptualisation of Sacred Space', pp. 267–325.

[107] Gittos, *Liturgy*, pp. 212–45.

has offered similar explanations of the building materials of wood and stone in the Anglo-Saxon world,[108] suggesting that while stone (deeply ingrained with associations of Rome) and wood (endemic to the Anglo-Saxon tradition of building), present a comprehensive binary division between the materials employed to create secular and scared structures,[109] their use may in fact represent the understanding that these materials have clear and distinct functions in the Anglo-Saxon consciousness, with timber being particularly appropriate for spaces of the living and 'eternal' material of stone being employed to construct spaces which housed God, 'the temporal locus of the eternal Church'.[110] Materials, in modern scholarship, are thus recognised to be imbued with social meaning, employed as conscious acts,[111] to be carefully chosen and employed coherently for their ability to create societal meanings, concepts and even memories.[112]

Considered in the light of such understandings, it may be said that while associations with Rome (expressed through material choices, architectural styles and the replication of dedications) served to lend authority to the Anglo-Saxon Church and determined its liturgical and political identity, associations with Jerusalem, constructed through the implicit triumphalism of these architectural articulations, functioned in a slightly different manner. When the earthly Jerusalem was indicated directly in Anglo-Saxon ecclesiastical space, mainly through references made to the Temple, or the Holy Sepulchre, or through the conceptual association of ecclesiastical triumph and earthly architecture, it was arguably less a matter of denoting earthly authority and power, as did the evocation of Rome; rather, articulations of Jerusalem served to remind the earthly of the unearthly, the temporal of the a-temporal, and the present of the omnipresent. It can thus be suggested that the architecture of the Church in Anglo-Saxon Kent was designed to produce symbolic spaces and references which allowed those encountering them to actualise the disparate sacred spaces across the geographies of the earthly Church: namely, Rome and Jerusalem, and were further intended to render the sacred spaces of the heavenly city present and apparent.

It also seems that this architectural articulation of the City of God, the heavenly Jerusalem, when combined with the vertical emphasis present in the biblical and exegetical texts describing heaven, taken together with the relative scale and height of the ecclesiastical buildings constructed in Anglo-Saxon England by the Church, compared with the vernacular wooden structures, and indeed, considered alongside

---

[108] Shapland, 'Meanings of Timber and Stone'.
[109] See Taylor and Taylor, *Anglo-Saxon Architecture*, vol. 1, pp. 222–6.
[110] Bintley and Shapland, 'Introduction', p. 11.
[111] Shapland, 'Meanings of Timber and Stone', pp. 27–8; See also Hawkes, '*Iuxta Morem Romanorum*'; Boulton, 'Conceptualisation of Sacred Space'.
[112] M. Carruthers, *The Book of Memory: A Study of Memory in Medieval Culture* (Cambridge, 1990); M. Carruthers, *The Craft of Thought: Meditation, Rhetoric, and the Making of Images, 400–1200* (Cambridge, 1998).

the very nomenclature of the 'heavenly' Church itself, all served to lend an illusion of solidity to the abstract space of Heaven for the early Christian community of Kent. As such these spaces and artefacts can be considered as providing important evidence for the 'attitude' and ideas which surrounded the eschatological events that were so prevalent in early Christian theology, providing a coherent system of space and structure in the present which spoke to both an institutional past, and a future 'last time'.[113] Given this, Rome and Jerusalem, and their architectural invocations, must be considered as central in the Anglo-Saxon world view, sharing many of the same attributes and identities and performing similar roles within the C/church, articulating authority and eschatology in the Christian past, present and future.

The Anglo-Saxon Church in Kent remains fundamental to our understanding of the early Church in England, but the ways in which it can be considered to articulate the identity of that institution, symbolically, are clearly extraordinarily rich and complex, invoking the temporal, the spiritual and the salvational by means that involved architectural form, design and material, ensuring that the coming of the Church was a predominant and permanent feature of the earthly landscape of Anglo-Saxon England.

Appendix: The Date Ranges of the Anglo-Saxon Churches of Kent[114]

DATING RANGES

c. 600–*c.* 800	*c.* 950–1100	*c.* 1050–1100
Canterbury, St Martin	Canterbury, St Mildred	Canterbury, St Mildred (cont.)
Canterbury, St Augustine's Abbey:	Cheriton	Canterbury, St Dunstan
St Peter and St Paul	Darenth	Aldington
St Mary	Dover, St Mary's at Castle	Coldred
St Pancras		
Lyminge	Leeds	Lower Halstow
Reculver	Lydd	Kingsdown
Stone by Faversham	Northfleet	Kingston
	Shorne	East Langdon
	Swanscombe	Lullingstone
	West Peckham	Milton Regis
	Wouldham	Orpington
		Paddlesworth
		St Mary at Cliffe
		West Stourmouth
		Willesborough
Whitfield	Whitfield (cont.)	Willmington
Minster-in-Sheppey	Minster-in-Sheppey (cont.)	Minster-in-Sheppey (cont.)

---

[113] *Last Things: Death and the Apocalypse in the Middle Ages*, ed. C. Walker Bynum and P. Freedman (Philadelphia, 2000).

[114] The date ranges are largely those provided by Taylor and Taylor, *Anglo-Saxon Architecture*.

(7)
Landscapes of Conversion Among the Deirans: Lastingham and its Neighbours in the Seventh and Eighth Centuries

RICHARD MORRIS

The subject of this chapter is a group of early medieval monasteries around the Vale of Pickering, most of them in Ryedale in the North Rding of Yorkshire.[1] The size of the group is uncertain, but it included at least six and possibly eleven or more houses, among them several of the earliest Northumbrian houses about which know. Holy men and women appear to have been enshrined within at least three, and at four or five there was a Roman dimension to the place that appears to have mattered at the time. Written records, archaeological evidence and sculpture suggest that the foundations were made from the middle of the seventh into the earlier eighth century; sculpture implies that the majority flourished at least until the mid-ninth.

What could such a group signify, and to whom? How might it be defined, and why was it here rather than in some other part of Northumbria? Indeed, in what sense or senses was it a group at all? Nearness in distance need not equate with closeness in time or association. Conversely, there are signs that several monasteries in other parts of England had close links with houses here: should we be thinking in terms of virtual as well as geographical intimacy? The chapter sets out to explore these matters.[2] It begins by describing the area in which the group is found (Fig. 7.1).

The Vale of Pickering is a low-lying, gently undulating plain in the North Riding that is framed by uplands to the north, west and south, and the Scarborough coast to the east. The Vale's floor is the bed of a former lake, which at fullest extent after the last glacial period had shores extending for some 65 miles (105 km.). Moving clockwise from Seamer, the southern edge of this relict inland coastline is first of chalk on the flank of the Yorkshire Wolds. The western end of the Vale is delimited successively by the Howardian and the Hambleton Hills. The two ranges are

---

[1] For advice, help and discussion leading towards the preparation of this article my thanks go to Lindsay Allason-Jones, Paul Barnwell, Tracey Partida, Tom Pickles, Dominic Powlesland, Sarah Semple, David Stocker, Lorna Watts, and Ian Wood.

[2] Previous explorations of this subject include R. Morris, *Journeys from Jarrow*, Jarrow Lecture 2004 (Jarrow, 2008); I. Wood, 'The Gifts of Wearmouth and Jarrow', in *The Languages of Gift in the Early Middle Ages*, ed. W. Davies and P. Fouracre (Cambridge, 2010), pp. 89–115; and principally I. Wood, 'Monasteries and the Geography of Power in the Age of Bede', *Northern History*, 45 (2008), pp. 11–25.

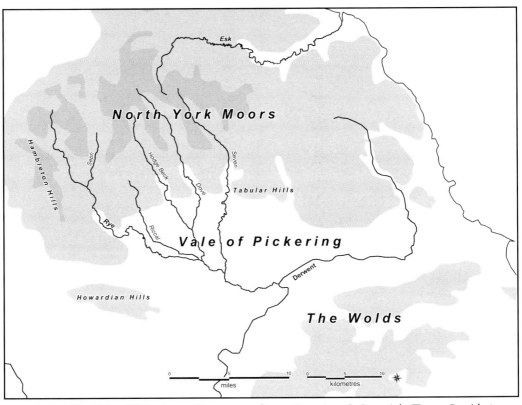

Fig. 7.1 The Vale of Pickering and its surroundings. (Drawing: © Copyright Tracey Partida.)

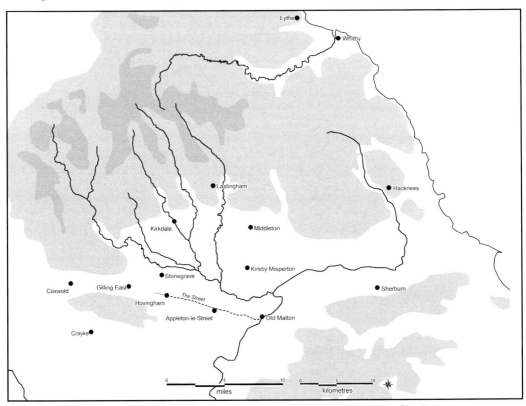

Fig. 7.2 Early-medieval religious houses in and around the Vale of Pickering. (Drawing: © Copyright Tracey Partida.)

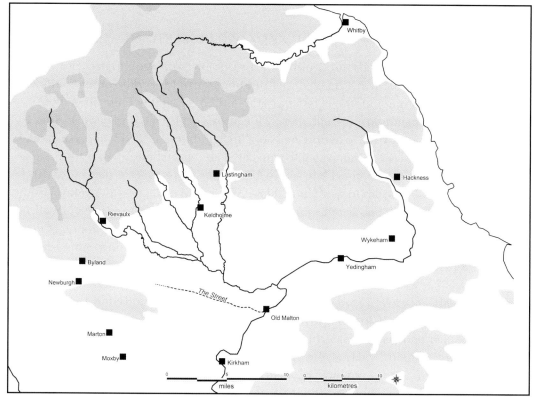

Fig. 7.3 (right) Later-medieval religious houses in and around the Vale of Pickering.
(Drawing: © Copyright Tracey Partida.)

separated by the Coxwold–Gilling gap, a pass about a mile and a half (2.5 km.) wide, created by geological faulting that runs east–west between the Vale of Pickering and the Vale of Mowbray. The Howardians and Hambletons are formed of Jurassic limestones and lime-rich sandstones. Today the area is characterised by secluded hollows, woodlands, designed parkland, and rolling arable on ridges.[3]

The northern rim of the Vale is made up of a series of flattish knolls known locally as a 'nabs'. Their form gives its name to the range: the Tabular Hills. Six of the eight rivers that rise on the North York Moors flow through steep-sided valleys between these hills. The south-eastern Moors are drained by the River Derwent,

[3] K. M. Clayton and A. Straw, *The Geomorphology of the British Isles: Eastern and Central England* (London, 1979), pp. 13–14; J. K. Wright, 'The Stratigraphy of the Yorkshire Corallian', *Proceedings of the Yorkshire Geological Society*, 39 (1972), pp. 225–66; J. K. Wright, 'The Geology of the Corallian ridge (Upper Jurassic) between Gilling East and North Grimston, Howardian Hills, North Yorkshire', *Proceedings of the Yorkshire Geological Society*, 57 (2009), pp. 193–216; Natural England, *National Character Area Profile 29: Howardian Hills* (Sheffield, 2013); G. D. Gaunt and P. C. Buckland, 'The Geological Background to Yorkshire's Archaeology', in *The Archaeology of Yorkshire: An Assessment at the Beginning of the 21st century. Papers Arising out of the Yorkshire Archaeological Framework Forum Conference at Ripon, September 1988*, ed. T. G. Manby, S. Moorhouse and P. Ottaway, Yorkshire Archaeological Society Occasional Paper, 3 (Leeds, 2003), pp. 16–23.

which descends into the Vale of Pickering from Fylingdales Moor through the Forge Valley. At this point the Derwent is but 4 miles (6.5 km.) from the North Sea, but instead of discharging into the sea it sets off inland, first heading west along the Vale. Three miles (5 km.) north east of Malton the Derwent is joined by the River Rye, which flows out of the eastern Moors past Helmsley and is itself joined by the Seph, Riccal, Dove and Seven, all of which emerge through the Tabular Hills. From Malton the Derwent leaves the Vale through a deeply incised winding valley that runs through the Howardian Hills to the plain beyond.

Most of the monasteries to be considered were clustered in the vicinity of Ryedale and the Coxwold–Gilling gap. The exceptions or outliers occur in comparable or otherwise distinctive settings: Hackness is in the valley of the Derwent, for instance, while Kirby Misperton and Crayke are on the summits of small hills (Fig. 7.2).

Ryedale is an area of distinctive character. Historically it was a communications nexus,[4] and productive: resources included arable, sheepwalk, woodland, wetland, stone (for building, sculpture, lime, grinding), jet, and iron.[5] Such a spectrum invites comparison with other sub-regions in which different kinds of asset existed in close proximity and in which monasteries are found in distinctive gatherings. The lower Tyne valley in Northumberland, is one example.[6] The Witham Valley in Lincolnshire is another.[7] Ryedale and the Witham Valley resemble one another in further respects. In each a river breaches a limestone upland; there are different kinds of sheltered place, and whether by coincidence or purpose founders of later medieval religious houses appear somehow to have referenced the presence of communities that existed several centuries previously. In Ryedale this successor group included the Cistercian abbeys of Rievaulx and Byland, the Augustinian house at Newburgh, and the Gilbertine priory at Old Malton. Also nearby were the priories of Marton and Moxby, and—briefly—the Benedictine revival at Lastingham (Fig. 7.3).[8] In Ryedale

---

[4] Morris, *Journeys from Jarrow*, pp. 21–2.
[5] D. J. Harrison *et al.*, *Mineral Resource Information in Support of National, Regional and Local Planning: North Yorkshire (comprising North Yorkshire, Yorkshire Dales and North York Moors National Parks and City of York*, British Geological Survey Commissioned Report CR/04/228N (Nottingham, 2006), 'Building Stone', pp. 15–16.
[6] Morris, *Journeys from Jarrow*, pp. 6-7; Wood, 'Monasteries and Geography of Power', pp. 15–17.
[7] P. Everson and D. Stocker, *Custodians of Continuity? The Premonstratensian Abbey at Barlings and the Landscape of Ritual*, Lincolnshire Archaeology and Heritage Report Series, 11 (Sleaford, 2011), pp. 4–5. For a bibliographical guide to work on all of the Witham monastic sites see P. Everson and D. Stocker, 'The Witham Valley: A Landscape with Monasteries?', *Church Archaeology*, 13 (2009), pp. 1–15.
[8] See now S. Harrison and C. Norton, 'Lastingham and the Architecture of the Benedictine Revival in Northumbria', *Anglo-Norman Studies*, 34 (2012), pp. 63–103 at 63–88.

and the Witham Valley we may encounter behaviours or perceptions that recurred across periods that are normally regarded as discrete.[9]

Peoples and Kingdoms

A Roman military complex and associated settlement existed at Malton from the later first century at least to the fifth. Its contemporary name was probably *Derventio*,[10] which was a familiar place-name in Roman Britain and a word ancestral to the River Derwent that flows through the town. (A case has been made for associating *Derventio* with Stamford Bridge, which gives a better fit with the distance from York given in the Antonine Itinerary and where a candidate settlement has been identified.[11] However, this adjustment would in turn introduce distance errors for the following two stages in the Itinerary. Both places are on the Derwent.) The name was once believed to have been derived from a British word meaning 'water' (cf. Welsh *dwfr*, 'water, river'), but for some years *Derventio* has been widely regarded as a British river name derived from British **dervā*, 'oak'; Ekwall considered it to mean 'river where oaks were common'.[12] *Derventio* is believed to share its root with Deira, which with Bernicia was one of the two main constituent political regions of seventh-century Northumbria. In this case Deira could be understood as 'The Land of the Oaks'. It has been argued that Deira is a forest name,[13] and Peter Hunter Blair remarked that a name deriving from 'water' would have been 'singularly inappropriate to the dry chalk of the Yorkshire Wolds'.[14] 'Land of the Waters', on the other hand, would be apt for an area like Ryedale in which six rivers meet.

Deira and Bernicia are usually conceptualised as kingdoms that were amalgamated during Bede's lifetime to form the greater kingdom of Northumbria.[15] Historians and archaeologists have accordingly tended to look upon Deira and Bernicia as geographical areas, seeking to map their borders, locate their capitals and identify their material correlates.[16] In the process a view has emerged that Deira's

---

[9] Everson and Stocker, *Custodians of Continuity?*, pp. 4, 7; M. Johnson, *Ideas of Landscape* (Oxford, 2006), p. 148.

[10] 'Derventione' (the ablative) in the Antonine Itinerary: A. L. F. Rivet and K. Jackson, 'The British Section of the Antonine Itinerary', *Britannia*, 1 (1970), pp. 34–82, at pp. 40–41.

[11] I. G. Lawton, 'Derventio: A Roman settlement at North Farm Stamford Bridge', *CBA Forum: The Annual Newsletter of CBA Yorkshire* (1994), pp. 8–13; cf. P. D. Horne and I. G. Lawton, 'Buttercrambe Moor Roman Camp, Buttercrambe with Bossall, North Yorkshire', *Britannia*, 29 (1998), pp. 327–9.

[12] E. Ekwall, 'Derwent', *The Concise Oxford Dictionary of English Place-Names*, 4th edn (Oxford, 1966), pp. 142–3.

[13] J. G. F. Hind, 'Elmet and Deira—Forest Names in Yorkshire', *Bulletin of the Board of Celtic Studies*, 28 (1978–80), pp. 541–52.

[14] P. Hunter Blair, *Northumbria in the Days of Bede* (London, 1976), p. 99.

[15] B. A. E. Yorke, *Kings and Kingdoms of Early Anglo-Saxon England* (London, 1990), p. 74.

[16] *Early Deira: Archaeological Studies of the East Riding in the Fourth to Ninth Centuries AD*,

royal city was York, that the province's northern frontier was probably the River Tees,[17] and that the 'original nucleus' was in eastern Yorkshire.[18]

Reservations have been voiced. David Rollason has asked if York really was the Deiran royal capital. He points to ambiguities in evidence for the status of York in the seventh and earlier eighth centuries, and to the fact that most of the key figures mentioned in association with York were ecclesiastical rather than royal.[19] It is the case that Alcuin tells us (as Bede does not) that King Edwin was born in York, and the Anonymous *Life of Gregory the Great* contains a passage that some regard as a depiction of York as a centre of power.[20] But Alcuin made more of the York connection than did Bede, and the purpose of his poem to accentuate York's significance and contribution to the development of an ecclesiastical province invites corresponding care over how it is read.[21] Ian Wood has argued that Deira and Bernicia were not territories with fixed borders at all, but 'fluid entities associated more with power groups'.[22] Wood points out that neither Bede nor other near-contemporary authors used the terms Deira and Bernicia as territorial terms. Bede talked instead of the 'kingdom, region or people of the *Deiri* or the *Bernicii*': that is, he sees the northern kingdom as being divided between two peoples, rather than as being two set regions.[23] Bede took a similar view of Northumbria, tending to refer to it as 'the *provincia*, *regnum* or *gens Northanhymbrorum*, rather than as a geographical entity called Northumbria.'[24] On this understanding, the meaning of 'Deiran' would turn less on where you lived than to whom you were related or whom you followed. This would allow intercalation between Deirans and Bernicians rather

---

ed. H. Geake and J. Kenny (Oxford, 2000); J. Lang, *The Anglian Sculpture of Deira: The Classical Tradition*, Jarrow Lecture 1990 (Jarrow, 1990).

[17] P. Hunter Blair, 'The Boundary between Bernicia and Deira', *Archaeologia Aeliana*, 4th ser. 27 (1949), pp. 46–59, reprinted in P. Hunter Blair, *Anglo-Saxon Northumbria* (London, 1984); Yorke, *Kings and Kingdoms*, p. 74.

[18] Yorke, *Kings and Kingdoms*, p. 74.

[19] D. Rollason, *Northumbria, 500–1100: Creation and Destruction of a Kingdom* (Cambridge, 2003), pp. 202–7.

[20] Alcuin, 'Versus de Patribus, Regibus et Sanctis Euboricensis Ecclesiae', ed. P. Godman, *Alcuin: The Bishops, Kings and Saints of York* (Oxford, 1982); *The Earliest Life of Gregory the Great*, ed. B. Colgrave (Cambridge, 1968), pp. 96–7; but see Rollason, *Northumbria 500–1100*, pp. 77–9.

[21] S. Ward, 'Church and State in Eighth-Century Northumbria: Alcuin's York poem', *Archaeologia Aeliana*, 5 ser. 41 (2012), pp. 217–36.

[22] F. Orton and I. Wood with C. A. Lees, 'Bernicii and Deiri', in *Fragments of History: Rethinking the Ruthwell and Bewcastle Monuments* (Manchester 2007), pp. 108–10; Wood, 'Monasteries and Geography of Power', pp. 11–13.

[23] Wood, 'Monasteries and Geography of Power', p. 11–12.

[24] Wood, 'Monasteries and Geography of Power', p. 12.

than their mutual exclusion either side of a frontier, and for fluctuations in that pattern as time passed.

Such interplay would have implications for the ways in and reasons for which religious houses were founded. The establishment of a monastery required the transfer of land in perpetuity. Hence, if we agree (following Ian Wood and Walter Goffart) that 'the main narrative sources of Bede's day are best seen as aspects of a debate, in which rival monastic communities—essentially Lindisfarne (Northumberland), Hexham (Northumberland) and Ripon (West Riding of Yorkshire), and Wearmouth and Jarrow (Durham)—attempted to interpret the recent past to their own ends', then the places in which such communities were put, and in what numbers, will be significant.[25]

Monasteries were both landlords and places of dynastic memorialisation. They were thus points where different kinds of temporal and spiritual power were aligned to particular interests. King Oswiu's gift of twelve 10-hide estates to enable monks to engage in continuous 'heavenly warfare' recalls the practice of *laus perennis* whereby relays of choirs provided unbroken adoration.[26] The giving of such praise would benefit the rule of the king who made it possible. And 'when kings and aristocrats founded monasteries they may have thought primarily of their own souls [...] but they certainly had an eye on the foundations set up by their predecessors and their neighbours.'[27] Such competition would in turn give circumstance for the varied motives that are attributed to royal founders. We hear of monasteries being instituted as thank offerings, for atonement, as prayer houses, as memorials, as stopping places, as gifts, as cenotaphs. A geographical cluster or characteristic grouping of monasteries should thus denote an area or type of landscape in which royal leaders and their relatives took sustained and active interest.[28] On this basis, the coast and estuaries were of keen interest to the Anglo-Saxon ruling class.[29] The mouths of Northumbria's rivers Tyne, Tees, Esk and Humber were all overlooked by monasteries, each headed by royal kinsfolk who were well placed to monitor comings, goings and trade. And between 650 and 750 at least five different kings are named in connection with monasteries in and around Ryedale.[30]

---

[25] Wood, 'Monasteries and Geography of Power', p. 14; W. Goffart, *The Narrators of Barbarian History (AD 550–800): Jordanes, Gregory of Tours, Bede, and Paul the Deacon* (Princeton, 1988), pp. 235–328.

[26] Bede, *Historia ecclesiastica gentis Anglorum*, ed. C. Plummer, *Venerabilis Baedae Opera Historica*, 2 vols (Oxford, 1896), bk. iii, c. 24. Six of the estates were 'in the province of the Deirans, and six in that of the Bernicians'.

[27] Wood, 'Monasteries and Geography of Power', p. 15.

[28] Cf. J. Blair, *The Church in Anglo-Saxon Society* (Oxford, 2005), pp. 84–8.

[29] R. Morris, *Churches in the Landscape* (London, 1989), p. 11, Fig. 3.

[30] Æthelwald, Oswiu, Ecgfrith, Eadbert, Æthelwald Moll: Wood, 'Monasteries and Geography of Power', p. 18.

Defining the Group

Evidence for earlier monastic character varies in type and strength. It is at its fullest for places where textual evidence, sculpture of relevant date and archaeology occur together and are mutually reinforcing.[31] This is the case at Lastingham and Crayke. Stonegrave and Hackness are witnessed by text and sculpture; Hovingham and Kirkdale by sculpture and archaeology; Coxwold by written record alone. In three cases—Gilling East, Kirby Misperton, and Sherburn—the case for monastic origin awaits clarification, while the presence of early sculpture at Middleton-by-Pickering will be argued to be the result of later redistribution. New evidence may sharpen or add to the picture, as it recently has at Hovingham and Sherburn (see below). Evidence for all these sites will now be introduced.

Lastingham

Lastingham lies in a sheltered hollow on the boundary between the Tabular Hills and the North York Moors (see Colour Plate 7.4). According to Bede a monastery was established here in the first half of the 650s at the instigation of Æthelwald, King Oswald's son, who ruled over the people of Deira from around 651. Bede reports that Æthelwald wished the monastery to be a place to which he might often 'come to pray and hear the Word and where he might be buried'.[32] Æthelwald disappears from the record after the battle of *Winwaed* (655);[33] it is reasonable to assume that the monastery came into being while he was still on the scene.

Æthelwald entrusted the formation of the community to Cedd, the brother of his priest, Cælin, and asked Cedd to accept a grant of land for the purpose. Bede records that it was the custom of Cedd's teacher (Aidan) to purify land so given by prayer and fasting.[34] At the start of Lent Cedd set out to cleanse the place, doing so with the king's permission. In the fifth week of Lent, Bede says, Æthelwald called for Cedd's attendance. Cedd obeyed, delegating completion of the consecration rite to another of his brothers, Cynebill. Cynebill, like Cedd, Caelin and a fourth brother, Ceadda, was an ordained priest. As boys the four had been educated at Lindisfarne, whereafter Cedd and Ceadda, at least, had travelled in Ireland.

---

[31] For seventh- to ninth-century sculpture at churches mentioned see J. Lang, *Corpus of Anglo-Saxon Stone Sculpture*, vol. 3: *York and Eastern Yorkshire* (Oxford, 1991), p. 133 (Gilling East 1); pp. 145–8 (Hovingham 3, 4, 5); pp. 153–4 (Kirby Misperton 1, 2, 3); pp. 157–8 (Kirkbymoorside 6); pp. 161–3 (Kirkdale 7, 8); pp. 168–74 (Lastingham 3–5, 7–12); p.187 (Middleton 9); pp. 201–6 (Sherburn 1–10).

[32] Bede, *Historia ecclesiastica*, bk iii, c. 23; T. M. Charles-Edwards, 'The Foundation of Lastingham', *The Ryedale Historian*, 7 (1974), pp. 13–21; R. Morris, '"Calami et iunci": Lastingham in the Seventh and Eighth Centuries', *International Bulletin of Medieval Research*, 11 (2005), pp. 3–21.

[33] A. Breeze, 'The Battle of *Uinued* and the River Went, Yorkshire', *Northern History* 41 (2004), pp. 377–83.

[34] Bede, *Historia ecclesiastica*, bk iii, c. 23.

7. LANDSCAPES OF CONVERSION AMONGST THE DEIRANS

Cedd and Ceadda played conspicuous roles in the conversion of different parts of England. Cedd, in addition to being abbot of Lastingham, was bishop of the East Saxons and ruled at least two communities in Essex, *Ythancæstir* and Tilbury.[35] Bede records that in 653 Cedd had been seconded to the leader of the Middle Angles for purposes of evangelisation.[36] A little later, King Oswiu of Northumbria sent him to preach to the East Saxons, to which purpose Finan, bishop of Lindisfarne, made him bishop.[37] It was during this ministry to East Anglia and Essex that Lastingham was founded. Following Cedd's death in 664 Ceadda succeeded him as abbot of Lastingham. Ceadda subsequently became bishop of York, later bishop of Lichfield (Staffordshire) and father of a monastery in Lindsey called *Adbaruae*, made possible by a royal grant of land.[38] Ceadda appears to have remained abbot of Lastingham throughout, and members of the Lastingham community accompanied him to Lichfield. These houses have often been regarded as separate entities founded at different stages in their fathers' careers. However, there are strong indications that members of communities ruled by Cedd and Ceadda in different parts of England thought of themselves as belonging to one community.[39] For example, we are told by Bede that shortly before his death Ceadda summoned the brethren at Lichfield. 'When they had come, he first of all urged them to live virtuously in love and peace with each other and with all the faithful; also to follow with unwearied constancy the Rule of life which he had taught them and which they had seen him carry out, or had learned from the words and deeds of the fathers who had gone before.'[40] Through the practical carrying out of the rule each brother was bound to the others regardless of distance, and emulation of the father meant that he lived on after his death through the daily re-enactment of his example. Bede's account of Ceadda's house at *Adbaruae* records that *vestigia* of Ceadda's rule of life were still evident in Bede's own day, eighty years later.[41] *Vestigia* has sometimes been translated as 'traces', with an implication of backsliding from original rigour. However, the underlying meaning of *vestigia* is 'footsteps' and Bede's intended sense was surely the opposite to lapsing: what he meant was that members of the community of *Adbaruae* still lived and behaved as their father had taught them. In this recollection we meet steadfastness and continuity, not decay. At *Adbaruae* Bede recognised a living link with the days of Aidan.

---

[35] Bede, *Historia ecclesiastica*, bk iii, c. 22.
[36] Bede, *Historia ecclesiastica*, bk iii, c. 21.
[37] Bede, *Historia ecclesiastica*, bk iii, c. 22.
[38] Bede, *Historia ecclesiastica*, bk iii, c. 23.
[39] Bede, *Historia ecclesiastica*, bk iv, c. 3; bk iii, c. 23.
[40] Bede, *Historia ecclesiastica*, bk iv, c. 3, translation from *Bede's Ecclesiastical History of the English People*, ed. B. Colgrave and R. A. B. Mynors (Oxford, 1969), p. 341.
[41] Bede, *Historia ecclesiastica*, bk iv, c. 3.

Ceadda died at Lichfield in 672. We are told that he was first buried close to the church of St Mary and later translated into the new-built church of St Peter.[42] The progress of Cedd's remains to a final resting place was likewise staged. According to Bede he was first buried outside ('Qui primo quidem foris sepultus est'). After some time 'a church was built of stone in the monastery in honour of the Mother of God'. Cedd's body was buried 'on the right side of the altar' of this church.[43] A subsequent translation, to Lichfield, undated and unremarked, is implied by Cedd's presence in the List of Saints' Resting Places that appears in two eleventh-century manuscripts. David Rollason has shown that the list as we have it combines several earlier sources,[44] the oldest of which contains the names of saints who lived between the seventh and later ninth century (the latest is probably St Edmund, d. 869). It is in this primary portion of the list that Cedd appears with his brother Ceadda, and an otherwise unknown saint called Ceatta.[45] Given these circumstances Cedd's translation must have taken place after the 730s (when Bede still has him at Lastingham) and the early tenth century (by which period the early part of the list seems likely to have been in existence). Given the argument above about the existence of a 'Lastingham Connexion', we can suggest that in taking this step it may have been imagined that Cedd was less being removed from Lastingham so much as transferred from one room of a virtual mansion to another (see further below).

Bede's description of the cleansing ritual undertaken by Cedd has attracted a considerable literature.[46] The fact that such a ceremony had been learned from Aidan does not necessarily make it Irish practice: little is known about purification ritual for newly received places in the seventh century; it is possible that such actions had a longer and broader context. At Lastingham, however, there may have been special

[42] Bede, *Historia ecclesiastica*, bk iv, c. 3.
[43] Bede, *Historia ecclesiastica*, bk iii, c. 23.
[44] D. Rollason, 'Lists of Saints' Resting-places in Anglo-Saxon England', *Anglo-Saxon England*, 7 (1978), pp. 61–94 at pp. 61–2. The Old English homily on St Chad in Oxford, Bodleian, MS. Hatton 116, is considered to be a product of no later than the early tenth century: J. M. Bately, 'Old English Prose Before and During the Reign of Alfred', *Anglo-Saxon England*, 17 (1988), pp. 93–138; A. Sargent, 'Lichfield and the Lands of St Chad', PhD thesis, University of Keele (2012), pp. 97–100.
[45] Ceatta could duplicate Ceadda: see J. Blair, 'A Handlist of Anglo-Saxon Saints', in *Local Saints and Local Churches in the Early Medieval West*, ed. A. Thacker and R. Sharpe (Oxford, 2002), pp. 495–565 at p. 520; however, relics believed to include bones of Ceadda were sequestered in 1538, variously held in the seventeenth and eighteenth centuries, and passed to the Roman Catholic cathedral of St Chad in Birmingham in 1841. Osteological analysis and radiocarbon determinations have identified the remains as deriving from at least three individuals, two probably from the seventh century and one from the eighth: M. W. Greenslade, *Saint Chad of Lichfield and Birmingham*, Archdiocese of Birmingham Historical Commission (Birmingham, 1996), pp. 14–17.
[46] Blair, *Church in Anglo-Saxon Society*, pp. 182–6 (with further references) and 191–5.

7. LANDSCAPES OF CONVERSION AMONGST THE DEIRANS

reason to cleanse (see below), while the need for a conventional cleansing routine may itself have been a consequence of so many new monastic sites being established on sites of previous ritual significance.[47] A question about Cedd's ritual concerns the scale at which it was undertaken. Did cleansing focus on the site of the intended buildings, or did it extend more widely? The question is worth pursuit. Bede drew attention to the 'high desert hills' surrounding Lastingham in a way that emphasises the setting as harsh and dangerous when in reality the church itself 'nestles comfortably in a sheltered stream valley'.[48] On one level the 'high desert hills' may simply be wilderness topos, but the description needs to be considered in the context of Bede's close links with the community. In the Preface to his *Ecclesiastical History* Bede records that the brethren at Lastingham had provided information about the conversion of the Mercians, about the restoration of faith in Essex, and about the ministries and deaths of Cedd and Ceadda. One of Lastingham's monks, Trumberht, was among those who had taught Bede the scriptures, and Trumberht had himself been educated in the monastery during the time of Ceadda's abbacy.[49] Andrew Sargent notes that an extraction of all references to Cedd and Ceadda from Bede's work points to the existence of a 'history' of these first two abbots, composed before 731, 'possibly in response to Bede's request for information'. Such a putative history 'bears comparison with Bede's *Historia Abbatum* (and the earlier anonymous version) of Wearmouth-Jarrow, or with the house chronicle that informed Bede's narrations concerning the minster at Barking, or with that represented by the Kentish Royal Legend'.[50]

Given that Bede was so well informed about Lastingham we should look for significance in what he says about it. Recent observations on Spaunton Moor just above the village may provide a context for doing so.[51] On the north side of the eleventh-century crypt under the church is a doorway that leads into a short vaulted passage. The original function of the passage is uncertain; it may never have been more than a side chamber.[52] However, in the early nineteenth century it was 'traditionally reported to have led to Stone Houghs, three hills, or barrows, at between

---

[47] D. Stocker and P. Everson, 'The Straight and Narrow Way: Fenland Causeways and the Conversion of the Landscape in the Witham Valley, Lincolnshire', in *The Cross Goes North: Processes of Conversion in Northern Europe, AD 300–1300*, ed. M. Carver (Woodbridge, 2003), pp. 271–88; Everson and Stocker, *Custodians of Continuity?*.

[48] Bede, *Historia ecclesiastica*, bk iii, c. 23; Blair, *Church in Anglo-Saxon Society*, p. 194.

[49] Bede, *Historia ecclesiastica*, Preface; bk iv, c. 3.

[50] Sargent, 'Lichfield and the Lands of St Chad', p. 67; A. Breeze, 'Bede's Castella and the Journeys of St Chad', *Northern History*, 46 (2009), pp. 137–9, points to a specific sign of Bede's reliance on a written source provided by Lastingham.

[51] R. Morris, 'Calvary by Rosedale Chimney', in *Making Christian Landscapes in the Early Medieval Atlantic World*, ed. T. Ó Carragáin and S. Turner (Cork: forthcoming).

[52] Norton and Harrison, 'Lastingham and Architecture of Benedictine revival', p. 75.

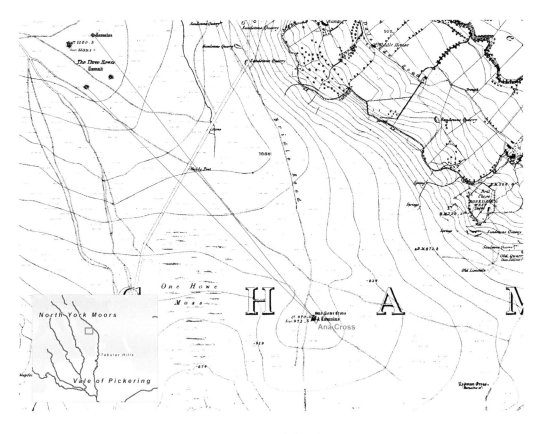

Fig. 7.5 Ana Cross and the Three Howes.
(Drawing: © Copyright Tracey Partida, based on first edition of Ordnance Survey.)

two and three miles distance.'[53] The 'howes' are a group of Bronze Age barrows that lie 2.5 miles (4 km.) north of the church on Spaunton Moor, close to Rosedale Chimney. They are known locally as the 'Three Howes'. The initial question is why they acquired this name, since on-the-spot inspection and mapping at least since the first edition of the Ordnance Survey show four of them, while on approach across Spaunton Moor one can only see two. Only from one point on Spaunton Moor, apparently, can three howes be seen: this is from a monument called Ana Cross that stands on a tumulus beside a track leading up onto the moor from Lastingham village. The name appears to derive from that of the tumulus on which it stands: Ainhowe. The effect is dramatic: as a walker approaches Ana Cross only two barrows can be seen on the skyline, but as one arrives at Anacross a third mound appears. The essence of the moment is that one has been granted a vision. It seems to follow, then, that Ana Cross stands where it does because Ainhowe is the one place from which the Three Howes can be seen (Fig. 7.5). This may explain the name Ainhowe, which is assumed

[53] J. Britton, *The Architectural Antiquities of Great Britain, Represented and Illustrated in a Series of Views, Elevations, Plans, Sections, and Details, of Ancient English Edifices: With Historical and Descriptive Accounts of Each*, 5 vols (London, 1807–26), vol. 5, p. 200.

to derive from Old English *ān*, 'one', the one being in contradistinction to the three. The same conclusion applies to the name 'Three Howes' for a group of four of which only two are ordinarily visible.

The existing Ana Cross is a recent replacement of an older monument, itself successor to an earlier head which following damage was removed for safekeeping in the crypt of Lastingham church. The link between the monument and the church suggests a longstanding connection between the two, as does the name of the area through which runs the track that connects them: Holiday Hill.

When these things are put together a hypothesis emerges: Ana Cross marks a place whereat an observer is granted a vision of Calvary—an image particularly appropriate at the end of Lent, and one that is, incidentally, suggested in variant forms in the imagery on some coinage that circulated among Deirans in the eighth century.[54] The possibility of liturgical journeys from the monastery up onto the moor on certain holy days is hinted by the name of the intervening area, while the tradition of sequestering the heads of worn-out crosses in the church invites consideration of the original functions and locations of parts of yet older cross heads that are kept there. Among them is a cross head dating from around 800 that from its size implies a complete monument that stood above 25 feet (7.5 m) tall.[55] While we cannot, of course, suggest that this might be a pre-existing version of Ana Cross, its weathering and subsequent wear allows us to say that in the later eighth or the ninth century it stood on an exposed site with one side facing the prevailing wind.

Bede's account of the death of Ceadda supports a connection between the church and the vicinity of Ana Cross in another, unlooked for, way. A week before Ceadda's death at Lichfield, Bede relates, a monk called Owine beheld a vision of singing angels. Owine had accompanied Ceadda from Lastingham to form the offshoot community at Lichfield, and had previously worked as a royal official for Queen Æthelthryth in East Anglia.[56] Owine reported the vision to Ceadda, who interpreted it as a sign of his own impending death that had been granted to enable him to prepare for it.[57] A similar premonition was recorded in Ireland. Supernatural warning of death was a sign of sanctity. A sub-text of the vision is that the brotherhood of Lichfield and Lastingham were one. At this point Bede introduced an anecdote about Ceadda that had been told to him by Trumberht, the Lastingham-educated monk who had been one of Bede's tutors. The memory concerned Ceadda's reactions to extreme weather at Lastingham. A high wind would cause him 'to invoke the mercy

---

[54] T. Abramson, *Sceatta List: An Illustrated and Priced Catalogue of Sceats for Collectors* (Leeds, 2012), pp. 166–82; see also pp. 130–1, 141–2, 154–6.
[55] Lang, *Corpus*, Lastingham 3, and see note 30.
[56] Bede, *Historia ecclesiastica*, bk iv, c. 3.
[57] For the construction and sources of this narrative see Sargent, 'Lichfield and the Lands of St Chad', pp. 77–8.

of the Lord'; in the presence of a gale he would prostrate himself in prayer; in a thunderstorm he would go into the church and with 'still deeper concentration' would 'devote himself to prayers and psalms until the sky cleared'. When members of the community asked Ceadda why he behaved thus he would remind them of the biblical symbolism of lightning and thunder. The Lord is one who 'hurls the lightnings'; thunder reminds us of our future judgment; disturbance of the sky is akin to threat followed by mercy.[58] The flank of Rosedale beside Ana Cross and the Three Howes is rich in ironstone.[59] The iron is close to the surface and has magnetic properties unique in the region. The area regularly attracts lightning strikes. Holiday Hill thus emerges as a place both of visions and of divine gestures. The phenomenological properties of these 'high desert hills' perhaps help to explain Cedd's interest in the area, and why Bede's account of Ceadda's last moments turns into a meditation on the devotional meaning of lightning.

The name 'Lastingham' may link to this wider picture, albeit in yet another direction. The original form *Læstinga ēg* 'the island of the people of the *Læstingas*', later changed to *Læstingahām*, can hardly apply to site of the present village.[60] However, the medieval parish of Lastingham was a huge elongated area running more than 15 miles (24 km.) from the central upland of the North York Moors down through the Tabular Hills and into the Vale of Pickering. Townships within this *Ur*-district included Middleton-by-Pickering and Kirby Misperton, both of became parishes in their own right. More on Middleton below; here we note (following David Stocker) that Kirby Misperton is situated on a low hillock of Kimmeridge Clay, surrounded by streams, wetland and carr—and that it is a former island in Lake Pickering. In the early middle ages it would have been seen as an *ēg*, and its position within the area that was later parochially delineated as 'Lastingham' points to its status as a component of the 'grant of land' ('possessionem terrae') made over to Cedd by Æthelwald around 654. Hence, while the home monastery was over 7 miles (11 km.) to the north the area initially assigned to it took in a cross-section of rural resources from the Vale floor up onto the Moors. This argument about the place-name Lastingham originally referring to an island within the wider territory of a 'people' parallels the argument made by Stocker and Everson about the place-name 'Barlings' in the Witham valley.[61] In some sense, then, 'Lastingham' applied to a constellation of places and landscape types that in later centuries became separated out—although in 1086 Stephen, Abbot of St Mary's, York, lately transferred from Lastingham, was

---

[58] Bede, *Historia ecclesiastica*, bk iv, c. 3.
[59] S. Chapman, *Rosedale and its Ironstone Mines* (Cleveland, 2004); R. H. Hayes and J. G. Rutter, *Rosedale Mines and Railway*, Scarborough and District Archaeological Society Research Report, 9 (Scarborough, 1974).
[60] Eillert Ekwall, *English Place-Names In* –Ing, 2nd edn (Lund, 1962), p. 155.
[61] Everson and Stocker, *Custodians of Continuity?*, pp. 380–1.

7. LANDSCAPES OF CONVERSION AMONGST THE DEIRANS

holding land in this *Chirchebi* as well as retaining Lastingham itself.[62] Several pieces of sculpture bolster the proposition that Kirby Misperton forms part of the early story. Three of them are described and discussed in the *Corpus of Anglo-Saxon Stone Sculpture*, where part of a cross shaft (now in the Yorkshire Museum) and part of a cross or impost built into the north wall of the church are assigned to the ninth century.[63] A fourth item seems not previously to have been discussed; it is built into the exterior of the east wall of the chancel, where a four-petalled equal-armed cross encircled by a double border appears on an ashlar. The ashlar has been cut from some larger feature, which to judge from the form of the carving is very early indeed, perhaps of the age of Bede.

There was also a Roman dimension to Cedd's Lastingham. The collection of carved stones held in the church includes two stones of Roman origin.[64] One is a dumpy, free-standing pillar with a simple chamfered plinth is at the base and a more complex moulding to delineate the capital platform. The pillar has been broken into two. If the parts are refitted they reconstruct as a statue base. The presence of such an object invites consideration of the underlying character of the site. The church stands on the edge of a bluff (an exposure of rock is still visible at the south-east side of the churchyard) overlooking a fast flowing stream. A lesser flow emerges from the churchyard itself. The working hypothesis is that in later prehistory this was a nemeton involving a water cult, that this was subsequently Romanised and then re-adopted for monastic use in the mid-seventh century. Such a past would give further context for Cedd's zeal for cleansing the site.

In a second phase, the stone was re-cut for a new use. The length of column between capital and the base was hollowed out while the front face was carefully pierced. The former pillar thus became the architrave for an opening. In this second use the external embrasure was treated with a continuous neat chamfer, and provision was made for a bar or grille to be inserted across the opening. This adaptation of the pillar is not in itself datable, although a potential context for the new barred opening is outlined below.

The other stone was originally part of the base of a parallel-sided sarcophagus. It is now in four abutting pieces. What survives is a portion of the sarcophagus floor with stubs of its cut-down walls rising to either side. The survival of this piece derives from its reworking as a vesica-shaped embrasure that was once fitted with shutters and set upright within a larger structure. From the well-detailed scale of this feature,

---

[62] Domesday Book, vol. 1, f. 314; J. Burton, *The Monastic Order in Yorkshire 1069–1215* (Cambridge, 1999), pp. 39–40.

[63] See note 30.

[64] This is a preliminary and outline account. Publication of these and other discoveries will follow in David Stocker, Richard Morris and Dominic Powlesland, *Ritual in Ryedale*, forthcoming. Descriptions of the stones given here are based on David Stocker's work.

the smooth finish on the outer face and lack of splay in the opening it is likely that the vesica opening fitted into an item of furniture or screen rather than a wall.

Reassessment of two of Lastingham's pre-Conquest carved stones (Lastingham 7 and 8 in the *Corpus of Anglo-Saxon Stone Sculpture*) provides a setting for the embrasure. Lastingham 8 is a re-cut length of rebated stone decorated with finely carved plant scroll, dated by Lang to the later eighth century and interpreted by him as part of a door frame. Lastingham 7 is a length of stone with carving on one long face, identified by Lang (who was following Collingwood) as 'probably a lintel or jamb from a doorway'.[65] Both stones are broken and have seen secondary use. Lang's interpretations of their function are problematic. The rebate on Lastingham 8, for example, is in the wrong place for a door jamb: if it were such then the door would open outwards, away from the embrasure, and such a door would close flush against the front face of the jamb, which is unlikely. Moreover, the door's leaf would be implausibly thin: at just over 1½ inches (40 mm) there are no contemporary significant doors as slim as this.

Re-examination of the stones indicates that they derive not from a building but were parts of a shrine composed of carved stone panels supported by upright carved stone posts, all standing on a boldly decorated sculpted plinth.[66] The detailed argument will be given in the substantive publication but the methodology has involved measurement of the widths and techniques of tooling on the primary surfaces of both stones (providing information about contemporaneity or difference of workmanship), deductions about thicknesses of panels enabled by study of the positions of scribed setting-out lines, the manner of breakage, measurement and comparison of rebate widths, signs of counter-rebating and abrasion to do with the seating of absent components. While there is room for debate about the exact form of reconstruction, the cumulative weight of the observations leaves little doubt that Lastingham 7 and 8, and the vesica were structurally connected, and that their context was a piece of furniture. The vesica, with its connotations of Christ in Majesty, Revelation and the End of Time, would be wholly appropriate as an aperture through which pilgrims might be granted a view of relics within (the shutters implying that this was granted on special occasions), or through which to reach for a pinch of dust irradiated by the saint's *virtus*. On style critical grounds the shrine is likely to have been created after *c.* 750. If Cedd was its occupant then a second translation is implied. There is striking correspondence with Bede's description of Ceadda's earlier interral in 'sepulchra tumba lignea in modum domuncili facta' ('in a wooden tomb/coffin made in the form of a little house'), with an opening in the side.[67]

---

[65] Lang, *Corpus*, pp. 170–1; Lang, *Anglian Sculpture of Deira*, pp. 6–7.
[66] Stocker *et al.*, *Ritual in Ryedale*.
[67] Bede, *Historia ecclesiastica*, bk iv, c. 3; J. Blair, 'A Saint for Every Minster? Local Cults in Anglo-Saxon England', in *Local Saints and Local Churches*, pp. 455–94, at p. 491.

7. LANDSCAPES OF CONVERSION AMONGST THE DEIRANS

To summarise: Lastingham's foundation was at royal behest, its consecration was under royal control, it was at a place where royal messengers came and went, and a key ceremony could be interrupted by secular command. Lastingham thus looks to be a counterpart to a nearby royal centre, as Lindisfarne was to Bamburgh (Northumberland). At the least we should see the area as having been much frequented by the Deiran elite.

Archaeology and landscape add detail. The re-use of the statue base suggests that the site Cedd chose was on or near a Romano-British shrine. The only other prospective context for such a feature would be civic or military, which would imply a substantial Romanised settlement like Malton, York, or Hovingham (see below). It is unlikely that such a piece would have been brought so far. We are left with the probability of a cult site in the vicinity. Evidence reinforcing this is in the walls of the western portion of the eleventh-century crypt, where the size, dressing and proportion of many stones suggests that they were taken from a Roman building. If we are further correct in our suspicion that the vesica embrasure was cut from a Roman rather than an early medieval sarcophagus, then it would also appear that at least one burial was made at or near the shrine. All of this would be consistent with Bede's account of Cedd's Lenten work of prayer and fasting to purify the site. In the surrounding landscape there are indications of special places: the positioning of a great cross at a point wherefrom there was a unique view of a scene that represented the crucifixion, and around which—we now guess for geochemical reasons—God often reminded the community that 'He will come in the clouds in great power and majesty, to judge the living and the dead, while the heavens and the earth are aflame.'[68]

The Neighbours

Crayke occupies a small but prominent hill about 12 miles (19 km.) north of York and four miles south of the western entrance to the pass that runs between the Hambleton and Howardian ranges—the Coxwold–Gilling gap. There are long views from the summit. The place-name is British (the *Creic* in Domesday Book is alike to Old Welsh *creic*, 'a rock'). The presence of a religious house here at least from the eighth century is indicated by a number of sources. Limited archaeological excavation has traced a sequence that included a cemetery on the hilltop containing burials made between *c.* 700 and 1100. The monastery was apparently slightly downslope (see Colour Plate 7.6).[69] Associated sculpture includes fragments of a cross arm and a ninth-century shaft. Alcuin's poem about the bishops and saints of York mentions Eccha, an anchorite of prophetic mind who died here in 767 and is remembered in the

---

[68] Bede, *Historia ecclesiastica*, bk iv, c. 3, translation from Colgrave and Mynors, citing Luke, xxi, 27; II Timothy, iv, 1; II Peter, iii, 12.

[69] K. A. Adams, 'Monastery and Village at Crayke, North Yorkshire', *Yorkshire Archaeological Journal*, 62 (1990), pp. 29–50

core list of the *Liber Vitae* of Durham.[70] According to a later source Crayke was given to Cuthbert by King Ecgfrith as a staging point to assist the saint on visits to York.[71] *Adbaruae* served a similar purpose for Ceadda between Lastingham and Lichfield. Survival of a community at least until the late ninth century is indicated by its status as one of the places in the travels of Cuthbert's relics between 875 and 883. The village and its fields may have been laid out in the late Saxon period, giving rise to an assumption that the monastery had by then been abandoned. However, given Crayke's status as a Durham outpost, and the nature of the Durham community itself in the later tenth and eleventh century, perhaps no hard-and-fast distinction between an ecclesiastical and secular settlement should be assumed. Crayke's later medieval parish traces the circuit of a surrounding zone more or less concentric to the hill that must be older and could go back to the claimed grant of land in the 680s.[72] Crayke's link with the community was sustained beyond the middle ages: the bishops of Durham held a fortified manor on the hill, the parish remained part of the Diocese of Durham until 1837, and part of the Palatinate and County of Durham until 1844.[73]

Less than three hours' walk from Crayke were three, possibly four, monasteries sited along the length of the Coxwold–Gilling gap. The existence of two, *Staningagrave* (Stonegrave) and *Cuchawalda* (Coxwold), is attested by a papal letter written in reply to a grievance lodged by an Abbot Forthred in 757–8.[74] Forthred had complained that Eadberht (king of Northumbria 737–58) and Ecgberht (archbishop of York 735–66—Eadberht's brother) had dispossessed him of three monasteries—the third being *Donemutha* (near the mouth of the Tyne, Northumberland)[75]—and assigned them to an aristocrat, Æthelwold Moll. According to Forthred the monasteries had come into his own hands as a gift from an abbess, and it appears that

---

[70] Alcuin, *Versus*, ll. 1388–93; British Library, Cotton MS. Domitian A VII, f. 18r.

[71] *Historia de Sancto Cuthberto: A History of Saint Cuthbert and a Record of His Patrimony*, ed. T. Johnson South (Cambridge, 2002), c. 5, p. 47.

[72] Adams, 'Monastery and Village at Crayke', pp. 29–32; J. Kaner, 'Crayke and its Boundaries', in *Yorkshire Boundaries*, ed. H. E. J. Le Patourel, M. H. Long, and M. F. Pickles (Leeds, 1993), pp. 103–11; Blair, *Church in Anglo-Saxon Society*, p. 222.

[73] F. Barlow, *Durham Jurisdictional Peculiars* (London, 1950); M. S. McCollum, 'Changes in the Pattern of Ecclesiastical Jurisdictions in and connected with the Diocese of Durham during the Nineteenth Century, with a Note on the Location of the Records of these Jurisdictions', *Transactions of the Architectural and Archaeological Society of Durham and Northumberland*, n.s. 6 (1982), pp. 61–65; A. J. Piper, 'The Diocese of Durham and its Organisation, 995–1995', in *Churches of the Diocese of Durham: A Pictorial Guide*, ed. J. E. Ruscoe (Durham, 1994), pp. 25–35.

[74] Letter of Pope Paul I, in *Councils and Ecclesiastical Documents Relating to Great Britain and Ireland*, ed. A. W. Haddan and W. Stubbs, 3 vols in 4 (Oxford, 1869–78), vol. 3, *The English Church During the Anglo-Saxon Period, 595–1066*, pp. 394–6.

[75] I. Wood, *The Origins of Jarrow: The Monastery, the Slake and Ecgfrith's Minster*, Bede's World Studies 1 (Jarrow, 2008), pp. 18–28.

Moll was either Forthred's brother or that the abbess was his sister.[76] These circumstances are not easy to disentangle. Was this royal repossession of lands formerly granted for proper monastic purpose but since secularised, or venal seizure (Eadberht and Ecgberht were brothers, and Moll a future king of Northumbria)? As for the places, Stonegrave and Coxwold are but 7 miles (11 km.) apart, nicely placed to overlook travellers at either end of the Coxwold–Gilling gap. *Donemutha* is 58 miles (93 km.) to the north—although it too was well situated to observe arrivals and departures. Were these individual communities (in which case, as John Blair notes, Forthred 'looks like an absentee monastic pluralist'[77]) or would they have regarded themselves—as did the brothers of Lastingham, *Adbaruae* and Lichfield—as members of a Connexion spread between several places? The episode is difficult to assess without more context.[78]

Stonegrave invites attention for more reasons. First is its substantial collection of pre-Conquest sculpture. This includes parts of a cross, dated style-critically after *c.* 920, with imagery and detailing that Lang thought suggestive of connections with Wales, Ireland, and Galloway.[79] Behind the place-name is the Old English word *stāngræf*, 'quarry'. Ekwall surmised that *Staningagrave* implies a modified sense along the lines of 'the quarry of the *Stāngræf* people'.[80] A quarry bench is indeed on the slope above the church. The bench runs for some miles, side-on access to rock being assisted by the fault that forms the northern side of the Coxwold–Gilling gap.[81] The occurrence of the name in the letter of 757–8 indicates that by this time the area was already used for stone extraction. It is a reasonable supposition that substantial quarrying had taken place under Roman auspices;[82] whether quarrying had since been practised continuously or intermittently the area had acquired, or retained, a specialised reputation by the eighth century. This may have been connected with a third factor, namely that in 1086 berewicks of the nearby manor of Hovingham are found in Stonegrave and the neighbouring township of Gilling East (below), and that Gilling East and Hovingham are next on our list of candidate Deiran monasteries.

---

[76] W. Richardson, 'The Venerable Bede and a Lost Saxon Monastery in Yorkshire', *Yorkshire Archaeological Journal*, 57 (1985), pp. 15–22, at p. 20; Wood, *Origins of Jarrow*, n. 83, p. 37.
[77] Blair, *Church in Anglo-Saxon Society*, p. 131.
[78] Wood, 'Gifts of Wearmouth and Jarrow', pp. 101–2.
[79] Lang, *Corpus*, Stonegrave 1, see note 29 above.
[80] Ekwall, *Dictionary of English Place-Names*, p. 446.
[81] R. Morris, 'Local Churches in the Anglo-Saxon Countryside', in *The Oxford Handbook of Anglo-Saxon Archaeology*, ed. H. Hamerow, D. A. Hinton and S. Crawford (Oxford, 2011), pp. 172–97, at pp. 186–7.
[82] P. C. Buckland, 'The "Anglian Tower" and the Use of Jurassic Limestone in York', in *Archaeological Papers from York Presented to M. W. Barley*, ed. P. V. Addyman and V. E. Black (York, 1984), pp. 51–7; P. C. Buckland, 'The Stones of York: Building Materials in Roman Yorkshire', in *Recent Research in Roman Yorkshire: Studies in Honour of Mary Kitson*

A case can be made for identifying Gilling East with the place called *Ingetlingum* where Oswine, king of the Deiri (*c.* 644–51), was murdered on the orders of Oswiu, king of the Bernicii (642–70) in 651.[83] Oswine and Oswiu were the son and brother of King Oswald (634–42), respectively, and such identification would have implications for this discussion. *Ingetlingum* was the home of a *gesith* whom Oswine believed to be a loyal friend. Prompted by his wife Eanflæd, daughter of Edwin, Oswiu founded a monastery at *Ingetlingum* to atone for the crime. The monastery's first abbot was one of Oswine's kinsman. A successor abbot was Cynefrith, the elder brother of Ceolfrith who joined the community in about 660 at the age of eighteen. Cynefrith departed for concentrated study in Ireland, handing Gilling into the rule of another kinsman, Tunbercht. A little later, possibly in 664 or 665, Tunbercht, Ceolfrid and several more Gilling brothers accepted an invitation from Bishop Wilfrid to join his community at Ripon.[84] Tunbercht went on to be bishop of Hexham (681–4), Ceolfrid to be abbot of Wearmouth-Jarrow.

Such overlapping allegiances, interconnecting royal and family interests, other royal foundations nearby and ready access to Ripon would provide a context for Oswiu's monastery. Unfortunately the case for associating *Ingetlingum* with Gilling East is inconclusive; the intuitive case for associating it with Gilling West, 32 miles (51 km.) away, is no less strong.[85] Regardless of this, what is not in doubt is that some sort of religious settlement did exist at Gilling East. A fragment of sculpture found in the south wall of the church is regarded as 'one of the earliest Anglian stones in Ryedale, without local parallels' that has 'more in common with Acca's cross at Hexham, Northumberland, than with any monument in eastern Yorkshire'.[86] In view of the report in the *The Anonymous Life of Ceolfrith* that members of the *Ingetlingum* community had joined Wilfridian—and subsequently Hexham—circles several generations earlier, the stylistic connection gives pause for thought.

Some of these questions begin to resolve themselves when we look at our next candidate, Hovingham. Hovingham and Stonegrave lie at the eastern end of the Coxwold–Gilling gap. The two places are but a mile and a half (2.5 km.) apart and face each other across the floor of the pass, Stonegrave on the south-facing slope of

---

Clark, ed. J. Price and P. R. Wilson with C. S. Briggs and S. J. Hardman, British Archaeological Reports British Series, 193 (Oxford, 1988), pp. 237–87; Gaunt and Buckland, 'Geological Background to Yorkshire's Archaeology'.

[83] Bede, *Historia ecclesiastica*, bk iii, c. 14. The case for Gilling East is given by Morris, *Journeys from Jarrow*, pp. 21–2, and Wood, 'Monasteries and Geography of Power', p. 17.

[84] *Vita Ceolfridi*, in *The Abbots of Wearmouth and Jarrow*, ed. C. Grocock and I. N. Wood (Oxford, 2013), cc. 2, 3.

[85] Andrew Breeze identifies *Uilfaresdun* (the place where Oswine disbanded his army) with Diddesley Hill, which is a mile north of the village of Gilling West: A. Breeze, 'Where were Bede's *Uilfaresdun* and *Pægnalæch*?', *Northern History*, 42 (2005), pp. 189–91.

[86] Lang, *Corpus*, Gilling 1, see note 30 above.

7. LANDSCAPES OF CONVERSION AMONGST THE DEIRANS

the Hambleton Hills and Hovingham in the corresponding position below the north-facing slope of the Howardians. Geographically, if not once institutionally, they look like a pair. Oswaldkirk and Gilling East occupy similar relative positions 3 miles (5 km.) or so to the east. Extensive woods grow on the limestone hills to either side; while these woodlands may differ from the exact distribution of woodland in the earlier middle ages, medieval sources suggest that they maintain the personality of earlier land use. Hovingham is important to this discussion for the presence and implications of part of a shrine-tomb of *c.* 800 in the parish church; for evidence of a structure under the church that was built between the sixth and eighth centuries; for its setting in relation to Roman cultural geography; and for evidence of its relationships with surrounding places.

To begin with the place-name, the conventional reading is 'the hām of Hofa's people'. Other readings have been suggested. The first element was once thought to have derived from Old English *hof* 'temple', while Wood has recently suggested 'dwelling', 'house' or 'court', as in Beowulf (l.1507)'.[87] Ekwall preferred 'place of Hofa's people' on grounds of probability,[88] but the other readings are philologically possible. Ekwall may have been unaware that sites of Romano-British temples lie nearby, that Hovingham has mineral springs, or that Roman buildings underlie the adjoining parkland of Hovingham Hall. The presence of a villa in the area has been assumed since the finding of a hypocaust, bath, and portions of mosaic pavement in the course of works in the grounds of the Hall in 1745. Recent geophysical survey suggests that the eighteenth-century excavators glimpsed outlying parts of a lavish complex, the main building of which is revealed by ground-penetrating radar to have been of palatial scale (Fig. 7.7).

Hovingham is linked to Malton by a 7-mile (11 km.) length of road known locally as 'The Street'. The road follows the boundary between the Vale and the sloping edge of the Howardians. It is assumed to be of Roman origin (Margary 814), and the consistent way in which later settlements and parishes were laid out in relation to it recalls the Cliff parishes along Ermine Street north of Lincoln.[89] However, The Street differs from many Roman roads in that it does not appear to have been strictly aligned. Even so, it has a logical path: it follows an outcrop of stone which has been quarried in a line of intermittent exposures and extractive workings. In places The Street runs along the shelf so created (see Colour Plate 7.8). The arrangement indicates extraction on a substantial scale and with Stonegrave points to the specialised significance of the area at least from the Roman period onwards.[90]

[87] Wood, 'Monasteries and Geography of Power', p.18.
[88] Ekwall thought 'temple' should be dropped 'since an OE pers[onal] N[ame] *Hofa* is on record': *English Place-Names in* -Ing, p. 155.
[89] Morris, *Churches in the Landscape*, p. 122, Fig. 26; p. 236, Fig. 64.
[90] Morris, 'Local Churches in the Anglo-Saxon Countryside', pp. 186–7.

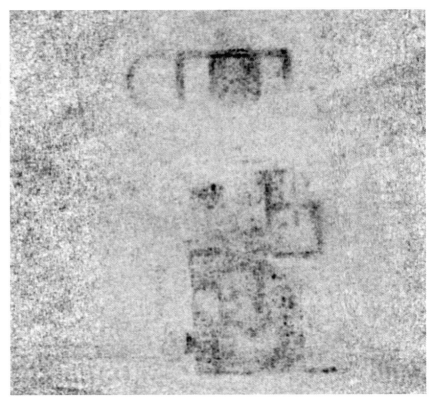

Fig. 7.7 Ground penetrating radar plot (2013) of Roman building in Hovingham Park. (© Copyright Landscape Research Centre.)

The relationship between The Street and quarrying flags the matter of to where it was that The Street ultimately led. Did it continue beyond Hovingham or was Hovingham its destination? There are hints of continuation towards Coxwold, but beyond this the trail is cold. If the road did end in the area, or even at Hovingham, then this could have implications for the status of the buildings under Hovingham Park: a 'villa' of sufficient importance to be connected to Roman Malton by its own road implies singular rank, such as the centre of an imperial estate, or even the legate's palace that presumably stood somewhere in the vicinity of *Eburacum*. Bearing in mind recent arguments for the emergence of the early Northumbrian leadership from already resident Roman auxiliary elements,[91] it becomes a question whether the status of Hovingham's Roman occupants has implications for their Deiran successors.

More questions and clues accumulate as we turn to look at the church, which stands about 550 yards (503 m.) north east of the Roman complex. Today it consists of a chancel with a north aisle, an aisled nave, and a tower. The nave and chancel were rebuilt in 1860. The nave arcades stand on the cut-down walls of an earlier stone structure. Small excavations in 1977 identified nearby traces of a yet earlier structure.[92] A charcoal sample from the filling of the foundation trench for the stone

[91] Orton, Wood and Lees, *Fragments of History*, pp. 110–15.
[92] A. Pacitto and L. Watts, 'Excavations at the Church of All Saints, Hovingham, Yorkshire,' *Church Archaeology*, 11 (2007), pp. 51–60.

Fig. 7.9 Hovingham panel.
(© Copyright Corpus of Anglo-Saxon Stone Sculpture, photographer T. Middlemass.)

building gave a radiocarbon determination which at 95 *per cent* confidence lies in the range cal AD 610–890, and gives cal AD 650–780 at 68 *per cent* confidence. Corresponding results from a second sample, from a superimposed but associated context, are cal AD 420–690 and AD 540–660.[93] The authors warn 'that both samples were unqualified as to whether heartwood or sapwood, and identified a risk of old heartwood making the obtained date up to 500 years too old if the charcoal had originated from the centre of a very old tree.'[94] This accepted, we still have *prima facie* signs for a pre-present church structure dating from the seventh to ninth century (at 95 *per cent* confidence) or of the seventh to eighth century (at 68 *per cent*).

The ghost of the western end of an older nave may be seen in quoins that clasp the tower and in the west wall of the nave against which the tower was built. The tower itself is divided into three stages by string courses and is likely to date from the later eleventh century.[95] Its builders used quantities of Roman building material, including megalithic blocks and ashlar, together with monolithic window heads that may have been derived either from an Anglo-Saxon or Roman building, or by turn from both. On the west face, below the first string course, above the west door, is a squarish (approx. 20 × 22 inches, 510 × 560 mm.) stone plaque upon which is embossed a cross dated on style-critical grounds to the ninth century. The plaque may have been cut from the lid of a sarcophagus (see below).

[93] Pacitto and Watts, 'Excavations at All Saints, Hovingham', pp. 53–4.
[94] Pacitto and Watts, 'Excavations at All Saints, Hovingham', pp. 55–6.
[95] H. M. and J. Taylor, *Anglo-Saxon Architecture*, 3 vols (Cambridge, 1965–78), vol. 1, pp. 326–8.

Two other pieces of sculpture were built into the tower, both in the south face: a cross head, above the belfry opening, and a decoratively carved slab that was taken into the church in 1924 (Fig. 7.9). The date of the cross head is judged as mid tenth-century, the slab, perhaps somewhere in c. 775 × 825.[96] Re-use of the two crosses has been assessed as 'iconic' whereas insertion of the slab seems to have been casual. The slab is now used as a reredos for an altar in the south aisle. Functionally it is most likely to be one of the long side panels of a composite box shrine; it has been described as 'one of the most complex and ambitious of Anglian monuments in Ryedale'.[97] The carved face of the panel evokes a Roman arcaded sarcophagus. It bears an arcade of eight bays above a strip of plant scroll in which dwell pecking birds. Each arch is occupied by a single figure, now heavily weathered. The first two are certainly the archangel Gabriel and the Virgin—the Annunciation. The Virgin seated with a weaving basket is a scene from the Protoevangelium of James that entered Annunciation iconography from the fifth century and begins to fade from the ninth—the weaving corresponds with a biblical idea that an infant is woven by God in the womb.[98] The next two figures are generally seen as Mary and Elizabeth—the Visitation. The rightmost figure is another angel, balancing Gabriel. Debate has attended the identities of the intervening three, but Jane Hawkes has surely settled this by recognising them as the Three Women at the Sepulchre. Hawkes draws attention to an iconographic progression from incarnation to fulfillment through resurrection that provides a connecting theme of salvation for the panel as a whole.[99]

Hawkes notes a dependence on early models for the postures of the three women. This is so, although the images of mourning in western resurrection scenes to which Hawkes points as referents bear less resemblance to what we see at Hovingham than do the gestures for sorrow and mourning of earlier classical theatre upon which early Christian artists drew. The seated figure in the seventh bay, half turned towards the woman standing with raised arm in the sixth, is uncannily close to the attitudes, grouping and hand positions of Phaedra and her maid in 'the quiet farewell scene' on the Hippolytus sarcophagus (of around 230) in Florence.[100] It is not suggested that the Hippolytus sarcophagus was an actual model, but that the means of expression at

---

[96] Lang (*Corpus*, p.148) proposed 'late eighth to early ninth century'; J. Hawkes says early ninth century: 'Mary and the Cycle of Resurrection: The Iconography of the Hovingham Panel', in *The Age of Migrating Ideas: Early Medieval Art in Northern Britain and Ireland. Proceedings of the Second International Conference on Insular Art, Held at the National Museums of Scotland in Edinburgh, 3–6 January 1991*, ed. R. M. Spearman and J. Higgitt (Edinburgh and Stroud, 1993), pp. 254–60, at p. 254.
[97] Lang, *Corpus*, p. 147.
[98] Psalms, cxxxix, 13.
[99] Hawkes, 'Mary and the Cycle of Resurrection', pp. 258–9.
[100] P. Zanker and B. C. Ewald, *Living with Myths: The Imagery of Roman Sarcophagi* (Oxford, 2012), p. 92.

Hovingham are ultimately derived from the gestural language of Graeco-Roman theatre.[101] How the Hovingham sculptor and his audience acquired that classical grounding is a question.

Who was the saint? Marian iconography would be appropriate for a female, and Hawkes has entertained production of the panel 'within, or for a nunnery or double monastery'—which is wholly imaginable, although as Hawkes reminds us, Mary was pre-eminent as dedicatee of religious houses of all kinds.[102] To say more about the saint within the shrine we would need to know how the panel's images fitted into the iconography of the whole. However, the world of ideas and associations to which the panel belongs does point to a monastic institution rather than to something more specialised, like a royal prayer house or chapel.

We are on firmer ground if we consider the period when the panel was made. Accepting that saint-making is as much a function of biographers, audiences and reception as of original deeds, it is periods of mission, challenge and change that tend to be more productive of saints than times of stability or consolidation. Fewer saints emerged from northern England between 700 and 1100 than from the seventh century. Hence, while it possible that the Hovingham shrine was produced for the remains of an eighth- or early ninth-century figure, the subject is more likely to have flourished in *c.* 640 × 700. In that case, the shrine represents a translation. We recall that a new shrine was made at Lastingham after *c.* 750 and that if it was for Cedd it was a second translation.

More translations in the later eighth or early ninth century are indicated at a third site, Kirkdale, where rectangular grave covers in the church of St Gregory were intended to mark the resting places of holy men or women. Today the church stands alone in the narrow, wooded, secluded valley of the Hodge Beck that flows south from the North York Moors to a confluence with the River Dove two miles (3.2 km.) downstream. Kirkdale is well-known for an inscription recording a rebuilding in the earlier 1060s on the site of an older church, which itself has a Roman context.[103] Excavation points to a monastic context for the site at least from the eighth century, while study of the building and antiquarian records reveals that the panel bearing the inscription was derived from the side of a sarcophagus—the third example of such re-use in a devotional or commemorative context to be met here.[104]

---

[101] Dorota Dutsch, 'Towards a Roman Theory of Theatrical Gesture', in *Performance in Greek and Roman Theatre*, ed. G. W. M. Harrison and V. Liapis, Mnemosene, bibliotheca classica batava, supplementum 353 (Leiden, 2013), pp. 409–32.

[102] Hawkes, 'Mary and the Cycle of Resurrection', pp. 259–60.

[103] J. Blair, 'The Kirkdale Inscription and its Latin Models: *Romanitas* in Late Anglo-Saxon Yorkshire', in *Interfaces Between Language and Culture in Medieval England: A Festschrift for Matti Kilpiö*, ed. A. Hall, Northern World, 48 (Leiden, 2010), pp. 139–45.

[104] L. Watts, P. A. Rahtz, E. Okasha, S. A. J. Bradley and J. Higgitt, 'Kirkdale—The Inscriptions', *Medieval Archaeology*, 41 (1997), pp. 51–99, at p. 89; L. Watts and P. A. Rahtz, 'Three Ages

Kirkdale can be identified as the monastery 'which is located at the place called Horn Vale', *Cornu Vallis*, where abbot Ceolfrid paused on his journey to the coast in the summer of 716.[105] The community was then headed by one Ælberht. It links to the preceding discussion in three ways. First, at least one of the grave covers that were introduced around a century later signifies a tomb cult.[106] The draping of a richly embroidered cloth over a free-standing tomb was a proclamation of sainthood, and the edges of the monument that is now kept under the eastern bay of the north nave arcade are carved to resemble a woven pall.[107] A skeuomorphic *palla* might denote a well-established cult, the monument being a perpetual embodiment of the moment when the cloth was spread. This would accord with a translation; we have seen evidence for other contemporary or near-contemporary translations at Lastingham and Hovingham.

The likely correspondence with Hovingham introduces the second aspect, which is that the medieval parish of Kirkdale included the vill of Hoveton, which as the place-name implies had at some time in the past been a dependency of Hovingham. (*Cornu Vallis* was still used as a personal name in the area in the twelfth century, when Hoveton was given to Rievaulx together with land previously held by Samson de Cornuwala.) Nearby place-names suggest that there were other trans-Vale links like this, as between Gilling East (which adjoins Hovingham), Gillamoor, 'moor belonging to Gilling', and Appleton, which recurs. The impression is thus of a network or federal manor, or manors, that took in rural resources of different kinds across a sub-region. The impression is reinforced by Hovingham's manorial relationships. Berewicks listed in Domesday included Grimston (which is in Gilling East), East Newton (which is in Stonegrave), Broughton (in Appleton-le-Street[108]) and several other vills along The Street.[109] What we see here is a great estate in decay, its former

---

of Conversion at Kirkdale, North Yorkshire', in *The Cross Goes North*, pp. 289–309; S. Paynter, 'St Gregory's Minster, Kirkdale, North Yorkshire: Analysis of a Glass Rod', English Heritage Research Department Reserach Series, 18 (2009).

[105] *Vita Ceolfridi*, c. 29; Morris, *Journeys from Jarrow*, pp. 22–3. David Petts's suggestion that *Cornu Vallis* may equate with Spurn Head ('Coastal Landscapes and Early Christianity in Anglo-Saxon Northumbria', *Estonian Journal of Archaeology*, 13 (2009), pp. 79–95, at p. 83) repeats an old notion that does not reconcile with the words: there is no 'vale' at Spurn, whereas 'vallis' translates directly into the 'dale' of Kirkdale—and Cornuualia occurs as a personal name in the parish in the later Middle Ages.

[106] Lang, *Corpus*, Kirkdale 7 and 8: note 29, above.

[107] A. Thacker, 'The Making of a Local Saint', in *Local Saints and Local Churches* (Oxford, 2002), pp. 45–72, at p. 64.

[108] Appleton-le-Street provides archaeological evidence for a pre-Conquest church: P. A. Rahtz, L. Watts and K. Saunders, 'Appleton-le-Street: All Saints Church', *Ryedale Historian*, 20 (2000), pp. 24–31. If All Saints is found to pre-date the onset of village church-building it could join the cluster of Gilling and Stonegrave centred on Hovingham.

[109] Domesday Book, vol. 1, f. 327v.

range extending from the west end of the Coxwold–Gilling gap to Malton, and from the Howardians across the Vale up onto the southern flank of the North York Moors.

Final things to register about Kirkdale are, firstly, that it appears to have had a connection with Wearmouth-Jarrow. Richard Bailey points out that while the form of the cross on the grave cover bearing the skeuomorphic *palla* (Kirkdale 7 in the *Corpus of Anglo-Saxon Stone Sculpture*) is not unusual in manuscripts, its use in sculpture is confined to three places: Monkwearmouth (with one example), Jarrow (with three or four), and Kirkdale.[110] The Wearmouth-Jarrow stones are perhaps three-quarters of a century older than Kirkdale 7, and a simple correspondence between sculptural similarities and monastic affiliation is neither suggested nor to be expected. Nonetheless, given the restricted occurrence of this form in this medium, the resemblance is unlikely to be coincidental. And secondly, another possible connection is suggested by the dedication to Christ and St Gregory on the mid-eleventh-century Kirkdale sundial. If the reference is to Gregory the Great then it evokes the age of conversion as recorded by Bede, the Life of Gregory composed at *Streanæshalch* in 704 × 714,[111] and the council of 664 in which the venerable Cedd was 'uigilantissimus' as an interpreter on behalf of both parties, and the results of which he put into effect.[112]

Lastly, Sherburn. The village is situated apart from the main group, on the southern side of the eastern end of the Vale of Pickering on a sandy margin that runs between the foot of the Yorkshire Wolds and the wetlands left by the former lake. Domesday Book identifies it as royal vill and records two churches. The modern village spans the Wykeham–Sherburn moraine, a low ridge projecting northward into the former wetlands that historically provided a natural causeway across the Vale. One church survives. It was virtually rebuilt shortly before the First World War, but retains a collection of pre–Conquest carved stones, of which three have been dated to the tenth or eleventh century, and four from the ninth century or later.[113]

Aerial photography and large scale geophysical survey around the village reveal a settlement that in the early Middle Ages extended more than 62 acres (25 ha.). This settlement included a large number of cavity floor buildings (see Colour Plate 7.10). East of the village aerial reconnaissance has detected the cropmark of a D-shaped enclosure maybe 110 yards (100 m.) across. Just outside it to the north is a rectangular structure aligned east–west. 'The enclosure is unusual and internal details, visible in the cropmark, geomagnetic and electronic resistance surveys, indicate that it is

---

[110] Richard Bailey, letter to author, 1 July 2004.
[111] *The Earliest Life of Gregory the Great by an Anonymous Monk of Whitby*, ed. B. Colgrave (Lawrence, Kansas, 1968); for the likelihood of female authorship see now A. Breeze, 'Did a Woman Write the Whitby Life of St Gregory?', *Northern History*, 49 (2012), pp. 343–50.
[112] Bede, *Historia ecclesiastica*, bk iii, cc. 25–6.
[113] Note 30, above.

exceptional. Very strong magnetic anomalies, possibly indicative of burnt structures, are situated just inside the ditch that defines the enclosure in a situation that is not dissimilar to the distribution of industrial structures in early Irish monastic enclosures.'[114]

Pilot excavation in 2011 confirmed the presence of the cavity floor buildings, and found some of them to have been of enormous size. One, for instance, measured 33 × 26 ft (10 × 8 m.) and there were others of similar scale. The reconnaissance also identified a grain drying kiln, again of exceptional dimensions, that had processed grain on an industrial scale. A wattle fragment from the grain dryer gave a radiocarbon determination of cal AD 605–674 (at 95.4 *per cent* probability); and a fragment of charcoal from one of the cavity floor buildings dated in the range cal AD 772–952 (at 95.4 *per cent* probability).[115]

Excavation on a larger scale will be needed to ascertain what kind of place this was, but on the strength of what we already know several points can be made. One of the benefits of the 11.5 square miles of (30 square kilometres) of contiguous geophysics that have been carried out in the Vale in recent years is that they enable comparison and generalisation about what was typical or unusual.[116] From this we can see that Sherburn in the seventh and eighth centuries was unusual in comparison with those others that have been studied through excavation and large-scale geophysics in other parts of the Vale. Second, the enormity of the cavity floor buildings and capacity of the grain dryer imply processing of agricultural produce on a huge scale. This might well point to Sherburn as a royal centre for the reception of renders, or as a religious house receiving produce from its estates, or both. In either case the unencumbered nature of the site makes fuller understanding of Sherburn both an opportunity and priority to assist understanding of the early medieval economy in the region as a whole.

Groups and Meanings

A case has been made for seeing some houses in Ryedale as members of monastic connexions. The Lastingham Connexion has already been discussed; it is likely to have included Kirby Misperton and had members like Lichfield and *Adbaruae* that lay far afield. Also linking to Lastingham, though for different reasons, were several later village churches which came to serve parishes detached from that of the mother. One of them was Middleton-by-Pickering where a late-eighth- or early ninth-century

---

[114] D. Powlesland, *Archaeological Excavations in Sherburn, Vale of Pickering, North Yorkshire, September 2011*, http://www.landscaperesearchcentre.org/Archaeological%20-Excavations%20in%20Sherburn%202011.pdf, accessed 22 June 2013.
[115] Powlesland, *Excavations in Sherburn*.
[116] D. Powlesland, *Twenty-Five Years of Archaeological Research on the Sands and Gravels of Heslerton* (Yedingham, 2003).

cross plaque has been iconically set above the door in the west face of the tower—an arrangement similar to the one already described at Hovingham. The cross (Middleton 9 in the *Corpus of Anglo-Saxon Stone Sculpture*) has a feature in common with Lastingham 4 and Kirkdale 7: a recess at the intersection of the cross which was 'probably the seating for a metalwork appliqué or semi-precious stone'.[117]

Such a cross almost certainly originated in a monastic milieu. However, it is a question whether the community in question was at Middleton. Middleton is a planned village of a rectangular form commonly seen in eastern Yorkshire with house plots and garths laid out at right angles to a linear central street and parallel back lanes. A further feature of such layouts was the way in which parallel fields come into the village. Debate continues about the date of such arrangements, with opinions spread between the later Saxon period to the eleventh and twelfth centuries.[118] The place-name reinforces the impression of a village being laid out in relation to existing settlements. The church houses a series of crosses bearing well-known carvings of armed, helmeted men (Middleton 2, 4A, 5A in the *Corpus of Anglo-Saxon Stone Sculpture*). The carvings date from the tenth century. It may be that the individuals commemorated were the founder-leaders of the planned community and fields.[119] Whether or not this is accepted, the churchyard in which they were presumably buried is integral to the planned village. Hence, the site of the church must either have been set out at the time of initial planning or inserted at a later date. This leaves no obvious context for an eighth-century cross. However, the plaque could have been a gift from a mother church to a daughter.[120] The mother church here was Lastingham, which would also help to explain the iconic re-use of the piece.

The Middleton plaque, like that at Hovingham, may have been cut from a Roman sarcophagus. Grave covers 1–3 excavated at Wharram Percy were similarly

---

[117] Lang, *Corpus*, p.162.
[118] J. A. Sheppard, 'Medieval Village Planning in Northern England: Some Evidence from Yorkshire', *Journal of Historical Geography*, 2 (1976), pp. 3–20; J. A. Sheppard, 'Metrological Analysis of Regular Village Plans in Yorkshire', *Agricultural History Review*, 22 (1974), pp. 118–35; M. Harvey, 'Regular Field and Tenurial Arrangements in Holderness, Yorkshire', *Journal of Historical Geography*, 6 (1980), pp. 3–16; M. Harvey, 'Planned Field Systems in Eastern Yorkshire: Some Thoughts on Their Origin', *Agricultural History Review*, 31 (1983), pp. 91–103; J. S. Brown, 'The Organisation of the Early Church in the East Riding of Yorkshire, c. 700–1100: The churches of 1086 and their Origins', MPhil thesis, University of York (2009), pp. 22–29; for recent contextual discussion P. Everson and D. Stocker, 'Why at Wharram? The Foundation of Nucleated Settlement', in *Wharram: A Study of Settlement on the Yorkshire Wolds, XIII: A History of Wharram Percy and its Neighbours*, ed. S. Wrathmell, York University Archaeological Publications, 15 (York, 2012), pp. 208–20.
[119] R. Morris, *Time's Anvil: England, Archaeology and the Imagination* (London, 2012), pp. 177-8; Morris, 'Local Churches in the Anglo-Saxon Countryside', pp. 189–90.
[120] Morris, 'Local Churches in the Anglo-Saxon Countryside', p. 189, with more examples.

derived,[121] and we have seen that Roman funerary furniture was reworked for the mid-eleventh-century inscription at Kirkdale and for part of the shrine at Lastingham. The grave covers at Wharram are thought to have marked a burial group of founders.[122] It has been suggested that the recurrence in the region of *spolia* in tenth- and eleventh-century ecclesiastical contexts may reflect a desire on the part of archbishops of York to establish physical links between themselves and newly founded local graveyards and churches.[123]

Turning to other groups, Crayke was firmly in the hands of the Community of St Cuthbert by the eleventh century, and there is no reason to doubt the view then held that it had been so since the seventh.

Hackness was a dependency of *Streanæshalch*, and whether seen as Whitby or Strensall, or as an association involving both, it adjoins the Ryedale group.[124] *Streanæshalch* was the burial place of Edwin, Oswiu, Eanflæd and Ælfflæd, and Edwin's wife may have been commemorated at its dependency at Hackness.[125] As Wood has noted, '*Streanæshalch* played a more central role in the commemoration of the kings of Northumbria than did any other single monastery.'[126]

The new Connexion to have emerged here appears to have centred on Hovingham. It included Stonegrave, Gilling East, and Kirkdale (Horn Vale), although it remains a question whether these travelled together from the start or became associated through transfer or purchase of the kind recorded for Stonegrave and

---

[121] D. Stocker, 'Pre-Conquest Stonework—the Early Graveyard in Context', in *Wharram: A Study of Settlement on the Yorkshire Wolds, XI: The Churchyard*, by S. Mays, C. Harding and C. Heighway, York University Archaeological Publications, 13 (York, 2007), pp. 271–87.

[122] Stocker, 'Pre-Conquest Stonework', pp. 284–5.

[123] Stocker, 'Pre-Conquest Stonework', pp. 284–5; D. Stocker, 'Monuments and Merchants: Irregularities in the Distribution of Stone Sculpture in Lincolnshire and Yorkshire in the Tenth Century', in *Cultures in Contact: Scandinavian Settlement in England in the Ninth and Tenth Centuries*, ed. D. M. Hadley and J. D. Richards, Studies in the Early Middle Ages, 2 (Turnhout, 2000), pp. 179–212.

[124] For later medieval equation of Streanæshalch with Whitby: Symeon, *Libellus de exordio atque procurso istius hoc est Dunelmensis ecclesie*, ed. and trans. D. Rollason (Oxford, 2000), bk iii cc. 21–2; *Cartularium abbathiae de Whiteby, ordinis s. Benedicti, fuindatae anno MLXXXVIII*, ed. J. C. Atkinson, Surtees Society 69, 72, 2 vols (1879–81), vol.1, pp. 1–6, no. 1. For doubts: P. S. Barnwell, L. A. S. Butler and C. J. Dunn, 'The Confusion of Conversion: Streanæshalch, Strensall and Whitby and the Northumbrian Church', in *The Cross Goes North*, pp. 311–26. For recent survey of debate concluding that the 'evidence is sufficient to identify Streanæshalch with Whitby', with further references: Thomas Pickles, 'Streanæshalch (Whitby), its Satellite Churches and Lands', in *Making Christian Landscapes*.

[125] C. E. Karkov, 'Whitby, Jarrow and the Commemoration of Death in Northumbria', in *Northumbria's Golden Age*, ed. J. Hawkes and S. Mills (Stroud, 1999), pp. 125–35.

[126] Wood, 'Monasteries and Geography of Power', p. 21; see also K. Veitch, 'The Columban Church in Northern Britain, 664–717: A Reassessment', *Proceedings of the Society of Antiquaries of Scotland*, 127 (1997), pp. 627–47.

7. LANDSCAPES OF CONVERSION AMONGST THE DEIRANS

Coxwold. Indeed, we should probably add Coxwold to the group on grounds both of propinquity and of it being co-owned with Stonegrave when it was passing from hand to hand in the eighth century. For the same reason, and given that we have seen distance to be no necessary obstacle to membership of a monastic confederation, perhaps the Tyneside house of *Donæmuthe* should also be visualised as belonging to the group. This could offer a context for the sculptural link between Kirkdale and Wearmouth-Jarrow. Ian Wood has shown *Donæmuthe* to have been in the vicinity of Jarrow, probably at the point where the River Don originally flowed into the Tyne.[127] Wood has further pointed out that this may be the house described in Bede's *Life of Cuthbert* as having existed on the south side of the Tyne close to the mouth of the river. *Donæmuthe* and Jarrow faced each other across the tidal mudflats of Jarrow Slake (a relationship akin to that between Hovingham and Stonegrave) and although they were distinct their histories were intertwined. The house at the mouth of the Don had first been occupied by monks but later passed to nuns. Another name for *Donæmuthe* seems to have been *Ecgferthes mynster*, and with Wood 'we might guess that Ecgfrith was responsible for handing the monastery over to a community of women, and that the monks were transferred to the new foundation of Jarrow.'[128]

This introduces a caution: while there must have been royal involvement in the foundation of many if not all monasteries in the seventh and early eighth centuries we cannot assume that the factors of kinship and patronage that brought them into being remained steady thereafter. The early disappearance of Lastingham's founder-king illustrates this, and both Ryedale and Tyneside provide examples of transfers of ownership, changes of occupancy and switches of affiliation: we recall key members of the community at *Ingetlingum* transferring themselves to Wilfrid's Ripon in the 660s. A recurrent theme in the Anonymous *Life of Ceolfrid* and the *Lives of the Abbots* is the risk of Wearmouth-Jarrow falling into inappropriate hands, and as far as Jarrow's foundation goes the trope of Wearmouth-Jarrow being one monastery in two places is contradicted by the earliest sources.[129] Once established, connections between monasteries may have been fostered as much by friendships developed in formative years and later sustained as followers of early leaders spread to become heads of other houses.[130]

It seems likely, then, that a similarly wide range of factors could have acted to influence which monasteries and saints within them were later to be remembered and which not. After Bede, Gilling, *Adbaruae* and *Cornu Vallis* drop out of the written record, while Lastingham and Hackness subside until the late eleventh century when

---

[127] Wood, *Origins of Jarrow*; I. Wood, 'Bede's Jarrow', in *A Place to Believe In: Locating Medieval Landscapes*, ed. C. A. Lees and G. R. Overing (Pennsylvania, 2006), pp. 67–84.
[128] Wood, 'Monasteries and Geography of Power', p. 19.
[129] I. Wood, *The Most Holy Abbot Ceolfrid*, Jarrow Lecture 1995 (Jarrow, 1996).
[130] Sargent, 'Lichfield and the Lands of St Chad', pp. 89–90.

Benedictine religious travelled north to seek out and revive ancient sites.[131] Material evidence, on the other hand, demonstrates a continuing rich cultural life at these places in the eighth and earlier ninth centuries, and indeed at other places that do not appear in the written record at all. And we have seen evidence for active saints' cults at three sites, and their renovation through translations in *c.* 775 × 825.

It has been pointed out that 'most of the Northumbrian ecclesiastics missing from the original core of the *Liber Vitae* were connected with Deira. In particular there are no names which can be connected definitely with the Deiran monasteries of Gilling and Lastingham.'[132] However, while it may be that the Ryedale houses fell victim to what Ian Wood has called 'competitive remembrance',[133] presumably because their shrines contained the remains of royal saints or members of the Deiran aristocracy, the larger commemorative picture actually shows an interspersal of Bernician and Deiran families. 'The Vale of Pickering may have been essentially Deiran, but Bernician royalty was remembered there; so too the Bernician Lower Tyne culted at least one Deiran king'.[134]

Arguably a strong factor behind the minimisation and eventual forgetting of Ryedale's monasteries, and with it their links with the conversion of other parts of England and role in the conversion of the Deirans, was the emergence of York as the pre-eminent economic, political and ecclesiastical focus of southern Northumbria. In his York poem Alcuin departed from Bede in selecting Oswiu, not Oswine, as one of his three exemplary kings, and in eulogizing his city and the cultural golden age that emanated from it.[135] In this narrative York and its leaders are in the foreground, and York is the centre of a great ecclesiastical province. For the bishops, kings and saints of York to achieve this dominance it was necessary for roles played by others to be understated, or not stated at all. Wilfrid and Aidan were marginalised. Cedd and Ceadda disappear. *Streanæshalch*, far from being the 'coenobium famosissimum' it had been in the early eighth-century life of Gregory the Great that had been written there,[136] was omitted, and with it the synod held in 664. 'To read the *Versus [...] de Sanctis Euboricensis Ecclesiae* it is as if the synod [...] had not needed to be held.'[137] In his use of Bede, Alcuin was in places 'effectively manufacturing a picture of

---

[131] D. Knowles, *The Monastic Order in England: A History of its Development from the Times of St Dunstan to the Fourth Lateran Council, 940–1216*, 2nd edn (Cambridge, 1963), pp. 163–71; R. Cramp, *Wearmouth and Jarrow Monastic Sites*, 2 vols (Swindon, 2005–6), vol. 1, pp. 35–7.

[132] E. Briggs, 'Nothing But Names: The Original Core of the Durham *Liber Vitae*', in *The Durham Liber Vitae and its Context*, ed. D. Rollason, A. J. Piper, M. Harvey and L. Rollason, Regions and Regionalism in History, 1 (Woodbridge, 2004), pp. 63–86, at p. 82.

[133] Wood, 'Monasteries and Geography of Power', p. 23.

[134] Wood, 'Monasteries and Geography of Power', p. 24.

[135] Sue Ward, 'Church and State in Eighth-Century Northumbria, pp. 227–8.

[136] *Earliest Life of Gregory the Great*, c. 18.

[137] P. Godman in Alcuin, *Versus*, p. li.

supremacy acquired by York in the eighth century which was not there in his source.'[138] If the Ryedale monasteries were important in the later seventh and eighth centuries—and from what we know of their arts, founders, and clues to their scholarship, they were—they would have presented a prime target for such expurgation. It may be significant that Crayke, the one house in the area that Alcuin did mention, was part of a confederation centred elsewhere that posed no direct threat to the re-remembering of York.

A further factor may have been York's response to the rise of Mercian power. Alcuin's poem was written at or close to a time of strain between Offa and Jænberht, archbishop of Canterbury (d. 792), which in 787 culminated in the transfer of part of the province of Canterbury to a new metropolitan province of Lichfield.[139] York seems not to have felt threatened by this: Offa, shown by Alcuin's correspondence to have been 'the secular head of the Southumbrian church', was apparently balanced by the king of Northumbria who was head of the Northumbrian church.[140] However, Lichfield's new status might have provided an occasion for the enhancement of its relics through the translation of Cedd's remains from Lastingham. The reuniting of Cedd and his brother Ceadda would simultaneously have served Alcuin's purpose by transferring a powerful rival focus from the archdiocese of York to another kingdom.[141] Whether so or not, Alcuin's highly selective account shows how still-flourishing communities in a region formerly in the forefront of Deiran royal interests could have been eased from public memory.[142] But Ryedale would re-emerge as a nexus of monasteries, saints and conversion, embodied most prominently by the house that still bears its name—Rievaulx.

---

[138] Ward, 'Church and State in Eighth-Century Northumbria', p. 226.
[139] Synod of Chelsea, Anglo-Saxon Chronicle s.a. 785 (*recte* 787): C. R. E. Cubitt, *Anglo-Saxon Church Councils c. 650–c. 850* (London, 1995), p. 271; Ward, 'Church and State in Eighth-Century Northumbria', pp. 229-31; S. Coates, 'The Bishop as Benefactor and Civic Patron: Alcuin, York, and Episcopal Authority in Anglo-Saxon England', *Speculum* 71 (1996), pp. 529–58.
[140] Cubitt, *Anglo-Saxon Church Councils*, p. 213; Sargent, 'Lichfield and the Lands of St Chad', pp. 55-6. Offa consulted Alcuin about the consecration of Jænberht's successor: W. Levison, *England and the Continent in the Eighth Century* (Oxford, 1943), pp. 245–6.
[141] Rollason, 'Lists of Saints' Resting-Places', pp. 61–62.
[142] This said the empty grave of a translated saint could be as potent as the bones that had been taken out of it, making it possible for a saint to be in two places at once. Did this have a bearing on the survival of the Lastingham shrine fragments?

Fig. 8.1 Sites with Anglo-Saxon churches and sculptures in Counties Durham and Northumberland. (© Copyright R. Cramp.)

(8)
Northumbrian Churches

ROSEMARY CRAMP

Northumbria is rich in Anglo-Saxon ecclesiastical sites and standing churches, but this paper concentrates on a smaller core, focussing on sites and buildings mainly located in the old kingdom of Bernicia—northern Northumbria—and within the *parochiae* of the episcopal monasteries of Lindisfarne and later Hexham (both in Northumberland).[1] It also concentrates on those churches which have substantial remains and are of the period from the seventh to the ninth centuries, but most of the features they demonstrate are a bench mark for lesser survivals in other churches. The potential density of ecclesiastical sites within the region is indicated by a map of sites with pre-Conquest sculptures, many of which are located in churches of which at least part of the surviving fabric is pre-Conquest (Fig. 8.1). This distribution also illustrates the pre-Conquest propensity for settlement in the lower-lying landscapes of the coastal plain and major river valleys. The sites to be considered first are the well-known monastic centres at Hexham (Northumberland), in the Tyne Valley, Wearmouth and Jarrow (County Durham) at the mouths of the rivers Wear and the Tyne, all documented foundations of the later seventh century[2] which are influential centres with important surviving architectural features. Then, along the Tyne there is Bywell (Northumberland), documented as in existence by 802,[3] and Corbridge (also Northumberland) by 786,[4] both of which are recorded, at one time, as monastic sites. In addition there are two churches of uncertain status and date—Seaham on the coast

---

[1] I am grateful to Belinda Burke for her invaluable help in preparing the copy of this text, and to Derek Craig for his editorial corrections. I would also like to thank Paul Bidwell for allowing me to use his Hexham paper in advance of publication. It has not otherwise been possible to take account of work published since the 2010 weekend at which this paper was to be delivered, and in particular, of E. Cambridge, 'The Sources and Function of Wilfrid's Architecture at Ripon and Hexham', in *Wilfrid: Abbot, Bishop, Saint. Papers from the 1300th Anniversary Conferences*, ed. N. J. Higham (Donington, 2013), pp. 136–51.

[2] The foundation date of the monastery at Wearmouth is 673, with a church constructed between 674 and 675, *Historia Abbatum, auctore Anonymo* (hereafter *HAA*) 7, in *Venerabilis Baedae Opera Historica*, ed. C. Plummer, 2 vols (Oxford, 1896), c. 7, and Bede, *Historia Abbatum* (hereafter *HAB*), ibid., c. 4. The twinned foundation at Jarrow was founded in 681/2 with a church dedicated in 685. The foundation date of Hexham is not certain but, according to Wilfrid's biographer, the church was constructed in the 670s. Eddius Stephanus, *The Life of Bishop Wilfrid,* ed. and trans. B. Colgrave (Cambridge, 1927), c. 22.

[3] Symeon of Durham, *Historia Dunelmensis ecclesiae, Symeonis monachi opera omnia*, ed. T. Arnold, Rerum Britannicarum medii aevi scriptores 75, 2 vols (London, 1882–5), vol. 1, p. 52.

[4] Symeon of Durham, *Historia Regum, Symeonis monachi opera omnia*, vol. 2, p. 51.

and Escomb along the River Wear, both in County Durham. Their locations, near to Roman sites, rivers or the sea and centres of settlement, are common to many Anglo-Saxon church sites and where there have been excavations, as at Wearmouth, Jarrow and Seaham,[5] and (as suggested below) Hexham, there is a probable attachment to earlier burial grounds. All the churches, with the exception of Seaham and Bywell, have engendered a large body of scholarly comment particularly on their form and architectural development. This discussion concentrates on what seem to be still the outstanding issues as well as the links between them.

Although there is some evidence that stone churches with apsidal ends existed in Roman Britain,[6] rural churches were most commonly unicellular rectangles,[7] and many of the later structures seem to have been built in part or totally in wood. In this region the best evidence for such a church is the round-ended building excavated at Vindolanda (Northumberland), in the *praetorium* courtyard. The stone foundations of what appears to be a late Roman or sub-Roman building could have supported low stone walls, but it is plausibly suggested that they had been levelled to support timber sill-beams.[8] Some of the northern forts seem to have been occupied into the fifth century and there is evidence for seventh/eighth-century occupation at sites such as South Shields, County Durham, but on the whole in this area there is the lack of any unequivocal evidence for continuity of Christian church sites from the sub-Roman into the Anglo-Saxon period. On current evidence it would seem that most churches were new foundations from the seventh century onwards, and also that the earliest churches in this region were of wood. At the excavated site of the royal vill at Yeavering (Northumberland), a building, with an adjacent burial ground, in phases IV and V of the site's history,[9] has a claim to be the earliest complete example of an Anglo-Saxon wooden church. From the moment the Yeavering buildings with rectangular annexes were discovered comparison was made with the plans of stone churches in the north such as Escomb (see Colour Plate 8.2), and, as discussed below, some features in that church imitate wooden construction, although the masonry throughout is re-used Roman. Bede's well-known statement that the main church at Lindisfarne was of hewn oak in the manner of the Irish[10] could imply not just a

---

[5] For the early burials at Wearmouth and Jarrow see R. Cramp, *Wearmouth and Jarrow Monastic Sites*, 2 vols (Swindon, 2005–6), vol. 1, pp. 78–80, Fig. 8.3. In 1860–1 burials between the church and Seaham Hall were reported: a short account is to be found in B. Griffiths *et al.*, *Old Seaham in Anglo-Saxon and Medieval Times* (Newcastle, 2001), pp. 10–12; 35–8. In the 1990s a burial ground, near to the church, with Anglo-Saxon burials, was professionally excavated, but is not yet published.

[6] D. Petts, *Christianity in Roman Britain* (Stroud, 2003), pp. 54–6.

[7] Petts, *Christianity*, pp. 67–74.

[8] Petts, *Christianity*, p. 75, Fig. 26.

[9] B. Hope-Taylor, *Yeavering. An Anglo-British Centre of Early Northumbria* (London, 1977), Figs. 78, 79.

[10] Bede, *Historia ecclesiastica gentis Anglorum*, ed. and trans. B. Colgrave and R. A. B. Mynors

difference between wooden and stone traditions but discernible differences in construction and ornament in the timber architecture of that period which are impossible to reconstruct now from archaeological evidence. Secular timber buildings with rectangular or square annexes are of course known in the south,[11] but it is in the north that there is the more persistent local tradition for stone churches with rectangular annexes, serving both as chancels and western porches. Early commentators on Anglo-Saxon churches, such as Baldwin Brown and Clapham,[12] cited long narrow naves of considerable height and the rectangular chancel as Northumbrian features, although the latter was seen as of 'Celtic' influence. Rectangular chancels may indeed be part of an Insular tradition, but they also occur on the continent. In contrast, in Kent, south-eastern England and parts of the Midlands, apsidal east ends are relatively common in the earliest church buildings, and have been considered to reflect a Roman tradition.

But the aspiration of Benedict Biscop, founder of Wearmouth/Jarrow was, according to Bede, to build 'in the Roman manner', and the same aspiration seems to apply to Wilfrid, founder of Ripon (West Riding of Yorkshire) and Hexham. Both were major travellers on the continent where they would have seen more impressive Roman buildings than in their homeland, and early Christian buildings of outstanding grandeur. These travels no doubt put the churches in their homeland in perspective, but also opened their eyes to the prolific Roman ruins in their native landscape. Their aspiration was to join Northumbria to the Early Christian tradition with its great buildings which were directly associated with the companions of Christ like St Peter's in Rome, and indeed, as others have suggested, to evoke in distant England the very buildings at Jerusalem: the temple and the tomb of Christ.[13] Nevertheless at the outset, it is important to remember that their buildings are reminiscences rather than close copies of greater buildings. Craftsmen in stone had to be brought in from outside the area: Wilfrid is said to have returned to his native kingdom in *c.* 665 with singers 'and with masons and artisans of almost every kind', although it is not certain whether he acquired them abroad or in Kent,[14] but the contemporary testimony of Bede is that the founder of Wearmouth imported masons from Gaul.[15] Yet some details of these

---

(Oxford, 1969). bk. iii, c. 25.
[11] M. Millett with S. James, 'Excavations at Cowdery's Down, Basingstoke, Hampshire, 1978–81', *Archaeological Journal*, 140 (1983), pp. 151–279.
[12] G. B. Brown, *The Arts in Early England, vol. 2: Anglo-Saxon Architecture*, 2nd edn (London 1925), pp. 118–48; A. Clapham, *English Romanesque Architecture Before the Conquest* (Oxford 1930), pp. 38–46.
[13] R. Bailey, 'St Wilfrid, Ripon and Hexham', in *Studies in Insular Art and Archaeology*, ed. C. Karkov and R. Farrell, American Early Medieval Studies 1 (Oxford, Ohio, 1991), pp. 3–25 at pp. 20–2.
[14] Stephanus, *Life of Wilfrid*, c. 14.
[15] HAB, 5.

buildings are not easily paralleled elsewhere and there seems to be individual input (probably from their founders) in features which are inventive, imaginative, and suited to local conditions, and which distinguish the surviving architecture.

Wilfrid's two Northumbrian foundations can be dated between 671 and 678, with Ripon the first, and this could be the earliest of the group, with Hexham near to Wearmouth in date. Wearmouth monastery was founded by Benedict Biscop in 673 and St Peter's church was built between 674 and 675 with additions later. Jarrow monastery was founded in 682 and the church of St Paul's was dedicated in 685.

Wilfrid's biographer Stephanus says of Ripon 'he built and completed from the foundations in the earth up to the roof a church of dressed stone supported by various columns and side aisles or chambers [*porticus*].'[16] Since nothing remains above ground of the church, which was dedicated to God and St Peter, one cannot say whether there were free-standing columns, as one huge base which survives could suggest,[17] or more probably engaged columns. What is unambiguous is that on this site, which had been one of the Irish foundations, and so presumably constructed in wood, he built in cut stone, and what does survive is a remarkable stone built crypt (Fig. 8.3); it is not mentioned by Stephanus although he does mention a crypt at Hexham, and there is no reason to believe that it was not built with the original church, and it is very like that surviving at Hexham.

These crypts are two remarkable structures, as Bailey says '[...] only on these two sites is it possible to stand completely enclosed within walls and roofs built during the first century of Anglo-Saxon Christianity'.[18] No close parallels for the complex form of the crypts has been found, despite extensive discussion. They seem an individual invention drawing on reminiscences of a variety of religious buildings. Indeed at Hexham on an estate given by the queen, Wilfrid built a house in honour of the apostle St Andrew for which it is claimed, in Stephanus' glowing description, that he was his own architect:

> the depth of foundations in the earth, and its crypts, of wonderfully dressed stone, and the manifold buildings above ground supported by various columns and many side aisles [*porticus*], and adorned with walls of notable length and height surrounded by various winding passages with spiral stairs running up and down, for our holy bishop, being taught by the spirit of God, thought out how to construct these buildings; nor have we heard of any building on this side of the Alps, built on such a scale.[19]

---

[16] Stephanus, *Life of Wilfrid*, c. 17. For a recent commentary on Ripon and its church see R. Hall, 'Observations on Ripon Cathedral Crypt', *Yorkshire Archaeological Journal*, 65 (1993), pp. 39–53.

[17] E. Coatsworth, *Corpus of Anglo-Saxon Stone Sculpture*, vol. 8: *Western Yorkshire* (Oxford, 2008), ill. 676.

[18] Bailey, 'St Wilfrid', p. 3.

[19] Stephanus, *Life of Wilfrid*, c. 22.

Fig. 8.3 (a): Hexham (Northumberland) and Ripon (West Riding of Yorkshire): crypts. (After Brown, as n. 12.)

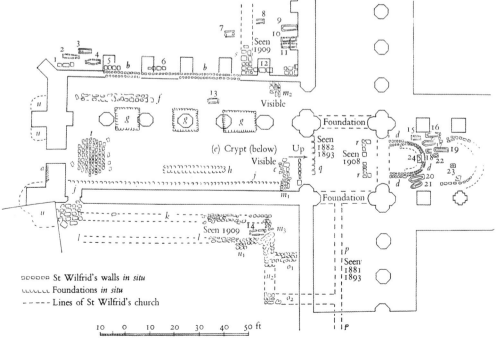

(b): Hexham church plan. (After Hodges and Gibson, as n. 20.)

In other words it rivalled anything in Gaul, but not, of course, Rome. Nothing is left above ground now of this complex church, but extensive discussions (notably by Harold Taylor and more recently, Richard Bailey, Eric Cambridge), on the possible form of the church, use as a starting point the plans of the architect Charles Hodges who recorded the walls he saw between 1880 and 1910 (Fig. 8.3b),[20] when the standing church was reconstructed. Recent reconstructions suggest complex aisled churches with similarities to those at Wearmouth and Jarrow discussed below. The differing thickness of walls and their inter-cutting, as Hodges recorded it, indicate, however, different phases of building, and of particular interest is a small apsidal building which lies to the east of the major church and is cut by later walls.

But, to consider first what can still be seen—the crypts of both Hexham and Ripon. There are features which could indicate that initial ideas tried at Ripon were improved on at Hexham: in both a long narrow passage on the north leads into ante-chamber fronting main chambers of similar size, and in both another narrow passage on the south leads out of the main chambers, but, at Hexham, an additional steep flight of steps leads from the west of the ante-chamber into the main body of the church. In both the lighting (eight lamps at Ripon and four at Hexham) seems directed towards the east and north walls.

What has struck commentators from the first discovery of the Hexham crypt is the distinctive Roman tooling and decoration on the stonework, which shows through the plaster at eye level, particularly in the north passage and the main chamber. It has long been supposed that the stones came from the nearby Roman settlement at Corbridge (*Corstopitum*) although amongst the extensive remains at the fort and settlement nothing like them survives. Now the source of the stone has been convincingly demonstrated by Paul Bidwell, who in a detailed survey and analysis of the crypt and this distinctive stonework, has traced the tooled stone to the bridges at Corbridge and Chesters (Northumberland), and the decorative elements (which include dentils, cables and leaf and berry ornament) to a huge tower tomb at Shorden Brae cemetery (Northumberland), now completely robbed.[21] His work also includes

---

[20] See especially, C. Hodges, *Ecclesia Hagustaldensis: The Abbey of St Andrew, Hexham* (London, 1888); C. Hodges and J. Gibson, *Hexham and its Abbey* (Hexham, 1919); H. M. Taylor and J. Taylor, 'The Seventh-Century Church at Hexham: A New Appreciation', *Archaeologia Aeliana*, 4th ser., 39 (1961), pp. 103–34; R. Bailey 'The Anglo-Saxon Church at Hexham' *Archaeologia Aeliana*, 5th ser., 4 (1976), pp. 47–67; R. Bailey and D. O'Sullivan 'Excavations over St Wilfrid's Crypt at Hexham, 1978', *Archaeologia Aeliana*, 5th ser., 7 (1979), pp. 114–57; E. Cambridge, 'C. C. Hodges and the Nave of Hexham Abbey', *Archaeologia Aeliana*, 5th ser., 7, (1979), pp. 159–68; E. Cambridge and A. Williams, 'Hexham Abbey: A Review of Recent Work and its Implications', *Archaeologia Aeliana*, 5th ser., 23 (1995), pp. 51–138.

[21] P. Bidwell, 'A Survey of the Anglo-Saxon Crypt at Hexham and its Reused Roman Stonework', *Archaeologia Aeliana*, 5th ser., 39 (2010), pp. 53–146.

8. NORTHUMBRIAN CHURCHES

the most recent review of current opinions of the church and crypt and a full compilation of drawings of the crypt.

There were plenty of Roman ruins in this northern landscape and Bidwell has calculated, in a text which must be read to be appreciated, roughly how much stone would be needed for St Andrew's church, and how it could be obtained using the abutments of the bridges at Corbridge and Chesters and the entire monument at Shorden Brae. Nothing was derived from the main Roman site of Corbridge except a Severan inscription from the central granaries, but the stonework was gathered from the periphery of that site. We do not know here, as elsewhere in Anglo-Saxon England at this time, who was considered to 'own' Roman ruins although it could have been the king. Perhaps the stone from the central site was used instead nearby at St Andrew's church in the market place of the modern town of Corbridge which is documented as existing in 786 and seems to have been in the king's possession.[22] All of the Northumbrian churches considered here incorporate some Roman stone, but nowhere else does one get the dramatic display of inscriptions and different types of Roman ornament found at Hexham. Was this because Wilfrid had seen in Rome churches being constructed or reconstructed which utilised Roman *spolia* and he too, in the Roman manner, wished to stress that there was also a Roman past in his region? There has been much recent discussion of the significance of the frequent use of Roman stone in Anglo-Saxon churches,[23] whether as an appropriation of the past or to confer authority, and certainly it would seem that there was more to the use of Roman stone than the utilisation of conveniently ready shaped building material. But that aspect should not be dismissed, there are the constraints in a less sophisticated technology, and Bidwell has demonstrated what a large proportion of any building process is absorbed in quarrying and shaping stone and how much time and effort the use of ready-cut stone can save. The huge megalithic quoins, which are a distinctive feature of all of these Northumbrian churches, would not have been easy to quarry and shape and also, in many churches, Roman blocks which had been cut to irregular shapes were not recut into rectangular blocks, but the cavities were filled in jigsaw-fashion with small fragments or even pebbles. (This is particularly visible at Escomb.) It is also feasible that in robbing standing stone buildings their methods of construction could have been copied, so that what we see now as typical Anglo-Saxon features in early Northumbrian buildings could have been copied from Roman

---

[22] Corbridge was a central place on major routes, and St Andrew's church which fronts onto the present market-place, supports the late reference to it being a trading centre, which in the Anglo-Saxon period could have been controlled from a royal monastery. D. Pelteret 'Slave Raiding and Slave Trading in Early England', *Anglo-Saxon England*, 9 (Cambridge, 1981), pp. 108–9.

[23] A convenient summary of recent views is to be found in T. Eaton, *Plundering the Past: Roman Stonework in Medieval Britain* (Stroud, 2000).

structures which alas do not survive to support or refute this view. Bidwell has found parallels for the ribbed vaults in Wilfrid's crypts in the construction of Roman strong rooms for example at Great Chesters. At both Corbridge and Escomb churches there are major arches which are claimed as reused Roman because of their neat voussoired heads. Both openings are formed from massive upright and flat jambs which are normally considered to be of Anglo-Saxon type, but could be Roman.

As well as copying architectural forms from the Roman world, it is clear from the complexity of layout as well as some textual references that both Wilfrid and Benedict Biscop wished to emulate Roman liturgy.[24] How the Hexham crypt operated is also still a matter for debate, its form is unique in its time—it is neither a mausoleum nor a ring crypt, but credibly the central chamber was to display a relic or relics. The present consensus is that the entrance to the journey to the relic chamber was by the northern passage, with exit either through the south or the western openings, but it would be easier to determine the route for visitors or processions if we knew the functions of the areas from which they began and ended their visit to the crypt, and especially where the monastic buildings were, since these could have been open only to religious.

The narrow turned passages to the north and south were certainly meant to induce a disorientating feeling of entry into another world, and a more ancient world in which there were visible signs of the Roman past with the sculptures and inscriptions. Then could have come a sense of awe when the flickering lights of the main chamber illuminated an altar and relics encased in their golden jewel-incrusted reliquaries came into view. The widening of the passages at the end of the north and south stairs at Hexham, which are not features at Ripon, could well have been one of Wilfrid's innovations to deal with the turn into the viewing space of the main chamber where one would naturally stop. Was the addition of another entrance to the west a similar invention based on experience, or does it reflect a liturgical change or option? Was it so that the main body of pilgrims would not have to pass through the main chamber as they did at Ripon, but were diverted west? It is not easy to provide conclusive answers to these questions. The idea that the southern passage, which led directly into the relic chamber, was an entrance for the clergy has attractions, since the major monastic buildings at Wearmouth/Jarrow and indeed the later medieval monastery at Hexham were on the south side of the building. If the laity were sent directly up the steep stairs to the west, however, that could have been straight into the

---

[24] Wilfrid claimed that he had introduced to Northumbria the practice of antiphonal singing with the alternate chanting of two choirs (Stephanus, *Life of Wilfrid*, c. 47 with note on p. 180). For a discussion of the stational liturgies of Rome with their processions between churches, and between shrines within individual churches (which both Wilfrid and Benedict would have known) see É. Ó Carragáin, *The City of Rome and the World of Bede*, Jarrow Lecture 1994 (Jarrow, 1994).

choir enclosure. On the other hand were there large numbers of lay pilgrims at this stage in seventh-century Northumbria or was Wilfrid hopeful that in building these structures he could recreate what he had seen in Italy? In default of a local saint he may have acquired a relic of St Andrew whilst in Rome, but in Bernicia only St Cuthbert's tomb at Lindisfarne seems to have had the pulling power to have attracted pilgrims seeking healing.[25] But there direct contact with his body in the shrine tomb seems to have been possible and the tomb was apparently on the floor of the church. There may have been more pilgrimage in Northumbria in the seventh and eighth centuries than we know of, but Cuthbert's cult was pre-eminent and since his incorrupt body was preserved from the relic snatching of the Viking Age, it survived even the dislocations of the Norman Conquest.

If the relics at Hexham were smaller and more portable, then wide straight stairs which led directly to and from the main chamber could have been more convenient for solemn processions in which the relics would be brought out and displayed. Bidwell has noted that there is no provision for a door at the west entrance and the chamber could be viewed from the church. The opening could however have been closed by a curtain, rather than planked over as Bidwell has suggested,[26] so that there was not a direct view into the relic chamber, but in the enclosed space of the choir it would not be so visible or accessible for the laity.

Richard Bailey's suggestion that the inspiration for the form of these unique crypts with winding narrow entries could have been the catacombs, where narrow passages open on to burial chambers, and also that there could be a reminiscence for the tomb of Christ, stresses the funerary associations for the buildings. Although there is no evidence for a burial in the Hexham crypt, it is tempting to suggest that it was inserted into an old cemetery or cult focus centred around the small apsed building to the east. This structure is an anomaly in Anglo-Saxon Northumbria, as mentioned above, but is curiously constructed; it is cut by the later transept, but west of the cut the west wall is only one stone thick, and east of it the walling is differently constructed and two stones thick, whilst Hodges' section shows the west and east walls of different depths. There is the trace of an internal bench around the interior of the apsidal end. In form this is like some Roman shrines such as the shrine of the nymphs sited amongst a complex of Roman shrines at Carrawburgh (Northumberland) on Hadrian's Wall,[27] and it is possible that in siting the church in an ancient holy place, whether or not it had been already used as an Anglo-Saxon burial

---

[25] Anonymous, *Vita sancti Cuthberti*, *Two Lives of St Cuthbert*, ed. and trans. B. Colgrave (Cambridge, 1940), cc. 15–18; Bede, *Vita sancti Cuthberti*, ibid., cc. 43–6.

[26] Bidwell, 'Anglo-Saxon Crypt', pp. 127–30.

[27] D. Smith 'The Shrine of the Nymphs and the Genius Loci at Carrawburgh', *Archaeologia Aeliana*, 4th ser., 40 (1962), pp. 59–81, Fig. I and pl. IX. Cambridge and Williams 'Hexham Abbey', pp. 79–80, considered that the structure could have been a mausoleum, but notes there is no burial inside and that the apsidal end is without parallels.

ground, the structure was reshaped into a funerary shrine around which later clustered important burials, including that of Bishop Acca. Many years ago I commented on the early burials surrounding St Andrew's, Hexham, and the possibility that some may have been earlier than the church.[28] What is clear is that the church is surrounded by burials on the north and east and indeed possibly on other sides as has been discovered by excavation at Wearmouth, Jarrow and Seaham. The currently isolated position of Hexham on the south bank of the Tyne (see Fig. 8.1) could be explained by an earlier cult focus.

There is textual evidence that there were two other churches at Hexham,[29] St Peter's, which was at some distance away, and St Mary's to the east of St Andrew's, which is plausibly where the medieval church of St Mary's was located across the market place. Market places to the west of a medieval church are of course known elsewhere, but this juxtaposition could have existed already in the Anglo-Saxon period since there is the same relationship with St Andrew's, Bywell, and St Andrew's, Corbridge, and there is pre-Conquest evidence that Corbridge was a market centre.[30] What is, however, still lacking at Hexham is evidence for the monastic layout. Other Northumbrian sites can, however, provide clearer answers to the ecclesiastical topography, notably sites with several churches such as Bywell with its standing churches dedicated to St Andrew and St Peter some distance apart and Wearmouth/Jarrow, where more extensive twentieth-century excavations, can relate the churches to the monastic buildings.

At Wearmouth (see Colour Plate Fig. 8.4) the building of the church began in 674 on land donated by the king, and with the aid of craftsmen from Gaul (probably from north-east France) and in 675/6 glaziers brought from the continent to glaze the windows in the church, the porticus (side chapels or other adjuncts as discussed below) and upper storeys or refectories. In 675 the church was dedicated to St Peter.[31] What survives is the west wall, a one-storey porch which is secondary but of the same construction, and which was raised later into a tower. The massive quoins show the width of the original nave, and its line has been traced, by small scale interventions inside, giving an interior width of 18 ft 6 in. (5.6 m.); height *c.* 30 ft (9.20 m.) and potential length of 64 ft (19.5 m.). There is evidence for side chambers on the north, but no conclusive evidence about the east end or whether the burial porticus mentioned by Bede was a separate or attached structure.[32] The proportions of the

[28] R. Cramp, 'Early Northumbrian Sculpture at Hexham', in *Saint Wilfrid at Hexham*, ed. D. P. Kirby (Newcastle, 1974), pp. 115–40 at pp. 126–7.
[29] For St Mary's church, see Stephanus, *Life of Wilfrid*, c. 56.
[30] See note 21.
[31] The church is fully discussed in Cramp, *Wearmouth and Jarrow*, vol. 1, pp. 43–75, especially pp. 66–72, Fig. 6.17.
[32] It is referred to in *HAA*, c. 18; for a discussion see Cramp, *Wearmouth and Jarrow*, vol. 1, pp. 67–8.

building, the massive quoins, and the forms of the splayed windows are all features found elsewhere in early Northumbrian churches. There is however little use of Roman *spolia* save for the quoins and door openings and the fabric of rubble set in poured concrete, which is the same in the early monastic buildings, but is not paralleled in churches elsewhere. The west porticus is the part of the church directly linked to the monastic buildings (Fig. 8.5a). It has openings on all four sides, closed with doors except on west, and in this *porticus ingressus* Abbot Eosterwine was buried before 716. So, if the central chamber was used for burial, to what did the other doors lead? The southern led down to monastic buildings and a cemetery, as was demonstrated by the excavations; the northern could have housed a stairway to the upper chamber through a door still visible in the north wall. How such stairs worked could be illustrated by a later development in Corbridge church. The stairs and the present form of the door are medieval as David Parsons pointed out long ago,[33] but the form of the opening on the opposite (south) side indicates something earlier and there could have been an upper chamber alongside the western porch before later developments destroyed the chamber. The Wearmouth upper chamber, with its east window into the church, may have functioned as a sort of *Kaiserhalle* for visiting dignitaries with a view into the church, as found in later Carolingian churches, but since there appears to be no safe crypt here, it could have functioned as a treasury, and the window used for the demonstration of important relics (in reminiscence of the *sacrarium* at St Peter's Rome, which was to the left of the entrance porticus). I will return to the uses of upper spaces later.

The decorated façade of the Wearmouth porch with its animal frieze and figure of St Peter or Christ provides an *in situ* context for similar items at Hexham now displaced, but Wearmouth is unique in the quantity of decorative sculpture which has survived and, in the use of insular as well as classical motifs,[34] seems to provide a transition between the familiar secular world and the more unfamiliar early Christian world which was reflected in the paintings imported by Benedict Biscop to enhance the interior. There was new technology also at Wearmouth: the lathe-turned shafts (which are also found at Jarrow) could be derived from a secular wood-working tradition, but the mortar mixers excavated on the site are a technology derived from Roman models, and were used for the fabric of the church and monastic buildings.[35]

Despite the fragmentary nature of the evidence, with a loss of floor levels so that the functions of buildings could not be determined, the site has provided an

---

[33] D. Parsons, 'The West Tower of St Andrew's Church, Corbridge', *Archaeologia Aeliana*, 5th ser., 23, pp. 185–218.

[34] R. Cramp, *Corpus of Anglo-Saxon Stone Sculpture, vol. 1: County Durham and Northumberland*, 2 vols (Oxford, 1984), vol. 2, Hexham, ills. 184–5; Wearmouth, ills.113–24; Cramp *Wearmouth and Jarrow*, vol. 1, pp. 43–75.

[35] Cramp *Wearmouth and Jarrow*, vol. 1, pp. 93–5.

illuminating picture of the church in its setting, with an enclosed space to the south reminiscent of a Roman villa. The long corridor leading from the centre of St Peter's church through the cemetery to ranges of buildings and beyond is a distinctive and unusual feature. It seems to have functioned as a processional way leading probably to the dormitory and on to the river, and it also appears to serve as a division between lay and monastic burials. It may however have had a deeper meaning if it is considered as a porticus. The most recent and fullest discussion by Ó Carragáin concludes that the word can refer to a variety of structures that can include aisles inside and outside buildings, as well as chambers, and at Wearmouth the long corridor linking the church and monastic buildings could be a reminiscence of processional ways in Rome which ran to St Peter's or St Paul's Outside the Walls, but a similar structure ran between the churches at Luxeuil in France, although this too could have copied the Roman buildings.[36] The stational liturgy whereby throughout the year Mass was said at different major churches and shrines in Rome, was known in England and in a compressed itinerary could be enacted between the various churches and chapels of a monastery. At Wearmouth at least two churches other than St Peter's are recorded: St Mary's by 686, which like Hexham could have been round, and possibly some way away, and the chapel of St Lawrence which was on the south side of St Peter's on the way to the river. A formal progress between them is recorded in the account of abbot Ceolfrid's departure to Rome in 716.[37] He went in procession with the singing of psalms and antiphons, preceded by candles and a processional cross, from the chapel of St Mary to St Peter's and then to the chapel of St Lawrence which was 'near to' or 'in' the dormitory of the brethren, then on to the river. There he was ferried across the river accompanied by deacons holding the golden cross and lighted candle until he reached the south shore and then, having venerated the cross, he mounted his horse and left the grieving community.

Other reminiscences of Roman custom may be seen in Eosterwine's burial in the *porticus ingressus*. Benedict Biscop was the first person to be buried in the church in 689 on the east side of the altar in the porticus of St Peter and in 716 Eosterwine and Sigfrid's remains were translated inside also to the side of the altar. Ó Carragáin has seen this as an imitation of what happening in Rome where the body of the earlier Pope Leo was taken in 688 from the entrance porticus of St Peter's to a place near the altar.[38]

As part of Ceolfrid's farewell peregrinations he had first visited St Paul's, Jarrow, the second foundation, which Bede was at pains to point out constituted with St Peter's, Wearmouth, one monastery in two places. It was built by monks from Wearmouth and its church was dedicated in 685, as is recorded in its learned dedication stone—the earliest surviving in Britain.[39] Here there were two churches on

---

[36] Ó Carragáin, *City of Rome*, pp. 12–14 and 62.
[37] *HAA*, cc. 25–7.
[38] Ó Carragáin, *City of Rome*, p. 15.

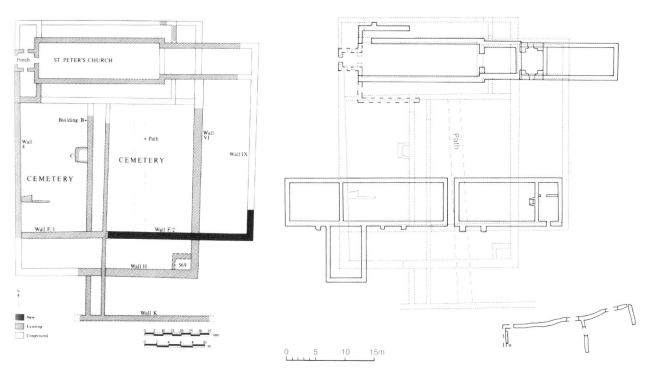

Fig. 8.5 (a): Wearmouth: reconstruction plan of Phase 3 church and monastic buildings.

(b): Comparative reconstruction plans of Wearmouth and Jarrow (both County Durham); Jarrow shown by the heavier lines. (both © Copyright R. Cramp.)

the same axis, the small eastern church had the same characteristics as other Northumbrian churches, huge side alternate quoins, small splayed windows with monolithic heads, doors to the north and south into burial grounds, the church being apparently inserted into an old burial ground.[40] It may well have been a funerary chapel serving the same purpose as the eastern porticus at Wearmouth. The basilica to which the dedication stone refers was altered in the post-Conquest period and a plan was made in the eighteenth century, before it was swept away when a new church was built, in 1782. The church was then largely reconstructed by Gilbert Scott whose church, completed in 1866, still stands. Limited excavation supports the accuracy of the eighteenth-century plan and has revealed an outline which in size is almost identical with Wearmouth (Fig. 8.5b), with a narrow north aisle in the first phase which is paralleled in some contemporary churches in France.[41] Later, if we can trust the eighteenth-century drawing, side chambers were developed, and finally the two churches were joined by a narrow structure leaving a passage through on the ground

[39] Cramp, *Wearmouth and Jarrow*, vol. 1, Fig. A1.1, pp. 365–6.
[40] Cramp, *Wearmouth and Jarrow*: for a full discussion of the east church see vol. 1, pp. 146–54, and Figs. 13.15 and 13.16.
[41] N. Duval *et al.*, *Naissance des arts chrétiens: atlas des monuments paléochrétiens de la France* (Paris, 1991), pp. 200–1.

floor and an upper chamber communicating both east and west with a door possibly into a gallery in the east wall.[42] This could be an early ninth-century development with a central low tower, useful for safe storage, or possibly for choir use. Such a structure has been suggested for a Northumbrian church described in an Old English poem *De Abbatibus*. The poet describes a monastic church in which he and another brother saw two bands of angels who entered their church and sang for a long time 'by the doors under the roof of the church'.[43] In a dream he sees an even more elaborate church with large and small chapels ('porticus') closed by doors, and in the western porticus an especially elaborate altar. There are several ways of reconstructing the churches in the poem as there are for churches already considered such as Hexham, Wearmouth and Jarrow where so much of the upper structures hinted at in surviving documentary or archaeological sources must remain speculative.[44]

Striking similarities in plan between the churches of Wearmouth and Jarrow may also be reflected at Hexham,[xlv] and the surviving sculptural decoration at Hexham and Jarrow has so many likenesses, in for example the baluster imposts and friezes, that if one could reconstruct the interiors these similarities might be reinforced. But local differences were dealt with in different ways and with the inventiveness I mentioned at the beginning of the paper. Despite the plans of the churches being almost identical at Wearmouth and Jarrow, and the site layout with burial grounds surrounding the churches through which one passed to parallel ranges of buildings, the impression of the two sites is very different.[46]

If the location of the churches at Jarrow was dependent on the east church being sited in an earlier burial ground, then it left a smaller space than at Wearmouth between the churches and monastic buildings and the area leading to the river. There was no processional way, and the buildings opposite the churches were not a range, and enclosed, but two separate buildings with a layout more like the Yeavering halls. Yet these great stone halls were of the same construction and as lavishly decorated as churches, with sculptured panels, painted plaster and coloured window glass, and in this they are a unique testament, so far, in Anglo-Saxon England to the grandeur of some of the monastic buildings.

The influence of great centres such as Hexham and Wearmouth/Jarrow seems without question, but much of it must be inferred when considering other less documented and unexcavated individual churches. Other churches dedicated to St Andrew near to Hexham, such as Corbridge or Simonburn (Northumberland),[47]

---

42   Cramp, *Wearmouth and Jarrow*, vol.1, Figs. 13.17; 13.19.
43   Æthelwulf, *De Abbatibus*, ed. A. Campbell (Oxford, 1967), pp. 54–7.
44   H. Taylor, 'The Architectural interest of Æthelwulf's "*De Abbatibus*"', *Anglo-Saxon England* 3 (1974), pp. 163–73, at Figs. 9 and 10.
45   Bailey, 'St Wilfrid', Fig. 6; Cambridge and Williams, 'Hexham Abbey', pp. 76–79.
46   Cramp, *Wearmouth and Jarrow*, vol. 1, Figs. 9.40, 16.88, 24.3.

could have been influenced by or even be subsidiaries of Hexham. Seaham (now St Mary's but said to have been originally dedicated to St Andrew) certainly was within the territory of Wearmouth/Jarrow, and was possibly a subsidiary. It has many of the features discussed so far with huge megalithic quoins, single-splayed windows north and south similar to those at Jarrow and a simple plan with a rectangular east end.[48] It has however been rebuilt in the pre-Conquest period with larger and more decorated windows in the north wall, and this style of architecture is possibly of a later date than the seventh-century churches discussed so far.

St John's Escomb, mentioned already, presents an interesting problem as to its relationship with other centres. It has an indigenous plan with rectangular adjuncts east and west—the east the chancel and the west (as revealed by excavation) a funerary porticus.[49] It has north and south doors and is almost identical in size with Jarrow east church, but, like Hexham, it is built almost entirely of Roman stone with inscriptions clearly displayed, and there is an impressive arch (probably Roman, re-erected) dividing the nave and chancel. This is in direct contrast with the evidence for carpentry techniques in the dowelling of the lintel into the jambs of the north door. Leading from the chancel is a north door into a secondary porticus, which is a strange construction, possibly of timber on a cobbled foundation, and may have been a sacristy. The only evidence that we have for a similar northern adjunct which is entered from a door closely fitted against the nave wall is St Peter's church at Bywell on Tyne.

Bywell on Tyne is now a shrunken village in which two churches survive, St Peter's and St Andrew's, positioned at some distance from each other but intervisible, and stational processions between them can be envisaged. In the Middle Ages, there was a market place between them as mentioned above. St Peter's stands on higher ground surrounded by a loop in the river (a favoured position for early Northumbrian churches), but St Andrew's, with its eleventh-century tower (see Colour Plate 8.6), like Wearmouth, is set in what seems to be a circular churchyard—which is considered to be an early feature also, so both churches could have co-existed from the beginning. Both reflect several building periods.[50] At St Andrew's an earlier west front is visible under the tower with the types of features now familiar—large Roman stones used as quoins and a western adjunct. Inside, an impost is identical with one from Hexham

---

[47] Cramp, *Corpus of Anglo-Saxon Stone Sculpture*, vol. 1, ills. 223–4, vol. 2, ills. 1233–40.
[48] H. M. Taylor and J. Taylor, *Anglo-Saxon Architecture*, 3 vols (Cambridge, 1965–78), vol. 2, pp. 534–6.
[49] For the excavated features at Escomb see M. Pocock and H. Wheeler, 'Excavations at Escomb Church', *Journal of the British Archaeological Association*, 3rd ser., 34 (1971), pp. 11–29.
[50] See, E. Gilbert, 'New Views on Warden, Bywell, and Heddon-on-the-Wall churches', *Archaeologia Aeliana*, 4th ser., 24 (1946), pp. 163–7 (St Andrew's), pp. 167–76 (St Peter's); Taylor and Taylor, *Anglo-Saxon Architecture*, vol. 1, pp. 122–6.

and there is evidence from a burial monument of Viking age, as well as the late tower, that it continued as a congregational church. St Peter's also has early features. It is a long narrow church with a series of high windows, providing light above side chambers, the scars of which can be seen on the outside north wall. Some windows are reset but, like Seaham, they are rather larger than Wearmouth/Jarrow and Corbridge, and could be later. The south wall is partly obscured by a later medieval chantry chapel, but the quoins which end the nave are visible, and tucked into the junction of the nave and chancel is a rectangular headed door in the same position as that at Escomb, and the roof line of the porticus it led into is also visible. Inside that area, now covered up and largely forgotten, is a well indicating that it was an adjunct for baptism. There is plenty of evidence for the siting of early churches alongside earlier ritual sites particularly in the Celtic west, where many holy wells survive, but also it is evident that these could be used for drawing living water for baptisms before fonts became common in tenth to eleventh century.[51]

We began with Yeavering, a place where Paulinus the first Christian missionary to the Northumbrians baptised King Edwin's subjects for thirty-six days in the River Glen, and probably St Peter's, Bywell was sited originally alongside the river Tyne for the same purpose. Baptism was part of the pastoral care that some monasteries provided as well as the skills of their teachers and their doctors and craftsmen. Such essential spiritual care was probably not the primary vision of their founders, when they imported craftsmen, singers and works of art to embellish their buildings. But, in attempting to imitate at the most northerly limit of the old Roman Empire, the new Rome which was the image of Jerusalem, they must have opened the eyes of all who entered their churches to a more colourful and more exotic world, and to the beauty that was a foretaste of heaven.

---

[51] R. Morris, *Churches in the Landscape* (London, 1989), pp. 84–8; J. Blair, 'The Prehistory of English Fonts', in *Intersections: the Archaeology and History of Christianity in England, 400–1200: Papers in Honour of Martin Biddle and Birthe Kjølbye-Biddle*, ed. M. Henig and N. Ramsey, British Archaeological Reports British Series 505 (Oxford, 2010), pp. 149–77.

(9)
The Early Medieval Church at Brixworth, Northamptonshire

DAVID PARSONS

Introduction

Brixworth is situated centrally in Northamptonshire in the East Midlands of England. In the Anglo-Saxon period it lay in the outer or eastern part of the kingdom of Mercia. It is 7 miles (11.25 km.) north of Northampton, and 25 (40 km.) south of Leicester, both important Anglo-Saxon centres. There is evidence for occupation in the Romano-British period in the shape of a villa some half mile (0.8 km.) north of the church, and in the early and middle Anglo-Saxon periods there were three, possibly four, mixed-rite cemeteries and a settlement site towards the southern end of the parish, part of which has been excavated archaeologically.[1] Settlement is further attested by significant scatters of middle Saxon pottery down the western side of the parish.[2]

The church of All Saints stands on rising ground towards the northern end of the parish (see Colour Plate 9.1). Its importance as an early place of worship was first recognised by the antiquary and self-trained architect Thomas Rickman, who visited the church in 1823, as recorded in his daybooks; his account of All Saints' was incorporated into the third and subsequent editions of his seminal work on English architecture.[3] Shortly after, the Revd C. F. Watkins became Vicar of Brixworth and during his long incumbency made a series of observations about the fabric of the church, and in 1865–6 instigated a far-reaching restoration, part of whose purpose was to recreate as far as possible what he thought was the Anglo-Saxon form of the building. His activities and the publication of his account of these and of his interpretation of his findings[4] drew academic attention to All Saints', leading to a

---

[1] A. L. Meaney, *A Gazetteer of Early Anglo-Saxon Burial Sites* (London, 1964), pp. 187–8; S. Ford, 'The Excavation of a Saxon Settlement and a Mesolithic Flint Scatter at Northampton Road, Brixworth, Northamptonshire, 1994', *Northamptonshire Archaeology*, 26 (1995), pp. 79–108 at pp. 81–8.

[2] D. Hall and P. Martin, 'Brixworth, Northamptonshire—An intensive Field Survey', *Journal of the British Archaeological Association*, 132 (1979), pp. 1–6.

[3] T. Rickman, *An Attempt to Discriminate the Styles of Architecture in England, from the Conquest to the Reformation*, 3rd edn (London, 1825), pp. 265–7.

[4] C. F. Watkins, *The Basilica; or, Palatial Hall of Justice and Sacred Temple; its Nature, Origin and Purport; and a Description and History of the Basilican Church of Brixworth* (London, 1867).

steady stream of articles and references in books over the ensuing one and a half centuries.

One such account, by the eminent archaeologist and architectural historian Sir Alfred Clapham, has supplied the oft-quoted appreciation of Brixworth church as 'the most imposing seventh-century architectural monument yet surviving north of the Alps',[5] and while it is now clear from both archaeological and architectural evidence not available when Clapham wrote that his proposed date was incorrect, his appraisal of the church in the context of places of worship in the early Middle Ages remains a measure of its historical significance.

Clapham's mis-dating of the existing building was based on an acceptance at face value of a statement of the twelfth-century Peterborough chronicler Hugo Candidus.[6] The genuineness and value of Hugo's text are highly dubious, and have been examined in detail recently by several historians.[7] Though the structure of the existing church must be dissociated from it, his text was formerly held to imply that a church was founded at Brixworth towards the end of the seventh century. As Barnwell has made clear, this implication cannot be sustained, and there is no evidence for a church predating the existing one. On general grounds, however, the possibility of an earlier church on the site should not be entirely discounted. Clapham's claim that it was a *monasterium* is incapable of proof, though there are various suggestive features that would not be inconsistent with such a status, not least the scale of the surviving building (which when complete was even larger than the present church). But there is no evidence to show what kind of community the church served or what its purpose was, in short how it should be described and defined in terms of the criteria proposed by Professors Foot and Blair and others.[8]

This all serves to emphasise the lack of documentary evidence for All Saints'. Nothing survives from before the Norman Conquest, and material from the post-Conquest period is very limited and sheds little light on its origins. The historical importance of the church depends very largely on the evidence of its fabric and comparisons with other contemporary places of worship both at home and abroad, together with information recovered by archaeological excavation and geophysical

---

[5] A. W. Clapham, *English Romanesque Architecture Before the Conquest* (Oxford, 1930), p. 33.
[6] *The Chronicle of Hugh Candidus, a Monk of Peterborough*, ed. W. T. Mellows (London, 1949), p. 15.
[7] A. M. Morris, 'Forging Links with the Past: The Twelfth-Century Reconstruction of Anglo-Saxon Peterborough', Ph.D. thesis, University of Leicester, 2 vols (2006); *Charters of Peterborough Abbey*, ed. S. E. Kelly, Anglo-Saxon Charters, 14 (Oxford, 2009); P. S. Barnwell, 'Documentary and Textual Evidence: Brixworth in History', in D. Parsons and D. S. Sutherland, *The Anglo-Saxon Church of All Saints, Brixworth, Northamptonshire: Survey, Excavation and Analysis, 1972–2010* (Oxford, 2013), pp. 220–9.
[8] S. Foot, *Monastic Life in Anglo-Saxon England*, c. 600–900 (Cambridge, 2006); J. Blair, *The Church in Anglo-Saxon Society* (Oxford, 2005).

survey. On the documentary front, the granting of All Saints' to Salisbury Cathedral (Wiltshire) as a prebend after the Conquest is a measure of its enhanced status in comparison with a 'normal' parish church.[9]

All Saints' Church now and in the Anglo-Saxon period: An Outline Development

The church as it exists today is impressive, and consists of three main compartments—nave, choir and apse, a west tower with an attached stair turret—and a two-bay south-eastern chapel. Around the apse a subterranean passage, now open to the sky, is the remnant of a ring-crypt, which was originally vaulted over and accessed by doorways low in the east wall of the choir (Fig. 9.2a). The basic fabric of the nave and choir is the original structure of the late-eighth to early-ninth century, though the dividing wall between them was largely replaced in the late middle ages by a standard two-centred arch. In the side walls of the nave the arches of the original four-bay arcades survive, but are filled with masonry of mid nineteenth-century date, including a window in each bay, with the exception of the most westerly arch on the south side, in which the main entrance is set, a doorway of late Romanesque form. These major arches once led into side chambers (porticus) or aisles subdivided by masonry cross walls into separate compartments. There is clear archaeological evidence for the range of chambers on the north side of the church; the most easterly porticus overlapped the choir and the small connecting door can still be seen, blocked, in the north wall of the choir. Excavation has revealed that there was also a door to the exterior in the porticus east wall. The restored plan of the Period I church is given in Figure 9.2b.

The lower half of the west tower is also Anglo-Saxon in origin, but of two distinct dates. The bottom 6 to 10 feet (2–3 m.) of masonry are comparable with the lower nave walling, this fabric being recognisable by the inclusion of igneous rocks foreign to Northamptonshire. This was the central compartment of a range of chambers across the west front of the church; there were five in all, those at the north and south ends of the series roughly comparable in area with the one in the centre; the compartments between the central and end chambers on either side were very narrow, only about 6 ft 6 in. (2 m.) wide. The form that this western forebuilding took is discussed below. Later in the Anglo-Saxon period the upper storey and flanking chambers of the forebuilding were removed, and the lower part of the present tower built up on the surviving central compartment. Simultaneously the stair turret was built against the west face of the tower, blocking the original great entry arch into the church (which is still visible in the vestry at the base of the tower). A new first-floor room (now the bell-ringing chamber) was created, with a doorway from the staircase and a triple-arched window looking down into the nave. Above this the stairway gave access to another room, but what height the Anglo-Saxon tower reached is not

[9] *Vetus registrum Sarisburiense alias dictum registrum sancti Osmundi*, ed. W. H. Rich Jones, Rerum Britannicarum Medii Aevi Scriptores, 78, 2 vols (London, 1883–4), vol. 1, p. 196.

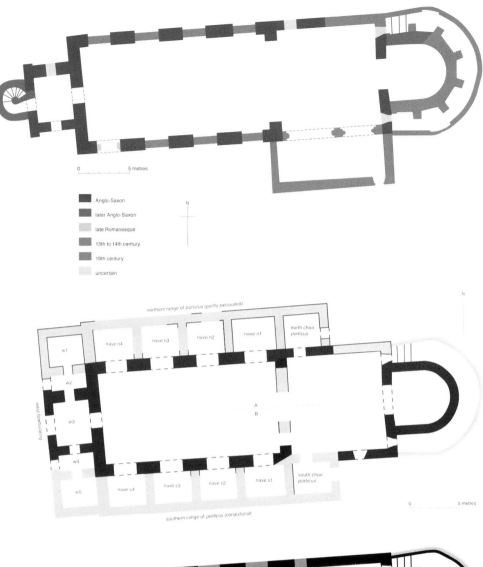
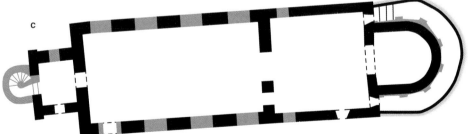

Fig. 9.2 Brixworth All Saints': plans. (C. Unwin, © Copyright D. Parsons.)
(a): present
(b): Anglo-Saxon Period I
(c): Anglo-Saxon Period II

known.

At the east end of the church the apse, which is likely to have had the form of a stilted semi-circle in Period I, was either refaced or rebuilt with seven straight panels separated by vertical pilaster strips on the exterior, much as it appears today, though only the two panels adjacent to the choir on the north side preserve their original masonry. The outer faces of the apse panels were supported on the haunch of the ambulatory vault, suggesting that the ring crypt was still in existence, if not in active use. Whether the apse reconstruction took place at the same time as the building of the west tower and its turret is not known, but the use of a new building material, a form of limestone called tufa, for both projects suggests that they may have been contemporary.

A further change took place in the structure of the church, namely the removal of the porticus flanking the nave, though it is possible that those attached to the choir remained for the time being. It is uncertain when this change came about, but the porticus on the south side must have gone before the present south doorway and its porch (since demolished) were built around 1200. The developments just outlined resulted in a very different form of church from that in Period I; the footprint of the building at the end of Period II is shown in Figure 9.2c.

Recent Archaeological Investigations

The establishment in 1972 of the Brixworth Archaeological Research Committee added impetus to the study of the church and has resulted in a huge increase in the information available for the understanding of the building and its history.[10] The Committee's programme of research included geophysical prospecting, excavation, the study of antiquarian accounts and illustrations, a stone-by-stone survey of the church fabric with petrological identification of the building materials, and sampling below and above ground for radiocarbon, luminescence and other scientific procedures.

While geophysical prospecting has been inconclusive in relation to the existing building, excavation has produced a great deal of positive evidence for the church and its original precinct. The investigation of the site of the new vicarage in 1972 uncovered a ditch that may be the boundary of the church's enclosure and what appears to be the farthest westerly extent of the early graveyard,[11] and an excavation to the south of the church in what is now the car park showed that burial had extended beyond the present churchyard wall in the late Anglo-Saxon period.[12] The location of

---

[10] R. Cramp, 'The Brixworth Archaeological Research Committee', *Journal of the British Archaeological Association*, 130 (1977), pp. 52–4; 'Introduction', in Parsons and Sutherland, *Anglo-Saxon Church of All Saints*, pp. 1–4.

[11] P. L. Everson, 'Excavations in the Vicarage Garden at Brixworth, 1972', *Journal of the British Archaeological Association*, 130 (1977), pp. 55–132.

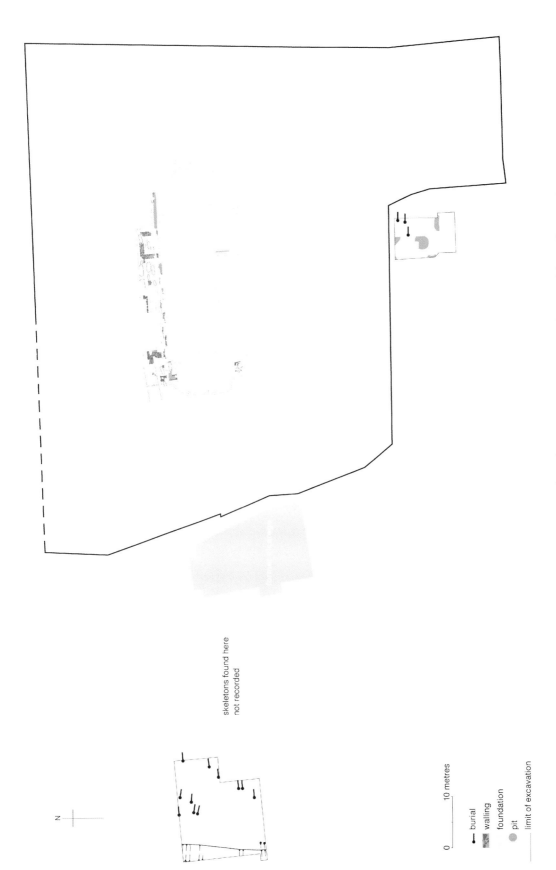

Fig. 9.3 Brixworth All Saints': composite plan of excavations. (C. Unwin, © Copyright D. Parsons.)

9. THE EARLY MEDIEVAL CHURCH AT BRIXWORTH, NORTHAMPTONSHIRE

these sites is shown in Figure 9.3. In relation to the church itself two important excavations clarified the nature of the porticus on the north and west sides of the building, whose existence had been known since the mid-nineteenth century. In 1981–2 both ends of the north range were examined: the two most easterly porticus were found to be seriously damaged by later burials, while at the west end the junction between the north and west ranges was revealed. Not only was it shown that the north wall of the western range was slightly offset to the south of the wall-line of the northern range, but its foundations had been dug into a ditch, whose fill contained material of eighth-century date.[13] The implications of this unexpected evidence for the dating of the church are discussed below. An earlier excavation north of the tower had established that there was an intermediate wall in line with the north arcade of the nave.[14] Rather than the single chamber north of the tower, which had been assumed by previous commentators, it was now shown that there were two, one approximately square at the north end of the range and a very narrow one between it and the tower. Assuming that the same arrangement had existed on the south side, the western range of porticus consisted of five chambers, including the lower part of the tower. The intermediate wall found by Hall had a central doorway to the end porticus, and this, together with the blocked doorway still visible in the north wall of the tower, suggests that all five chambers of the western forebuilding were originally interconnected.

The survey of the standing building began in 1976 and continued annually in tandem with the programme of maintenance and repair directed by the church's architect. It was carried out manually from the contractors' scaffolding, using a string grid dividing the wall surface into one-metre squares; the bench mark on the north-east corner of the choir was used to define the horizontal datum line. Small areas of masonry were drawn to scale and later assembled as a mosaic to show complete elevations stone by stone at 1:20. The development of sophisticated computer technology during the lifetime of the project made it possible ultimately to scan these master drawings electronically.

As each field drawing was completed it was handed over to Dr Diana Sutherland, a local geologist attached to the Geology Department of Leicester University. By visual inspection of the masonry she was able to identify each individual stone in geological terms; overall some forty different stone types were recognised petrologically, and

---

[12] P. J. Woods, 'Northamptonshire: Brixworth', in 'Medieval Britain in 1969', *Medieval Archaeology*, 14 (1970), pp. 205–7, and D. N. Hall, 'Northamptonshire: Brixworth', in 'Medieval Britain in 1972', *Medieval Archaeology*, 17 (1973), p. 181.

[13] M. Audouy *et al.*, 'Excavations at Brixworth, 1981–82', *Journal of the British Archaeological Association*, 137 (1984), pp. 1–44, at pp. 5–6, 30.

[14] D. N. Hall, 'Excavations in Brixworth Churchyard, 1971', *Journal of the British Archaeological Association*, 130 (1977), pp. 123–32.

each was assigned an alpha-numeric code. Each drawn stone was labelled with the appropriate code. The codes were then converted to colours, using different shades within a given rock type to denote the variants. In the Committee's interim report on the fabric of the nave west wall the various colours were applied by hand to the stone outlines of the master drawing, an extremely tedious process.[15] It eventually became possible to do this electronically (see Colour Plate 9.4), and by putting each colour variant on a different layer the coded drawings could be used interactively by means of an appropriate computer programme to study the significance of the stone distributions in the church fabric.

The contribution of the petrological survey to our understanding of the development of the building and its sequence of construction has been enormous. It was already apparent in the interim report that the geological information would play a big part in unravelling the structural history of the west tower; this potential has been fully realised in the monograph which presents all the evidence available for the whole church and the conclusions that have been drawn from it.[16] In addition to its contribution to the detailed study of the fabric the petrological survey has cast light on wider themes such as the sources of the building materials, the significance of burnt stone and its distribution in the fabric, and the widespread reuse of reclaimed stone and brick. For instance, the recognition that much of the early masonry of the church is Roman material recycled, and brought from as far away as Leicester (25 miles/40 km. or more), indicates both the undeveloped nature of the quarrying industry and the existence of transport networks at the time of the building of the church (Period I) and its later reconstruction (Period II).

Form and Function: The Church in Period I

The church as originally constructed has a number of potentially archaic as well as some forward-looking features (Fig. 9.2b). The porticus flanking the nave are reminiscent of the arrangement in Kentish churches of the earliest period of church construction in Anglo-Saxon England, seventh to eighth centuries, especially the example at Reculver, where the nave was totally surrounded by porticus, as at Brixworth. This appears to have been a secondary development and not part of the original layout of the church, supposedly *c*. 669.[17] Access to the side chambers was by doorways 3ft 2 in. (965 mm.) wide; the large open arches at Brixworth were an innovation, and must have some bearing on the use intended for the chambers. Although the function of the porticus at Reculver is not known, the examples at SS. Peter and Paul in Canterbury were designated burial areas for the royal family of Kent

---

[15] D. S. Sutherland and D. Parsons, 'The Petrological Contribution to the Study of All Saints' Church, Brixworth, Northamptonshire: An Interim Study', *Journal of the British Archaeological Association*, 137 (1984), pp. 45–64, esp. Fig. 3.

[16] Parsons and Sutherland, *Anglo-Saxon Church of All Saints*.

9. THE EARLY MEDIEVAL CHURCH AT BRIXWORTH, NORTHAMPTONSHIRE

and its archbishops respectively.[18] There is no clear evidence for primary burial in the Brixworth chambers; the 1981 excavation encountered only one inhumation which may have been dug in the lifetime of the northern range of porticus,[19] and its radiocarbon date (cal AD 985–1300) shows that this would have been towards the end of the Anglo-Saxon period.[20] It is unlikely therefore that the porticus were originally intended for this purpose, and the wide arches of entry from the nave are inconsistent with the privacy which a mortuary chapel might be expected to require. This accessibility also argues against the use of the chambers as offices for clergy or church officials of the sort indicated for the chambers of the outer north aisle in the parchment plan of St Gallen, dated to around 830. Public access for liturgical purposes seems to be the best explanation, though it must be admitted that no traces of altar positions were discovered in the excavation.

Another possibly archaic feature was the connection between the nave and the choir. This has been widely accepted as having been a triple arcade of the type also known from Reculver and some other early Kentish churches since the discovery by the Watkins in the mid-nineteenth century of the bases of the jambs of the central arch. Watkins interpreted what he had found as rectangular pier bases and proposed smaller arches flanking the one in the centre (see his published plan and Taylor's proposed reconstruction elevation[21]). Investigations by a later vicar, and one of the early drawn plans of the church, suggest, however, that these supposed bases were simply the ends of long tongues of wall at right angles to the line of the nave/choir side walls, and that there was a conventional single arch between the nave and the choir. A recent ground penetrating radar survey recorded the north face of the southern jamb of the central arch, but was unable to confirm whether it was part of a rectangular pier. It is therefore not possible to be precise about what view of the choir and east end of the church a congregation in the nave would have had or how a possible altar in front of the central choir arch would have been served.[22]

The arcade arches in the nave are supported on substantial masonry piers rather than the columns characteristic of the classical basilica to which the form of All Saints' is related. This kind of arcade support was used in classical antiquity and continued into the early middle ages, with examples north of the Alps at Glanfeuil (sixth century) and Saint-Pierre, Jumièges (now dated to the eighth or ninth century), in France, and at St Emmeram, Regensburg (probably late eighth), Steinbach and Seligenstadt (early ninth century) in Germany, the two last being built of brick.[23] Although not

---

17 H. M. and J. Taylor, *Anglo-Saxon Architecture*, 3 vols (Cambridge, 1965–78), vol. 2, pp. 503–9.
18 Taylor and Taylor, *Anglo-Saxon Architecture*, vol. 2, pp. 135, 140.
19 Audouy *et al.*, Excavations at Brixworth, p. 13.
20 A. Millard, 'The Radiocarbon Dates', in Parsons and Sutherland, *Anglo-Saxon Church of All Saints*, pp. 271–82.

frequently used, the masonry pier was a form current at the time when Brixworth church is likely to have been constructed.

The introduction of the square choir bay between the nave and the apse, however, is an innovation in Anglo-Saxon architecture, and foreshadows the development in later churches, such as Breamore (Hampshire) and Repton (Derbyshire), of a central liturgical space. Those examples were flanked by narrower transeptal porticus, and the north choir porticus at Brixworth, with its assumed counterpart on the south side, may hint at this arrangement. The size of the surviving arch at Breamore suggests that the south porticus there had some sort of liturgical importance in relation to the choir space, but the scale of the blocked doorway in the north choir wall at Brixworth implies that the porticus there had a separate function. The analogy of chambers in a similar position on the St Gallen plan suggests possible uses as a vestry or sacristy, but the doorway discovered in the east wall of the porticus seems inconsistent with this and may indicate rather an entrance vestibule giving direct access to the choir for the members of the religious community. Whatever the interpretation of the porticus, however, the choir itself must have played a central role in the liturgy of Brixworth church.[24]

Whether or not there was an altar in the choir space, at least one may be assumed in the apse to its east. The investigation of the interior of the apse in 1841 and the subsequent discussion of the floor levels were at best inconclusive, and arguments based on the sill level of the window in the present north-east panel of the apse can only refer to the situation in Period II. Nevertheless the floor of the Period I apse is not likely to have been below the crown of the ambulatory vault surrounding it, and that can be reconstructed as having been marginally above the local datum line; in its turn this equates closely with the present floor level, which may therefore be taken as an approximate indication of the Period I level. Since the interventions of the nineteenth century there have been arguments about what lay below this raised floor level, summed up in recent times by Lord Fletcher.[25] Any physical evidence that there may have been was disturbed by the construction in the late middle ages of a square-ended chancel, which is shown in all the pre-restoration illustrations, and whose floor was clearly at a lower level than the Anglo-Saxon ones.

The removal of that chancel in the 1860s gave the opportunity to reveal the whole of the ambulatory passage surrounding the original apse. The inner wall of the passage survives, and supports the fabric of the apse above. Much of its plaster finish also survives, concealing the detail of the masonry, but where that is visible it appears

---

21 Watkins, *Basilica*, facing p. 45; Taylor and Taylor, *Anglo-Saxon Architecture*, vol. 3, Fig. 653.
22 R. Gem, 'The Liturgical Context of the Church', in Parsons and Sutherland, *Anglo-Saxon Church of All Saints*, pp. 212–20.
23 E. Fernie, *The Architecture of the Anglo-Saxons* (London, 1983), p. 72.
24 Gem, 'Liturgical Context'.

to be consistent with the Period I fabric of the rest of the church. However, in the most easterly of the bays into which the nineteenth-century buttresses divide the wall the masonry consists entirely of stonework which matches that of the restoration. It is possible that this represents the making good of a previous opening giving access to a chamber beneath the apse floor. This arrangement of a circulatory passage leading to a feature below the apse with its altar has been compared with the ring crypt installed *c.* 600 inside the apse of Old St Peter's in Rome and its imitators elsewhere in Europe.[26] In reviewing the evidence, Taylor concluded that, since the latter were mainly datable to the late-eighth or ninth century, that must be the date of the Brixworth example; in view of the then accepted late seventh-century date for the body of the church the ambulatory must have been a later addition.[27] This is difficult to sustain, since the addition of a passage more than 6ft 6 in. (2 m.) below ground level would have required the underpinning of the east wall of the choir for which there is no evidence in the fabric. The argument has become redundant, however, since the 1982 excavation showed that the church as a whole must date from the late-eighth century or later. Examples of ring crypts do occur before the ninth century, one of which is at St Emmeram in Regensburg, where there is documentary evidence that the crypt was in existence by 791. This is a very instructive parallel to Brixworth, since the passage lies outside the apse, whereas in most cases ring crypts were constructed inside the apse, as at St Peter's. There is thus no longer any difficulty in accepting the Brixworth ambulatory as a primary feature.

The exact purpose of the ring crypt is not known but the comparanda elsewhere imply three possible uses, which are not mutually exclusive. First, if there was a passage or chamber below the apse it is likely that this was to house important relics, which were often placed beneath an altar in the church above, and the ambulatory would have afforded access for the veneration of the relics. One relic, a throat bone, has survived at Brixworth, having been found in 1809 in a stone reliquary of fourteenth-century date. There is circumstantial evidence that this may have been a relic of St Boniface; if so, it is likely to have been acquired soon after the saint's death in 754.[28] Second, there are two recesses in the outer wall of the ambulatory; these were rebuilt along with the wall in the 1860s, but are supposed to represent original features. They resemble the *arcosolia* of catacombs, and may have been the burial places of important members of the Brixworth community. The ambulatory would have given access for celebrations on significant dates, such as the anniversary of their deaths. Third, several continental examples of ring crypts lead to subterranean

---

[25] Lord [E. G. M.] Fletcher, 'Brixworth: Was there a Crypt?', *Journal of the British Archaeological Association*, 3rd ser. 37 (1974), pp. 88–96.

[26] H. M. Taylor, 'Corridor Crypts on the Continent and in England', *North Staffordshire Journal of Field Studies*, 9 (1969), pp. 17–52.

[27] Taylor and Taylor, *Anglo-Saxon Architecture*, vol. 1, p. 109.

chapels or outer crypts to the east of the crown of the passage. If there had been such an extension to the crypt at Brixworth, it would lie beneath densely packed graves of the nineteenth century to the east of the present apse, and these preclude any investigation, including geophysical prospecting. Without such an investigation this interpretation must remain in the realm of speculation.

At the opposite end of the church the new interpretations of the predecessor of the west tower are one of the exciting outcomes of the Research Committee's work. Previous assumptions about what was often referred to as a 'narthex' (for example in Audouy's excavation report[29]) were largely based on the observations of the highly respected Alexander Hamilton Thompson.[30] He did not however present a reconstruction drawing or even a photograph of the evidence on which he based his hypothesis, and most subsequent commentators similarly omitted to provide any visual interpretation. The present author's attempt to do so in 1979[31] has now been shown to be unworkable, and the reconstructions now proposed take account of evidence of whose existence—or of whose significance—Thompson was unaware. In the side walls of the tower, about 13 ft (4 m.) above ground level, are roughly square areas of ironstone patching separated by short piers of brick (Colour Plate 9.4); there is complementary evidence inside the tower, where the patching contains the limestone variety known as tufa. These patches are the infilled sockets of large beams which ran across the central compartment of the west range of porticus and continued beyond its north and south walls. The scantling of the beams is indicated by the dimensions of the patching, approximately 500mm across, suggesting an original size of 18 inches. Not only is this unnecessarily massive simply to support a floor in the central compartment, but the evidence that the beams continued through the side walls also indicates that they covered one or both of the flanking compartments on either side. The tower north and south walls above this level are in a fabric different from that below, and belong to Period II. It is therefore suggested that the upper floor of the western forebuilding was continuous across compartments 2, 3 and 4, equating with the full width of the nave, or over the whole of the western range. Judging by the lack of Period I masonry in the west wall of the tower above the level of the tops of the beams, the entire superstructure may have been timber-built.

Access to this upper chamber would have been by staircases in one or both of the end compartments or even at the west end of the nave. Communication between the upper chamber and the nave was through the doorway, now blocked, above the

---

[28] D. Parsons, 'Brixworth and the Boniface Connexion,' *Northamptonshire Past and Present*, 6.4 (1980–81), pp. 179–83.
[29] Audouy *et al.*, 'Excavations at Brixworth', p. 5 and *passim*.
[30] A. H. Thompson, 'Brixworth Church', *Archaeological Journal*, 69 (1912), pp. 505–10.
[31] D. Parsons, 'Past History and Present Research at All Saints' Church, Brixworth', *Northamptonshire Past and Present*, 6.2 (1979), pp. 61–71: Fig.3.

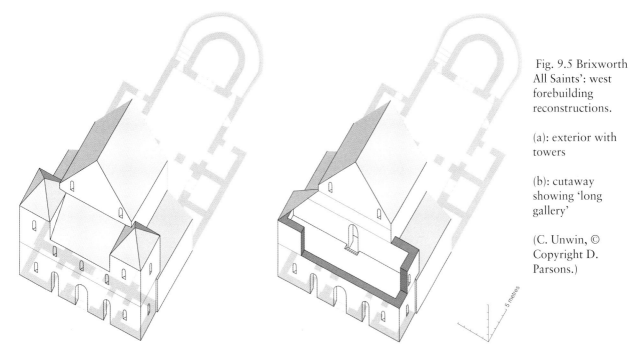

Fig. 9.5 Brixworth All Saints': west forebuilding reconstructions.

(a): exterior with towers

(b): cutaway showing 'long gallery'

(C. Unwin, © Copyright D. Parsons.)

door connecting the present tower with the nave at ground-floor level, though it would have required two or three steps down to walk from the forebuilding onto a landing or gallery in the nave. Two of the various permutations of this interpretation are shown in Figure 9.5, and are fully published elsewhere.[32] The function of the upper chamber could have been liturgical, ceremonial or domestic. It might have been an assembly point for a small choir proceeding to the gallery in the nave to sing perhaps antiphonally with the main body of singers in the choir (the upper doorway into the nave seems too small to make singing in the forebuilding itself practical), or it might have housed subsidiary altars, possibly used in the course of a stational liturgy. Alternatively, the upper room may have been for a personage of importance, either lay or ecclesiastical, to observe the liturgy in the nave, enthroned and looking down through the upper doorway, through which he could pass to make a ceremonial appearance on the gallery in the nave. Finally, in the reconstruction showing a long open room at first-floor level (Fig. 9.5b and the Period I south-west view of Fig. 9.6), the space could have been used by the religious community for meeting ('chapter house') or even for sleeping (dormitory) with direct access to the nave by means of the staircase at the west end ('night stair'?).

Form and function: The Church in Period II

The replacement of the western forebuilding was one of three major events that took place in Anglo-Saxon Period II. The upper floor was confined to the area over the central compartment and the side chambers were removed. The walls of the central

[32] Parsons and Sutherland, *Anglo-Saxon Church of All Saints*, Fig.11.9.

Fig. 9.6 Brixworth All Saints': reconstruction perspectives. Clockwise from top left: Period I from south west; Period I from north east; Period II from north east; Period I from south west. (M. Kneen, © Copyright D. Parsons.)

compartment were raised by about 10 ft (3 m.) in a limestone fabric sharply contrasting in colour with the mixed Period I assemblage below (see Colour Plate 9.4). Limestone was also used to block the opening into the nave at first-floor level and the great western entrance arch in the west wall of the central compartment. To the west of this a new element was added to the structure: a turret, on plan a stilted semi-circle, containing a helical stone vault supporting the treads of a winding staircase (see Fig. 9.6, Period II south-west view). This replaced the previous stairway(s) leading to the upper level, and was entered by a doorway fashioned in the blocking of the former entrance arch. The first phase of this reconstruction rose to about 21 ft (6.5 m.) above ground level, roughly where the first floor now is inside the tower. At this point a doorway led from the staircase to the new upper floor; this is still in use for access to the bell-ringing chamber. The doorway is surrounded by the same limestone fabric as is seen on the exterior, but this masonry gives way to a fabric rich in local sandstone. The junction between the two fabrics is clear, and with the horizontal line of the floor forms a depressed triangular shape. It is possible that this represents the gable seen by Thompson from which he deduced a two-storeyed porch. This may have been part of

9. THE EARLY MEDIEVAL CHURCH AT BRIXWORTH, NORTHAMPTONSHIRE

a temporary roof over the still incomplete tower, which was subsequently removed in order to carry the tower up to its full height. This was done using sandstone, as noted in the ringing chamber but more clearly visible externally, though increasingly mixed with tufa, which is characteristic of the upper parts of the tower below belfry level and of the top section of the stair turret. The new arrangements were then consolidated by the removal of the beams which had supported the original upper floor and the insertion of new floors more or less in the positions they occupy at present. At first-floor level (the present ringing chamber) a new opening was inserted into the west wall of the nave: a triple arch with baluster supports and heads made of brick and tufa. The lower part of this opening destroyed part of the head of the former first-floor doorway into the nave. The use of tufa makes it clear that the triple opening was built at the same time as the upper parts of the tower; it also occurs in the blocking of the beam holes internally, suggesting that the former upper floor remained in use, probably as a construction platform, until the end of the building operation.

The use of tufa also characterises the second event in Period II. The apse was rebuilt or refaced in the form of a polygon with seven plane faces. These faces, or panels, oversail the haunches of the Period I ambulatory vault, which supports them. It is not certain whether the crypt remained in use, though it has been suggested that the small quantities of tufa identified at ambulatory level in the east choir wall indicate a refurbishment of the crypt at this stage. The new apse panels were separated by projecting pilasters, three of which remain on the north side of the apse, flanking the two surviving Anglo-Saxon panels. In the angle between the apse and the choir east wall the top of the pilaster has a slightly projecting stone and the beginning of a curved section of masonry, which implies that the pilasters were joined by blind arches, framing the panels in the manner that still survives at Wing (Buckinghamshire) and Deerhurst (Gloucestershire). This interpretation is shown in the Period II north-east view in Figure 9.6.

Whether the renovation of the apse was contemporary with the building of the tower and turret at the west end of the church is not known, but the common use of tufa suggests that it may have been. If the two events were carried out in sequence, it is likely that the rebuilding of the apse followed the completion of the tower, since that is when tufa appears to have been available. The motives for the two developments were not necessarily the same, although architectural fashion may have played a part in both. The tower with its substantial staircase access must have been a response to an intended change of use. Insofar as the Period I forebuilding had a liturgical function, this must have been modified in Period II; if its original purpose was ceremonial or if it was used as some form of accommodation, then these must have been abandoned in favour of a new liturgical use. The key to this use is the triple arch which unlike its predecessor did not afford physical access to the nave, but was a means of visual or auditory communication. Its purpose may have been the kind of synchronisation between the main liturgy in the church and the ringing of the bells, which were presumably the ultimate reason for the building of the tower,[33] for which there is evidence in the late Anglo-Saxon *Regularis Concordia*.[34] It is not possible to know whether there was a similar liturgical imperative for the rebuilding of the apse, but the two developments clearly indicate a desire to enhance the church both functionally and cosmetically.

In this context, it is unclear where the third major event, the loss of the north and south ranges of porticus, fits chronologically. It is arguable that the reduction of the church in size by the removal of the porticus is not consistent with the enhancement represented by the two reconstructions just described. It could also be claimed that the demolition of the north range at least was occasioned by some unconnected external event. At the base of the clerestory on the north side of the church there is a continuous band of several course of fire-reddened masonry, which suggests the possible destruction of the roof of the north range.[35] If the porticus were seriously fire-damaged, this may have been the occasion for their removal. The most easterly porticus, that flanking the choir, may have survived, however, since there is no fire-reddening on the choir wall; this could be accounted for by the assumption of a two-storey elevation for the choir porticus, whose continued existence was postulated in the 1981–2 excavation report.[36] The possible form of the church at the end Period II—aisleless but with porticus flanking the choir—could suggest that a virtue was made of necessity, and that the church was deliberately reduced to a form not unlike the late Anglo-Saxon type, unaisled and with a central space with flanking transeptal porticus. To this extent the removal of the porticus could be regarded as the final stage in the transformation of the Period I church to accord with prevailing church planning norms. New and revised radiocarbon dates available since this paper was first delivered[37] support the suggestion that the removal of some or all of the porticus was a separate event from the reconstructions of Period II, and it is now assigned to Period III.

Dating and Conclusions

In the course of the research project the dating of the Period I church has become relatively clear. Excavation evidence shows that it cannot be earlier than about the middle of the eighth century, and the dates of comparable buildings on the continent range from the late eighth to the early ninth century, so a date for All Saints around

---

[33] N. Christie, 'On Bells and Bell-Towers: Origins and Evolutions in Italy and Britain, AD 700–1200', *Church Archaeology*, 5–6 (2004), pp. 13–30.

[34] *Regularis Concordia / The Monastic Agreement*, ed T. Symons (London, 1953), c. 52.

[35] D. S. Sutherland, 'Burnt Stone in a Saxon Church and its Implications', in *Stone: Quarrying and Building in England AD 43–1525*, ed. D. Parsons (Chichester, 1990), pp. 102–13, esp. Fig. 29.

or just before 800 seems likely. In historical terms, assuming that there must have been a high-status patron for such a grand building project commanding the transportation of materials over comparatively long distances, the reign of King Offa of Mercia (d. 796) offers a suitable context.

No such clarity is possible in Periods II and III, however. The three separate events in the development of the church did not necessarily take place simultaneously. Despite the previous dating of the stair turret to the eleventh century, a recent radiocarbon determination on charcoal from the mortar in its foundations suggests a date before 900, while comparanda for the polygonal apse (Wing, Deerhust) and for the central space with quasi-transepts (Repton) now seem to lie in the ninth century, with later examples of the latter in the tenth or eleventh (Breamore, Dover (Kent)). Although the remodelling of the church appears to take place hard on the heels of the original construction, a date before the disruptions of the Danish incursions and settlement of the late-ninth century is probable, with the removal of the porticus at a later date, perhaps still in the late Anglo-Saxon period or even after the Norman Conquest.

---

36 Audouy *et al.*, 'Excavations at Brixworth', p. 36.
37 For this and for the dating generally see now Section 9 and Appendix 6 in Parsons and Sutherland, *Anglo-Saxon Church of All Saints*.

(10)
The Church of St Mary, Deerhurst, Gloucestershire, in the Ninth Century

MICHAEL HARE AND MAGGIE KNEEN

Introduction

The church of St Mary at Deerhurst, Gloucestershire (NGR 870299), is one of the major surviving monuments of Anglo-Saxon date.[1] It has attracted much study and comment since the 1840s.[2] Many Anglo-Saxon features were discovered during a restoration in 1861–2.[3] In the 1970s there was a programme of excavation and structural study under the direction of Philip Rahtz, published in 1997.[4] Perhaps the major achievement of Rahtz and his colleagues was the identification of a building phase ('Period IV') during which an earlier church, surviving to no more than about head-height, was raised to the full height of the surviving building. It is the Period IV structure which is the subject of the present study, which also incorporates the results of observations made during liturgical reorganisation in 2012. Reconstruction drawings have been prepared (see Figs 10.3, 10.4), and one of the aims of this paper is to set out the rationale which underpins them.

    A major feature of the church at Deerhurst is the survival of a substantial quantity of sculpture *in situ* in the Period IV structure. It is only following the publication of the archaeological and structural studies carried out in the 1970s that this sculptural material has received detailed study. Richard Bailey's 2002 Deerhurst

---

[1] We are most grateful to Richard Bryant and Helen Gittos for reading and commenting on an early draft of this text; Malcolm Thurlby kindly allowed us to make use of two of his photographs. We are also much indebted to the parochial authorities of Deerhurst for the ready help which they have provided during our work on the building. Especial gratitude is due to Will Morris of Priory Farm, Deerhurst and to his late wife Shelagh, and this paper is dedicated to Will and Shelagh.

[2] The first study of the church is D. H. Haigh, 'Deerhurst Church, Gloucestershire', *Journal of the British Archaeological Association*, 1 (1846), pp. 9–19.

[3] The principal sources for the restoration are two works by the incumbent: G. Butterworth, 'The History of Deerhurst Church, Gloucestershire', *The Ecclesiologist*, 23 (1862), pp. 89–101; G. Butterworth, *Deerhurst, A Parish in the Vale of Gloucester*, 2nd edn (Tewkesbury, 1890).

[4] P. Rahtz and L. Watts with H. Taylor and L. Butler, *St Mary's Church, Deerhurst, Gloucestershire: Fieldwork, Excavations and Structural Analysis, 1971–84*, Reports of the Research Committee of the Society of Antiquaries of London, 55 (Woodbridge, 1997); for the excavation of the east end, see also P. Rahtz, *Excavations at St Mary's Church, Deerhurst, 1971–73*, Council for British Archaeology Research Report, 15 (London, 1976). The best general description of the Anglo-Saxon fabric remains H. M. and J. Taylor, *Anglo-Saxon Architecture*, 3 vols (Cambridge, 1965–78), vol. 1, pp. 193–209.

Lecture, the first discussion of the sculptures as a body of material, was a major step forward; on art-historical grounds he argued for a date in the first half of the ninth century.[5] Richard Gem has advanced further arguments for such a date in a study of the sculpture of the Virgin and Child at the western entrance;[6] a ninth-century date is also maintained by Richard Bryant in the recent Western Midlands volume of the *Corpus of Anglo-Saxon Stone Sculpture*.[7]

The date suggested by the art-historical evidence also enables something to be said about the patronage which led to the construction. A document bearing the date 804 records that Æthelric son of Æthelmund intended to bequeath four estates to the community at Deerhurst; it was also his wish to be buried at Deerhurst, and it would seem to be implied that his father Æthelmund had been buried there before him.[8] Æthelmund was in all likelihood the son of Ingeld, an ealdorman of King Æthelbald of Mercia (716–57); he is also very probably one and the same as the Ealdorman Æthelmund who was killed in battle against the men of Wiltshire in 802.[9] It seems likely that it was the patronage of this family which lay behind the construction of the Period IV church; Deerhurst is perhaps one of the earliest surviving English buildings erected by a family whose members were of comital rank.

Deerhurst was a significant minster church and retained its importance throughout the Anglo-Saxon period.[10] However, around the time of the Norman Conquest, the church was granted to the French abbey of St-Denis and became an alien priory.[11] While the church continued to evolve, rebuilding on a major scale was never undertaken. Substantial elements of the ninth-century church are thus preserved for us.

The Existing Church

The present church (Figs 10.1, 10.2, 10.5, 10.6) consists of a nave with north and south aisles; the aisles extend eastwards to flank what is now the chancel and

---

[5] R. N. Bailey, *Anglo-Saxon Sculptures at Deerhurst*, Deerhurst Lecture 2002 (Deerhurst, 2005).

[6] R. Gem, *Deerhurst and Rome: Æthelric's Pilgrimage c. 804 and the Oratory of St Mary Mediana*, Deerhurst Lecture 2007 (Deerhurst, 2008).

[7] R. M. Bryant, *Corpus of Anglo-Saxon Stone Sculpture, vol. 10: The Western Midlands* (Oxford, 2012), pp. 161–90.

[8] P. H. Sawyer, *Anglo-Saxon Charters: An Annotated List and Bibliography*, Royal Historical Society Guides and Handbooks, 8 (London, 1968), no. 1187; *Cartularium Saxonicum*, ed. W. de G. Birch, 3 vols (London, 1885–93), vol. 1, pp. 438–40 (text); *English Historical Documents, vol. 1: c. 500–1042*, ed. D. Whitelock, 2nd edn (London, 1979), pp. 512–13 (translation).

[9] For a detailed study of the family, see M. Hare, 'Deerhurst's Earliest Patrons: Æthelmund and Æthelric', *Transactions of the Bristol and Gloucestershire Archaeological Society*, 130 (2012), pp. 151–82.

[10] For Deerhurst as a minster church see S. Bassett, *The Origins of the Parishes of the Deerhurst Area*, Deerhurst Lecture 1997 (Deerhurst, 1998).

[11] P. Wormald, *How Do We Know so much about Anglo-Saxon Deerhurst?*, Deerhurst Lecture 1991 (Deerhurst, 1993), pp. 17–19.

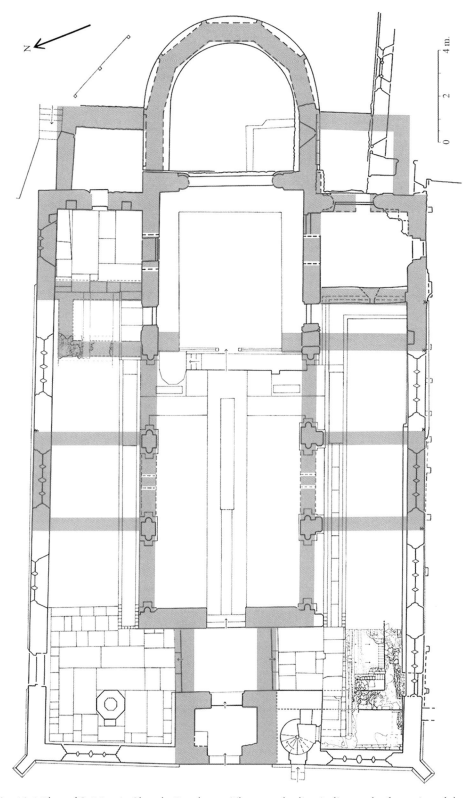

Fig. 10.1 Plan of St Mary's Church, Deerhurst. The grey shading indicates the footprint of the Anglo-Saxon church. (Based, with permission, on a plan in the Deerhurst excavation archive, London, Society of Antiquaries, MS. 952; © Copyright R. Bryant.)

Fig. 10.2 St Mary's Church, Deerhurst, from the south. (© Copyright M. Thurlby.)

westwards to flank a tall western tower. In plan the tower is one-and-a-half times as long (east–west) as it is wide (north–south); a cross wall, which extends through all the stages of the tower except the belfry, divides the tower into a square eastern compartment and a rather smaller western compartment. There is now no structural division between nave and chancel. The chancel furnishings are of special interest as a unique survival of an arrangement much favoured at the time of the Elizabethan settlement, with seating to the north, south and east of the communion table.[12] In the east wall of the choir, there is a substantial blocked arch (Fig. 10.5). Originally this arch led to a seven-sided apse, now largely demolished. Fortuitously, one bay of the apse was incorporated in farm buildings and thus survives; the semicircular foundation of the rest of the apse has been excavated. The remains of a ruined structure to the north of the apse also survive, while part of the east wall of a similar structure has been excavated on the south side.

The Anglo-Saxon elements in this building consist first of the lower part of the tower, originally a porch; the upper part of the tower is of fourteenth-century date. Secondly, the four walls of what is now the undivided space of nave and chancel

---

[12] R. H. Murray, 'The Arrangement of the Chancel at Deerhurst', *Transactions of the Bristol and Gloucestershire Archaeological Society*, 25 (1902), pp. 285–93; on the liturgical context of this type of arrangement, see K. Fincham and N. Tyacke, *Altars Restored: The Changing Face of English Religious Worship, 1547–c. 1700* (Oxford, 2007), pp. 25–6, 50–61.

consist of Anglo-Saxon masonry; the term 'basic rectangle' was coined in the 1970s to refer to this space as a whole and is adopted here to avoid confusion as to the liturgical functions of the different parts of this space over the centuries. In the thirteenth century, arcades were cut through the standing walls, and there was much refacing of the walling, especially at clerestory level, in the restoration of 1861–2.

At the east end of the south aisle, the east, south and west walls remain from a two-storeyed adjunct or porticus flanking the eastern end of the 'basic rectangle';[13] the west wall is now cut through by an arch of late eleventh-century date. The vestry is housed in the ground floor of this adjunct, while the first floor is used for storage.[14] The east and north walls of a similar porticus survive at the east end of the north aisle; in this case the west wall no longer exists, but its foundations were identified in excavations in the 1970s.[15] Recent structural study has also demonstrated the former existence of further two-storeyed porticus halfway along the nave; part of the south wall of one of these porticus is preserved in the south aisle wall. In this paper the adjuncts flanking the chancel are termed the choir porticus, while those flanking the nave are termed the nave porticus. The remains of the ruined apse and of the adjuncts to its north and south are also of pre-Conquest origin.

The standing remains of pre-Conquest date are all considered to belong to the Period IV church; a number of features of later Anglo-Saxon date were inserted in the Period IV masonry, and some of these later insertions are mentioned below. The Period IV church is sufficiently intact to enable reconstruction drawings to be prepared (Figs 10.3 and 10.4), though inevitably some problems remain and some aspects of the reconstruction are conjectural.

Reconstructing the Period IV Church
The Apse
Only a single bay of the apse now survives on the south side, with just enough remaining for the angle to the next bay to be visible. The apse has elaborate stripwork formed of pilasters, and the design visible in the surviving bay has been assumed to have been used in each of the other bays. The surviving bay does not stand to its full height, but there is a scar against the east wall of the 'basic rectangle' indicating where the wall of the apse has been removed; the apse walls seem unlikely to have been any higher than indicated by this scar. The pitch of the apse roof has been assumed to be 51° in line with the pitch of the nave roof.

---

[13] On the term 'porticus', which was used in contemporary sources for a variety of adjuncts to churches, see É. Ó Carragáin, 'The Term *Porticus* and *Imitatio Romae* in Early Anglo-Saxon England', in *Text and Gloss: Studies in Insular Learning and Literature*, ed. H. C. O'Briain, A. M. D'Arcy and J. Scattergood (Dublin, 1999), pp. 13–34.

[14] Until 2012 this was the organ-chamber, but a new organ has now been installed at the east end of the south aisle.

[15] Rahtz *et al.*, *St Mary's Church, Deerhurst*, pp. 44–7.

10. THE CHURCH OF ST MARY, DEERHURST, GLOUCESTERSHIRE

There seems to have been no original window in the standing bay of the apse; the existing small window is probably of late-medieval date. Windows have been assumed to have existed in alternate bays (bays 2, 4 and 6) of the apse. In the surviving bay, the false pediment formed by the stripwork encloses the famous angel sculpture. Bailey has suggested that there were originally similar angels in the other six bays and that they were in fact all archangels, corresponding to the seven canonical archangels; he sees the surviving angel as 'the last remaining sentinel of a seven-strong detachment of spiritual guards set over the church and its community'.[16] A slight variation on Bailey's hypothesis may be proposed. Some sources name not seven but six archangels. For instance only six archangels are listed in a prayer in the Book of Cerne, a Mercian manuscript of early ninth-century date which, as Bailey noted, provides the closest art-historical parallels for the existing angel.[17] The sculpture of the Virgin and Child at the entrance would seem to imply that Deerhurst has always been dedicated to St Mary, and it is worth noting that representations of the Virgin in her guise as Queen of Heaven frequently show her accompanied by archangels.[18] It may therefore be suggested that in the bay of the apse facing east, there could have been a hieratic image of the Virgin looking out over Deerhurst's minster parish.[19]

Deerhurst is one of three Mercian churches with seven-sided apses, the two others being Brixworth (Northamptonshire) and Wing (Buckinghamshire).[20] Brixworth and Wing both had crypts; at Deerhurst there is some evidence for a sub-floor space beneath the apse, but it is hard to see how the limited space available could possibly have functioned as a proper crypt.[21] While the present floor of the church is just above the flood-level of the River Severn (as could be seen in 2007), the sub-floor space beneath the apse would have been subject to periodic flooding.

The Central Space and the Nave
Although the 'basic rectangle' is now a single undivided space, it is evident that a

---

[16] Bailey, *Anglo-Saxon Sculptures*, pp. 11–14.
[17] For the relevant text, see *The Prayer Book of Aedelualdl the Bishop, Commonly Called the Book of Cerne*, ed. A. B. Kuypers (Cambridge, 1902), p. 153; the fullest recent discussion of the manuscript is M. P. Brown, *The Book of Cerne: Prayer, Patronage and Power in Ninth-Century England*, British Library Studies in Medieval Culture, 1 (London, 1996).
[18] A near-contemporary example is for instance found in the painted scene of Mary surrounded by archangels in the western arm of the crypt of Abbot Epiphanius (824–42) at San Vincenzo al Volturno (Molise, Italy): J. Mitchell, 'The Crypt Reappraised', in *San Vincenzo al Volturno: The 1980–86 Excavations*, ed. R. Hodges, Archaeological Monographs of the British School at Rome, 7 and 9, 2 vols (London, 1993–5), vol. 1, pp. 75–114.
[19] Deerhurst stands on the east bank of the Severn, and its early minster parish seems likely to have lain entirely on the east side of the river: see Bassett, *Origins of the Parishes*, pp. 10–19.
[20] Taylor and Taylor, *Anglo-Saxon Architecture*, vol. 1, pp. 108–14 (Brixworth), vol. 2, pp. 665–72 (Wing); for Brixworth, see also D. Parsons, this volume.
[21] Rahtz, *Excavations*, p. 13.

Fig. 10.3 St Mary's Church, Deerhurst: conjectural reconstruction of Period IV seen from the south-east. (© Copyright M. Kneen.)

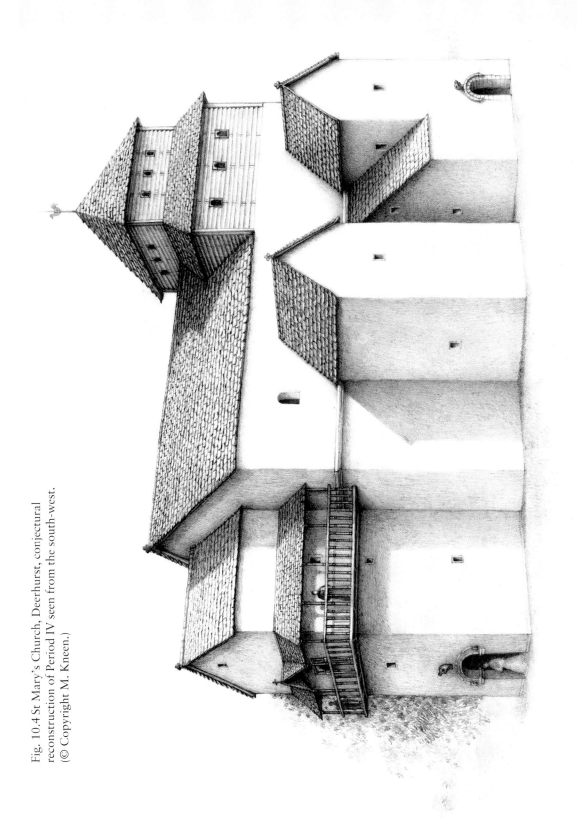

Fig. 10.4 St Mary's Church, Deerhurst, conjectural reconstruction of Period IV seen from the south-west. (© Copyright M. Kneen.)

square central space originally existed. During the restoration of 1861–2, the scars left when the west wall of the central space was demolished were visible running up the entire height of the side walls of the 'basic rectangle'; foundations which presumably supported the responds of an arch in this wall were also discovered.[22] The fact that the scars extended up the full height of the walls would tend to indicate that the cross wall was an original feature, but the point cannot be regarded as established beyond all doubt. A broad arch opens from the central space to the apse, and it seems likely that the arch in the west wall of the central space was similar.[23]

The staged timber tower shown over the central space in the reconstruction drawings is entirely conjectural, but such structures are known to have existed in both continental and English churches in the early middle ages.[24] The relationship between the staged timber tower and the nave roof is based on that surviving at Breamore (Hampshire), where the timber tower may perpetuate an arrangement of tenth- or eleventh-century date.[25] Whether or not such a timber tower existed, it seems unlikely that the central space received much natural light.

The most distinctive surviving feature of the nave is the 'great string-course'. This string-course ran from the western porch to the two-storeyed nave porticus; from these porticus to the choir porticus; and from the choir porticus to the apse.[26] Battered fragments of this string-course may still be seen high up in the nave walls just beneath the aisle roofs, and a well-preserved section may be seen embedded in the south wall of the tower.[27] The pitch of the nave roof has been taken as 51°, based on the surviving weathering (Fig. 10.2).[28] The weathering also indicates that the original nave walls are likely to have extended to about the same height as the present walls. There is no surviving evidence for windows in the nave, and high-level windows have been

22 Butterworth, 'History of Deerhurst Church', pp. 94–5.
23 Butterworth, 'History of Deerhurst Church', p. 95, notes that 'arch-stones and fragments of columns of a kind similar to those' of the arch opening into the apse were discovered in the course of the restoration; nothing of this sort survives at Deerhurst today.
24 R. Gem, 'Staged Timber Spires in Carolingian North-East France and Late Anglo-Saxon England', *Journal of the British Archaeological Association*, 148 (1995), pp. 29–54.
25 Taylor and Taylor, *Anglo-Saxon Architecture*, vol. 1, pp. 94–6.
26 No trace of the string-course now survives between the choir porticus and the apse, as the eastern angles of the 'basic rectangle' were rebuilt in 1861–2, but there is evidence for it in eighteenth- and nineteenth-century drawings. The clearest evidence is provided by two unpublished drawings by E. A. Freeman dating to the 1840s or 1850s (Manchester, John Rylands Library, FA4/1/492 and 494); the string-course is also visible in S. Lysons, *Etchings of Views and Antiquities in the County of Gloucester* (London, 1791–6), pl. LV.
27 E. Gilbert, 'Deerhurst Priory Church and its First String Course', *Transactions of the Bristol and Gloucestershire Archaeological Society*, 83 (1964), pp. 49–69, at pp. 63–4.
28 Rahtz *et al.*, *St Mary's Church, Deerhurst*, pp. 103–7. The weathering is of the same fourteenth-century date as the tower, but seems likely to preserve the pitch of an earlier nave roof.

assumed to have existed to either side of the nave porticus; these are in the position of two of the the three late-medieval clerestory windows on the south side.

The Choir Porticus

The two-storeyed adjuncts or porticus which flank the central space to the north and south still stand in large measure. The porticus on the south side was evidently constructed at the same time as the 'basic rectangle'. Though the lower part of this porticus is not in bond with the 'basic rectangle', it does display the same petrological assemblage; the upper part of the porticus is in bond with the 'basic rectangle'.[29] However, on the north side the equivalent porticus was clearly not built at exactly the same time as the 'basic rectangle'. There is a straight joint between the 'basic rectangle' and the east wall of the porticus (now the east wall of the north aisle) throughout its height; moreover the petrological assemblage in the north porticus is different.[30] Nevertheless there is clear evidence that the two-storeyed north porticus was planned as an integral part of the Period IV structure. The upper floor of the southern porticus opens to the central space through a broad arch (Fig. 10.5), and there is a similar arch on the north side which was undoubtedly constructed while the 'basic rectangle' was being built; this must mean that there was an intention to build a north porticus, and it was presumably built very soon after the rest of the Period IV structure was completed.[31]

The east end of the south aisle is now covered with a flat roof continuous with the roof of the south aisle (Fig. 10.2). However, until the restoration of 1861–2, the walls of the former porticus supported a pitched roof abutting the central space.[32] In the surviving masonry of the south wall of the clerestory, a large piece of oolite covers what seems to be a blocked socket. This is in the right position to have been the socket for the ridge-piece of the original south porticus roof. There is a surviving window in the west wall which would have lit the first floor, and a similar window has been assumed in the south wall, where there is now a window of fourteenth-century date. The two-storeyed porticus on the north side was built simultaneously with a low porticus to its east flanking the apse, and the foundations of the east wall of a similar structure have been excavated on the south side.[33] The north wall of the small ruined north-east porticus is in bond with the east wall of the two-storeyed porticus, and it seems unlikely that it could have been any higher than the present wall, as it would

---

[29] S. Bagshaw, *The Building Stones of St Mary's Church, Deerhurst*, Deerhurst Lecture 2003 (Deerhurst, 2014), pp. 12–17.
[30] Bagshaw, *Building Stones*, pp. 17–20.
[31] Rahtz et al., *St Mary's Church, Deerhurst*, pp. 166–70.
[32] An early photograph showing this arrangement was published in W. H. Knowles, 'Deerhurst Priory Church: Including the Result of the Excavations Conducted During 1926', *Archaeologia*, 77 (1927), pp. 141–64, at Fig. 1 (opposite p. 141).
[33] Rahtz, *Excavations*, pp. 15–17; Rahtz et al., *St Mary's Church, Deerhurst*, pp. 166–70.

have left a visible scar. The south wall of the south-east porticus has been assumed to have been of similar height. The form of the roof is uncertain, but a lean-to roof offers the simplest solution; the roof must in part have obscured the stripwork of the apse. A small window in the south wall is suggested to have lit this room.

Two narrow adjuncts have also been identified immediately to the west of the two choir porticus (Fig. 10.1) and were evidently built simultaneously with them; these two adjuncts are here termed vestibules. The west wall of the north vestibule was first identified at its southern end during excavations in the 1970s;[34] in the course of a watching brief in January 2012, the full extent of the wall was observed, and its eastern return was recorded.[35] At the same time examination of the external face of the south aisle showed that the south wall of a similar vestibule still survives; the vestibule on the south side was rather longer, but also a little narrower than the north vestibule.

It seems probable that the two vestibules were connected with the provision of access to both levels of the porticus. There seems to have been no direct access between the central space and the ground floor of the choir porticus. The triangular-headed doorway, which opened directly from the central space to the ground floor of the north porticus, is a later Anglo-Saxon insertion;[36] the door opening directly into the south porticus is of post-Conquest date.[37] Instead access to the two porticus would seem to have been via the square-headed doorways just east of the cross wall dividing the central space from the nave. These doorways led into the vestibules, from which further doorways presumably led through the west walls of the porticus. It also seems probable that the two vestibules contained stairways, providing access to the upper floors of the porticus, again through doorways in their west walls. A small piece of evidence on the south side supports this suggestion. The lower part of the west wall

Fig. 10.5 (opposite) Interior view of St Mary's Church, Deerhurst, showing the east wall and the south wall of the present chancel. The heads of two doorways may be seen above the seating in the chancel; the doorway close to the east wall is a later insertion, while the doorway further west is original. The large round-headed opening led to the first floor of the south porticus; the square-headed doorway to the west at the same level is a rood stair of fifteenth-century date, and this doorway marks the position of the now-lost cross wall dividing the nave from the central space. (© Copyright M. Hare.)

[34] Rahtz et al., *St Mary's Church, Deerhurst*, pp. 44–7.
[35] R. Bryant, M. Hare and C. Heighway, 'Excavations at St Mary's Church, Deerhurst in 2012: An Interim Report', *Glevensis: Gloucester and District Archaeological Research Group Review*, 45 (2012), pp. 20–6, at p. 20, Figs 1, 2.
[36] This doorway is described as 'a crude insertion [...] with very poor mortar': Rahtz et al., *St Mary's Church, Deerhurst*, p. 52.
[37] The jambs of this doorway are built of Highley stone (a green sandstone), first used in the late eleventh century for the construction of Wulfstan's cathedral at Worcester: M. Thurlby, *The Architecture and Sculpture of Deerhurst Priory: The Later 11th-, 12th- and Early 13th-Century Work*, Deerhurst Lecture 2009 (Deerhurst, 2014), pp. 15–16.

of the south choir porticus was cut away in the eleventh century by an arch, but at first-floor level the restorers of 1861–2 found traces of a doorway close to the south wall of the 'basic rectangle'; the remains of this doorway are marked in the plaster, though no structural details can be seen.[38] The length of the vestibules suggests that the staircases which they contained were not excessively steep and that members of the community and others could have processed up them. Two windows have been shown in the west wall of the south vestibule in the reconstruction drawing.

The Nave Porticus

The realisation that there were two-storeyed porticus flanking the nave is a recent development. An excavation at the west end of the south aisle in January 2012 provided the opportunity to examine the south wall of the south aisle in the adjacent private garden at a time of year when it is not covered in foliage. The south wall of a porticus was clearly defined by a quoin formed of rubble at its south-west corner, with a rather more ragged joint at the south-east corner. Examination of the stonework indicated that it was largely built of Lower Lias Limestone with an admixture of Old Red Sandstone, a petrological assemblage characteristic of the earliest phase of work at Deerhurst.[39] The east and west walls of the south nave porticus do not survive, but the south-facing responds of two former arches are built against the piers of the south arcade;[40] these arches were doubtless cut through the east and west walls of the porticus.

The south nave porticus was evidently of two storeys. Above the south arcade there is a small triangular opening. There are also similar small triangular openings at the same level in the north arcade and in the west wall of the nave (Fig. 10.6). These openings are cut straight through the wall and measure between 1 ft 5 in. and 1 ft 9 in. (44–53 cm.) wide at the base and between 2 ft 1 in. and 2 ft 4 in. (64–72 cm.) in height. There are grounds for suspecting that they may be original features of the ninth-century church; Knowles reported that the openings are of corbelled construction, a technique which would have been awkward to use if the openings were inserted at a later date.[41] The southern opening would have been centrally placed in relation to the south nave porticus, and the northern opening would seem to have been similarly located with reference to a lost north nave porticus; these openings presumably provided communication between the first floor of the porticus and the nave.

[38] On the discovery of this doorway, see Butterworth, 'History of Deerhurst Church', p. 97; the position of the doorway is shown in Rahtz *et al.*, *St Mary's Church, Deerhurst*, Fig. 96 (p. 123).
[39] Bagshaw, *Building Stones*, pp. 12–24, 28 n. 57.
[40] These responds may be glimpsed in Fig. 10.6.
[41] Knowles, 'Deerhurst Priory Church', pp. 149–50. Knowles evidently removed plaster from one of these openings; in November 1926, he received permission to remove an area of plaster from the south wall of the nave (Gloucestershire Archives, P112 VE 2/3).

Fig. 10.6 Interior view of St Mary's Church, Deerhurst, showing the west wall of the nave with the north and south nave arcades. (© Copyright M. Thurlby.)

One further observation has encouraged us to reconstruct the nave porticus as equal in height to the two choir porticus. As noted above, battered remnants of the great string-course may be seen along the side walls of the nave, though they are conspicuously lacking above the central arch of both north and south arcades. There are, however, fragments of the string-course visible above the two western piers of the arcade, in line with the west walls of the two nave porticus. On the south side the string-course at this point has been cut back flush with the wall, but on the north side a short section has been preserved for use as a corbel. What is striking about this short section is that it appears to be unweathered;[42] it may be contrasted with two long sections further east which are heavily weathered. We suggest that this section of string-course has survived in good condition because it was originally embedded in the west wall of the north nave porticus, in similar fashion to the section of string-course embedded in the south wall of the porch. When the north nave porticus was demolished, the surviving short section of string-course was preserved by being adapted for use as a corbel supporting the aisle roof.

[42] This observation is made on the basis of examination through binoculars.

The south wall of the south nave porticus survives to a height of about 11 ft (3.5 m.) above ground level, and there is no trace of any opening. In the reconstruction drawings a window has been shown in the west wall to light the ground floor and in the south wall to light the first floor.

The Western Porch

The lower three storeys of the western porch survive largely intact. The west doorway was replaced in the fourteenth century, but traces of the original doorway survive and enable its reconstruction. The side walls of the square eastern compartment of the porch were cut away at ground-floor level by arches *c.* 1200, and a small window to light the eastern compartment has been suggested. The first floor was also removed *c.* 1200, but the windows in the north and south walls which lit the eastern compartment at this level remain. In the west wall there is a square-headed window, which is evidently of later construction in its present form; a rather smaller window in the same position has been assumed to light the western compartment.

The cross wall dividing the porch into two compartments originally rose only through the lower two storeys, and the second floor was thus open throughout the length of the porch. There was an elaborate chapel at this level; in its west wall there was a doorway which opened onto a wooden walkway round three sides of the porch. The existence of this walkway has recently been deduced from a series of sockets for substantial timbers in the walls of the porch and in the west wall of the nave.[43] Many of the details are of necessity hypothetical; it has, for instance, been assumed on the basis of parallels elsewhere that the walkway was roofed.

The height to which the original porch rose is uncertain, as is the form of its roof; no entirely satisfactory solution could be identified.[44] In the reconstruction drawings the porch is shown with walls about 6 ft 6 in. (2 m.) higher than the surviving early medieval masonry; the walls are thus shown as rising to the same height as the side walls of the nave. In the west gable of the nave, there is a doorway with its sill in the eastern face at about this level, with steps leading down to the west. The proposed solution thus allows for a (rather cramped) third floor in the porch; a small window in the west wall to light this room is postulated. There is evidence of fire damage in the remaining upper parts of the porch, and it may be that it was fire damage which led to the removal of the original superstructure.

---

[43] M. Hare, 'The 9th-Century West Porch of St Mary's Church, Deerhurst, Gloucestershire: Form and Function', *Medieval Archaeology*, 53 (2009), pp. 35–93. That paper also argues that the second floor of the porch is part of the Period IV structure; earlier studies considered the porch at this level to be an addition (see for instance Rahtz *et al.*, *St Mary's Church, Deerhurst*, pp. 171–4, 176–9).

[44] This point is discussed further in Hare, '9th-Century West Porch', pp. 68–70.

10. THE CHURCH OF ST MARY, DEERHURST, GLOUCESTERSHIRE

St Mary's Church, Deerhurst and the Liturgy

The improved understanding gained of the church in recent years—and especially of the Period IV structure—means that we can begin to ask questions about how the building was used. These questions are, however, fraught with difficulty. Although we know that there was a community at Deerhurst in 804, nothing of its character is known; the document recording Æthelric's bequest uses the neutral term *congregatio*.[45] We do not even know whether the community was predominantly male or female at this early date. Sims-Williams has explored the wide range of influences which operated on the church in the dioceses of Worcester and Hereford in the seventh and eighth centuries;[46] these early influences may have produced correspondingly varying patterns of liturgical practice. The general difficulties inherent in attempts to understand how early medieval churches were used have recently been stressed by Gem and Gittos.[47]

A consideration of the liturgical dispositions of the church should necessarily begin with the apse and the central space, which must have been the main focus of the liturgical life of the community, emphasised externally by the elaborate stripwork on the apse. The exact position of the principal altar cannot now be ascertained. It must have sited somewhere between the centre of the apse (as on the St Gallen plan of *c.* 820) and a position just to the west of the arch dividing the central space from the apse (Fig. 10.5); such limited English evidence as is available from elsewhere would tend to favour a location just west of the arch.[48] This arch retains substantial painted remains of ninth-century date, which have recently been the subject of detailed study.[49] The beast-head at the northern end of the arch retains its polychromy; more importantly for present purposes the fragmentary remains of a vine scroll have been detected on the west face of the voussoirs of the arch. Whatever the exact position of

---

[45] See n. 8 above.

[46] P. Sims-Williams, *Religion and Literature in Western England, 600–800*, Cambridge Studies in Anglo-Saxon England, 3 (Cambridge, 1990).

[47] R. Gem, 'How much can Anglo-Saxon Buildings tell us about Liturgy?', in *The Liturgy of the Late Anglo-Saxon Church*, ed. H. Gittos and M. Bradford Bedingfield, Henry Bradshaw Society Subsidia, 5 (London, 2005), pp. 271–89; H. Gittos, 'Architecture and Liturgy in England *c.* 1000: Problems and Possibilities', in *The White Mantle of Churches: Architecture, Liturgy and Art around the Millennium*, ed. N. Hiscock, International Medieval Research, 10 (Turnhout, 2003), pp. 91–105.

[48] W. Horn and E. Born, *The Plan of St Gall*, California Studies in the History of Art, 19, 3 vols (Berkeley, 1979), vol. 1, pp. 131–3, 139–44, 150 (Fig. 99); H. M. Taylor, 'The Position of the Altar in Early Anglo-Saxon Churches', *Antiquaries Journal*, 53 (1973), pp. 52–8; P. S. Barnwell, 'The Laity, the Clergy and the Divine Presence: The Use of Space in Smaller Churches of the Eleventh and Twelfth Centuries', *Journal of the British Archaeological Association*, 157 (2004), pp. 41–60, at pp. 48–51.

[49] R. Gem and E. Howe with R. Bryant, 'The Ninth-Century Polychrome Decoration at St Mary's Church, Deerhurst', *Antiquaries Journal*, 88 (2008), pp. 109–64.

the altar, this arch would have acted as a frame for it. The vibrant symbolism of the vine scroll, representing Christ and his Church and their power to act as sources of sustenance and protection, would carry particular resonance in this setting.[50]

In considering the further arrangements in the apse and central space, something of a conundrum is encountered. Blair has argued that every minster community in Anglo-Saxon England could well have had its own local saint or saints;[51] as an important minster probably enjoying comital patronage *c*. 800, it seems highly likely that a significant local cult once existed at Deerhurst. Other Mercian minster churches of ninth- and tenth-century date with surviving architectural remains seem to have had eastern crypts which were the main focus for relic cults; this includes Brixworth and Wing, mentioned above, as well as Repton (Derbyshire), St Oswald's at Gloucester, and Cirencester (Gloucestershire).[52] At Deerhurst there was no crypt, as noted above, and this raises the question of where a shrine would have been placed. In Merovingian and early Carolingian Francia, the most common arrangement was a shrine set in an elevated position immediately east of the principal altar, thus often sheltered by the apse; such shrines are also known to have existed in seventh- and eighth-century England, sometimes to one side of rather than behind the altar.[53] Other arrangements are, however, also possible. For instance, in Ireland the principal reliquary focus was usually distinct from the main congregational church and was often located in a small separate shrine chapel.[54] There would certainly have been subsidiary churches within the minster complex at Deerhurst (though nothing is known of them), and it is possible that the shrine with Deerhurst's principal relics may have stood within one of these buildings; at nearby Winchcombe (Gloucestershire), there is evidence to suggest that there was a relic cult in a chapel dedicated to St

---

[50] On the symbolism of the vine scroll, see R. N. Bailey, *England's Earliest Sculptors*, Publications of the Dictionary of Old English, 5 (Toronto, 1996), p. 52.

[51] J. Blair, 'A Saint for Every Minster? Local Cults in Anglo-Saxon England', in *Local Saints and Local Churches in the Early Medieval West*, ed. A. Thacker and R. Sharpe (Oxford, 2002), pp. 455–94, at p. 456.

[52] M. Biddle, 'Archaeology, Architecture, and the Cult of Saints in Anglo-Saxon England', in *The Anglo-Saxon Church: Papers on History, Architecture, and Archaeology in honour of Dr H. M. Taylor*, ed. L. A. S. Butler and R. K. Morris, Council for British Archaeology Research Report, 60 (London, 1986), pp. 1–31, at pp. 16–22 (Repton); C. Heighway and R. Bryant, *The Golden Minster: The Anglo-Saxon Minster and Later Medieval Priory of St Oswald at Gloucester*, Council for British Archaeology Research Report, 117 (York, 1999), pp. 11–12, 62–7; D. Wilkinson and A. McWhirr, *Cirencester Anglo-Saxon Church and Medieval Abbey*, Cirencester Excavations, 4 (Cirencester, 1998), pp. 23–39. The sites in question have all undergone complex changes in the course of their evolution, and crypts are by no means always part of the initial structure erected on the site.

[53] J. Crook, *The Architectural Setting of the Cult of Saints in the Early Christian West c. 300–1200* (Oxford, 2000), pp. 68–79.

[54] T. Ó Carragáin, 'The Architectural Setting of the Cult of Relics in Early Medieval Ireland', *Journal of the Royal Society of Antiquaries of Ireland*, 133 (2003), pp. 130–76.

Pancras, close to but perhaps detached from the two major churches in the minster complex.[55]

Nevertheless, the elaborate architecture of Deerhurst's apse inclines us to think that any shrine is likely to have been located in or close to it. The location of the shrine is relevant to whether the Mass in the ninth century was celebrated by a priest standing to the east or west of the altar.[56] It also has a bearing on where the clergy were seated. Traditionally apses contained a bench running round the curve of the apse, which served as the seating for the clergy, as in England at Hexham (Northumberland) and Reculver (Kent).[57] Though there is no sign of any bench on the existing fragment of apse walling at Deerhurst, such a bench could easily have existed; the existence of a wooden floor above a sub-floor space means that it is likely to have been of timber rather than of stone. However, if a substantial shrine existed to the east of the altar, this would have interfered severely with any such arrangement, preventing the clergy from viewing proceedings at the altar and elsewhere in the central space. Such a shrine might well imply that the clergy did not on any occasion sit on a bench in the apse but were displaced to seating which lay to the west of the altar in the central space.[58] Whatever the arrangements in and adjacent to the apse, most of the central space is likely to have functioned as a choir space in which the clergy celebrated the daily office.[59]

One of the major functions of the porticus flanking the central space and apse is likely to have been the burial of important figures connected with the minster community, such as senior clerics and major lay patrons. In a brilliant analysis Éamonn Ó Carragáin has shown how such structures were citations of the Roman basilicas, in particular providing reminiscences of the burial customs of the popes at St Peter's basilica.[60] It may be well be that it was in one of these flanking porticus that Æthelmund and Æthelric were buried. It is at least worth noting that the one early grave cover known at Deerhurst is built into the head of the inserted doorway leading from the ground floor of the north choir porticus to the central space;[61] it might previously have been used within the porticus.

[55] S. Bassett, 'A Probable Mercian Royal Mausoleum at Winchcombe, Gloucestershire', *Antiquaries Journal*, 65 (1985), pp. 82–100.
[56] For discussion of this issue, see Barnwell, 'Laity', pp. 52–3.
[57] Barnwell, 'Laity', pp. 46, 48–9.
[58] Note the comments in Barnwell, 'Laity', p. 53.
[59] For a discussion of the similar (though notably larger) choir space at Brixworth (Northamptonshire), which is broadly contemporary with Deerhurst, see R. Gem, *Architecture, Liturgy and Romanitas at All Saints' Church, Brixworth*, Brixworth Lecture 2009 (Brixworth, 2011). I am grateful to Dr Gem for allowing me to see a copy of his text in advance of publication.
[60] Ó Carragáin, 'The Term *Porticus*'.
[61] Rahtz *et al.*, *St Mary's Church, Deerhurst*, pp. 52–3. The grave cover is probably of ninth-century date: see Bryant, *Corpus*, pp. 162–3.

The use of the porticus for burials would not exclude other functions. The presence of a doorway in the centre of the east wall of the main north porticus (Fig. 10.1) suggests that there is unlikely to have been an altar in the ground floor of this porticus, and the north-east porticus seems too low and small for such a purpose; the arrangement on the south side was probably similar. The principal south porticus has a fine doorway in the south wall with a neatly-cut hood-mould terminating in label stops with beast heads (Fig. 10.2);[62] formerly there was also a large *prokrossos* (projecting beast-head) above the doorway, though only the neck now remains. This doorway seems likely to have served as the principal entry into the church for the minster clergy of Deerhurst; the porticus on the south side may thus also have served for the storage of liturgical vestments, books and vessels.

It is also worth giving some consideration to the original location of Deerhurst's font, now situated at the west end of the north aisle. The art-historical evidence indicates that this font belongs to the same general date as the Period IV church, that is to say the first half of the ninth century.[63] While there has been some debate as to whether this stone originated as a font, detailed study has shown that it was designed as a bowl from the outset;[64] it is, however, an exceptionally rare feature, as no other tub-font in Europe north of the Alps can be dated earlier than the eleventh century with any conviction.[65] The normal position for the font in the central and later middle ages was at the west end of the nave, as already in the St Gallen plan of *c*. 820.[66] However, there is some evidence from pre-Conquest England to suggest that the arrangements for baptism were located in separate compartments distinct from the main body of the church.[67] At the Old Minster at Winchester (Hampshire), established in the middle of the seventh century, there was an octagonal structure containing a well in the north porticus;[68] at Barton-upon-Humber (Lincolnshire),

---

[62] There are two types of hood-mould at Deerhurst; hood-moulds such as those round the south doorway and the chancel arch are carefully cut in dressed stone. For the lesser grade of hood-moulds, see below n. 72.

[63] Bailey, *Anglo-Saxon Sculptures*, pp. 14–23.

[64] Bryant, *Corpus*, pp. 163–8. Bryant concurs with Bailey's dating, but considers the stem (put together with the bowl only in the nineteenth century) to be part of a separate monument.

[65] On the origin of fonts, see now J. Blair, 'The Prehistory of English Fonts', in *Intersections: The Archaeology and History of Christianity in England, 400–1200. Papers in Honour of Martin Biddle and Birthe Kjølbye-Biddle*, ed. M. Henig and N. Ramsay, British Archaeological Reports British Series, 505 (Oxford, 2010), pp. 149–77.

[66] Horn and Born, *Plan of St Gall*, vol. 1, p. 135.

[67] On this topic, see now P. S. Barnwell, *The Place of Baptism in Anglo-Saxon and Norman Churches*, Deerhurst Lecture 2013 (Deerhurst, 2014).

[68] B. Kjølbye-Biddle, 'Anglo-Saxon Baptisteries of the 7th and 8th Centuries: Winchester and Repton', *Radovi XIII međunarodnog kongresa za starokršćansku arheologiju (= Acta XIII Congressus Internationalis Archaeologiae Christianae)*, ed. N. Cambi and E. Marin, Studi di antichità cristiana, 54, 3 vols (Vatican City, 1998), vol. 2, pp. 757–78, at pp. 758–62.

there was a font sited in a western porticus of the turriform church, and at Potterne (Wiltshire), the excavated timber church had a baptistery to the south of the chancel.[69] A location in one of the flanking porticus, perhaps the north choir porticus, would therefore seem at least possible for Deerhurst. Burial and baptismal functions could go hand-in-hand, as seems to have been the case with the mausoleum and baptistery dedicated to St John the Baptist built at Canterbury by Archbishop Cuthbert (740–60);[70] a similar arrangement has also been suggested at Repton in the eighth century.[71]

As already noted the ground floors of the principal porticus flanking the central space were separated from the central space by solid walls. However, the upper floors of the porticus were linked to the central space through arches about 4 ft 11 in. (1.5 m.) wide and 6 ft 10 in. (2.1 m.) tall (Fig. 10.5); these arches had roughly-formed hood-moulds on the outer faces, now cut back on the north side but still in place on the south side.[72] The use of these upper rooms must have been closely connected with the liturgy in the central space and apse. One possibility is that these upper chambers were occupied by high-status lay patrons, such as Æthelmund and his family. An arrangement of this type would seem to be shown in the final miniature of the Benedictional of St Æthelwold of *c*. 973; this scene depicts a bishop standing in front of an altar, blessing clerics and monks standing in front of him with the laity (including a woman) apparently seated in an upper gallery or balcony.[73] Alternatively members of the community itself may have viewed proceedings in the central space and apse through these openings; if there was a female component to the community in the ninth century, the ladies of the community may have sat in the upper storeys of the porticus, just as nuns were to sit in raised galleries in later centuries in some

---

69   W. Rodwell and K. Rodwell, 'St Peter's Church, Barton-upon-Humber: Excavation and Structural Study, 1978–81', *Antiquaries Journal*, 62 (1982), pp. 283–315, at pp. 296–9; N. Davey, 'A Pre-Conquest Church and Baptistery at Potterne', *Wiltshire Archaeological and Natural History Magazine*, 59 (1964), pp. 116–23.

70   N. Brooks, *The Early History of the Church of Canterbury: Christ Church from 597 to 1066* (Leicester, 1984), pp. 80–3; it should be noted that the information about Cuthbert's construction of this church is first recorded in a source of late eleventh-century date and may not be entirely reliable.

71   Kjølbye-Biddle, 'Anglo-Saxon Baptisteries', pp. 762–8.

72   The hood-moulds to these arches at Deerhurst are built of thin blocks of lias rubble and are less well formed than the neat hood-moulds of dressed stone found in the most important locations (for which see n. 62 above). However, it is evident from the arch opening at ground-floor level from the eastern compartment of the porch into the nave that hood-moulds of this character were plastered so as to smooth out the irregularities; the hood-mould at the west end of the nave also retains much red paint, probably original.

73   London, British Library, MS. Add. 49598, f. 118v; see A. Prescott, *The Benedictional of St Æthelwold: a Masterpiece of Anglo-Saxon Art: A Facsimile* (London, 2002).

continental churches.⁷⁴ It should, however, be noted that no more than a modest handful of people could have obtained a satisfactory view of the proceedings in the choir and apse from these upper chambers. Klukas, who interpreted the design of Deerhurst as an expression of the liturgical provisions of the late tenth-century *Regularis concordia*, suggested that these openings were for musical performance.⁷⁵ The church is now considered to be of ninth-century origin (as previously noted) and it is in fact uncertain whether Deerhurst was a Benedictine monastery at any point in time during the Anglo-Saxon period.⁷⁶ Klukas's specific interpretation is thus problematic, but the idea that these upper rooms opening through arches to the central space were used for antiphonal singing remains possible.

As noted above, there was probably a broad arch separating the central space from the nave. There is no evidence to indicate whether or not there were screens or curtains in place at this point. The nave was presumably used primarily to accommodate the lay congregation of Deerhurst's minster parish.

The nave and central space were occupied on several levels. At the west end of the nave there was a timber gallery at the same height as the upper floors of the various flanking porticus and as the first floor of the porch; there is a doorway opening from the porch to the nave at this level, and there are also corbels in the western corners of the nave (Fig. 10.6). At the level of the second floor of the porch, there was certainly activity at the west end of the nave, as the northern half of the double opening in the east wall of the upper chapel was subsequently cut down to act as a doorway;⁷⁷ there was also at least one timber projecting through the west wall of the nave into the interior at this level.⁷⁸ In addition the external string-course along the walls of the nave marks this level. Whether there was a balcony at the west end of the nave or a more extensive floor remains uncertain, but there is also evidence for a floor at the same level above the central space, and it is difficult to see how this could have been reached except from the nave. The floor over the central space opened in turn through a series of apertures into a space within the apse roof (in the tenth century two of these apertures were blocked by triangular-headed panels (Fig. 10.5); the panel on the north side retains traces of a painted figure).⁷⁹ The openings to the roof-space above the

---

74   Galleries in the south transept and at the west end of the nave are for instance found at the church for canonesses at Meschede (North Rhine-Westphalia, Germany) of *c*. 900: see C. Jäggi and U. Lobbedey, 'Kirche und Klausur—zur Architektur mittelalterlicher Frauenklöster', in *Krone und Schleier: Kunst aus mittelalterlichen Frauenklöstern*, ed. J. F. Hamburger *et al.* (Munich, 2005), pp. 88–103, at pp. 91–3.
75   A. W. Klukas, 'Liturgy and Architecture: Deerhurst Priory as an Expression of the Regularis Concordia', *Viator*, 15 (1984), pp. 81–106.
76   Wormald, *How Do We Know so much*, pp. 7–9.
77   Taylor and Taylor, *Anglo-Saxon Architecture*, vol. 1, pp. 197–8.
78   Hare, '9th-Century West Porch', p. 62.
79   S. Bagshaw, R. Bryant and M. Hare, 'The Discovery of an Anglo-Saxon Painted Figure at St

apse seem to have been designed for viewing rather than for access, and it has been conjectured that there may have been a subsidiary shrine at this point placed above the principal shrine located in the apse beneath.[80] Finally the west gable of the nave retains a doorway, which shows that at least at the west end of the nave, there was an upper chamber between a flat ceiling and the nave roof.[81] The extent of these upper floors is uncertain, and it is therefore difficult to discuss their use.[82] It is likely that the blocked sockets for the joists of the floors and for other timbers remain in the walling concealed beneath plaster; these blocked sockets may enable a future generation of archaeologists to trace the extent of upper floors in more detail.

The two nave porticus would have provided further areas for burial for members of the community and their benefactors; they would also provide an alternative location for the font. The curious triangular openings are the only features of the upper storeys to survive, and they are without any known parallel in the corpus of early medieval architecture.[83] These openings (and the similar opening in the west wall of the nave) would only have provided a very limited field of view; they are perhaps better suited for the transmission of sound.[84]

The western porch at Deerhurst is an elaborate structure. At ground-floor level, the visitor would need to pass through three arches when entering the nave of the church, first the outer doorway, then an arch through the cross wall and finally an arch into the nave. Above the central arch there is a carving of the Virgin and Child, showing an iconography of Byzantine origin current in Rome in the second half of the eighth century. Gem has suggested that the arrangement may be a deliberate reminiscence of the oratory of St Mary Mediana sited at the entrance to the atrium of St Peter's in Rome. Gem is inclined to view this in the light of the pilgrimage to Rome known to have been made *c.* 804 by Deerhurst's patron, Æthelric, though he recognises that such a specific identification goes beyond what the evidence permits.[85]

Mary's Church, Deerhurst', *Antiquaries Journal*, 86 (2006), pp. 66–109.

[80] Bagshaw *et al.*, 'Discovery', pp. 84–100.

[81] It was suggested by the late Harold Taylor that this roof-space was occupied as a dormitory (quoted in Rahtz *et al.*, *St Mary's Church, Deerhurst*, p. 178). It seems to us most improbable that this doubtless cold and draughty space could have functioned effectively in such a fashion (one might ask what provision there could have been for a reredorter); this interpretation also depends on the assumption that the clerics of Deerhurst lived according to a strict monastic rule, and it is far from clear that this was ever the case.

[82] Bagshaw *et al.*, 'Discovery', pp. 97–100.

[83] A drawing by E. A. Freeman shows that the opening above the south arcade was open before the restoration of 1861–2 (Manchester, John Rylands Library, FA4/1/495); this suggests that it may never have been blocked. If similar openings survive elsewhere but are blocked, it is doubtful whether they would readily be recognised.

[84] I owe this point to Richard Bryant.

[85] Gem, *Deerhurst and Rome*, pp. 19–27.

The function of the eastern compartment of the first floor is presumably to be linked to the upper floors of the two nave porticus, as there is a similar triangular opening towards the nave. The triangular opening is not centrally placed in relation to the width of the nave. However, its position may make sense if the arrangements within the eastern compartment of the porch at first-floor level are considered. The northern part of this compartment may have served simply as a corridor, since there are doorways close to the north wall in both the west wall of the nave and the cross wall. Within the first floor of the porch, the triangular opening is placed centrally between the southern jamb of the doorway and the south wall of the porch; it was thus placed centrally in relation to that part of the room which did not act as a corridor.

The upper chapel in the second floor of the porch may be paralleled in numerous churches of early medieval date in England and on the continent, but the projecting walkway round it is a most unusual feature. Its possible function has been discussed in detail elsewhere;[86] it has been suggested that the principal purpose of the walkway is likely to have been the display of relics to pilgrims gathered beneath. A major shrine could not conveniently have been manœuvred round the walkway, and it is more likely that relics in small portable reliquaries (possibly including a fragment of the True Cross) may have been displayed. The argument is not, however, without problems, as the display of relics on a regular basis is not attested in written sources before the second half of the ninth century. Other functions are possible; for instance the walkway might have been used for the ringing of handbells. The walkway also provided a fine view up and down the Severn valley (now obscured by the vast Wellingtonias planted in the churchyard in the nineteenth century), and might on occasion have been used as a look-out post. Such uses are not mutually exclusive.

Conclusion

As recently as 1985, Warwick Rodwell wrote of Deerhurst that 'It is an undated building, of many phases, with a substantially incomplete plan. Fundamentally, we do not know whether to class it as a simple box-like church with a more or less random collection of appendages, a full-scale basilica from which deletions have been made, or a cruciform building achieved by tortuous conversion'.[87] Since Rodwell wrote, the work of a number of scholars from different disciplines has done much to clarify the development of the building and the date of at least the principal episode of construction. Nevertheless, there is still much about this building which remains mysterious, and there is considerable scope for further study.

[86] Hare, '9th-Century West Porch', pp. 79–86.
[87] W. Rodwell, Review of E. Fernie, *The Architecture of the Anglo-Saxons* (London, 1983), *Medieval Archaeology*, 29 (1985), pp. 237–8.

(11)
Conclusion: Churches, Sites, Landscapes

P. S. BARNWELL

The early Christian sites of England, or at least of those areas with the strongest Anglo-Saxon presence, have tended to be studied apart from those of the rest of Britain and Ireland. Part of the reason lies in the nature of written sources, since for much of England Bede's *Historia ecclesiastica gentis Anglorum* provides a coherent narrative of the development of the Church which has no counterpart elsewhere. Further, the model of conversion it reveals differs from that which can be discerned for other parts of Britain and Ireland as it shows a relatively tightly controlled foundation of churches by powerful rulers, especially kings. In Ireland, by contrast, the process was more diffuse, with greater local initiative, while in Wales and Scotland there may have been some variation with time and place.[1] The variation reflects differing structures of power: in fifth- and sixth-century Ireland there were no rulers with sufficient strength to impose centralised control over the process of conversion or church foundation; but in substantial areas of seventh- and eighth-century England there were. It is also related to the nature of the conversion: in contrast to the disparate efforts of individual missionaries, particularly in Ireland, or of the possibility of the growth of Christianity from residual Roman Christianity in areas such as south Wales, the Augustinian mission to the English was centrally directed, ultimately by the Papacy. Not only did it seek to work through the most powerful English rulers in the hope that they would encourage their followers and subjects to convert, but it was also a means of reinforcing the growth of royal power.

The centrality of Rome to the process of conversion in England from the seventh-century onwards is reflected in the fact that many churches were built of mortared stone. They have therefore survived, and the physical remains of the early Church in Anglo-Saxon England have largely been studied through church buildings in ways which are not possible elsewhere in Britain and Ireland. In Wales (chapter 3), there are no standing churches of the period—the few archaeologically recognisable remains suggest that the buildings were timber;[2] in Ireland (chapter 4) and Scotland (chapter 5) mortared stone buildings were and are rare, though drystone structures are known. This means that other forms of evidence, especially various forms of

---

[1] For comparisons between England, Ireland and Wales, see T. Charles-Edwards, *Wales and the Britons 350–1064* (Oxford, 2013), pp. 609–14; for Ireland, see also H. Mytum, *The Origins of Early Christian Ireland* (London and New York, 1992), pp. 62–3.

[2] D. Petts, *The Early Church in Wales* (Stroud, 2009), pp. 55–8.

sculpture and inscribed stone, assume greater importance than in England, though that is not to suggest that Anglo-Saxon sculpture has been neglected. Further, where early churches survive in England, later town and village development has often destroyed their context, leaving little of their complexes of associated buildings available for archaeological study,[3] reinforcing the tendency for English sites to be studied through their churches, whereas in more northern and western areas, where the pressure of later development has generally been less, there is greater scope for understanding complete sites.

At one level the present volume reinforces these differences. Because of its primary emphasis on buildings for worship, churches, where they exist, take centre stage. In seeking to draw out some conclusions, therefore, rather than attempting to pull together all the themes which emerge from the foregoing essays, many of which are foreshadowed in Barbara Yorke's opening chapter, what follows is a brief and tentative attempt to tease out some things which link what at first appear diverse forms of religious buildings, sites and landscapes.

Churches

In addition to being constructed of mortared stone, most surviving early Anglo-Saxon churches are also distinguished by having integrated plans, bringing into one structure several different functions—especially the main place of cult (with the principal altar), and the place of burial (in porticus)—which in early Christian tradition were often accommodated in individual structures, and which remained separate in other parts of Britain and Ireland. As Meg Boulton and Jane Hawkes discuss in chapter 6, both these features of structure and plan appear from the earliest Augustinian churches of Kent and are specifically associated with Rome. Even if mediated through Merovingian Gaul,[4] they were made in the specific context of Gregory I's mission to England. That mission was, as Martin Henig notes (chapter 2), as much concerned with bringing British Christians to full acceptance of Roman authority as it was with the conversion of pagans, and the use of Roman types of building must have visibly marked out the churches of the Roman mission, have associated them with the power and prestige of the Roman Church, and have distinguished them from British places of worship. Although the architectural articulation differed, both the structure and

---

[3] Cf. R. Cramp. 'Anglo-Saxon Monasteries of the North', in *Scottish Archaeological Forum*, 5 (1973), pp. 104–24, at p. 104. The point may be further illustrated by the inevitably quite tight focus of the excavations at Wearmouth and Jarrow reported in R. Cramp, *Wearmouth and Jarrow: Monastic Sites*, 2 vols (Swindon, 2005–6), and the recent date of the first sustained attempt to look at the setting of the two monasteries more widely: S. Turner, S. Semple and A. Turner, *Wearmoth and Jarrow: Northumbrian Monasteries in an Historic Landscape* (Hatfield, 2013).

[4] E. Cambridge, 'The Architecture of the Augustinian Mission', in *St Augustine and the Conversion of England*, ed. by R. Gameson (Stroud, 1999), pp. 202–36, at pp. 216–27.

plans of early Northumbrian churches exhibit the same interest in Rome, perhaps also mediated through Gaul,[5] as Rosemary Cramp discusses in chapter 8. It is equally apparent, though in different ways, at Wearmouth–Jarrow (County Durham) and at Wilfrid's foundations of Ripon (West Riding of Yorkshire) and Hexham (Northumberland).[6] In the case of Ripon, the association between the mortared stone building and the authority of Rome is underlined by the fact that, on being given a pre-existing monastery to convert from British to Roman traditions, Wilfrid replaced the church from its foundations ('a fundamentis in terra') with one of dressed stone ('polite lapide').[7] Not only was this a powerful symbol of the new religious allegiance of the house, but it is also likely to have marked it out in the landscape as something new and clearly distinct from the British 'loca sancta' which were subject to Ripon.[8]

The association of mortared stone with authority, particularly Roman authority, worked at more than one level. It was, perhaps most obviously, a material associated with the Church of Rome and the church buildings of Rome. Stone was also associated with the Roman past in Britain itself, and the re-use of Roman stone, as well as in many cases being for practical considerations, may have been a conscious attempt to take possession of the powerful remains of the Roman past, to harness them to the new age, to demonstrate that the patrons of the new buildings were in some way heirs to ancient (Roman) power, to demonstrate their wealth and ability to command the resources necessary for obtaining, transporting and re-working the costly and exotic building material.[9] This was not only the case during the missionary phase of the Anglo-Saxon Church, but continued much later, and may be exemplified by Brixworth (Northamptonshire), to which Roman building materials were transported over the quite considerable distance from Leicester.[10]

---

[5] E. Cambridge, 'The Sources and Function of Wilfrid's Architecture at Ripon and Hexham', in *Wilfrid: Abbot, Bishop, Saint. Papers from the 1300th Anniversary Conferences*, ed. by N. J. Higham (Donington, 2013), pp. 136–51.

[5] For the close association of Wearmouth–Jarrow and Hexham, despite differences between them, see I. N. Wood, *The Most Holy Abbot Ceolfrid*, Jarrow Lecture 1995 (Jarrow, 1995), pp. 7, 9.

[7] For the British foundation, see Bede, *Vita sancti Cuthberti*, in *Two Lives of St Cuthbert: Text, Translation and Notes*, ed. by B. Colgrave (Cambridge, 1940), pp. 141–307, c. 7; and for the explicit reason for its transfer to Wilfrid, Bede, *Historia ecclesiastica gentis Anglorum*, ed. by B. Colgrave and R. A. B. Mynors (Oxford, 1969), bk iii, c.25. On the rebuilding, see Stephen, *Vita Wilfridi*, in *The Life of Bishop Wilfrid by Eddius Stephanus*, ed. and trans. by B. Colgrave (Cambridge, 1927), c. 17.

[8] Stephen, *Vita Wilfridi*, c. 17.

[9] In addition to the specific instances discussed in earlier chapters, see the broader discussion in T. Eaton, *Plundering the Past: Stonework in Medieval Britain* (Stroud, 2000), especially chapter 5.

[10] D. Parsons and D. S. Sutherland, *The Anglo-Saxon Church of All Saints, Brixworth, Northamptonshire: Survey, Excavation and Analysis, 1972–2010* (Oxford and Oakville,

There is also some evidence of an association of mortared stone with the Roman church in other parts of Britain and Ireland, to which its use spread from Northumbria. The clearest case, perhaps because the evidence comes from Bede, is that of King Nechtan of the Picts, whose adoption of the Roman method of calculating the date of Easter and of the Roman form of tonsure was accompanied by a desire to build a stone church after the Roman fashion as part of an overall commitment to follow the customs of the Roman Church.[11] At Armagh, evocations of Rome associated with its claim to be pre-eminent in Ireland included the building, in 789, of a mortared-stone congregational church, perhaps inspired by knowledge of Bede's works.[12] Mortared stone buildings were not, however, the only means of evoking Rome, even in areas subject to direct Anglo-Saxon influence. At Kildare, also a site with pretensions to authority over all of Ireland, the church described by Cogitosus, conjured up Rome through its internal layout, which, it has been suggested, was a simplified imitation of Roman basilicas,[13] even though the structure was almost certainly of timber; and, as Sally Foster points out (chapter 5), the arrangement of the timber Northumbrian church at Whithorn (Wigtownshire) was not dissimilar.

The fact that there are surviving stone buildings in England, and that Bede draws a distinction between them, built *more Romanorum*, and timber churches, built *more Scottorum*, is a reflection of his distinction between the traditions of Church authority; it does not imply that the 'Irish' had a monopoly of building timber churches. Although the evidence is fragmentary, it is clear that Anglo-Saxon adherents of the Roman Church sometimes built in timber. At York, for example, Bede himself records that the first church of the Roman mission at York was timber, though the choice of material may have been for reasons of haste, and the building was soon replaced in stone;[14] similarly, the destruction by fire of the early church at *Campodunum* (North Riding of Yorkshire), where Paulinus baptised into the Roman church, may imply a timber structure, with the material again perhaps chosen for reasons of haste at the time of conversion.[15] Perhaps more significantly, even so great a champion of the Roman church as Wilfrid, when in exile and without royal patronage, seems to have built a timber church for when, after his death, his

---

2013), pp. 150–3.
[11] Bede, *Historia ecclesiastica*, bk v, c. 21.
[12] T. Ó Carragáin, this volume; for greater discussion, see T. Ó Carragáin, *Churches in Early Medieval Ireland: Architecture, Ritual and Memory* (New Haven and London, 2010), pp. 61–6.
[13] C. Neuman de Vegvar, 'Romanitas and Realpolitik in Cogitosus' Description of the Church of St Brigit, Kildare', in *The Cross Goes North: Processes of Conversion in Northern Europe, AD 300–1300*, ed. by M. Carver (Woodbridge, 2003), pp. 153–70, especially at pp. 161–7.
[14] Bede, *Historia ecclesiastica*, bk 2, c. 14.
[15] Bede, *Historia ecclesiastica*, bk 2, c. 14.

monastery in or near Oundle, Northamptonshire, was attacked and burnt everything was destroyed apart from the house ('domus'—it is clear that it is not the church) in which Wilfrid died and the wooden cross which marked the place where his body was washed.[16] Nor were timber churches in any sense unique to Britain and Ireland: there is substantial textual and archaeological evidence for their existence in parts of Merovingian Gaul, with some hint that it was the greater churches which were built of stone.[17] The fact that it is only relatively recently, in the last three decades, that archaeological evidence for timber churches in Gaul has become at all plentiful should caution against any assumption that there may not have been a considerable number in England. Later in the Anglo-Saxon period, from the late ninth century onwards, there is more plentiful evidence for timber construction, most of it in smaller churches of non-royal patronage, but including what was either a palace chapel or a minster church at Cheddar, Somerset,[18] and the early tenth-century royal church built at Colchester, Essex, in the wake of the conquest of the area from the Danes by Edward the Elder.[19]

Timber buildings were not necessarily impoverished: parts of their structure might be carved,[20] painted[21] (as were stone buildings, including Ripon[22] and Deerhurst) or plastered and painted,[23] and adorned with decorative metalwork, in the

[16] Stephen, *Vita Wilfridi*, c. 67.

[17] See in particular, C. Bonnet, 'Les Églises en bois du haut moyen-âge d'après les recherches archéologiques', in *Grégoire de Tours et l'espace gaulois: actes du congrès international, Tours, 3–5 novembre 1994*, ed. by N. Gauthier and H. Galinié, 13e Supplément à la *Revue archéologique du centre de la France* (Tours, 1997), pp. 217–36, with, in the same volume, N. Gauthier, 'Note annexe: les églises en bois du VIe siècle d'après les sources littéraires, pp. 237–40; cf., also in the same volume, J. Guyon, 'L'Architecture religieuse chez Grégoire de Tours', pp. 197–207. Further examples are conveniently gathered together in E. James, 'Archaeology and the Merovingian Monastery', in *Columbanus and Merovingian Monasticism*, ed. by H. B. Clarke and M. Brennan, British Archaeological Reports, International Series 113 (Oxford, 1981), pp. 33–55.

[18] P. Rahtz, *The Saxon and Medieval Palaces at Cheddar*, British Archaeological Reports, British Series 65 (Oxford, 1979), pp. 198–203, 206–10; for re-interpretation as a minster, see J. Blair, 'Palaces or Minsters? Northampton and Cheddar Reconsidered', *Anglo-Saxon England*, 25 (1996), pp. 97–121, at pp. 108–21.

[19] P. J. Drury, 'Aspects of the Origins and Development of Colchester Castle', *Archaeological Journal*, 139 (1982), pp. 302–419, at pp. 328–33, 350–4, 390, 396.

[20] *Betha Máedóc Ferna I* [Life of Maedoc of Fearns I], in *Bethada náem n'Érenn: Lives of the Irish Saints*, ed. and trans. by C. Plummer, 2 vols (Oxford, 1922), vol. 1, pp. 183–9 (translation vol. 2, pp. 177–82), c. 34.

[21] Cogitosus, *Sanctae Brigidae virginis vita*, in *Patrologia cursus completes, series latina*, ed. by J.-P Migne, 221 vols (Paris, 1844–65), vol. 72, cols 775–90, at col. 789.

[22] Stephen, *Vita Wilfridi*, c. 17.

[23] As in the later Anglo-Saxon period at Colchester: see E. C. Rouse and P. J. Drury, 'Late Saxon Painted Wall Plaster, in Drury, 'Aspects of Colchester Castle', pp. 350–4, P. J. Drury, 'Anglo-Saxon Painted Plaster Excavated at Colchester Castle, Essex', in *Early Medieval Wall*

same way as were secular halls,[24] and they might contain painted sculpture and fixtures in the same way as did stone churches, as well as textiles (such as curtains),[25] elaborate altars covered in metal and gems, and vessels and altar ornaments of precious and eye-catching materials.[26] The tomb of St Brigit at Kildare was covered in gold silver, gems and precious stones, and the costly sculptures of Govan (Renfrewshire) and St Andrews (Fife), particularly when painted, are evidence of considerable opulence and investment no matter what the nature of the buildings in which they stood, and may be paralleled in England by the early tenth-century timber church, described as of wonderful workmanship, built for the relics of the leading English saint, Edmund, at *Beadericesworth* (Suffolk).[27]

No matter what the structural material of the churches, it was not only the buildings which conveyed the association with Rome, but also their fittings, such as the turned baluster shafts of Wearmouth (chapter 8). The same is true of liturgical and devotional artefacts including the painted image of Christ processed by Augustine on his way to meet King Æthelberht of Kent,[28] the similarly painted panels acquired from Rome for Wearmouth–Jarrow by Benedict Biscop,[29] and the creation of icon-like stone sculpture particularly in Northumbria.[30] Books—not only liturgical ones—could also have Roman associations, as most notably exemplified by the three pandects commissioned by Abbot Ceolfrith, of which the *Codex Amiatinus* is the survivor: although the translation is that we know as the Vulgate, the order of the books is that of the *Vetus Latinus*, presented—wrongly—as having been established, amongst others by Pope Hilary (rather than Hilary of Poitiers), emphasising the importance of the authority of Rome.[31]

Painting and Painted Sculpture in England: Based on the Proceedings of A Symposium at the Courtauld Institute of Art, February 1985, British Archaeological Reports, British Series 216 (1990), pp. 111–22.

[24] *Beowulf*, in *Beowulf and the Finnesburgh Fragment*, ed. by C. L. Wrenn (London, 1953), ll. 721–2, 773–6.

[25] Cogitosus, *Sanctae Brigidae virginis vita*, col. 789.

[26] Cogitosus, *Sanctae Brigidae virginis vita*, col. 789.

[27] Abbo of Fleury, *Passio sancti Edmundi*, in *Memorials of St Edmund's Abbey*, ed. by T. Arnold, *Rerum Britannicarum medii aevi scriptores*, 96, 3 vols (London, 1890–6), c. 19.

[28] Bede, *Historia ecclesiastica*, bk i, c. 25, discussed by Boulton and Hawkes, this volume.

[29] Bede, *Historia abbatum*, in *Abbots of Wearmouth and Jarrow: Bede's Homily i. 13 on Benedict Biscop, Bede's History of the Abbots of Wearmouth and Jarrow, the Anonymous Life of Ceolfrith, Bede's Letter to Ecgbert, Bishop of York*, ed. by C. W. Grocock and I. N. Wood (Oxford, 2013), cc. 6, 9.

[30] J. Hawkes, 'Stones of the North: Sculpture in Northumbria in the "age of Bede"', in *Newcastle and Northumberland: Roman and Medieval Architecture and Art*, ed. by J. Ashbee and J. Luxford, British Archaeological Association Conference Transactions, 36 (Leeds, 2013), pp. 34–53.

[31] See the discussion in Wood, *Most Holy Abbot Ceolfrid*, pp. 12–13.

11. CONCLUSION

Rome had a particular significance as the source of authority and touchstone of the universal Church, but it was not the only point of reference for church buildings across Britain and Ireland. At least as important was an association between churches and the Temple at Jerusalem, providing a link with the centre of Christianity and the life of Christ himself. There is a particularly rich range of reference in Irish sources, where *templum* is often the word used for a church, and the simple quadrilateral form of the buildings reflects the way in which the Temple was seen a mirror of the quadrangular form of the world and its fourfold organisation through the cardinal directions, seasons and elements, as well as in the four virtues and the four gospels which are represented by the corners of the building. The Temple, and those churches which in some way alluded to it, was therefore both a representation of this world and a prefiguration of the next.[32] Although there is little relationship between the proportions of Irish church buildings and any of the successive forms of the Temple, the proportions of St Peter's, Wearmouth, may evoke the Temple of Solomon.[33] The crypts of Ripon and Hexham may also contain allusions to the Holy Sepulchre[34] as well as to the St Paul's outside the walls of Rome;[35] similarly, as Meg Boulton and Jane Hawkes argue, the apsidal churches of Kent, while of Roman form also conjure up to the New Jerusalem: for the medieval mind, multiple, simultaneous, points of reference were unexceptional.[36]

Plan and Liturgy: Form and Function
Differences in building materials and in symbolic references do not necessarily reflect differences in belief or in the basics of worship either as formal liturgy or as private devotion. Although a formalist interpretation of architecture might suggest that differing forms of church plan relate to significant differences in liturgical ceremonial, such does not appear to be the case.

The relationship between liturgy and the forms of early churches can most easily be considered through the plans of the east ends of churches. Stripped to its barest essentials, the celebration of the Mass was centred on the main altar which was placed

---

[32] Ó Carragáin, *Churches in Early Medieval Ireland*, pp. 38–42; J. O'Reilly, 'Patristic and Insular Traditions of the Evangelists: Exegesis and Iconography', in *Le isole britanniche e Roma in età romanobarbarica*, ed. by A. M. Luiselli Fadda and E. Ó Carragáin (Rome, 1998), pp. 49–94 at pp. 54, 79–81.
[33] Wood, *Most Holy Abbot Ceolfrid*, p. 15, with references.
[34] E. Cambridge, 'The Sources and Function of Wilfrid's Architecture at Ripon and Hexham', in *Wilfrid: Abbot, Bishop, Saint*, pp. 136–51, at pp. 144–50.
[35] C. B. McClendon, *The Origins of Medieval Architecture: Building in Europe, AD 600–900* (New Haven and London, 2005), pp. 66–8.
[36] R. Krautheimer, 'Introduction to an "Iconography of Medieval Architecture"', in R. Krautheimer, *Studies in Early Christian, Medieval and Renaissance Art* (New York, 1969), pp. 115–50.

in the central vessel of the church between a clergy area to the east and the congregational area to the west; one or more clergy approached the altar from the east and returned to the east end at the end of the service. The near-universality of this pattern has been to some extent obscured by debate concerning whether the celebrant faced east or west while at the altar, though it seems almost certain that he came round the altar and faced east, acting as the leader of the congregation.[37] Even if that were to be incorrect, the basic functional and spatial arrangement would be the same. The pattern can most clearly be read in the churches of Kent, particularly Reculver, where the plan of eastern clergy area, transverse screen (or triumphal arch)[38] and altar footing[39] are readily apparent and form a recognisable basilican plan. The layout of many later high-status churches, including the late eighth-century church of All Saints', Brixworth (chapter 9), and ninth-century St Mary's, Deerhurst, Gloucestershire (chapter 10), are elaborated variations of the basilican form.

The same fundamental relationship between clergy, altar and laity, encompassing the same basic forms of ceremonial and movement, is also apparent in spaces which are differently architecturally expressed. One step away from the Kent model is a cross-shaped plan in which there was a single rectangular nave, at the east of which were north, east and south porticus. At the seventh-century Old Minster, Winchester, Hampshire, there is archaeological evidence that the altar stood towards the east of the nave, between the lateral porticus; the clergy approached it from the east porticus which therefore served the same function as the apse, and can be described as a 'square apse'.[40] This kind of plan is not dissimilar from that of some of the Northumbrian churches discussed by Rosemary Cramp. Even in simpler buildings, plain rectangles without the porticus, the same physical relationship could be maintained by the use of screens and/or hangings to compartmentalise the space, as revealed both by the excavations of the mid eighth-century phases of St Ninian's,

---

[37] The work of C. Vogel seems definitive on this point: '*Versus ad orientem*: l'orientation dans les *ordines romani* du haut moyen âge', *La Maison-Dieu*, 70 (1961), pp. 67–99; 'L'Orientation vers l'est du celebrant et des fidèles pendant la celebration eucharistique', *L'Orient syrien*, 9 (1964), pp. 3–37; '*Sol aequinoctialis*. Problèmes et technique de l'orientation dans le culte chrétien', *Revue des sciences religieuses*, parts 3–4 (1962), pp. 175–211.

[38] Cf. L. Izzi, 'The Visual Impact of Rome in Anglo-Saxon Eyes: The Evidence of Architecture', in *Making Histories: Proceedings of the Sixth International Conference on Insular Art*, ed. by J. Hawkes (Donington, 2013), pp. 105–20, at p. 116.

[39] Discussed by H. M. Taylor, 'The Position of the Altar in Early Anglo-Saxon Churches', *Antiquaries Journal*, 53 (1973), pp. 52–8.

[40] See M. Biddle, 'Excavations at Winchester 1967. Sixth Interim Report', *Antiquaries Journal*, 48 (1968), pp. 250–84, at p. 270; for context, see also P. S. Barnwell, 'The Laity, the Clergy and the Divine Presence: The Use of Space in Smaller Churches of the Eleventh and Twelfth Centuries', *Journal of the British Archaeological Association*, 157 (2004), pp. 41–60.

Whithorn,[41] and by the description of the church of St Brigit, Kildare, by Cogitosus:[42] it has indeed been independently suggested that the latter was designed to accommodate aspects of the Roman liturgy, particularly as revealed by *Ordo Romanus I*.[43]

The significance of the east end, beyond the altar, and its association with the clergy can be explored further though consideration of the implications of the ceremonial for the reconciliation of penitents. The seventh-century Penitential of Theodore records that in Roman practice penitents were reconciled during Mass, by the bishop or priest, in the apse ('intra absidem').[44] The arrangement is practical and follows the logic of the space as used in the Mass: the penitent was taken to the place where the priest would be except when at the altar. It is also possible to read the ceremonial in symbolic terms, for the space in which reconciliation was conducted was beyond the altar, where the means of redemption was commemorated, and therefore, as Meg Boulton and Jane Hawkes suggest, an evocation of heaven, the New Jerusalem, the place attained by salvation, a symbolic place of forgiveness. At the same time, taking the penitent into the place of privilege could be read as a re-enactment of the return of the Prodigal Son:[45] the penitent was readmitted to the Church (the father's house), led through the church (the household or *ecclesia*), past the common table (the altar) to the place of privilege with the priest (father). Although the Penitential refers to an apse, and is most easily understood in relation to a church of the Kent type, the ceremonial would have needed little adaptation for the same range of association to be appreciated in a church with a square apse or eastern porticus, or in a simple rectangular building with a space to the east of the altar, particularly if that space was demarcated by screens or hangings.

Similar issues of the relationship of ceremonial to space can be explored in relation to care for the dead. According to Theodore's Penitential, in the Roman tradition, upon death the body of a monk or person in orders was taken to the church for anointing and the Mass; the corpse was then taken its burial place accompanied by singing; prayers were offered, and the body was covered in earth or stone. Thereafter, commemorative Masses were to be chanted at intervals which varied in

---

[41] Period II Phase 3, *c.* 735–60, and Period II Phase 4, *c.* 760: see P. Hill, *Whithorn and St Ninian: The Excavation of a Monastic Town 1984–91* (Stroud, 1997), esp. pp. 135–62.

[42] Cogitosus, *Sanctae Brigidae virginis vita*, cols 788–90.

[43] Neuman de Vegvar, 'Romanitas and Realpolitik', pp. 161–5; *Ordo romanus I*, in *Les Ordini romani du haut moyen âge*, ed. by M. Andrieu, Spicilegium sacrum loviniense, 11, 23, 24, 28, 29, 5 vols (Louvain, 1931–61), vol. 2, pp. 65–108.

[44] 'Poetentiale Theodori', in *Councils and Ecclesiastical Documents Relating to Great Britain and Ireland*, ed. by A. W. Haddan and W. Stubbs, 3 vols in 4 (Oxford, 1869–78), vol. 3, pp. 173–213, bk i, 14, c. 1.

[45] Luke, xv, 11–32.

accordance with the status of the deceased and the wishes of the community; much the same was done for members of the laity.[46] Parts of this appear to be reflected in what is reported to have happened after Wilfrid's death for, even though Wilfrid was buried at Ripon, rather than at Oundle where he died, the community at Oundle celebrated a daily Mass in his honour, with that on each Thursday, the day of his death, treated like a feast day.[47] There is also some similarity with Bede's narrative of the burial of Cuthbert,[48] though it is not clear whether Bede gave an accurate account of what actually happened at Lindisfarne, which was an Irish foundation, or whether he made an assumption based on his experience of the Roman traditions of Wearmouth–Jarrow; whichever is the case, however, what Bede says is likely to relate to practice in at least one of the two traditions present in England.

The kind of liturgical activity of which these early written sources provide the merest outline can be envisaged in more than one type of church layout. In churches of the Kent tradition, porticus were used for burial, as is most clearly apparent, from written and archaeological sources, at SS. Peter and Paul, Canterbury.[49] By extension porticus became places of commemorative prayer for those buried within, or of supplication of the deceased, not least for healing miracles (perhaps an evolution of the idea of incubation in the side chambers of some Roman temples—chapter 2), and could be provided with altars for commemorative Masses.[50] The early Kent buildings are so small that there may have been little scope for singing as the body was taken to the place of burial after Mass, unless a deliberately circuitous processional route was taken, perhaps even going outside the building; there was greater potential at larger and later churches such as Brixworth and Deerhurst. The fundamentals of all stages of the process could equally well have been accommodated in simpler churches of the kind exemplified by the Old Minster, Winchester, or at Wearmouth, where Abbot Eosterwine at first buried in the 'porticus ingressus', the west porticus which served as a porch[51] (another example of imitating Rome, since popes were buried in the west porticus of St Peter's).[52] There is, furthermore, no reason why every aspect of the

---

[46] *Poenitentiale Theodori*, bk ii, 5, cc.1–6.
[47] Stephen, *Vita Wilfridi*, cc. 65–6.
[48] Bede, *Vita Cuthberti*, c. 40.
[49] Bede, *Historia ecclesiastica*, bk ii, cc. 3, 5; Goscelin of S.-Bertin, *Historia translationis sancti Augustini episcopi Anglorum apostoli*, in *Patrologia latina*, vol. 155, cols 13–46, bk i, cc. 17, 29, and bk ii, cc. 3, 28; W. St J. Hope, 'Recent Discoveries in the Abbey Church of St Austin of Canterbury', *Archaeologia Cantiana*, 66 (1915), pp. 377–400.
[50] On the evolution of porticus in general, and particularly on the way in which porticus in England fulfilled functions similar to those found on the continent, see E. Ó Carragáin, 'The Term *porticus* and *imitatio Romae* in Early Anglo-Saxon England', in *Text and Gloss: Studies in Insular Learning and Literacy Presented to Joseph Donovan Phiefer*, ed. by H. C. O'Briain, A.-M. D'Arcy and J. Scattergood (Dublin, 1999), pp. 13–34.
[51] Bede, *Historia abbatum*, c. 20.
[52] Ó Carragáin, 'The Term *porticus*', pp. 20–1.

11. CONCLUSION

ceremonial could not be accommodated at sites, typical of Ireland (chapter 4) and Wales (chapter 3),[53] where burial was in a separate building: indeed, such an arrangement gave greater scope for the procession from the Mass to the place of burial. A similar variety of arrangements is found in the medieval churches of Constantinople, where chapels, known as houses of prayer (*euktērioi* or *euktērioi oikoi*), which originated as places of commemoration of saints, monks and founders, and might or might not contain altars, could either be attached to the church, often in an aisle or outer aisle, or be freestanding nearby.[54]

In churches with porticus, the position of, and access to, the subsidiary compartments varied. At Reculver the eastern lateral porticus (the only original ones) were both entered from the chancel,[55] whereas at Bradwell-on-Sea (Essex), a church of similar type, the porticus on the north was entered from the chancel, that on the south from the nave;[56] at Escomb (County Durham) a north porticus was originally entered from the nave, and a western porticus appears only ever to have had external access.[57] Rather than view such variations as indicating major differences in function or in the most fundamental building-blocks of rite, it may be better to see them a reflecting local preference, and variations in who—clergy, kin, high-status laity, the local lay community, visitors and pilgrims—was to be provided with access to the funerary and commemorative chapels of particular individuals.

That is not, however, to suggest that the functions of all porticus were identical or that they were only connected to burial and commemoration. Some, particularly those entered only from the chancel, may have been used as sacristies, though the suggestion tentatively made by Alfred Clapham that they may have originated as the been a reflection of the *prothesis* (where the laity present their offerings) and *diakonikon* (sacristy) of the Orthodox liturgy, is unlikely since more recent scholarship has shown that the appropriation of flanking compartments to those functions in the eastern Church was a development of the mid-Byzantine period.[58]

---

[53] See also Petts, *Early Church in Wales*, p. 74; J. Knight, *South Wales from the Romans to the Normans: Christianity, Literacy and Lordship* (Stroud, 2013), p, 107.

[54] V. Marinis, *Architecture and Ritual in the Churches of Constantinople, Ninth to Fifteenth Centuries* (New York, 2014), pp. 77–9. Although there were significant differences between many aspects of eastern and western liturgies, medieval Byzantine practice in relation to the dead may reflect something of early practice in general since it evolved without the intrusion of belief in Purgatory which fundamentally altered patterns of commemoration in the west.

[55] H. M. Taylor and J. Taylor, *Anglo-Saxon Architecture*, 3 vols (Cambridge, 1965–78), vol. 2, pp. 503–9.

[56] Taylor and Taylor, *Anglo-Saxon Architecture*, vol. 1, pp. 91–3.

[57] Taylor and Taylor, *Anglo-Saxon Architecture*, vol. 1, pp. 234–8.

[58] A. Clapham, *English Romanesque Architecture: Before the Conquest* (Oxford, 1930), pp. 26–7. For discussion of the Byzantine material, see, for example, G. Descoudres, *Die Pastophorien im syro-byzantinischen Osten: Eine Untersuchung zu architektur- und liturgiegeschichtlichen Problemen*, Schriften fur Geistesgeschichte des östlichen Europa, 16

Others were used for baptism, the most notable early case being that of the Old Minster, Winchester, where a baptismal cistern has been excavated;[59] this could be combined with a funerary function, since baptism is a form of death and rebirth, though the lack of permanent fonts makes it impossible to understand how common such arrangements may have been.[60]

The analysis offered here does not seek to minimise the fact that that there were differences in liturgy across Britain and Ireland, particularly the contrast between the Gelasian forms used in the British Church and non-Anglo-Saxon areas, and the greater Roman influence in post-Augustinian England.[61] In practice, however, in many foundations the liturgy is likely to have been of hybrid form: Pope Gregory I instructed Augustine to adopt what he found good in non-Roman traditions,[62] and the existence of variation in England a century and a half later may be inferred from attempts to impose Roman 'uniformity' at the 747 Council of *Clofesho*.[63] Most of the variety lay in the calendar, the forms of prayers, the order of some items in the liturgy, and in some aspects of ritual gesture; none of those had a significant impact upon the basic building-blocks of the liturgy, particularly in the Mass and concerning the commemoration of the dead, where there were underlying similarities in the broad patterns of ceremony and movement. All liturgy, unless performed in the individual building for which it was first designed, had to be adapted to fit churches of varied and local plan and different kinds of institution with varying numbers of priests and other participants, and local variants were customary and seldom written down.[64] It

---

(Wiesbaden, 1983), esp. pp. 46–7. The complicated and contentious twentieth-century historiography of the issue is discussed in English in A. Mailis, *The Annexes at the Early Christian Basilicas of Greece (4th–6th Centuries): Architecture and Function*, British Archaeological Reports, International Series 2312 (Oxford, 2011), pp. 5–16; there is a convenient further discussion in Marinis, *Architecture and Ritual*, pp. 30–41.

[59] B. Kjølbye-Biddle, 'Anglo-Saxon Baptisteries of the 7th and 8th Centuries: Winchester and Repton', in *Radovi XIII međunarodni kongressa za starokršćansku arheologiju, Split–Poreč, 25.9–1.10.1994 = Vjesnik za arheologiju i historiju dalmatinsku*, supplementary vols 87–9; *Acta XIII congressus internationalis archaeologiae christianae* = Studi di antichità christiana, 54, ed. by N. Cambi and E Marin, 3 vols (Split and Rome, 1998), vol. 2, pp. 757–78.

[60] For further evidence and exploration of this issue, see P. S. Barnwell, *The Place of Baptism in Anglo-Saxon and Norman Churches*, Deerhurst Lecture 2013 (Deerhurst, 2014), pp. 4–11.

[61] For what can be gleaned concerning England, see R. W. Pfaff, *The Liturgy in Medieval England: A History* (Cambridge, 2009), pp. 30–55. For a summary account relating to Scotland (and Ireland), see I. Muirhead, 'The Beginnings', in *Studies in the History of Worship in Scotland*, ed. by D. B. Forrester and D. M. Murray, 2nd edn (Edinburgh, 1996), pp. 1–17, at pp. 9–11.

[62] Bede, *Historia ecclesiastica*, bk i, c. 27.

[63] Acts of the 747 Council of *Clofesho*, in *Councils and Ecclesiastical Documents*, vol. 3, pp. 362–75, cc. 13, 15, 16, 18. See the discussion in C. R. E. Cubitt, *Anglo-Saxon Church Councils c.650–c.850* (London and New York, 1995), pp. 130–2; but also note the different emphasis suggested by Pfaff, *Liturgy*, pp. 45–53.

[64] *Les Ordini romani*, vol. 2, pp. xlvi–xlviii.

is not possible, beyond a very broad level, to determine the form of the liturgy from the form of a building, only to discern whether a particular liturgy could have been performed in a particular building or kind of building. This is not peculiar to the early middle ages or the Insular context: it was as true of the later middle ages, when the Use of Sarum, designed for use in the cathedral of Salisbury, which had a large staff, multiple chapels, processional routes and a cloister, was adapted in myriad ways to fit into a wide variety of much smaller, simpler, parochial churches and chapels, some with only one or two clergy; the same is also true today, and even in our text-based culture local adaptations of the liturgy are rarely written down. Variations in the form of churches, including early medieval churches, cannot be taken to result from significant differences of liturgical practice; it is at least as likely they mask some underlying similarities in patterns of worship.

Sites

Similarities are more readily apparent in relation to the wider complexes of buildings on religious sites. Sites in all traditions and in all parts of Britain and Ireland could have more than one church, most notably in England at the extra-mural site of SS. Peter and Paul, Canterbury, at Jarrow and at Hexham, though the functions of the various buildings, which need not have been the same everywhere, are far from clear. In Ireland, the functions of at least some of the churches at places such as Armagh and Clonmacnoise (County Offaly) are clearer (chapter 4), and in Wales most seem to have been associated with burial and perhaps relics.[65] The pattern, and the lack of clarity concerning function, are also found on the continent, particularly in Francia, and the reasons for it need to be sought in that broader geographical context.[66] Also common across the whole area were many of the other elements of the sites: accommodation for the religious, cemeteries, storage for agricultural produce, craft and industrial production, and pits for waste disposal. Places as diverse as Lyminge (Kent),[67]

---

[65] Petts, *Early Church in Wales*, pp. 72–4; D. Petts and S. Turner, 'Early Medieval Church Groups in Wales and Western England', in *The Archaeology of the Early Medieval Celtic Churches: Proceedings of a Conference on the Archaeology of the Early Medieval Celtic Churches, September 2004*, ed. by N. Edwards, Society for Medieval Archaeology Monograph 29, Society for Church Archaeology Monograph 1 (Leeds, 2009), pp. 281–99.

[66] For a recent overview, see H. Gittos, *Liturgy, Architecture, and Sacred Places in Anglo-Saxon England* (Oxford, 2013), pp. 55–87. For an excavated Frankish example, see J. Mertens, 'Recherches archéologiques dans l'abbaye mérovingienne de Nivelles', *Archaeologia belgica*, 61 (1962) = *Miscellanea archaeologica in honorem J. Breuer*, pp. 89–113.

[67] G. Thomas and A. Knox, 'A Window on Christianisation: Transformations at Anglo-Saxon Lyminge, Kent, England', *Antiquity*, 334 (2012), online supplement: www.antiquity.ac.uk/projgall/thomas334 [accessed 26 December 2014]; G. Thomas, 'Life Before the Minster: The Social Dynamics of Monastic Foundation in Anglo-Saxon Lyminge, Kent', *Antiquaries Journal*, 93 (2013), pp. 109–45 at p. 129.

Bernician Hartlepool (County Durham),[68] Pictish Portmahomack (or Tarbat, Ross and Cromarty),[69] and Irish Armagh and Clonmacnoise,[70] provide evidence that each function was restricted to a discrete part of the site. Such zoning of activity has been proposed as one of the defining characteristics of 'monastic towns' in Ireland, and both it and the list of the elements of monastic sites (functional zoning around a core of major church buildings; dwellings and workshops; evidence for streets or rows of buildings; some kind of trading function; an enclosure; evidence that of association with a political centre)[71] could with relatively little adaptation be applied to a wide range of the places discussed in this volume.

Evidence for industrial production, particularly metal-working, seems particularly widespread. It has been found at sites ranging from the tiny island monastery of Illaunloughan (Kerry)[72] to the royal church centre at Govan,[73] Hartlepool,[74] and even the very centre of the Roman mission to England, SS. Peter and Paul, Canterbury.[75] Other crafts and industries are represented on some of the same sites as well as elsewhere, notably at Lyminge,[76] Clonmacnoise[77] and, as Sally Foster shows (chapter 5), at a large number of sites in Scotland.

Although the functions represented by the buildings were similar, the forms of the buildings were more varied. In many instances, the buildings reflected local traditions of plan and structure. In Ireland and much of Scotland, for example, domestic accommodation was mostly in huts built in varying combinations of wattle, turf, unmortared stone and timber: plans are annular, as at Illaunloughan, Luchubran (Pigmie's Isle, Lewis, Ross-shire), and St Cuthbert's Isle (Northumberland),[78] or

[68] R. Daniels, *Anglo-Saxon Hartlepool and the Foundation of English Christianity: An Archaeology of the Anglo-Saxon Monastery*, Tees Archaeology Monograph Series, 3 (Hartlepool, 2007), pp. 142.

[69] M. Carver, 'An Iona of the East: The Early Medieval Monastery at Portmahomack', *Medieval Archaeology*, 48 (2004), pp. 1–30, at pp. 8, 13.

[70] J. Bradley, 'The Monastic Town of Clonmacnoise', in *Clonmacnoise Studies 1: Seminar Papers 1994*, ed. by H. A. King (Dublin, 1999), pp. 42–56, at pp. 44, 45–50.

[71] Bradley, 'Monastic Town', p. 45.

[72] J. W. Marshall and C. Walsh, *Illaunloughan Island: An Early Medieval Monastery in County Kerry* (Bray, 2005), pp. 19–22.

[73] C. Dalglish and S. T. Driscoll, *Historic Govan: Archaeology and Development* (York and Edinburgh, 2009), pp. 28–50.

[74] Daniels, *Anglo-Saxon Hartlepool*, p. 142.

[75] C. Jarman, 'Christ Church College', *Canterbury's Archaeology 1995–6 (20th Annual Report)*, (Canterbury, 1997), pp. 2–4; M. Houliston, 'Christ Church College', *Canterbury's Archaeology 1996–7 (21st Annual Report)*, (Canterbury, 1998), pp. 1–4.

[76] Thomas and Knox, 'Window on Christianisation'.

[77] H. A. King, 'The Economy and Industry of Early Medieval Clonmacnoise: A Preliminary View', in *Archaeology of Early Medieval Celtic Churches*, pp. 333–49.

[78] C. Thomas, *The Early Christian Archaeology of North Britain: The Hunter Marshall Lectures delivered at the University of Glasgow in January and February 1968* (London, Glasgow and

11. CONCLUSION

rectangular with rounded ends, reflecting the form of construction, as at Canna (Inverness-shire) or in Orkney and Shetland.[79] In Anglo-Saxon parts of England, rectilinear buildings are the norm, though the Irish-type monastery at Burgh Castle (Norfolk) had oval buildings of wattles.[80] In Northumbria, at Whitby, wattles may have been used for rectilinear buildings in a first phase of construction, before stone cills were added.[81] At Hartlepool, by contrast, the seventh-century buildings were post-in-trench structures, more characteristic of the region, before also having stone cills added,[82] as were those at Lyminge.[83] Of particular significance is a suggestion that the establishment of the Northumbrian minster at Whithorn may have been accompanied by a change in the method of construction employed,[84] though it is unclear whether the change resulted from an importation of craftsmen from Northumbria, from an ideological decision to follow the Northumbrian Roman-Church pattern, or a combination of the two.

The change in construction at Whithorn was accompanied by a change in the plan of the site from a curvilinear earlier phase to what is described as a 'rigorously-planned rectilinear settlement'.[85] Although the excavator saw these changes as being from an Irish-type monastery to a 'Roman' Northumbrian one, this has, as Sally Foster notes in chapter 5, been contested, and it is perhaps more likely that it marks a transition from a secular to an ecclesiastical site. The difficulty of distinguishing between secular and ecclesiastical use is not peculiar to Whithorn or to the fifth to seventh centuries. Similar uncertainties exist both in early Ireland,[86] and in relation to eighth- and ninth-century Brandon (Suffolk) and Flixborough (Lincolnshire);[87] and it is debated whether Cheddar and Northampton were royal

---

New York, 1971), pp. 85–7

[79] Canna: J. G. Dunbar and I. Fisher, 'Sgòr nam Ban-Naomha ("Cliff of the Holy Women"), Isle of Canna', *Scottish Archaeological Forum* 5 (1973), pp. 71–5; the Northern Isles: R. G. Lamb, 'Coastal Settlements of the North', in the same volume, pp. 76–98, at pp. 76–83.

[80] S. Johnson, *Burgh Castle: Excavations by Charles Green, 1958–61*, East Anglian Archaeology, 20 (Dereham, 1983).

[81] P. A. Rahtz, 'The Building Plan of the Anglo-Saxon Monastery at Whitby', in *The Archaeology of Anglo-Saxon England*, ed. by D. M. Wilson (Cambridge, 1976), pp. 459–62, at p. 461, reinterpreting the evidence originally presented in C. Peers and C. A. R. Radford, 'The Saxon Monastery of Whitby', *Archaeologia*, 89 (1943), pp. 27–88, especially at pp. 30–1.

[82] Daniels, *Anglo-Saxon Hartlepool*, pp. 32–73; cf. A. Marshall and G. Marshall, 'Differentiation, Change and Continuity in Anglo-Saxon Buildings', *Archaeological Journal*, 150 (1993), pp. 366–402.

[83] Thomas and Knox, 'Window on Christianisation'.

[84] For the seventh-century buildings at Whithorn, see Hill, *Whithorn*, especially pp. 138–9; for further discussion, Daniels, *Anglo-Saxon Hartlepool*, p. 73.

[85] Hill, *Whithorn*, p. 134.

[86] Mytum, *Origins of Early Christian Ireland*, pp. 61–6, 74.

[87] J. Blair, *The Church in Anglo-Saxon Society* (Oxford, 2005), pp. 204–12; T. Pestel, *Landscapes*

palaces or minster complexes.[88] At Lyminge, however, the buildings of the minster were laid out on a new site adjacent to the former royal estate centre, which was abandoned.[89] Further, the domestic structures were smaller than on contemporary secular sites, suggesting they were cells for individual occupants, and densely packed suggesting a semi-communal life,[90] features which have also been observed at Hartlepool.[91] Whithorn was also densely packed, and there is evidence for quite large halls, possibly for communal use, as well as smaller ones perhaps for individual occupation.[92] The density at Whitby led Philip Rahtz to suggest the layout had more in common with a claustral layout than individual cells,[93] while at Wearmouth and Jarrow there were more developed claustral plans (chapter 8).

Some of the differences between sites, particularly the distinctive forms at Wearmouth and Jarrow, may indicate varying degrees of communal life, but the cases of Lyminge and Whitby suggest that the line between the communal and the individual may not have been clear-cut. Since there was no prevalent monastic rule or way of life—even at Rome itself there was considerable variation[94]—and since building traditions varied across Britain and Ireland, it would be wrong to expect uniformity. However, as with the churches, a focus on the differences may divert attention from some underlying similarities, particularly in relation to the range of functions associated with early religious institutions, the accommodation of the economic activities pursued on many sites and to the widespread pattern of segregation of functions.

Landscapes

Although monastic and other church sites were demarcated by a boundary—whether a monastic *vallum*[95] or a hedge[96]—they were nevertheless part of the landscapes within which they stood. Churches founded in or next to secular centres demonstrated

---

of Monastic Foundation: The Establishment of Religious Houses in East Anglia, c.650–1200, Anglo-Saxon Studies, 5 (Woodbridge, 2004), pp. 31–48.

[88] See Blair, 'Palaces or Minsters?'.
[89] Thomas, 'Life Before the Minster', p. 128; Thomas and Knox, 'Window on Christianisation'.
[90] G. Thomas, 'Bringing a Lost Anglo-Saxon Monastery to Life', in 'Medieval Britain and Ireland in 2009', ed. by N. Christie, *et al.*, *Medieval Archaeology*, 54 (2010), pp. 409–14; Thomas, 'Life Before the Minster', p. 131; Thomas and Knox, 'Window on Christianisation'.
[91] Daniels, *Anglo-Saxon Hartlepool*, pp. 63–71.
[92] Hill, *Whithorn*, pp. 139–41.
[93] Rahtz, 'Building Plan at Whitby', p. 462.
[94] F. Ferrari, *Early Roman Monasteries: Notes for the History of the Monasteries and Convents of Rome from the V through the X Century*, Studi di antichità cristiana, 23 (Vatican City, 1957).
[95] Though few in England have been found archaeologically: R. Cramp, 'Monastic Sites', in *Archaeology of Anglo-Saxon England*, pp. 201–52, at p. 249.
[96] E.g., at Oundle: Stephen, *Vita Wilfridi*, c. 67.

11. CONCLUSION

the faith of the ruler and the interdependence of secular and religious authority, while those with stone churches showed their ecclesiastical affiliation. That some of the centres chosen for the Augustinian mission were Roman—Canterbury, Lincoln, London, York—was partly because they were centres of secular power, but it was also because of their association with the Roman past. Elsewhere, both within and beyond the area affected by the Augustinian mission, other forms of past association might be played upon—cult centres such as Yeavering (Northumberland), and ancestral burial places such as Taplow (Buckinghamshire). Such appropriation could be on a small scale—the placing of a cross or a chapel or church at a spring, well, or enclosure, as was widespread in the far south west of England[97]—or on an even larger scale as has been suggested in relation to north-west Scotland and to Pictland.[98]

The approach to the landscape so far discussed is more about worldly power, particularly secular lordship, than it is about religion. Many significant relationships between churches and earlier cult sites may have occurred accidentally as a function of the fact that the Church was given existing estates. Richard Morris's exploration of the Vale of Pickering in the North Riding of Yorkshire (chapter 7) is an example: a vast royal estate with Roman antecedents was given to the Church, rather than the Church seeking out the estate because of its history. The point might be strengthened by the way in which the Church felt obliged to purify the place of Roman cult at Lastingham,[99] taking it over by an act of rejection as much as of assimilation. As reconstructed by Richard Morris, however, Lastingham also provides striking evidence of a different aspect of the Christianisation of the landscape—its adoption into a lived, experienced, religion and an allegorical tradition of perception, Calvary being understood by the 'Three Howes' and Ana Cross on Spaunton Moor, the ever-presence of God's Judgement and the vision of the Book of Revelation by the prevalent thunder. The footprints of Augustine and Mildreth at Richborough and Minster-in-Thanet in Kent (chapter 6) reveal a like appreciation of the landscape, both cases having multiple and simultaneous levels of resonance. A similar allegorical approach to the landscape is comes from a story about the Irish saint, Berach. In the hope of preventing his monks from making the pilgrimage to Rome, he erected a cross to SS. Peter and Paul, so that when they went and prayed at it they might 'be' in Rome, the place being understood by the cross; when that failed, and a monk began the

---

[97] S. Turner, *Making a Christian Landscape: The Countryside in Early Medieval Cornwall, Devon and Wessex* (Exeter, 2006), pp. 131–69.

[98] M. Meredith-Lobay, *Contextual Landscape Study of the Early Christian Churches of Argyll: The Persistence of Memory*, British Archaeological Reports, British Series 488 (Oxford, 2009); M. Carver, *The Pictish Monastery of Portmahomack*, Jarrow Lecture 2008 (Jarrow, 2008). For general discussion, see S. Semple, *Perceptions of the Prehistoric in Anglo-Saxon England: Religion, Ritual, and Rulership in the Landscape* (Oxford, 2013), especially pp. 138–42.

[99] Bede, *Historia ecclesiastica*, bk iii, c. 23.

journey to Rome, saying he would not stop until he had seen Rome with his own eyes, Berach made the sign of the cross in front of his eyes, whereupon the monk was granted a vision of Rome, after which a church and two crosses were constructed at the spot where the vision was vouchsafed, and visiting the crosses was thereafter understood to be a visit to Rome itself.[100]

Conclusion

That the physical setting of churches and monasteries might be pressed into service as part of the understanding, teaching and experience of God's purpose is an extension of the allegorical means of Biblical exegesis characteristic of the early middle ages. So too is much of the interpretation of the church buildings discussed earlier, in which the churches evoke Rome, the Temple, the Heavenly Jerusalem and Judgement. It is more than symbolic: the holy places were brought into the lives of worshipers; through them worshipers were put into living contact with the events of the story of salvation, the saints, the working out of God's purposes on earth. This is perhaps the strongest unifying thread which runs through the sites and buildings discussed in this volume: although Govan and Reculver, Clonmacnoise and Jarrow, may in physical terms appear as opposed as green and purple, they are parts of a spectrum in their form, in what they represent in terms of belief, in the interpretation of that belief, and in the setting they provide for worship. The evidence of the buildings, sites and landscapes discussed in this volume complements arguments made elsewhere, using different forms of evidence, that, despite persistent popular perceptions, the Celtic Church was not a thing apart from the western, Roman, tradition.[101]

---

[100] *Betha Beraigh* [*Life of Berach*], in *Bethada náem n'Érenn: Lives of the Irish Saints*, vol. 1, pp. 23–43 (translation vol. 2, pp. 22–43), c. 87.

[101] W. Davies, 'The Myth of the Celtic Church', in *The Early Church in Wales and the West*, ed. by N. Edwards and A. Lane, Oxbow Monograph 16 (Oxford, 1992), pp. 12–21.

Index

Aaron, saint 16
Abernethy, Perthshire 73
Abraham, bishop of St Davids 50, *51*
Acca, bishop of Hexham 162
Adbarunae, Lindsey, Lincolnshire 127, 136–37, 146, 149
Adomnán, saint 3, 33, 65, 82–3, 79, 111
Ælberht, abbot of Kirkdale 144
Æthelbald, king of Mercia 7, 187
Æthelberht, king of Kent 93, 103–5, 214
Æthelmund, Ealdorman 187, 203, 205
Æthelric, son of Æthelmund 187, 201, 203, 207
Æthelthryth, queen of Northumbria 131
Æthelwald, king of Deira 126
Æthelwold Moll 136–7
Aidan, saint, bishop of Lindisfarne 126–8, 150
Aitchison, N. 84–5
Alban, saint 16, 30
Alcock, Leslie 76
Alcuin of York 96, 124, 150–1
Aldington, Kent 118
Anderson, Joseph 71
Andrew, saint 85
Anglo-Saxon architecture
   at Deerhurst, Gloucestershire 186–208
   in Kent
      historiography 92–100
      identification 100–1
      Roman *spolia*, re-use of 102–3, *107*, 107–9, 112, *115*
      Rome, as rebuilding of 104–18
   in Northumbria 154–68, *157*
   see also individual place names; *and under* building material
Annales Cambriae 43
Annals of Ulster 63

Appleton-le-Street, North Riding of Yorkshire *120*, 144
Ardwall Island, Kirkcudbrightshire 68, 77–8
Arfryn, Anglesey 36
Arles, Council of (314) 16
Armagh 5, 33, 58, 63–4, 67, 212, 221–2
Artmail 46
Audouy, M. 180
Augulius, saint 30
Augustine of Canterbury, saint 1, 30–2, 93–4, 102–5, 112, 209, 214, 220, 225
   footprint of 110–11, 225
   Gospels of 31
Auldhane, East Lothian, 68, 76–77, 80, 91

Baalbek 17
Bacchus 15, 19, 28
Bailey, Richard 145, 156, 158, 161, 186, 191
Balisclate, Argyll 76n24
Bamburgh, Northumberland 135, *152*
Bangor, Caernarfonshire 43–6, *44*, 48
baptism, baptisteries 12–13, 105, 204–5
   fonts 21–2, *22*, 25–8, *25*, 54, 204–5, 207
   in Scotland 76, 85, 91
   wells/cisterns 168, 220
Bardsey Island, Gwynedd 54
Barnwell, Paul 170
Barton-upon-Humber, Lincolnshire 204
Bath, Somerset, Sulis Minerva 16, 17
Beadericesworth, Suffolk 214
Bede, saint 2–3, 23, 31, 33, 82, 96–7, 110–11, 209, 63–4, 101–2, 212, 218
   on Canterbury, papal mission to 32, 101–5, 112

227

on Cuthbert, saint 12
on Northumbrian churches 154–5, 162
on Pickering, monasteries in Vale of 131–4, 145, 149–50
on saints' cults 7
Belach Mugna, battle of 67
Bellerophon 24
Benedict Biscop 155–6, 160, 164, 214
Benedictional of St Æthelwold 205
Benwell, Northumberland, Temple of Antenociticus 28, 32
Berach, saint 225–6
Berger, Rainer 64
Berinsfield, Oxfordshire, Wally Corner 29
Berllan Bach, Caernarfonshire 45
Bernicia 123–4, 150, 153, 222
Bertha, queen of Kent 93, 106–7
Biddle, M. 23, 29
Bidwell, Paul 158–61
Birinus, saint 29
Blair, John 107, 137, 170
Boniface, saint 179
Book of Cerne 191
Book of Kells 79
Borland, John 72
Boulton, Meg 116, 210, 215, 217
Bourton on the Water, Gloucestershire 27
Bradford on Avon, Wiltshire 25, *25*, 28
Bradwell-on-Sea, Essex 32, 219
Brandon, Suffolk 223
Breamore, Hampshire 177, 185, 194
Brechin, Angus 73
Brigit, saint 40, 65, 214
Britannia Prima 16
Britannia Secunda 16
Brixworth, Northamptonshire, All Saints' xiv, 169–6, *174*, 191, 211, 216, 218
    Period I 176–81, 183–5
    Period II 181–5
    reconstructions *181, 182*
    ring crypt 179–80, 191, 202
Brough of Deerness, Orkney 77

Brown, Baldwin 155
Brown, P. D. C. 22
Brown, Peter 23
Bryant, Richard 187
Brynach, saint 52–3
building material
    brick 93, 100, 102, 107–8, *107, 108*, 112
    sod 4, 58–9, *59*
    stone
        Anglo-Saxon 2–6, 93, 99–102, *98, 101*, 112, 117, 155–68, 171–85, 190–200, 209–11
        in Ireland 46, 56, 58, 60, 63–7, 209, 212
        Romano-British 154, 158–60, 163, 167
        in Scotland 73–3, 77, 82–5, 90–1, 209
        in Wales 6, 55
    timber
        Anglo-Saxon 4, 99, 117, 154–5, 194, 209, 212–14, 223
        in Ireland 4, 213–14
        in Scotland 73, 76–7, 81–3, 85, 89–91, 212
        in Wales 50, 55
    wattle 4, 223
Burgh Castle, Norfolk 223
burial 173, 176–7
    Christianisation of 12–14, 30–1, 210
    in Deerhurst, Gloucestershire 203–5, 207
    in Ireland 58–9, 64–5, *65*, 86, 88
    in Northumbria 154, 156, *157*, 158, 161–6
    in Pickering, Vale of 129–31, *130*, 147–8
    rituals 217–19
    royal 7, 176
    in Scotland 72, 74–8, *75*, 80–1, 88–9, 91

INDEX

in Wales 35–42, *37, 39*, 46, 49–50, 52, 55, 221
    capeli-y-bedd 6, 35
    see also saints' cults
Burry Holms, Glamorgan 49
Byland, North Riding of Yorkshire 122
Bywell, Northumberland *152*, 153–4
    St Andrew's *xiv, xv*, 162, 167
    St Peter's 162, 167–8

Caelin, priest 126
Caerleon, Monmouthshire 16
Caerwent, Monmouthshire 18, *18*, 21, 28–9
Caffo, saint 54
Caherlehillan, Kerry 59
Cambridge, Eric 158
Campodunum, North Riding of Yorkshire 212
Canna, Inverness-shire *68*, 73, 223
Canterbury, Kent 5, 92, 101–5, 151
    Christ Saviour 113
    mausoleum and baptistery 205
    and Rome 100, 102–3, 105–6, 111–18, *115*, 225
    Quatro Coronati 97
    St Augustine's 7, 32, 118
    St Dunstan 118
    St Martin 23, 29, 93–4, 105, 107, *107*, 111–13, 118
    St Mary 118
    St Mildred's 118
    St Pancras *98, 99*, 106, 113–14, *115*, 118
    SS. Peter and Paul *98, 99*, 105–6, 117, 176, 218, 221–2
Capel Eithin, Anglesey 36, *37*, 38–9
Capel Maelog, Radnorshire 36, 50
Carrawburgh, Northumberland 18, *19*, 28, 32, 161
Carver, Martin 74
Cashel, Tipperary 58–9

Ceadda, abbot of Lastingham 126–9, 131–2, 134, 150–1
Ceatta, saint 128
Cedd, abbot of Lastingham 126–9, 133–5, 143, 145, 150–1
Céli Dé (Servants of God) 3, 56
Cellach, bishop of the Scots 70
cemeteries *see* burials
Ceolfrith (Ceolfrid), abbot of Wearmouth 83, 138, 144, 164, 214
Cerrig Ceinwen, Anglesey 54
Cheddar, Somerset 213, 223
Chedworth, Gloucestershire 25–6, *26*
Cheriton, Kent 118
Chesters, Northumberland 158–60
Church Island, Kerry 58–9
Cilgwyn, Nevern, Pembrokeshire *vii*, 52
Cilrhedyn, Llanychaer, Pembrokeshire 53
Cirencester, Gloucestershire 202
Clapham, Alfred W. 95–6, 155, 170, 219
Clarke, D. V. 84
Clofesho, Council of (747) 220
Clonmacnoise, Offaly 58, 64–7, *66*, 221–2, 226
Codex Amiatinus 214
Cogitosus 4, 59, 63, 65, 81, 212, 217
Colchester, Essex 17, 23, 213
Coldred, Kent 100, *101*, 118
Colmán, abbot of Clonmacnoise 67
Cologne, Germany, St Severin 23
Columba, saint 6, 70, 80, 86
Columbanus, saint 8
Conlaed, archbishop of Kildare 65
Constantine, king of Alba 70
Constantine, Roman emperor 16–17, 106
Constantinople 219
Constantius, *Life of St Germanus* 28
Constantius, Roman emperor 16
Corbridge (*Corstopitum*), Northumberland 4, 17, *152*, 153, 158–60
    St Andrew's 159, 162–3, 166, 168
Coxwold, North Riding of Yorkshire *120*,

229

126, 136–7, 140, 149
Cramp, Rosemary 9, 211, 216
crann-chaingel 62–3
Crayke (*Creic*), North Riding of Yorkshire
    ix, *120*, 122, 126, 135–6, 148, 151
Crerar, B. 27
cross-carved stone *vii*, 50–4, *51*, 79, 83–4
    145–7
crosses, stone
    Acca's cross 138
    Ana Cross 130–2, *130*
    in Ireland 66, 67
    on Man, Isle of 53
    in Pickering, Vale of *130*, 132–3, 135,
        137, 142
    in Wales 45–6, *47*, 49–50, 52–5
Croughton, Northamptonshire, Rawler
    Manor 24–5
Currauly, Kerry 57
Cuthbert, archbishop of Canterbury 205
Cuthbert, saint 11, 13, 70, 80, 136, 161,
    218
Cybele *see* Magna Mater cult
Cybi, saint 54
Cynebill, priest 126
Cynefrith, abbot of Gilling East 138

Darenth, Kent 118
David (Dewi), saint 8, 34, 50, 53
Davies, Wendy 34
De Abbatibus 166
Deerhurst, Gloucestershire, St Mary's 183,
    185
    existing church 187–90, *188*, *189*, *197*
    foundation of 187
    liturgy 201–8, 218
    painted remains 201–2, 206, 213
    Period IV Anglo-Saxon church 186,
        190–208, *192*, *193*, 216
    sculpture 186–7, 191, 204, 207, 213
Deiniol, bishop of Bangor, saint 43
Deira 123–4, 126, 135, 137–8, 150–1

Derrynaflan, Tipperary 56
Derventio see Malton
Dinas Powys, Glamorgan 42
Diocletian, Roman emperor 16
Dochdwy, saint 40
Domesday Book 97, 100, 135, 144–5
Domesday Monachorum 100
Domitian, Roman emperor 109
Donemutha, Northumberland 136–7, 149
Dorchester, Oxfordshire 29, 31
Dover, Kent 185
    St Mary *in Castro viii*, 102, 108–9, 118
Downpatrick, Down 64
Driscoll, Stephen 85–6
Dull, Perthshire 86
Dunbar, East Lothian 68, 76, 82
Dunbarton Rock, Dunbartonshire 68, 70
Dunkeld, Perthshire, 68, 86
Durham 136, *152*
Dysert Aenghusa, Limerick 56
Dyserth, Flintshire 54

Eadberht, king of Northumbria 136–7
Eadmer of Canterbury 96
Eanflaed, daughter of King Edwin 138,
    148
East Langdon, Kent 118
Eboracum see York
Ecgberht, archbishop of York 136–7
Ecgfrith, king of Northumbria 136, 149
Eddius Stephanus, *Vita Wilfridi* 96
Edgar, king of England 45
Edinburgh Castle, Midlothian 73
Edmund, saint 214
Edward the Elder, king of England 45,
    213
Edwin, king of Deira and Bernicia 124,
    148, 168
Egilsay, Orkney 73
Eileach na Naoimh, Garvellachs, Argyll
    73
Ekwall, E. 123, 137, 139

Elfoddw, bishop of Bangor, archbishop of Gwynedd 43–4
Eosterwine, abbot of Wearmouth 163–4, 218
Escomb, Durham *xi*, 76, 85, *152*, 154, 159–60, 167–8, 219
Ethernan, saint 86
Everson, P. 132

Faunus 28
Faversham, Kent 30
Fernie, Eric 73, 96
Ffraid (Brigit), saint 40
Finan, bishop of Lindisfarne 127
Fisher, E. A. 96
Fisher, Ian 71
Flann, king of the Southern Uí Néill 67
Flavia Caesariensis 16
Flawborough, Nottinghamshire 27
Fletcher, Lord 178
Flixborough, Lincolnshire 10, 223
fonts *see under* baptism, baptisteries
Foot, S. 170
Forteviot, Perthshire 6, *68*, 84–5, *85*
Forthred, abbot 136
Fortingall, Perthshire *68*, 78, 86
Foster, Sally 212, 222–3
Frampton, Dorset 15, 24

Garvellachs *68*, 73
Geddes, J. 84
Gem, Richard 3, 92, 94, 96, 112, 187, 201, 207
Germanus, saint 29
Gerontius, son of Spectatus 48–9
Gildas 8, 29, 33
Gillamoor, North Riding of Yorkshire 144
Gilling East (poss. *Ingetlingum*), North Riding of Yorkshire *120*, 126, 137–9, 144, 148–50
Gittos, H. 96, 107, 110, 116, 201

Glanfeuil, France 177
Gloucester, St Oswald's 202
Glywysing 46
Goffart, Walter 125
Goscelin of Saint-Bertin 96, 110
Govan, Renfrewshire *68*, 70, 80, 88, 90, 214, 222, 226
Gratian, Roman emperor 15
Greenstead, Essex 59
Gregory I the Great, pope 1, 5, 13, 30, 32, 102–3, 113, 210, 220
Gruffudd ap Cynan, ruler of Gwynedd 44
Gwenfrewi, saint 55
Gwytherin, Denbighshire 55

Hackness, North Riding of Yorkshire *120*, 122, 126, 148–9
Hadrian's Wall 18, 32, 161
Hall, Mark 85
Harbison, P. 65
Hartlepool, Durham 9–10, 14, 222–4
Hawkes, Jane 142–3, 210, 215, 217
Hayden, A. 59
Heliopolitanus 17
Helmsley, North Riding of Yorkshire 122
Henderson, George 84
Henderson, Isabel 84
Henig, Martin 210
Hereford 201
hermitages 9, 42, 50, 53, 58, 73
Hexham, Northumberland *152*
    Acca's cross 138
    St Andrew's 32, 113, 125, 153–6, *157*, 162, 166–7, 203, 211
        crypt 4, 156, *157*, 160–1, 215
    St Mary's 162
    St Peter's 162
Hilary, pope 214
Hilda, abbess of Whitby 11
Hinton St Mary, Dorset 24, 28
The Hirsel, Berwickshire 76–7, 80, 91
Hoddom, Dumfries 10, *68*, 78, 80, 82,

89–90, *90*
Hodges, Charles 158, 161
Horák, Jana 54
Housesteads, Northumberland 28, 32
Hovingham, North Riding of Yorkshire *120*, 126, 135, 137–41, *140*, 148–9
   sculpture at 141–3, *141*, 147
Hoxne Treasure 28
Hugeburg, nun 13
Hugo Candidus 170
Hunter Blair, Peter 123
Hywel ap Rhys, king of Glywysing 46

Icklingham, Suffolk 26–7
Illaunloughan, Kerry *xvi*, 6, 9, 58, *59*, 222
Illtud, saint 46
Inchmarnock, Buteshire 68, 77, 80, 88–9
Iniscealtra, Clare 58
Inishmurray, Sligo 89
inscribed stones, in Wales 35, 38, 40, *41*, 42
Iona, Argyll 3, 64, 68, 72, 74, 79–80, 82–4, 88–9, 01
   and St Columba 6, 33, 86, *87*
   St Ronan's 77
Isiac cult 16, 19
Iuthahel, king of Glywysing 46

Jackson, Heather 54
Jænberht, archbishop of Canterbury 151
James, Heather 50
Jarrow, Durham 5, 32, 33, 113, 125, 129, 138, *152*, 153–5, 158, 163, 211, 221, 226
   burials 162, 166, 218
   communal buildings 9, 160, 224
   foundation of 156
   painted panels 214
   St Paul's 156, 164–8, *165*
   sculptures at 145, 149, 166
   see also Wearmouth
Jerusalem 5, 116–18, 168, 217

Holy Sepulchre (tomb of Christ) 65, 117, 155, 215
   Temple 61, 117, 215
Jesus Christ 18
   as Christological prototype 110–11
   images of 24, 26, 30–1, 214
Julius (Julian), saint 16
Jumièges, France, Saint-Pierre 177
Juno 17
Jupiter (Zeus) 17

Kells, Meath 86
Kevin, saint 59
Kildare 4, 59, 63, 81, 212, 217
Kilmalkedar, Kerry *viii*, 61
Kilree, Kilkenny *62*
Kingsdown, Kent 118
Kingston, Kent 118
Kirby Misperton, North Riding of Yorkshire *120*, 122, 126, 132–3, 146
Kirkdale, North Riding of Yorkshire *120*, 126, 143–5, 147–8
Kjølbye-Biddle, Birthe 23, 29
Klukas, A. W. 206
Knowles, W. H. 198

Labbamologa, Cork 64, *65*
landscapes 88–9, 224–6; *see also* Pickering, Vale of
Lane, Alan 34
Lang, J. 134, 137
Lastingham, North Riding of Yorkshire, St Mary's church *ix*, *120*, 122, 126–35, 137, 143–4, 146–50, 225
   Roman carved stones 133–5
Leeds, Kent 118
Leo I the Great, pope 106, 164
Liber Vitae 136, 150
Lichfield, Staffordshire 127–8, 131, 136–7, 146, 151
Lichfield Gospels 55
Life of Samthanne 59

lighthouses, Roman *viii*, 102, 108–9
Lincoln 16, 225
  St Paul in the Bail 31
Lindisfarne, Northumberland 125–6, 135, *152*, 153–4, 218
Littlecote, Wiltshire 20, 28
liturgy
  at Deerhurst, Gloucestershire 201–8, 218
  and plan 214–21
Llanbadarn Fawr, Cardinganshire 34, 43
Llancarfan, Glamorgan 40, 46
Llandaf, Glamorgan 34, 40, 46
Llandanwg, Merioneth 43, 48–9, *48*
Llandeilo Fawr, Carmarthenshire 42, 55
Llandough, Glamorgan 29, 40, 42, 46
Llaneln, Glamorgan 36, 50, 55
Llanfihangel Tre'r Beirdd, Anglesey 54
Llanfihangel y Traethau, Merioneth 49
Llangaffo, Anglesey 54
Llantwit Major (*Llanilltud Fawr*), Glamorgan 29, 43, 46–8, *47*
Llanychlwydog, Pembrokeshire 52
Llawhaden, Daugleddau 52
Loch Glashan, Argyll 79
London 16, 20, 31, 225
  Drapers' Garden 30
  Roman temples 17–19
  St Martin's-in-the-Fields 23, 28–9
  Walbrook 18–19
Long Wittenham, Oxfordshire 31
Loveluck, Chris 10
Lower Halstow, Kent 118
Luchubran, Pigmie's Isle, Ross-shire 222
Lullingstone, Kent 20, 24, 27–8, 118
Lundin Links 68
Luxeuil, France 164
Lydd, Kent 97, *98*, 113–14, 118
Lydney Park, Gloucestershire 18–19
Lyminge, Kent 113, 117, 221–4

Magna Mater cult 19

Maldonado, Adrián 80, 88
Malton (*Derventio*), North Riding of Yorkshire 122–3, 135, 139–40, 144
Man, Isle of 53
Manning, Conleth 65, 67
Mars Nodens 19
Marton, North Riding of Yorkshire 122; *see also* Old Malton
martyria 29–30
Maxima Caesariensis 16
Maximian, Roman emperor 16
May, Isle of, Fife *68*, 77, 80, 88
Meigle, Perthshire *68*, 84, 88
Melangell, saint 49
Mercury 26
Middle-by-Pickering, North Riding of Yorkshire *x*, 126, 132, 146–8
Milan, Italy, St Tecla 20
Mildrith, saint 110–11, 225
Milton Regis, Kent 118
Minerva 17; *see also* Bath, Somerset, Sulis Minerva
Minster-in-Sheppey, Kent 118
Minster-in-Thanet, Kent 110–11, 225
Mithraism and *mithraea* 16, 18–19, *19*, 28, 32
Molaga, saint 65
monasteries (*monasteria*) 9–12, 29, 32, 42–3, 58, 89, 99, 106–7, 153, 224
  in Pickering, Vale of 119–51
    number of 119, *120*, *121*, 125
    and saints' cults 128–32, 134–5, 143, 150
  see also individual place names
Monkwearmouth, Durham 32, 33
Monymusk, Aberdeenshire 79
Morglais, bishop of Bangor 44
Morris, Richard 225
mosaics 15, 20, 24–5, *25*, 28, 31, 139
mother churches (*mam eglwysi*) 42–9
Moxby, North Riding of Yorkshire 122

Nechtan, king of the Picts 5–6, 80n42, 83, 212
Nendrum, Down 10, 89
Neptune 15
Nettleton, Wiltshire 18
Nevern, Pembrokeshire 52–3
Newburgh, North Riding of Yorkshire 122
Ninian (Finnian), saint 70, 80
North Rona, Ross and Cromarty 68, 73
Northampton 223
Northfleet, Kent 118

Ó Carragáin, Éamonn 203
Ó Carragáin, Tomás 86, 114, 164
O'Reilly, Jennifer 61, 110
Offa, king of Mercia 30, 151, 185
Old Malton, North Riding of Yorkshire *120*, 122
open-air worship sites 12–13
Orpheus 20, 28
Orpington, Kent 118
Oswald, king of Northumbria 126, 138
Oswaldkirk, North Riding of Yorkshire 139
Oswine, king of Deira 138, 150
Oswiu, king of Bernicia 5, 125, 127, 138, 148–50
Oundle, Northamptonshire 213, 218
Owine, monk 131

Paddlesworth, Kent 118
pagan temples 17–20, *18, 19*; see also Mithraism and *mithraea*
Painter, Kenneth 23
Paor, Liam de 58
Papa Stronsay, St Nicholas' chapel 68, 76
Parsons, David 163
Patrick (Patricius), saint 2, 28–9, 33, 61, 63–4
Paul, saint 64, 225
Paulinus, saint 168, 212

Pelagius, Roman heresiarch 25
Pen-Arthur Farm, Pembrokeshire 50
Pen Parke, Pembrokeshire 52
Penitential of Theodore 217
Penmacho, Caernafonshire 40, *41*
Penmon, Anglesey 53
Pennant Melangell, Montgomeryshire 36, 49
Pertinax, Publius Helvius, Roman emperor 24
Peter, saint 64, 225
Petra, Jordan 21
Petts, David 15
Pickering, Vale of, monasteries 119–51, *120, 121*, 225
  Ana Cross 130–2, *130*, 225
  geology 119, 121–2
  Roman remains 119, 123, 133–5 137, 139–44, *140*, 147–8
  'The Street' 139–40, 144
  Three Howes 129–32, 225
  see also *individual place names*
Pistyll, Gwynedd 54
Portmahomack (Tarbat), Ross and Cromarty 6, 10, 33, *68*, 74, 78–80, 84, 88–91, 222
Potterne, Wiltshire 205
Presteigne, Radnorshire 34

Quintus Natalius Natalinus 20

Radford, Raleigh 77
Rahtz, Philip 186, 224
Raunds, Northamptonshire, Furnells Manor 14
Reculver, Kent 32, 97, 109, 113–17, *115*, 176–7, 203, 216, 219, 226
Redcastle 68
Regensburg, Germany, St Emmeran 177, 179
Regularis Concordia 184
relics 5, 110–11, 134, 136, 160–1, 179,

202–3, 208, 214, 221; *see also* saints' cults
Repton, Derbyshire 7, 178, 185, 202, 205
Restennth, Angus 73
Rhygyfarch 34, *50*
Richborough, Kent, 22, *22*, 25, 109–11, *109*, 225
Rickman, Thomas 92, 97, 169
Rievaulx, North Riding of Yorkshire 122, 144, 151
Ripon, West Riding of Yorkshire 125, 138, 149, 155–6, 211, 213, 218
   crypt 156, *157*, 158, 160, 215
Rochester, Kent 109, 113
Rodwell, Warwick 208
Rollason, David 124, 128
Romanesque churches *viii*, 6, 34, 54, 66, 171
romanitas 64, 81–2, 102, 112, 114, 116
Romano-British Christian churches, origin of 20–32
Rome 5, 64, 117, 158, 210–12, 214–15, 220, 225–6
   and Canterbury 100, 102–3, 105–6, 111–18, *115*, 225
   Lateran 23, 106
   Old St Peter's 99, 106 179
   SS Cosmas and Damian 113
   St Paul's 113
   Saint Paul's Outside the Walls 164, 215
   Saint Peter's 23, 113, 116, 155, 163–4, 203, 207, 218
   San Marco 113
   Sant' Agnese *fuori le mura* 113
   Santa Cecilia in Trastevere 113
   Santa Maria Maggiore 113
   Santa Prassede 113
   Santa Pudenziana 113
   Santa Sabina 113
Rosemarkie, Black Isle, Ross and Cromarty 83–4
Ryedale *see* Pickering, Vale of

St Albans (Verulamium), Hertfordshire 16, 23, 28–30
St Andrews, Fife 68, 73, 82, 214
   Hallow Hill *75*, 75–6
   sarcophagus 7, 84, 88
St Cuthbert's, Northumberland 222
St David's, Pembrokeshire 34, 50–2, *51*
St-Denis, France 187
St Gallen, Switzerland 177–8, 201, 204
St Ismael, Rhos 52
St Flanan's, Eilean Mor, Flannan Isles, Ross and Cromarty 73
St Justinian's chapel, Pembrokeshire 50
St MacDara's, Galway 61
St Mary at Cliffe, Kent 118
St Ninian's Isle, Shetland 68
St Ninian's Point, Buteshire 68, 77
St Non's chapel, Pembrokeshire 50
St Patrick's chapel, Pembrokeshire 50
St Vigean's, Angus 6, 68, 84, 88
saints' cults 7–8, 16, 29–30, 179, 202–3, 219
   in Ireland 5–6, 64–5, *65*
   in Northumbria 160–2
   in Pickering, Vale of 128–32, 134–5, 143, 150
   in Scotland 6, 64, 80–1, 83–8
   in Wales 6
Salisbury, Wiltshire 171
Samson, king of Glywysing 46
Samson de Cornuwala 144
Samson of Dol, saint 34, 46
Sargent, Andrew 129
Scarborough, North Riding of Yorkshire 119
Scone, Perthshire 68, 70
Scott, Gilbert 165
Scott, Ian G. 71
Seaham, Durham *152*, 153–4, 162, 168
Seamer, North Riding of Yorkshire 119
Seligenstadt, Germany 177
Serf, saint 86

Sgòr nam Bán-Naoimha, Canna, Inverness-shire 73
Shapland, M. G. 96, 116–17
Sherburn, North Riding of Yorkshire x, 126, 145–6
Shorden Brae, Northumberland 158–9
Shorne, Kent 118
Silchester, Hampshire 20–1, *21*
Simonburn, Northumberland *152*, 166
Sims-Williams, Patrick 38, 201
Sixtus, saint 30
Skellig Michael, Kerry 9
Smith, Ian 71, 78
South Shields, Durham 154
Spaunton Moor, North Riding of Yorkshire 129–30, 225
Spier, Jeffrey 17
Springhead, Kent 18
Sprouston, Roxburghshire 68, 78
Stamford Bridge, North Riding of Yorkshire 123
Steinbach, Germany 177
Stephanus of Ripon 156
Stephen, abbot of St Mary's, York 132
Stocker, David 132
Stone-by-Faversham, Kent 108, *108*, 118
Stonegrave (*Staningagrave*), North Riding of Yorkshire 126, 136–9, 148–9
Streanæshalch 145, 148
Strenshall, North Riding of Yorkshire 148
Strood, Kent 30
Sulien, bishop of St Davids 43
Sutherland, Diana 175
Swanscombe, Kent 118
Symmachus, Quintus Aurelius 15

Tanwg, saint 48
Taplow, Buckinghamshire 225
Tarbat *see* Portmahomack
Tatheus, saint 28
Tatton-Brown, T. 96, 99–100
Taylor, Harold 3, 93, 99–100, 158, 177, 179
Taylor, Joan 3, 93, 99–100
Taylor, Simon 72
Tecan 46
Terryglass, Tipperary 56
Thanet, Isle of, Kent 103, 110–11
Thetford, Norfolk 28
Thomas, Charles 15, 36, 71, 77
Thompson, Alexander Hamilton 180
Thornybank, Midlothian 68, 74
Thruxton, Hampshire 20, 28
Tiberius Claudius Togidubnus, British client king 17
Tilbury, Essex 127
Toynbee, Jocelyn 15
Traprain Law, East Lothian 31
Trawsfynydd, Merioneth 40
Tre-bulch, Pembrokeshire 52
Tre-haidd, Pembrokeshire 52
Trier, Germany 20
Trim, Meath 8
Trumberht, monk of Lastingham 129, 131
Tullich, Aberdeenshire 68, 74
Tunbercht, abbot of Gilling East, bishop of Hexham 138
Tŷ Mawr, Anglesey 36
Tywyn y Capel, Angelsey 39–40, *39*

Uley, Gloucestershire 18, 26
Unuist, Pictish king 84

Vegvar, Neuman de 81
Venus 27
Verulamium *see* St Albans
Vindolanda, Northumberland 28, 32, 154

Walesby, Lincolnshire 27
Water Newton, Cambridgeshire 16, 22–3
Watkins, C. F., Rev. 169, 177
Wearmouth 5, 9, 83, 113, 125, 129, 138, 153–6, 158, 160, 211, 224
 burials 162, 218

painted panels 214
St Lawrence's 164
St Mary's 164
St Peter's *xi*, *xii*, 156, 162–8, *165*, 215
sculpture at 145, 149
see also Jarrow
Wearmouth-Jarrow *see* Jarrow; Wearmouth
West Peckham, Kent 118
West Stourmouth, Kent 118
Wharram Percy, North Riding of Yorkshire 147–8
Whitby, North Riding of Yorkshire 148, 223–4
Synod of 5, 82
Whitfield, Kent 118
Whithorn, Wigtownshire 4, 33, 59, 63, *68*, 77–82, 88–9, 212, 223–4
mortuary chapel 89, 91
phasing of period II 81–2, *81*, 216–17
Wigginton, Oxfordshire 27
Wiglaf, king of Mercia 7
Wilfrid, bishop of York 4, 138, 149, 155–6, 159–61, 211–13, 218
Wilkinson, John 21
Willesbrough, Kent 118
William I, king of England 93
William of Malmesbury 96

Willmington, Kent 118
Winchcombe, Gloucestershire 202–3
Winchester, Hampshire, Old Minster 32, 204, 216, 218, 220
Wing, Buckinghamshire 183, 185, 191, 202
Winwaed, battle of 126
Witham, Essex 26
Wood, Ian 124–5, 149–50
Worcester 201
Wouldham, Kent 118
Wulfric, abbot of St Augustine's, Canterbury 111

Xanten, Germany 23

Yeoman, Peter 74
Ynys Dewi, Ramsey Island, Pembrokeshire 50
Ynys Seiriol, Anglesey 53
York (Eboracum) 16–17, 31, 123–4, 127, 135–6, 148, 150–1, 212, 225
St Mary's 132
Yorke, Barbara 210
Ythancæstir, Essex 127

Zeus *see* Jupiter

Rewley House Studies in the Historic Environment

Published

1. *The Medieval Great House*, ed. by Malcolm Airs and P. S. Barnwell (2011), ISBN 978-1-907730-07-8
2. *Country House Technology*, ed. by P. S. Barnwell and Marilyn Palmer (2012), ISBN 978-1-907730-20-7
3. *Sir George Gilbert Scott 1811–1878: an Architect and His Influence*, ed. by P. S. Barnwell, Geoffrey Tyack and William Whyte (2014), ISBN 978-1-907730-37-5
4. *Places of Worship in Britain and Ireland, 300–950*, ed. by P. S. Barnwell (2015), ISBN 978-1-907730-48-1

Forthcoming

Places of Worship in Britain and Ireland, 950–1150, ed. by P. S. Barnwell

Places of Worship in Britain and Ireland, 1150–1350, ed. by P. S. Barnwell

Places of Worship in Britain and Ireland, 1350–1550, ed. by P. S. Barnwell

Architect, Patron and Craftsman in Tudor and Jacobean England, ed. by P. S. Barnwell and Paula Henderson

Some Other Recent Titles of Related Interest

Monographs

Badham, Sally, *Seeking Salvation. Commemorating the Dead in the Late-Medieval English Parish*, with photography by Cameron Newman, ISBN 978-1-907730-47-4

Burfield, Diana, *Edward Cresy, 1792–1858, Architect and Civil Engineer*, with a foreword by Andrew Saint, ISBN 978-1-900289-65-8

Calder, Alan, *William Flockhart. A Maverick Architect for the Nouveaux Riches*, ISBN 978-1-907730-34-4

Hamilton, Alec, *Charles Spooner, Arts and Crafts Architect*, ISBN 978-1-907730-21-4

Karol, Eitan, *Charles Holden, Architect*, ISBN 978-1-900289-81-8

Kenyon, John R., *Castles, Town Defences and Artillery Fortifications in the United Kingdom and Ireland. A Bibliography 1945–2006*, ISBN 978-1-900289-89-4

Lindley, Phillip, *Tomb Destruction and Scholarship. Medieval Monuments in Early Modern England*, ISBN 978-1-900289-87-0

Litten, Julian, *The Mystery of Marquis d'Oisy*, with a foreword by Sir Roy Strong, ISBN 978-1-907730-49-8

Meara, David, *Modern Memorial Brasses 1880–2001*, ISBN 978-1-900289-85-6

Woods, Kim W., *Imported Images. Netherlandish Late Gothic Sculpture in England, c.1400–c.1550*, ISBN 978-1-900289-83-2.

Collections

Airs, Malcolm and William Whyte (eds), *Architectural History after Colvin: the Society of Architectural Historians of Great Britain Symposium, 2011*, ISBN 978-1-907730-32-0

Andrews, Francis (ed.), *Ritual and Space. Proceedings of the 2009 Harlaxton Symposium*, Harlaxton Medieval Studies, XXI, ISBN 978-1907730-09-2

Badham, Sally and Oosterwijk, Sophie (eds), *Monumental Industry. The Production of Tomb Monuments in England and Wales in the Long Fourteenth Century*, ISBN 978-1-907730-00-9

Barron, Caroline F. and Clive Burgess (eds), *Memory and Commemoration, Proceedings of the 2008 Harlaxton Symposium*, Harlaxton Medieval Studies, XX, ISBN 978-1-907730-04-7

Binski, Paul & Elizabeth New (eds), *Patrons and Professionals. Proceedings of 2010 Harlaxton Symposium*, Harlaxton Medieval Studies, XXII, ISBN 978-1-907730-12-2

Cooper, Trevor & Sarah Brown (eds), *Pews, Benches and Chairs. Church Seating in English Parish Churches from the Fourteenth Century to the Present*, published by the Ecclesiological Society, distributed by Shaun Tyas, ISBN 978-0-946823-17-8

Hawkes, Jane (ed.), *Making Histories. Proceedings of the Sixth International Conference on Insular Art, York 2011*, ISBN 978-1-907730-31-3

Jones, David & Sam McKinstry (eds), *Essays in Scots and English Architectural History. A Festschrift in Honour of John Frew*, ISBN 978-1-900289-94-8

Lindley, Phillip (ed.), *The Howards and the Tudors. Studies in Science and Heritage*, ISBN 978-1-907730-44-3

Oram, Richard (ed.), *'A House that Thieves Might Knock At': Proceedings of the 2010 Stirling and 2011 Dundee Conferences on 'The Tower as Lordly Residence' and 'The Tower and the Household'*, Tower Studies, 1 & 2 (in one volume), ISBN 978-1-907730-40-5

Penman, Michael (ed.), *Monuments and Monumentality across Medieval and Early Modern Europe*, ISBN 978-1-907730-28-3

Petre, James (ed.), *The Castles of Bedfordshire*, ISBN 978-1-907730-14-6

Ramsay, Nigel (ed.), *Heralds and Heraldry in Shakespeare's England*, ISBN 978-1-907730-35-1

Rogers, Nicholas (ed.), *The Friars in Medieval Britain. Proceedings of the 2007 Harlaxton Symposium*, Harlaxton Medieval Studies, XIX, ISBN 978-1-907730-03-0.